INSIGHT GUIDES

ROME

Discovery
CHANNEL

APA PUBLICATIONS
Part of the Langenscheidt Publishing Group

※ INSIGHT GUIDES

ROME

Project Editor
Cathy Muscat
Picture Editor
Hilary Genin
Art Director
Ian Spick
Cartography Editor
Zoë Goodwin
Production
Kenneth Chan
Editorial Director
Brian Bell

Distribution

United States
Langenscheidt Publishers, Inc.
36–36 33rd Street 4th Floor
Long Island City, NY 11106
Fax: (1) 718 784-0640
UK & Ireland
GeoCenter International Ltd
Meridian House, Churchill Way West,
Basingstoke, Hampshire, RG21 6YR
Tel: 44 (0) 1256 817987
Fax: 44 (0) 1256 817988
Australia
Universal Publishers
1 Waterloo Road
Macquarie Park, NSW 2113
Fax: (61) 2 9888 9074
New Zealand
Hema Maps New Zealand Ltd (HNZ)
Unit D, 24 Ra ORA Drive
East Tamaki, Auckland
Fax: (64) 9 273 6479
Worldwide
**Apa Publications GmbH & Co.
Verlag KG (Singapore branch)**
38 Joo Koon Road, Singapore 628990
Tel: (65) 6865 1600.
Fax: (65) 6861 6438

Printing

Insight Print Services (Pte) Ltd
38 Joo Koon Road, Singapore 628990
Tel: (65) 6865 1600.
Fax: (65) 6861 6438

©2008 Apa Publications GmbH & Co.
Verlag KG (Singapore branch)
All Rights Reserved

First Edition 1991
Sixth Edition 2008

No part of this book may be
reproduced, stored in a retrieval
system or transmitted in any form or
means electronic, mechanical, photo-
copying, recording or otherwise,
without prior written permission of
Apa Publications. Brief text quota-
tions with use of photographs are
exempted for book review purposes
only. Information has been obtained
from sources believed to be reliable,
but its accuracy and completeness,
and the opinions based thereon, are
not guaranteed.

www.insightguides.com
In North America:
www.insighttravelguides.com

ABOUT THIS BOOK

What makes an Insight Guide different? Since our first book pioneered the use of creative full-colour photography in travel guides in 1970, we have aimed to provide not only reliable information but also the key to a real understanding of a destination and its people.

Now, when the internet can supply inexhaustible (but not always reliable) facts, our books marry text and pictures to provide that more elusive quality: knowledge. To achieve this, they rely on the authority of locally based writers and photographers.

This book turns the spotlight on one of the most exhilarating cities in the world. Travellers have been drawn to Rome for centuries. Today they flock here in their millions not only to see the ancient city, the Vatican and to eat in traditional trattorias, but also to experience the newer side of the city – modern architecture, boutique hotels, and designer bars and restaurants. From the classical to the contemporary, *Insight Guide: Rome* covers the best of everything the city has to offer.

CONTACTING THE EDITORS

We would appreciate it if readers would alert us to errors or outdated information by writing to:

**Insight Guides, P.O. Box 7910, London SE1 1WE, England.
Fax: (44) 20 7403 0290.
insight@apaguide.co.uk**

THE CONTRIBUTORS TO THIS BOOK

This new edition of *Insight Guide: Rome* was edited by **Cathy Muscat**, editor and Italian specialist at Insight Guides' London office, implementing a vibrant new design by **Klaus Geisler**. A team of Rome experts was assembled to provide comprehensive updates and cover the latest hotspots.

Annie Shapero, a long-time resident and regular contributor to the Rome edition of *Where* magazine, trekked the city streets to update many of the chapters. She also provided an expert overview of the shopping scene with a comprehensive rundown of the best places to shop. Travel editor **Natasha Foges**, a former Rome resident recently returned to London, researched and updated all the restaurants and hotels to provide well-informed listings of both established favourites and exciting new haunts. Travel writer and journalist **Marc Zakian** contributed a number of the short

features, including *Rome on Film*, and also updated a selection of the city chapters. Writer and broadcaster **Lisa Gerard-Sharp** offers an incisive account of modern Rome and what makes the Romans tick.

This edition builds on excellent foundations laid down by many past contributors, including **Rowlinson Carter**, who wrote the original history chapter, **Jon Eldan**, who penned the food and drink chapter, and **Giovanna Dunmall**, who contributed to many of the previous updates. Additional material was supplied by **Jason Best**.

The majority of new photographs were by **Britta Jaschinski**, with other images by **Anna Mockford** and **Nick Bonnetti**, **Alessandra Santarelli** and **Bill Wassmann**. Invaluable editorial back-up was provided by **Siân Lezard** and **Nick Rider**. Proofreading was by **Neil Titman** and the index was by **Helen Peters**.

THE GUIDE AT A GLANCE

The book is carefully structured both to convey an understanding of the city and its culture and to guide readers through its attractions and activities:

◆ The Best Of section at the front of the book helps you to prioritise. The first spread contains all the Top Sights, while Editor's Choice details unique experiences, the best buys or other recommendations.

◆ To understand Rome, you need to know something of its past. The city's history and culture are described in authoritative essays written by

specialists in their fields who have lived in and documented Rome for many years.

◆ The Places section details all the attractions worth seeing. The main places of interest are coordinated by number with the maps.

◆ A list of recommended restaurants, bars and cafés is printed at the end of each chapter.

◆ Photographs throughout the book are chosen not only to illustrate geography and buildings, but also to convey the moods of the city and the life of its people.

◆ The Travel Tips section includes all the practical information you will need, divided into five key sections: transport, accommodation, activities (including nightlife, events, tours and sports), shopping, and an A–Z of practical tips. Information may be located quickly by using the index on the back cover flap of the book.

◆ Two detailed street atlases are included at the back of the book, complete with a full index. On the second one, you will find all the restaurants and hotels plotted for your convenience.

PLACES & SIGHTS

Colour-coding at the top of every page makes it easy to find each area in the book. These are coordinated by specific area on the orientation map on pages 82–3.

A locator map pinpoints the specific area covered in each chapter. The page reference at the top indicates where to find a detailed map of the area highlighted in red.

Margin tips provide extra little snippets of information, whether it's a practical tip, a whimsical quote, an historical fact or advice on shopping and eating.

A four-colour map provides a bird's-eye view of the area covered in the chapter, with the main attractions coordinated by number with the main text.

PHOTO FEATURES

Picture stories offer visual coverage of major sights or unusual attractions. The map shows where it is, while vital statistics convey practical information: address, contact details, website, opening times, and if there's a charge.

RESTAURANT LISTINGS

Restaurant listings feature the best establishments within each area, giving the address, phone number, opening times and price category followed by a useful review. The grid reference refers to the atlas at the back of the book.

Vecchia Locanda
2 Vicolo Sinibaldi 06-6880 2831 D only Mon–Sat. €€ [p335, D4] In a pedestrianised alleyway, this rustic restaurant offers decent if a little unadventurous food. A nice touch is that

TRAVEL TIPS

GETTING AROUND
From the Airport
From Fiumicino, there are frequent train services to the city – every 15–30 minutes to Trastevere Station and every 30 minutes to Stazione Termini. Trains to Stazione Termini (the Leonardo Express) run from 6.37am to 11.37pm; the journey takes 35 minutes and the ticket €11. If you're travelli

Advice-packed Travel Tips provide all the practical knowledge you'll need before and during your trip: how to get there, getting around, where to stay and what to do. The A–Z section is a handy summary of practical information, arranged alphabetically.

Contents

Best of Rome

Top Sights 8

Campo de' Fiori **170**
The Capitoline Museums **89**
The Colosseum **111**
The Forum **100**
The Pantheon **154**
Piazza Navona **158**
The Spanish Steps **129**
Trastevere **201**
The Trevi Fountain **117**
The Vatican Museums **141**
Villa Borghese **188**

Editor's Choice . . . . **.10**

Introduction

Guide at a Glance. **4**
Rome and the Romans **19**

History

The Making of Rome. **27**
Decisive Dates. **40**

Features

Art and Architecture **47**
The Shape of Modern Rome **57**
Food and Drink. **63**
Shopping. **69**

Insights

Mini Features:
Rome on Film. **44**
Mussolini's Legacy. **58**
Roman Fashion. **132**
Talking Statues **160**
EUR **216**
Lazio Beaches **254**

Photo Features:
Bernini and the Baroque **54**
Modern Architecture **60**
Shopping Areas. **72**
Markets in Rome. **74**
The Capitoline Museums **92**
The Colosseum **114**
Treasures of the Vatican **146**
The Sistine Chapel **148**
The Galleria Borghese **198**
Relics of the Catacombs **244**
Parks and Gardens. **262**

Places

Orientation **81**
- The Capitoline Hill **87**
- Ancient Rome **97**
- Fontana di Trevi
  and Quirinale **117**
- Piazza di Spagna
  and Tridente **125**
- The Vatican and Prati **137**
- Piazza Navona and
  the Pantheon **151**
- Campo de' Fiori and
  the Ghetto **169**
- Via Veneto and
  Villa Borghese **185**
- Trastevere and
  the Gianicolo **201**
- Aventino and Testaccio **211**
- Celio and San Giovanni **221**
- Monti and Esquilino **229**
- The Appian Way **239**
  ***Excursions from Rome....* 249**
- Ostia Antica.................... **251**
- Tivoli............................. **257**
- Castelli Romani **265**
- Etruscan Towns **273**

Restaurants & Bars

The Capitoline Hill **91**
Ancient Rome **113**
Fontana di Trevi and Quirinale **123**
Piazza di Spagna and Tridente **134**
The Vatican and Prati **145**
Piazza Navona
  and the Pantheon **166**
Campo de' Fiori
  and the Ghetto **181**
Via Veneto and Villa Borghese **197**
Trastevere and the Gianicolo ..**208**
Aventino and Testaccio **218**
Celio and San Giovanni **227**
Monti and Esquilino................**236**
The Appian Way......................**243**

Travel Tips

TRANSPORT
Getting There **282**
Getting Around **283**
  Public Transport **284**
  Car Hire **285**
  Driving **286**

ACCOMMODATION
Choosing a Hotel **288**
Fontana di Trevi, Via Veneto and
  Villa Borghese **289**
Piazza di Spagna and Tridente **290**
The Vatican and Prati **292**
Piazza Navona and the
  Pantheon **293**
Campo de' Fiori, the Ghetto and
  Trastevere **294**
Aventino and Testaccio **295**
Termini, Monti and Esquilino **296**
Excursions **297**

SHOPPING
What to Buy **298**
Where to Buy **299**
Size Chart **300**
Bargain Picks **301**

ACTIVITIES
The Arts **303**
Nightlife **304**
Children **306**
Annual Events **306**
Sport **308**
Festivals **308**
Sightseeing Tours **309**

**A–Z of PRACTICAL
INFORMATION 310**

**LANGUAGE and
FURTHER READING 318**

Maps

Rome
inside front cover and **84**

Map legend **325**

Street Atlas **326**

Restaurant & Hotel Atlas **334**

Capitoline Hill **88**
The Forum **98** and **100**
The Palatine **110**
Quirinale **118**
Tridente **126**
The Vatican and Prati **138**
Piazza Navona and
  the Pantheon/Campo de'
  Fiori and the Ghetto **152**
Via Veneto and
  Villa Borghese **186**
North and Central Rome **190**
Trastevere and the
  Gianicolo **202**
Aventino and Testaccio **212**
Celio and San Giovanni **222**
Monti and Esquilino **230**
The Appian Way **240**
Excursions from Rome **248**
Ostia Antica **252**
Vatican/Forum/Palatine
  back flap

THE BEST OF ROME: TOP SIGHTS

Here, at a glance, are the city's must-sees, from the iconic monuments of Ancient Rome to the vibrant squares of Campo de' Fiori and Trastevere, and the tranquil gardens of the Villa Borghese

△ The majestic ruins of the **Forum**, the civic centre of Ancient Rome, are best seen on a Sunday when the busy thoroughfare that cuts through the site is closed to traffic. *See page 100.*

◁ The **Vatican Museums** merit a lifetime's study, but if you only have a few hours, be sure to include the Sistine Chapel in your tour of this vast repository of art. Michelangelo's breathtaking ceiling is a triumph of fresco painting. *See page 141.*

◁ The **Colosseum** is a shadow of its marble-clad imperial days, but it's impressive nonetheless and, as the symbol of Rome, remains one of the city's key sights. *See page 111.*

△ For a real insight into life in Ancient Rome, follow a tour of the Forum with a visit to the **Capitoline Museums**, an imposing collection of ancient art and Roman statuary. Among its most famous exhibits is the original bronze statue of a she-wolf suckling Romulus and Remus. *See page 89.*

◁ All human life converges on the **Spanish Steps** at the heart of Rome's main shopping district. *See page 129.*

▷ The old working-class district **Trastevere** "across the Tiber" is now a trendy quarter full of boutiques, restaurants and wine bars. *See page 201.*

▽ The best-preserved of all Ancient Rome's buildings is Emperor Hadrian's perfectly proportioned **Pantheon**. *See page 154.*

▷ When a voluptuous Anita Ekberg frolicked in the **Trevi Fountain** in Fellini's *La Dolce Vita*, she turned it into a Roman icon. Throw a coin in the water and enjoy an ice cream on the steps. *See page 117.*

◁ Bernini's masterpiece, the Fountain of the Four Rivers, stands at the heart of elegant **Piazza Navona**, a totally enclosed square full of buskers, street performers, street artists and tourists. *See page 158.*

▽ By day the **Campo de' Fiori** is awash with the colour and activity of the daily market. It's also a great place to eat out at night. *See page 170.*

▽ Leafy **Villa Borghese** is perfect for picnicking and home to two world-class museums. *See page 188.*

THE BEST OF ROME: EDITOR'S CHOICE

Unique attractions, festivals and events, top shops, pizzas and piazzas, church art, family outings... here are our recommendations, plus some money-saving tips

BEST CHURCHES FOR ART

- **San Luigi dei Francesi** The dramatic paintings by Caravaggio in the Contarelli Chapel were the artist's first great religious works. *See page 157.*
- **Santa Maria in Trastevere** A pretty medieval church with spectacular mosaics on the façade and in the apse. *See page 202.*
- **Basilica di San Pietro** Michelangelo's tender and moving *Pietà* in St Peter's was completed when the artist was only 25 and remains one of his most famous works. *See page 139.*
- **San Pietro in Vincoli** This church houses another Michelangelo masterpiece, the newly restored statue of *Moses. See page 231.*

- **Santa Maria della Vittoria** So sensual is Bernini's famous sculpture of the *Ecstasy of St Teresa* that many suggest the rapture on her face is more than an expression of piety. *See page 187.*
- **Santa Prassede** The 9th-century church is filled with magnificent Byzantine mosaics. *See page 230.*
- **Santa Maria del Popolo** is a treasure house of art, with paintings by Pinturicchio, Raphael and two impassioned Caravaggios. *See page 125.*

BEST VIEWS

- **The Gianicolo hill** Worlds away from the tightly packed streets of Trastevere and the chaos of the city below. *See page 206.*
- **Piazza Venezia** Fine views from the Vittoriano monument have the added advantage of excluding the hulking monument itself. *See page 90.*
- **Caffè Capitolino** Romantic views of terracotta rooftops and countless cupolas from the Capitoline

Museum's pretty café. *See page 91.*
- **The Tabularium** Take in the Forum and the Palatine from a terrace in the ancient archive of Roman Law. *See page 89.*
- **Pincio Gardens** Views from the Villa Borghese Gardens stretch from Monte Mario to the Gianicolo and the piazza below. *See page 189.*
- **Castel Sant'Angelo** Views of the Tiber. *See page 143.*

- **Villa Borghese Gardens** Laid out over rolling hills, this is the perfect city park for picnicking and relaxing. Attractions include museums, a zoo, a boating lake and bikes for hire. *See page 188.*
- **Castel Sant' Angelo** Drawbridges, trapdoors, cannons, ditches and dungeons … everything but dragons in this ancient castle. *See page 143.*
- **Children's Museum** Explora is a delightful "playtown" where kids can touch, draw and play to their heart's content. *See page 306.*
- **Puppet shows** Free Punch and Judy shows on the Gianicolo hill. *See page 206.*
- **Coins in the fountain** A coin tossed in the Trevi Fountain is said to guarantee your return to Rome. *See page 117.*
- **A leisurely ride** on the No. 116 electric bus, which weaves its way from Via Veneto to the Vatican. Lovely for sightseeing and a welcome relief for sore feet. *See page 285.*
- **Luneur** When sightseeing saturation point has been reached head for the EUR district and let off steam in this amusement park or in the large open-air swimming pool. *See page 216.*

BEST GETAWAYS

- **Ostia Antica** Well-preserved ruins of an old Roman port town. *See page 251.*
- **Tivoli** See the sumptuous Villa d'Este and its fountain-filled garden, and the remains of Hadrian's magnificent villa. *See page 257.*
- **Etruscan tombs** Cerveteri is the most atmospheric of the many Etruscan necropolises outside Rome. *See page 276.*
- **Oasi di Ninfa** An enchanting wild garden with medieval ruins. *See page 263.*
- **Beaches** Sunseekers should head for Fregene or venture further afield to Lazio's southern coastal stretches. *See page 254.*

BEST PIAZZAS

- **Piazza Navona** Baroque grandeur, spectacular fountains and lively atmosphere. *See page 158.*
- **Piazza Farnese** A welcome relief from the chaos of neighbouring Campo de' Fiori. *See page 177.*
- **Piazza Mattei** A small piazza with a playful fountain and trendy café. *See page 173.*
- **Piazza Santa Maria in Trastevere** This neighbourly square buzzes with activity round the clock but never seems crowded. *See page 202.*
- **Piazza San Pietro** Vast, colonnaded square designed by Bernini to accommodate those on the papal pilgrimage. *See page 137.*
- **Piazza del Campidoglio** For the beautifully elegant staircase designed by Michelangelo. *See page 89.*
- **Piazza di Spagna** A spectacular urban space, perfect for people-watching. *See page 129.*

OPPOSITE FAR LEFT: views from the Vittoriano monument. **OPPOSITE LEFT:** Michelangelo's *Pietà*. **OPPOSITE BELOW:** mosaic in Santa Maria in Trastevere. **ABOVE:** Hadrian's Villa. **LEFT:** cycling in Villa Borghese. **RIGHT:** Piazza Navona.

ABOVE: a contented cat colony member. **BELOW LEFT:** arcane potions made by monks. **BELOW:** fireworks over the Colosseum.

BEST BUYS

- **Ice cream** Head for Gelato San Crispino for colouring- and preservative-free ice-cream. *See page 123.*
- **Valentino** Ready-to-wear from Rome's beloved designer. *See page 299.*
- **Handbags** from Fendi and Furla are the ultimate in classic chic. The less discerning can pick up a cheap designer knock-off from any of the street vendors that congregate around tourist hotspots. *See page 299.*

- **Shoes** from Bruno Magli, a prestigious shoemaker for over 70 years. *See page 300.*
- **Food** Two legendary delis for Roman specialities are Volpetti in Testaccio and charmingly old-fashioned Innocenzi in Trastevere. *See page 302.*
- **Jewellery** In New York there's Tiffany, in Paris there's Cartier, in Rome there's Bulgari, where extravagant jewellery reigns supreme. Serious money. *See page 301.*

ONLY IN ROME

- **Cat colonies** There are thousands of cats in Rome, many of them living wild among the ancient ruins. *See page 172.*
- **Priestly couture** Papal party gear, nuns' underwear, incense burners and more can be found in shops for religious garments and accessories on Via dei Cestari and Via di Santa Chiara. *See page 153*
- **Cappuccino** Rome is full of atmospheric cafés serving excellent

coffee. Piazza Rotonda and Piazza Farnese are prime spots, but the neighbourhood cafés frequented by locals are more fairly priced.
- **Catacombs** Three of the largest underground burial sites are to be found in the vicinity of the Appian Way. *See page 245.*
- **Made by monks** The potions and lotions, teas and preserves on sale at Ai Monasteri are all made by monks. *See page 301.*

BEST FESTIVALS AND EVENTS

- **RomaEuropa** An experimental arts festival held every autumn: a real breath of cosmopolitan air.
- **Estate Romana** "Roman Summer" is the collective name for all the events held outdoors in parks, villas, monuments and ancient sites, from June to September.
- **Easter week** torchlit processions and a

huge open-air Mass in St Peter's Square. Plus chocolate and pastries galore.
- **Photography Festival** held all over town from April to June.
- **Il Natale di Roma** On 21 April Rome celebrates its founding with fireworks, music and other events. *For more about Rome's festivals see pages 306–8.*

BEST PIZZAS

- **Dar Poeta** A special yeast-free dough is this Trastevere pizzeria's trademark. A local favourite. *See page 209.*
- **Formula Uno** The best and most down-to-earth pizzeria in the San Lorenzo university quarter, which is known as pizza central. *See page 237.*
- **Da Baffetto** A legendary pizza venue with fast-moving queues outside all night long. Brash but efficient service adds to the quintessential Roman experience. *See page 166.*
- **Clok** Fun and lively pizzeria with modern decor and a wine bar. *See page 145.*
- **O' Pazzariello** A Neapolitan pizzeria with lots of ambience in quite a small space. *See page 166.*
- **PizzaRé** Serves a huge range of crusty Neapolitan-style pizzas that are reliable and appetising. *See page 135.*
- **Zi' Fenizia** A kosher take-away in the Jewish Ghetto which has a permanent queue. *See page 183.*

ABOVE: inviting rooms at the Casa Howard. **RIGHT:** pizzas may have originated in Naples, but there are many excellent ones to be found all over Rome.

BEST SMALL HOTELS

- **Casa Howard, Via Capo Le Case** Tucked away in a secluded *palazzo*, the rooms are decorated with real flair. *See page 290.*
- **Aleph** Intriguing boutique hotel. Bedrooms inspired by 1930s design with hi-tech details, huge beds and a great spa. *See page 289.*
- **Locarno** Appealing Art Deco touches (the ornate cage lift alone is memorable). Oodles of charm and class. *See page 291.*
- **Due Torri** A delightful, historic hotel in a former cardinal's palace down a cobbled street. *See page 293.*
- **Teatro di Pompeo** Perched just off picturesque Campo de' Fiori, a homely mood prevails in the tasteful bedrooms. *See page 295.*

MONEY-SAVING TIPS

Free Forum
Free entrance to the Forum – you only pay when you get to the Palatine. *See page 98.*

Free churches
All the basilicas and churches in Rome are free, as is the Pantheon.

Settimana della Cultura
Cultural Week is held all over Italy in late April or May, when entrance is free to all state-run museums and historical sites (log onto www.beni culturali.it for more details). *See page 307.*

Bus tours
Buses in Rome are cheap and efficient. An army of small, electric buses (116, 117 and 119) wind their way through the most scenic parts of Rome where cars and "real" buses cannot venture. *See page 285.*

Cheap eats
Anywhere marked *tavola calda*, where you can choose from well-stocked buffets, or *pizza al taglio*, where you can buy slices of pizza to enjoy on the steps of a nearby fountain or square.

Free Vatican
Entrance to the Vatican Museums is free on the last Sunday of the month, but be prepared for long queues. *See page 141.*

"Roman Summer" events
Anything that is part of the Estate Romana programme is usually very cheap (€8–€15), and you can buy a season ticket that makes it even cheaper. *See page 309.*

ROME AND THE ROMANS

Dubbed the Eternal City by poets and artists, Rome is one of the world's most exhilarating and romantic travel destinations. It is a city that inspires the mind, appeals to the senses and captures the heart

Since its millennial revamp for Holy Year, Rome has rarely looked lovelier. The facelift to its ancient sites has been matched by subtle plastic surgery to its arts scene. Revamped galleries, new contemporary art museums, a cinema festival and the creation of a superb music complex have helped turn the city's face towards the future. While not a new *Dolce Vita*, there is a cinematic gloss to the emerging city: eclectic festivals, a funky club scene, sleek cafés, boutique hotels and a more cosmopolitan air. Cynics retort: but this is not why we flock to Rome. True, but to remain "Ancient Rome" and still be a contemporary city is the cleverest trick of all.

Not that Rome will ever wear its history lightly. The Eternal City remains chaotic but compact, bewildering but walkable, beguiling but exhausting. Unfortunately, the public transport system, from the pointless metro to the

The Eternal City has shaken off its dusty toga and slipped into contemporary clothes. As the mayor says: "Rome dares to dream again."

overcrowded buses, is woefully inadequate, with buses shunned by most middle-class Romans and the metro going nowhere relevant for most visitors. Work on a new metro line, running north-west to south-east, will slice through the heart of the Imperial city, but this is not due for completion until 2013 at the earliest. Fear of damaging ancient sites and becoming mired in bureaucracy are why radical measures have never been contemplated before now.

For now, cynical Romans see a decent transport system as a gift to their grandchildren, much as straight roads were a gift to the Empire's grateful colonies. Until then, the demented locals will continue to fume in traffic jams, flit by on flimsy Vespas or rattle around in speed-crazed buses. For visitors, the good news is that, with stoicism, sturdy shoes and enough caffeine-fuelled café stops, Rome is still a heavenly walking city.

PRECEDING PAGES: Castel Sant' Angelo; view from the Vatican. **LEFT:** shopping on the busy Via del Corso. **ABOVE:** sharing a quiet moment on Piazza del Popolo.

Neighbourhoods

The locals jest that Rome is not for Romans: few Romans live in the historic centre any more. In the 1960s the tradesmen moved to the suburbs in search of comfortable apartments while the *centro storico* succumbed to gentrification; once-crumbling *palazzi* were snapped up by astute investors, from bankers to politicians. Yet individuals remain attached to their *rione* or neighbourhood: the original 14 date from the time of the Emperor Augustus, but have grown to 22, each with its own civic crest. Moreover, Romans also harbour attachments to mythologised quarters in the *centro storico*, such as the Ghetto, the former Jewish district, or Campo de' Fiori, once peopled by mere fruit-sellers and furniture-restorers but now full of funky bars and fashion victims.

Outsiders often see Rome as devoted to Imperial posturing, whether of the ostentatious Colosseum-Forum variety or Mussolini's self-aggrandising EUR district. Yet local neighbourhoods can be both cosmopolitan and homely, ranging from the formalised domesticity of Parioli, framed by embassies, to mellow Trastevere, louche yet intimate, dotted with arty bars and galleries. Looming above Trastevere is the leafy, *fin de siècle* Gianicolo district, home to retiring residents and expatriate newcomers.

Rome can be rough around the edges, but its lack of manicured perfection is part of its charm. The Esquilino area,

---

ALL ABOARD

For the cheapest, most chaotic tour through the time machine that is Rome, hop on the 87 bus, which runs from east to west, scoring a cross-section of the city's history. The route runs from bustling Piazza Cavour to the rural Via Appia Antica archaeological park, replete with tombs, ruins, cats and ghosts. En route are swathes of the Imperial, Early Christian, Renaissance and Baroque city in all its glory, from the gladiatorial Colosseum to seductive Piazza Navona, the Tiber and the legendary Seven Hills of Rome.

Flashing past your eyes is all Roman history, from monumentality to murder most foul.

To see Rome as Fellini saw it, ride the No. 3 tram, which Fellini claimed gave him inspiration.

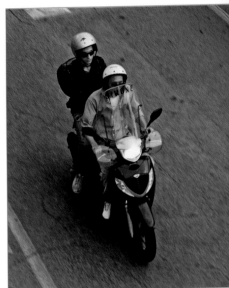

around the Fascist-Modernist Termini Station, nicknamed "the dinosaur", is a case in point, as is Testaccio, the former meat-packing district that is, with Ostiense, the pulsating heart of clubland. Once dilapidated, these districts are being gentrified but retain their edginess, youthful spirit and multi-ethnic flavour. Rome is more cosmopolitan than at any time since the Empire, though hardly on the same scale.

Yet beyond its bustle and bravado, the Eternal City feels static, imprisoned by its past. Rome is *the* place for contemplating the passage of time and the vanity of human wishes. "Within a short time you forget everything; and everything forgets you," said Marcus Aurelius. The world-weary population has little inclination to relive the glory, decline and fall. Nonetheless, there is a residual melancholy and romantic nostalgia for the grandeur of Imperial Rome.

The temporal and the spiritual

Novelist Alberto Moravia used to say: "Rome is an administrative city dominated by two institutions: the State and the Church." While an oversimplification, Rome *is* the meeting place of temporal and spiritual powers and, as the capital, lives and breathes politics. As for piety, the Vatican has traditionally been treated as a temporal power, as the corporate arm of the papacy. "Faith is made here but believed elsewhere," is the local dictum.

Essentially, the Romans are more ritualistic than religious, even if the death of John Paul

II saw an outpouring of emotion that surprised cynical Rome-watchers.

At work, Romans have an inbuilt resistance to Milanese efficiency, schedules and short lunch breaks. Life is too Latin for a Protestant work ethic. Indeed, there are few qualms about playing the tourist at home, from eating an ice cream on Piazza Navona to tossing a coin in the Trevi Fountain, visiting the Vatican museums on a Vespa, lolling around the Villa Borghese

> As the writer Alberto Moravia said: "There are no Romans, only people from all parts of Italy who adopt Roman characteristics."

Gardens, or peeking into the Pantheon while on a café crawl.

The first Pantheon was built by Marcus Agrippa. Even though Hadrian's later version in AD 117 was an improvement, he gave credit to his predecessor. Agrippa, who built aqueducts, baths and colonies, was too industrious to be a typical Roman. As the local saying goes: "*ce piace mangia bene ce piace poco lavora*" – we prefer eating and drinking to working.

FAR LEFT: guards outside the Quirinal Palace.
LEFT ABOVE: shopping on the Campo de' Fiori.
LEFT BELOW: in-line skating in the Villa Borghese.
ABOVE: Trastevere street. **ABOVE RIGHT:** Rome's most efficient form of transport.

Romans at play

Bar aficionados believe you can tell a lot about a Roman by his café of choice. Cardinals favour the upstanding Caffè San Pietro near the Vatican, while haunts such as Caffè Rosati on Piazza del Popolo are proud of being the place *not* to be seen; here, celebrity regulars unwind in a discreet Art Nouveau ambience.

Roman café-owners proudly announce that "this was Fellini's favourite place", "Mastroianni's haunt", or that "Bertolucci prefers our pastries". Bar Canova, near Piazza del Popolo, was Fellini's second home: he came straight from his Oscar success to a party in the bar. The back room, where the visionary director held meetings, is now a Fellini shrine.

Yet the best bars compel a sentimental attachment that goes well beyond celebrity-worship: the journalist wife of Francesco Rutelli, the Deputy Prime Minister, even dedicated a book to her local bar-owner in Caffè del Teatro Marcello.

Nightlife is less tribal than café culture, inspired by "*vivere e lascia vivere*," a "live and let live" philosophy. Party-goers start late and finish late, with clubbers calling into a bar for a *cornetto* (sweet croissant) and cappuccino before heading home. San Lorenzo, a city within a city, is an erstwhile immigrant district that is now the heart of the main university quarter, around Via dei Volsci. By night, books are exchanged for bar crawls, with Happy Hour an excuse for wine-tasting, tapas bars, emerging bands and, bizarrely, even board games.

Clubland is centred on Testaccio and Via Ostiense, particularly since the Roma Tre university campus has revitalised the area. How-

SLEEPLESS NIGHTS

Notte Bianche, the Sleepless Nights festival in September, has kick-started the city's nightlife, with gallery openings, wine-tastings and fireworks. But even outside the big festivals, the bars in Testaccio, Ostiense and Trastevere are rarely quiet. Supperclub has reached Rome, a recline-as-you-dine cool cabaret concept with Prosecco-sipping locals prostrate on sofas, all appropriately staged in Nero's former baths. Bloom is a celebrity haunt set in a medieval chapel that has been jazzed up by DJs, Philippe Starck lighting, Asian-Italian fusion food and gold-leaf walls. Its rival, Salotto 42, is a bohemian traveller's den set in a Roman temple, complete with chandeliers and ethnic snacks. In hip Ostiense, just south of Testaccio, Doppiozero is a slick bar to take the designer-clad crowd from *aperitivi* to *digestivi*. Nearby, Estrobar is a cool but atmospheric wine bar and gallery. At Fluid, you can sip your *aperitivo* while sitting on illuminated ice cubes in a fake water theme park. For those who crave tradition, Caffè Greco, a plush, hand-painted bar where Shelley once scribbled verse, is still popular with hip Romans. Night-owls might prefer Caffè della Pace, off Piazza Navona.

ever, more mellow visitors may feel more at home with Trastevere's arty ambience, and an evening spent in cool bars, listening to the Blues, followed by an *affogato* ice cream, drenched in liqueur.

High culture

As for high culture, Rome has seen a swathe of renovations and reopenings. The most radical project is MAXXI, a partially completed grand project by Anglo-Iraqi architect Zaha Hadid, which sees a former army barracks reborn as the Museum of 21st-Century Arts. More traditional is the major refurbishment of the Palazzo Barberini and Gallery of Ancient Art, set in a palace designed by Borromini and Bernini, the founder of the Italian Baroque style. The rest of this great collection resides in Palazzo Corsini over the river, but is due to be displayed under one roof in Palazzo Barberini – but only when the privileged Officers' Club decamps from its palatial residence there.

In leafy Villa Borghese, the city's best-loved gardens, the Orangery (Aranceria) has been transformed into a modern art museum dedicated to Carlo Bilotti, an Italo-American collector. Close to vibrant Campo de' Fiori, the new Museo Barracco showcases Egyptian, Etruscan and Roman sculpture and, unlike most didactic Roman museums, uses a multimedia approach.

The most controversial new site is the Ara Pacis Museum, a steel, glass and marble structure designed to house a 2,000-year-old Altar of Peace that, ironically, was used for sacrifices. Created by Richard Meier, this is the first new public monument erected in the historic centre since Mussolini's day, and it divides local opinion. Art critic Vittorio Sgarbi called it "an indecent cesspit", while others have praised it as an airy, accessible building that lets citizens see into the mindset of Emperor Augustus and Ancient Rome.

The Romans have a reputation for being artistic connoisseurs and cultural raiders rather than creative artists. As blasé sophisticates, they have seen it all before and bought the T-shirt. Yet despite their love of bread and circuses, contemporary citizens have cultivated a dynamic arts scene, with one of the most

FAR LEFT: waiter at the News Café. **LEFT:** party-goers start late and finish late. **ABOVE:** Easter concert performance at the Auditorium.

Venice, but seeks to involve the Roman public rather than outsiders.

In trendy Testaccio, the Mattatoio, a former slaughterhouse, houses a cultural centre and MACRO, a hip art gallery. In the San Lorenzo area, near Termini Station, galleries in unconventional settings combine literary cafes with installations, photographic displays and performance art. Dotted around the city are concept stores and bookshops that double as bars and multimedia venues. Rome playfully mixes art and entertainment: in the Supperclub, based in Nero's former baths, revellers feast and lounge on divans, just as their ancestors did in Nero's day.

Fashion parades

Shopping passes the time for world-weary city dwellers. Svelte Romans saunter down Via del Corso and Via Condotti to windowshop for chic designer names. As for Roman brands, the leading lights are Valentino, renowned for his

vibrant music venues in Italy. Much credit is due to the Parco della Musica, Renzo Piano's theatrical space, where beetle-like pods create perfect acoustics in settings suitable for symphonies or soul, Rachmaninov or Lou Reed. Casa del Jazz, in the gardens of Villa Osio, a property confiscated from a Mafia boss, has grown into the city's major dedicated jazz venue. The new Cinema Festival may not rival

EASTER IN ROME

Easter is the most heartfelt Roman festival, when history and tradition merge with common piety and cheerful consumerism. At Easter, the Eternal City is never more at ease with its Roman and Christian heritage, from St Peter's "Roman" relics to the Scala Santa, the marble staircase that Christ supposedly ascended to meet Pontius Pilate. In San Giovanni in Laterano, where the staircase arrived from Palestine, the faithful dutifully climb to the top on their knees. On Good Friday, the Pope retraces Christ's Via Crucis on a moving candlelit procession, ending in a huge open-air Mass on St Peter's Square on Easter Sunday. On becoming Pope, Benedict XVI opened up the Porta Santa Rosa entrance to the Vatican, as a gesture of openness, but the queues of pilgrims remain just as long. The Easter procession winds from the Colosseum to Monte Palatino, re-enacting the 14 Stations of the Cross, from Christ's death sentence to his entombment, with the Pope uttering a prayer at each station. Thousands of pilgrims gather with torches to follow this solemn procession, which coincides with classical concerts in many city churches. Not that Roman festivals eschew gaiety and self-indulgence. The city's pastry shops display Easter eggs stuffed with tiny silver picture frames or costume jewellery. Wealthier Romans even instruct their favourite chocolatiers to encase treasured gifts in the eggs, ranging from engagement rings to car keys or symbolic crosses. Despite their sophistication, Romans love the chocolate-wrapped trappings of piety, and tangible symbols of truth, a reminder that even Christian Rome was founded on relics.

red-carpet style, Brioni, dresser to James Bond, and Fendi, displaying bespoke bags and politically incorrect furs in the gorgeous Palazzo Fendi at the foot of the Spanish Steps. More individualistic shopping awaits in the art galleries and workshops of Trastevere or in the Borghetto Flaminio antiques market. Rome is full of *botteghe*, artisans' workshops that will copy a marble bust on demand. Come nightfall and *aperitivo* time, the fashionistas emerge, to parade around lively Campo de' Fiori and the beguiling Piazza Navona area.

Summer in the city

The summer heat drives most Romans out of the city in search of sea or mountain air. Those who remain are wooed by summer festivals and hedonistic nightlife, especially during the *Estate Romana* festival. Summer is a riot of outdoor events staged in villas, parks and squares, from open-air cinema on Tiber Island to concerts and parties in the park. Equally lovely are the Terme di Caracalla, the high-vaulted Roman baths, periodically used to showcase summer events.

In the lush Villa Borghese Gardens, the Globe Theatre Roma is a replica of London's Elizabethan theatre of the same name, and stages Shakespearean drama and experimental theatre from June to September.

Set in stone

Despite all the surface glitz, there is no escaping the architecture, which assails one's senses around every corner. The Romans were

FAR LEFT: lounging at the Supperclub. LEFT: leather craftsman at work in his San Lorenzo studio. ABOVE: AS Roma celebrate a win at a Rome derby against Lazio. ABOVE RIGHT: Via dei Condotti swarms with shoppers and tourists.

arguably the greatest builders of antiquity, combining monumentality and utility with Greek grace and a sense of creation for eternity. The Pantheon remains an inspiration to contemporary architects, while down-to-earth football fans are equally struck by the Stadio Olimpico, Mussolini's Olympic Stadium, which hosts the deadly rivals, Roma and Lazio.

For an architectural overview, the Crypta Balbi displays recent archaeological finds and traces the city's development from the pre-Imperial era to Early Christian and medieval times. While most city museums and galleries are unduly didactic, the theatrical streets are a revelation.

Given its cinematic glamour, Rome can't help resembling a film set. Memories of gladiatorial contests are inescapable, superimposed on scenes of Fellini-esque excess or *Dolce Vita* charm, a *Roman Holiday* with Gregory Peck and Audrey Hepburn. Not that Hepburn will suddenly hitch up her Givenchy skirt and hop on a Vespa – the *Dolce Vita* doesn't linger on, despite the retro sexiness of the city. But a certain sultriness seeps into the spirit of the stones, ensuring that Rome remains the Eternal City. ❏

THE MAKING OF ROME

Emperors and popes, dictators and rebels,
philosophers and barbarians, saints and
sinners, from immense wealth to pillage
and ruin; Romans really have seen it all

omulus and Remus, the twins famously suckled by a she-wolf, are not the only candidates for the title of founders of Rome. One account offered by Pliny the Elder was of a noblewoman who was surprised by a male organ rising from the ashes of a hearth. The resulting child became King Servius Tullius, builder of the first wall around Rome.

The Livy version

Implausible pregnancy is a feature of many of the legendary accounts, and this is no accident. Archaeology has unearthed evidence of scattered settlements in the Roman hills in 1200 BC, but these early Latins were culturally overshadowed by Etruscans and Greeks. Roman historians preferred a neat break with the past. Miraculous conception was just the ticket.

Rome is the only great city that has a birthday – 21 April, Il Natale di Roma, the precise day when, according to Livy, Romulus founded the city back in 753 BC.

A large part of Livy's vast *History of Rome*, written in the 1st century BC, is devoted to weighing up theories on its origins, including that of the poet Virgil, who relished the idea of the Greek world as Rome's spiritual cradle. Aeneas, the hero of Virgil's *Aeneid*, is a survivor

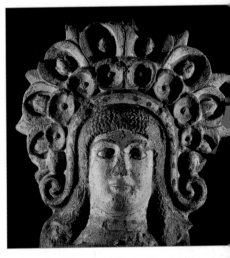

of the sack of Troy who drifted to North Africa and was sent by the gods to found Rome. Livy added more divine intervention: King Numitor of Alba Longa, the city founded by Aeneas's son Ascanius, was usurped, Livy explains, by his brother Amulius, and Numitor's daughter Rhea Silvia hid in a cave. She was visited there by the war god Mars, who became the father of her twins Romulus and Remus. Doubting this unlikely story, Amulius had her thrown into the Tiber, while the twins were put in a basket and cast adrift to meet their fate. The basket was washed up below the Palatine Hill, and the babies' cries attracted a she-wolf, who suckled the boys until they were rescued by a shepherd.

LEFT: detail showing battle scenes from the Column of Marcus Aurelius. **ABOVE:** an Etruscan head from the 4th century BC.

Mars later appeared to the twins and pointed them towards their glorious destiny. They founded Rome, wrote Livy, in 753 BC.

Relations between them then soured. Remus proposed a site on the Aventine, and the name Rema; Romulus demanded the Palatine and Roma. Remus ridiculed Romulus' new walls, jumping over them. Furious, Romulus killed his brother, and the walls were ritually annointed with his blood.

Again as Livy tells it, Rome's population grew fast, but with many more men than women. Romulus decided to lay on games so magnificent all the surrounding tribes were bound to attend. What they did not know was that their women would not be going home. This has been immortalised as the "rape of the Sabine women".

Republican virtues

Seven kings were said to have ruled Rome after Romulus.

Most – despite the legends – were Etruscans, indicating that Rome was still subordinate to the older civilisation. The city's institutions took shape: the patrician class provided priests and judges, while plebeians took care of agriculture, cattle-breeding and trade.

Tensions were frequent between Etruscans and Romans. They came to a head over another notorious rape, of Lucretia, the virtuous wife of a Roman, Collatinus, by the degenerate son of

ROMAN FAMILIES – THEORY AND PRACTICE

In Roman law men had absolute power over women – in theory. The head of a family or *pater familias* enjoyed total authority over all the women in it, and on marriage a woman simply passed from his authority to that of her husband. If she fell short of "virtue in all things" he could instantly divorce her, or punish her. Reality, though, often intervened. Wars sent high-born men away for years on end, leaving their wives in charge of their property, and created many wealthy widows. The rich woman with a string of lovers and a far-off husband was a stock figure for Roman gossips. Laws were relaxed to allow upper-class women to manage estates, or even engage in trade.

At the start of the Empire Augustus tried to re-establish old disciplines with fierce punishments for misbehaviour and restrictions on women, but without much success: one of their first victims was his own daughter Julia, who was exiled for adultery.

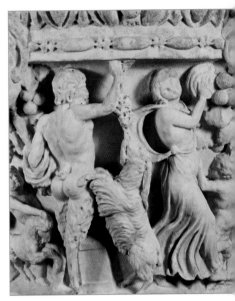

Rome's Etruscan King Tarquinius Superbus. As Roman historians tell it, the populace rose up against the licentiousness of the Etruscan court, and drove Rome's last Etruscan king into exile. In 509 BC Marcus Junius, leader of the revolt, was elected one of the two Consuls who ruled Rome, as it became a republic. An Etruscan attempt to retake the city was seen off at the bridge across the Tiber by the hero Horatius.

The Roman Republic was tightly organised, above all for war – to which every Roman citizen had to contribute – but had no democracy. Only patricians could vote and sit in the Senate, to which the Consuls were responsible. In 494 the post of Tribune was created to protect plebeian interests, and from 450 BC the Twelve Tables of laws were displayed in the Forum, but the thousands of slaves had no rights at all.

Continental domination

Rome made little effort to develop an economic base: it simply lived on the proceeds of conquest. The Republic prospered against the backdrop of an invasion by the Gauls in 390, when cackling geese sounded the alarm; the wars with Carthage, when Hannibal led his elephants across the Alps and almost brought Rome's progress to a dead stop; and the steady growth of its Empire, as the Romans expanded into Spain and to the banks of the Danube. With the final defeat of Carthage in 146 BC, Rome dominated the entire Mediterranean.

A mighty military machine was needed to control the conquered provinces, and successful generals became the most powerful figures

in the state, with violent rivalries between them. In 91 BC two generals, Marius and Sulla, put down a revolt in several Italian cities, but then fought each other, and the unscrupulous Sulla took advantage of the situation to seize

> *The Roman Republic was marked out among its neighbours by military organisation and its belligerent belief in its right to conquer allcomers.*

power and install Rome's first brief military dictatorship. The Roman Republic was dying.

Enter Caesar

The squabbles of the Roman élite continued after Sulla's death, but were interrupted by a vast slave revolt in 73 BC, led by the gladiator Spartacus. It was finally crushed by Crassus, which helped him become for a time the Empire's foremost general. From 59 BC he shared power in the First Triumvirate with Pompey and Julius Caesar, a brilliant commander who was about to conquer Gaul and lead his legions across the English Channel.

LEFT: the rape of the Sabine women, as seen by David in the 1790s. ABOVE: the Roman Senate in session. ABOVE RIGHT: carved column capital depicting Pan teasing a goat with a bunch of grapes.

While in Gaul, he made sure a generous share of his booty went back to the capital to buy political support, and the friendship between him and Pompey turned into bitter enmity. Caesar was forbidden to return to Italy, but in 49 BC he defied the Senate by crossing the River Rubicon with his army, with the aim of seizing power. Defeated by Caesar's legions in Greece, Pompey fled to Egypt, where he was killed by his former Egyptian friends. Caesar followed him, and lingered in Egypt, besotted by its young queen Cleopatra, with whom he

had a son. When he returned to Rome, she accompanied him.

Caesar now had unchallenged power, and endeared himself to the people with a spectacular building programme. Rome still had Republicans determined to resist dictatorship, however, and a band of senators led by Brutus cut Caesar down, on the Ides of March, 44 BC.

Gods and Empire

Caesar's murder did not lead to a restoration of the Republic but a new civil war, in which the conspirators were easily defeated by an alliance of Caesar's nephew and adopted son Octavian and Caesar's leading general, Mark Antony. These two, though, were also rivals, and became open enemies when Antony developed his passion for Cleopatra, which provided romantic interest for the next 13 years. After the two famous lovers committed suicide, Octavian, who took the name Augustus or "revered one", emerged as victor and – although the Senate remained in place, with little power – the first Roman emperor.

Cleopatra's expropriated treasure funded Augustus' transformation of Rome from "a city of brick into a city of marble". The Augustan Age was Rome's cultural apex, producing Virgil, Ovid and Livy. To end the political bickering of earlier years, Augustus gave Rome a much stronger civil service, which kept the Empire and its capital going throughout all the bizarre misbehaviour of his successors.

To reinforce his power (and ego) Augustus encouraged the worship of Julius Caesar and the rest of his family as gods, and this was taken to heart by his descendants, who literally believed they could do anything. Emperors such as Tiberius, Caligula and Nero acted like monsters at the pinnacle of society,

NERO'S DREAM HOME

Nero's extravagance was extraordinary even for one of the Caesars. After Rome's great fire in AD 64 – which many said he started – he seized 80 hectares (200 acres) of land by the Forum to build his Domus Aurea or "Golden House", with façades clad in gold, ivory and mother-of-pearl tiles and fountains sprinkling perfumes. "At last", he said when it was finished, amazingly quickly, "I can live like a human being." So hated was Nero, though, that demolition began immediately after his death in 68, and his artificial lake-bed was used as the site of the Colosseum, to entertain the masses.

rivalling each other in their decadence, gleefully related by the later writer Suetonius. Alongside Roman excess there was a strange devotion to formality; the Greek Plutarch

The satirist Juvenal said that Roman emperors ruled with "bread and circuses" – doling out free grain to the poor, and dazzling the masses with lavish spectacles and bloody gladiatorial combats.

wrote long treatises on morality and etiquette, including which subjects to discuss at dinner.

Honour was restored to the throne after the death of Nero in AD 68 by a succession of effective emperors, notably Trajan, Hadrian and the philosopher-emperor Marcus Aurelius, who between them led Rome to the height of its power in the second century AD. With over

1 million people, it was a city without equal anywhere in the world, attracting people from every part of its Empire and the known world.

Constantine and Christianity

Over the centuries, defending its vast possessions against a host of potential invaders imposed immense strains on the Empire. In 286, Emperor Diocletian decided ruling the Empire had become too big a job for one man, and divided it into two halves, Eastern and Western. After his death this led to more fighting between rival emperors, which ended, briefly, in 312 when Constantine the Great emerged as sole emperor. He, however, reaffirmed the division between East and West, and moved his main capital to the shores of the Black Sea, to the city he gave his name, Constantinople. Rome, once the *caput mundi* or "head of the world", was left just a shadow of its former self.

Constantine's other world-changing decision was to grant toleration to Christianity, which only recently had been fiercely persecuted. In 324, he effectively made it the state religion of the Empire. In Rome itself the new faith and old pagan traditions coexisted for decades, but Constantine's decisions established Christianity

---

FAR LEFT: the grape harvest, in a Roman mosaic.
LEFT: noble Romans: Caesar (left) and Brutus.
ABOVE TOP: portrayal of a Roman orgy with dancer.
ABOVE: the poet Virgil, from an early manuscript.
ABOVE RIGHT: philosopher-emperor Marcus Aurelius.

Western Roman emperor. In the next century, the Byzantine emperor Justinian sought to restore the old Empire and succeeded in regaining control of most of Italy, but even then his governors ruled from Ravenna, not Rome, and they were unable to resist another Germanic invasion, by the Lombards. The popes left Ravenna and returned to Rome, installing themselves in the Castel Sant'Angelo.

A major part in building up the role of the papacy was played by Gregory the Great, pope from 590–604. Seized by the beauty of Anglo-

as the religion of the Western world. In Rome the first great churches were built; eventually Christianity and paganism fused, and images of ancient goddesses metamorphosed into the Christian Madonna.

Hard times

Rome was still the seat of the so-called Western emperors, who clung on, relying on armies of barbarian mercenaries. In 410, Emperor Honorius failed to pay the Visigoth leader Alaric, who sacked Rome, an event seen as the real end of the Roman Empire in the West.

Political collapse left a leadership vacuum increasingly filled by the new religion, and especially the bishop of Rome, the Pope – in contrast to the East, where Christian patriarchs were subordinate to the Byzantine emperors. In 452, Pope Leo I played a major part in buying off the hordes of Attila, the "Scourge of God", but he was unable to stop another sack of Rome, by the Vandals in 455. The city's essential aqueducts were no longer maintained, and Rome was partly abandoned.

Germanic tribes dominated Italy, and in 476 the Ostrogoth king Theodoric finally deposed Romulus Augustulus, theoretically the last

Around AD 100 Rome's population was well over 1 million; by 600 it had no more than 20,000 people, living among the ancient ruins and using them as a quarry.

Saxon youths in Rome's slave market, it is said, he was inspired to send missionaries to convert their country to Christianity. Missionary expeditions across the Continent were also used to assert papal authority over all the Christian communities of Western Europe, which until then had largely gone their own way.

Nostalgic Empire

The papacy's search for a Christian ruler to protect the Church focused on an alliance with the Frankish kings, sealed on Christmas Eve 800 when Pope Leo III crowned Charlemagne as Holy Roman Emperor in Rome. By this act Leo sought to make it clear that popes preceded emperors, but this was only the prelude to centuries of struggle for supremacy between the two. The "Holy Roman Empire" evoked the stability of the past, but it was never clear what the powers or role of this Empire were.

Rome was attacked by Muslim Saracens, in 846, and Romans fought Romans in political factions. Pope Gregory VII, elected in 1073, established many characteristic institutions of the Catholic Church, including the College of Cardinals and compulsory celibacy for priests. He also attempted to claw back authority over the Holy Roman Empire at the expense of Emperor Henry IV. He looked for new allies in the Normans, but this led to disaster *(see below)*.

Popes frequently excommunicated rulers who displeased them, but this only encouraged disrespect for the papacy. In 1309 France imposed its own candidate as pope and even moved the papacy to Avignon, from where seven successive popes reigned in the papacy's "Babylonian captivity".

Return to splendour

The papacy returned to Rome in 1378, but this was just the prelude to the Great Schism, when there were two or even three popes at the same time. The papacy was only unified with the election in 1417 of Martin V, of the aristocratic Roman Colonna clan.

Rome was in a ruinous state, but the restored papacy enjoyed a new authority that enabled it to demand funds from across Europe, so immense wealth began to flow into the city. Pope Nicholas V (1447–55) is credited with bringing the Renaissance to Rome, founding the Vatican Library and first proposing the complete rebuilding of St Peter's, which was on the verge of collapse. Posterity is indebted to the

Renaissance popes for their lavish patronage of the arts, but it was viewed with suspicion at the time, as Northern Europeans suspected they were just Italian princes extending their power. Fears were reinforced by Machiavelli's *The Prince* of 1513, a study in political intrigue based on the life of Cesare Borgia, illegitimate son and soldier-henchman of the Spanish Pope Alexander VI (1492–1503). Stories circulated around Europe of the worldliness, love of luxury and sexual peccadilloes of the popes, and one,

*FAR LEFT: Ancient Rome's last great monument, the Arch of Constantine. **LEFT**: the founding of Constantinople, as depicted in a tapestry. **ABOVE**: Alaric and his Visigoths sack Rome. **ABOVE RIGHT**: Pope Gregory the Great, from an 11th-century manuscript.*

UNSUITABLE ALLIES

In his struggle with Emperor Henry IV, Pope Gregory VII lacked an army, so he tried to get Robert Guiscard *(pictured)*, the ferocious Norman warrior-ruler of southern Italy, to support him. However, when Guiscard reached Rome in 1084 he found that its people had already surrendered to Henry, and instead of protecting the Pope the

Norman army (which included many Saracen mercenaries, indifferent to squabbles among Christians) set about a sack of Rome that surpassed anything done by Goths or Vandals. Pope Gregory was blamed. Hated by Romans, he lived out his life in exile.

Julius II (1503–13) – as well as being one of the greatest patrons of art and architecture – sought to end the papacy's dependency on untrustworthy monarchs by building up a large army of his own. Called "the warrior-pope", he launched a war against Venice, and played a full-blooded part in all the intrigues of Italian and foreign rulers for dominance in Italy.

Enormous wealth had also made Italy, and Rome, great prizes over which the European powers, especially France and Spain, fought for 60 years. In the 1520s Pope Clement VII mistakenly favoured the French against the mighty Emperor Charles V – then ruler of Spain and Austria – and in 1527 the emperor's army, which included many German Lutherans, took revenge in the infamous Sack of Rome. The Swiss Guard were killed to a man, "old nuns beaten with sticks, and young nuns raped and taken prisoner". This was the end of the papacy's pretensions to be an independent power. Clement VII, fortunate to be alive in his Castel Sant'Angelo refuge, was the first of a series of popes who threw in their lot with Charles V and his Spanish successors. Artists who had fled Rome gradually drifted back, but with a changed spirit. Michelangelo's *Last Judgement* in the Sistine Chapel (1536) is said to reflect the sombre mood of the time.

Counter-Reformation

The shockwaves of the Reformation were soon felt in Rome. In 1545 Pope Paul III convened the Council of Trent to define the "Counter-Reformation", the Catholic

GOD'S BANKER

The richest man in Renaissance Rome was Agostino Chigi. He made a fortune trading in salt and alum (used in textile-dyeing), then made himself still richer by extending loans to several popes, to the point of being named Julius II's official treasurer. Dubbed *il magnifico*, he was a legendary bon vivant and art connoisseur; his mistress Imperia was famed as Rome's most beautiful courtesan. In 1508 he had a dazzling villa built by the Tiber, with paintings by (among others) Giulio Romano, Perugino and Raphael, including *The Triumph of Galatea*. So wealthy was he it was said that after banquets he had silver plates thrown into the Tiber rather than use them again (though it was also said he had his servants lay secret nets to catch them). His heirs were less successful, and in 1580 the villa was sold to the Farnese clan, to become the Villa Farnesina.

better, or have at least assumed the appearance of being so… the whole city has become much more Christian-like in life and manners."

Nevertheless, while the extravagances of Renaissance Rome may have faded, the papacy remained hugely wealthy, and the popes were now able to dedicate more time and resources to Rome itself. This was the background to the

Church's response to the crisis. A newly severe religious discipline was to be maintained, heretical ideas were to be stamped out, and militant new religious orders such as the Jesuits were encouraged to combat Protestantism. Art was required to have a far more emphatic religious message, seen in the growth of the Baroque.

In Rome, some saw an improvement in the social and religious climate. "Several popes in succession have been men of irreproachable lives," wrote Paolo Tiepolo, almost with surprise, in 1576, "hence all others are become

> The Medici Pope Leo X loved extravagant banquets. "God has given us the papacy," he said to his brother, "let us enjoy it."

extraordinary creativity that produced Baroque Rome, which perhaps marked the city visually even more than the High Renaissance. No longer a political power, Rome could still be a giant symbol of the glory of the Church. This could be kept up so long as the flow of wealth into Rome continued, but from around 1650 the papacy faced tighter times.

Napoleon upsets things

In 1796 Napoleon issued a proclamation: "Peoples of Italy, the French army comes to

LEFT: a procession of cardinals during the election of Pope Pius II, 1458, by Pinturicchio. ABOVE TOP: father and son: Pope Alexander VI and Cesare Borgia. ABOVE: detail from Michelangelo's *Last Judgement*. ABOVE RIGHT: warrior-pope and art patron, Julius II.

LE GATEAU DES ROIS,
Tiré au Congrès de Vienne en 1815.

break your chains... we have no quarrel save
with the tyrants who enslave you." After
defeating the papal army, he demanded
money and art treasures from the Vatican,
and sovereignty over the Papal States. Pope
Pius VI was bundled across the French border to Valence, but his successor, Pius VII,
agreed to recognise Napoleon and crown
him emperor in return for being allowed to
return to Rome. Napoleon installed his
mother in a palace in Piazza Venezia, and

married his scandalous sister Pauline to the
Roman Prince Camillo Borghese, who recip-
rocated by selling him the Borghese art collection, for 13 million francs.

Risorgimento

After Napoleon's fall papal rule was restored at
the Congress of Vienna in 1814–15, together
with Austrian dominance over Italy. This was
the background to the Risorgimento, the rise of
modern Italian nationalism, and the liberal and
nationalist conflagration that swept Europe in
1848. Pope Pius IX was perceived as a liberal
reformer, but was also terrified of revolution.

As unrest grew in Rome, he fled to Naples
in November 1848, and a Roman Republic
was proclaimed led by a "triumvirate" including the idealist Giuseppe Mazzini. France's
new ruler Napoleon III, however, needed
Catholic support, and saw the restoration of
the pope as a way to win it. Garibaldi's 4,000
red-shirted volunteers were no defence against
French troops, but after resisting for months
Garibaldi escaped with the remains of his band
across Italy, to gain immortality.

Pius IX was protected by French troops for
20 years, while the Italian states threw off their
princes and united, not behind Mazzini's
Republic but a kingdom of Italy under Victor
Emmanuel II of Piedmont. The Pope meanwhile convened the First Vatican Council,
which had just asserted the doctrine of Papal
Infallibility when in 1870, after Napoleon III's
downfall led to French withdrawal, an explosion rocked the old Aurelian Wall and the Italian army poured through the breach. The Pope
barricaded himself in the Vatican, and Rome
began to adjust to life after 11 centuries of
papal rule.

THE ORIGINAL TOURISTS

After 1700 Rome and the papacy were no longer major
players in European power politics. Instead, the city settled down into being the Continent's first great tourist
attraction, as a "Grand Tour" of Italy and its ancient
relics became an essential part of a Northern European
gentleman's education. Writers such as Gibbon, Smol-
lett, Goethe and Keats all
wandered the ruins of
Ancient Rome, pondering on
its lost civilisation. Romans
responded enthusiastically,
and streets like Via Condotti
were full of servants, guides
and "artists' models" looking
for tourist business.

The capital of united Italy

When Rome was proclaimed capital of united Italy in 1871, a third of its population, then about 200,000, were beggars. For decades the clerical élite had paid no attention to mundane matters like drainage, at which the ancients had excelled, and every flood on the Tiber cascaded through the Old City. The new state unleashed an unprecedented round of new building, as old *palazzi* were converted into ministries, wide new streets were laid out and giant edifices were put up to house governement offices. The spectre of the Paris Commune in 1871 persuaded the city fathers the new Rome would be better off without a resident working class, so the poor were forced into shanty towns on the city's edge.

World War I was, for Italy, virtually a private fight against the Austro-Hungarian forces in the north, and Rome itself was not directly affected. Repercussions came later in the person of Benito Mussolini, the former editor of a socialist paper who came out of the war "burning with patriotism and bursting with ambition, a *condottiere* of fortune... shrinking from no violence or brutality".

Garibaldi and Italian patriots called for "Rome o morte" – Rome or death – but the papacy bitterly resisted the city's incorporation into the new Italian nation.

Mussolini and Fascism

Mussolini named his black-shirted party after the *fasces,* the symbol of authority in Ancient Rome. In 1922 he marched on Rome, ostensibly to save Italy from Communism. With King Victor Emmanuel III nominally still on his throne, Mussolini pushed through sweeping changes in Italian society. He dreamed of creating a new Roman Empire, with Rome as its showpiece. Roads were bulldozed through the old centre to modernise the city and its traffic.

FOOD FOR WARRIORS

In 1930 the Futurist artist and Fascist Filippo Marinetti launched a campaign against pasta, which, he said, made Italians fat, lazy and apathetic. It had not been part of the diet of the ancient Romans, it was said, when they had conquered Europe. Mussolini himself often said he wanted to make Italians tougher and more dynamic, less addicted to pleasure and more to combat and heroism, and for a time the campaign was taken up by the regime – which also wanted to lower Italy's dependence on imported wheat. Most Italians, though, ignored it, and remained as devoted to pasta as ever.

FAR LEFT: the Tiber in the 18th century, with St Peter's in the background. **LEFT:** the "Kings' Cake" being cut at the Congress of Vienna. **ABOVE:** the Italian army ends papal rule, 1870. **ABOVE RIGHT:** patriarch of Italian nationalism, Garibaldi.

The next two years of war devastated Italy, but Rome – after some Allied bombing in 1943 – was declared an "Open City", which would not be directly fought over by either side, a period captured in Rossellini's remarkable film *Rome, Open City*. Acts of resistance were met with severe reprisals. Rome had no strategic value, but was a great symbolic prize. Rome fell on 4 June 1944, yet it was not until 28 April 1945 that Mussolini was captured, shot and hung from a lamp-post in Milan.

Slicing up the post-war cake

Conditions in Rome after the war were vividly portrayed in films of the era such as Vittorio de Sica's *Bicycle Thieves*. A common backdrop was the high-rise blocks that proliferated under Salvatore Rebecchini, mayor 1947–56. Property developers bribed bureaucrats, and empty spaces filled with illegal buildings.

The 1957 Treaty of Rome spelt out a vision of a European Common Market, but Italian political life was blighted by strikes and instability. The Communists were the largest single party, but all other parties agreed they must be kept from power by any means; no other party was big enough to form a government, so the result was a run of short-lived coalitions. Nevertheless, Italy managed an economic miracle, and instead of being associated with poverty, Rome began to attract new waves of tourists with the image of *La Dolce Vita*, enshrined in another film, by Fellini, from 1960.

In 1978, the Polish cardinal Karol Wojtyla became the first non-Italian pope in 450 years, as John Paul II. He brought a new international prestige to the Vatican, but it was also damaged by irregularities in its finances, and in 1985 the government ended Catholicism's status as the state religion of Italy.

Pope Pius XI, a semi-recluse in the Vatican, warmed to the dictator as he restored the crucifix to schools and worked towards a treaty between the Vatican and the Italian state, formalised in the concordat of 1929.

In pursuit of his imperial dreams, Mussolini invaded Ethiopia and Albania. He took Italy into World War II in June 1940, when he felt sure Germany would win. But Fascist power proved to be made of straw, and one military disaster followed another. By July 1943 the Allies were preparing to invade Sicily. With the

"All merely picturesque things are to be swept away", proclaimed Mussolini in his plans for Rome, "and must make room for the dignity, hygiene and beauty of the capital'".

support of the king senior generals had *Il Duce* arrested, and Marshal Badoglio made head of government. Hitler, however, guessing the new government would make peace with the Allies, sent German troops into Italy and paratroops to rescue Mussolini, who became puppet ruler of a Fascist republic in the north.

Modern times

Ever since 1945 the Christian Democrats had been the constant in every government coalition, but over the next decade their dominance disintegrated as the judicial system cracked down on organised crime. This campaign spread to the worlds of business and politics in 1992, under the name *mani pulite* (clean hands), and the system of corruption and kickbacks that had ruled post-war Italy began to crumble.

It seemed like an opportunity for a completely new beginning, but the hole left by the Christian Democrats on the right was filled by media mogul Silvio Berlusconi and his Forza Italia party. Bringing a new, brash, populist style to Italian politics, Berlusconi's response to corruption has often been to wink and suggest a certain amount of it doesn't really matter. After a brief Berlusconi government, the centre-left Olive Tree coalition took power in 1996 under Romano Prodi. The coalition was unstable, however, and in 2001 Berlusconi became prime minister for a second time, in Italy's longest-lived government since 1945.

In the same year Rome's mayoral elections were won by Walter Veltroni, a former Communist. Regularly voted most popular mayor in Italy, he has worked hard to improve services and extend them into Rome's neglected suburbs, and cultural events have proliferated. Rome's biggest threats today are pollution and traffic. Measures to make the city a better environment for the future and preserve its incomparable past are under way, but this will be an uphill struggle.

In 2005 an era ended with the death of Pope John Paul II, who was succeeded by another non-Italian pope, the German cardinal Joseph Ratzinger, as Benedict XVI. The following year saw national and local elections in Italy. While Veltroni was easily re-elected in Rome, on the national scene Berlusconi had polarised opinion. A tight election was only just won by the centre-left, again under Romano Prodi, but Berlusconi continues to intrigue, and the Prodi coalition's position remains insecure. ❑

FAR LEFT: Mussolini holds forth.
LEFT: Italians read of his fall from power, 1943.
ABOVE: Pope Benedict XVI, shortly after his election.
ABOVE RIGHT: popular mayor Walter Veltroni.

THE UNSTOPPABLE *CAVALIERE*

Two-times prime minister Silvio Berlusconi is also Italy's richest man, the owner of three TV channels, newspapers, AC Milan football club and much more. He's a modern phenomenon: time and again he has been accused of abuse of power, suppressing free speech or (notoriously) making bad-taste jokes about women or other countries, but instead of being embarrassed he just grins even harder and comes back with abuse or jokes in even worse taste. His admirers say he gives them confidence, and a new word, *berlusconismo*, has been coined for his particular brand of flamboyance.

DECISIVE DATES

The Roman Republic: 753–27 BC

753 BC
Traditional date when Rome is said to have been founded by Romulus, on 21 April.

c.600 BC
First parts of Forum built.

509 BC
Rome becomes a republic.

390 BC
Gauls sack Rome, but are then driven off.

264–146 BC
Punic Wars against Carthage: after its destruction in 146 Rome is the dominant power in the entire Mediterranean.

100 BC
Birth of Julius Caesar.

58–48 BC
Caesar conquers Gaul, invades Britain, then leads his army back into Italy, challenging the Senate. He defeats Pompey and is made dictator of Rome.

44 BC
Caesar assassinated.

31 BC
Octavian (Augustus) defeats Mark Antony and Cleopatra at the battle of Actium, in Greece.

The Roman Empire: 27 BC–AD 476

27 BC
Augustus declared Princeps or sole ruler, and founds the Empire. Peace is established and the arts flourish, especially in Rome.

AD 14
Death of Augustus, to be succeeded by Tiberius.

AD 64
Great fire in Rome: Nero builds his Domus Aurea or Golden House. First major persecution of Christians.

69–79
Emperor Vespasian builds the Flavian Amphitheatre (Colosseum). In AD 81 the Arch of Titus is erected to commemorate the destruction of Jerusalem by Vespasian and his son and successor Titus.

98–117
The Roman Empire achieves its greatest extent under Emperor Trajan, after his conquests in Dacia (Romania), Persia and Arabia, extending from northern England to the Persian Gulf. The arts flourish across the Empire.

117–38
Hadrian builds walls to secure the Empire's borders against barbarian invasions.

161–80
Reign of Marcus Aurelius. His column, with reliefs showing his victories over Danubian tribes, stands in Rome's Piazza Colonna.

193–211
Septimius Severus leads campaigns against the Parthians, commemorated by a grand arch in the Forum.

284–305
Emperor Diocletian divides Empire into Western and Eastern halves. Intense persecution of Christians.

312
Constantine defeats his rival Maxentius at the Milvian Bridge, near Rome.

313
Edict of Milan establishes toleration of Christianity; in 324 it is officially recognised.

330
Constantinople made the new capital of the Empire.

395
Division of the Roman Empire made permanent.

410
Rome sacked by Visigoths.

476
Romulus Augustulus, last Western emperor, deposed by Ostrogoth leader Theodoric, who declares himself king of Italy.

Surviving: 476–1378
536–68
Rome and most of Italy recaptured by Eastern Empire, with a stronghold at Ravenna, but the Byzantine armies are overwhelmed by another invasion, by the Lombards.

590–604
Pope Gregory the Great protects Rome by making peace with the Lombards, and sends missionaries throughout Europe.

750s
Pepin, king of the Franks, aids Pope Stephen III, returns lands taken by the Lombards, and lays the foundations of temporal sovereignty of the papacy.

800
Charlemagne is crowned Holy Roman Emperor by Pope Leo III in St Peter's.

962
Saxon King Otto I becomes Holy Roman Emperor.

1084
Rome is sacked twice, by Emperor Henry IV and by the Normans.

1309
Clement V moves the seat of the papacy to Avignon.

Papal Rome: 1377–1801
1377
Papacy returns to Rome under Gregory XI, but rival popes still contest the claims of his successors.

1417
Single papacy re-established in Rome, under Martin V.

1450s–1520s
Rome enjoys great prosperity during the High Renaissance. The popes attract great artists, among them Bellini, Botticelli, Bramante, Donatello, Michelangelo and Raphael.

1527
Charles V's army sacks Rome.

1545–63
Council of Trent initiates the Counter-Reformation.

1568
Jesuit order begins building of the Church of the Gesù.

1585–90
Pope Sixtus V orders major public works in Rome, including the restoration of ancient aqueducts and fountains.

1626
Consecration of St Peter's.

1796–9
The French Revolutionary armies under Napoleon take Rome and make it a Republic. Pope Pius VI dies in exile in France in 1799.

1801
Pope Pius VII agrees a concordat with Napoleon in order to be allowed to return to Rome.

1811
Napoleon makes his baby son the king of Rome.

Rome in Italy: 1814–1945
1814–15
Papal States are restored to Pius VII by the Congress of Vienna.

1848–50
Pope Pius IX gives Papal States a constitution but refuses to support Italian unification and flees Rome. Radicals declare Roman Republic; Rome is besieged by French troops, who restore papal rule and protect Rome until 1870.

1870
French troops withdraw: Italian troops take over Rome, which is declared capital of the kingdom of Italy. The popes refuse to recognise the state and withdraw to the Vatican.

1871–1910
New Italian government undertakes massive building works in Rome, including the Tiber embankments.

1922
Mussolini marches on Rome and seizes power. More new building, with broad avenues and monuments, and suburbs around the city.

1929
Lateran Treaty: Church recognises the Italian state which acknowledges the Vatican as an independent state, with the Pope at its head.

1940
Italy enters World War II.

1943
Mussolini arrested; Allies land in southern Italy; Germans occupy the north.

1944
The Allies liberate Rome, on 4 June.

1945
Mussolini is killed by partisans.

Modern times
1946
After a referendum, Italy becomes a republic.

1957
The European Economic Community (now the European Union) is established by the Treaty of Rome; Italy is one of six founder members.

1960
La Dolce Vita is released, and Rome hosts the Olympics.

1962–5
Second Vatican Council.

1978
Cardinal Karol Wojtyla becomes the first Polish Pope, as John Paul II.

1981
Ali Agca tries to assassinate Pope John Paul II in St Peter's Square.

1993
Corruption scandals rock Italy; national unity government formed. Francesco Rutelli becomes Rome's first directly elected mayor.

1994
Media magnate Silvio Berlusconi briefly becomes prime minister.

1995
Giulio Andreotti, seven times Italian prime minister, goes on trial for Mafia association.

1996
First left-wing government in Italian post-war history.

1998
Massimo D'Alema is first former Communist to head an Italian government.

2000
Millions flock to Rome for Holy Year celebrations, after a frenzy of restoration work. Centre-left government coalition falls.

2001
Berlusconi becomes prime minister for the second time. Walter Veltroni of the centre-left wins Rome's mayoral elections.

2005
Pope John Paul II dies: Cardinal Joseph Ratzinger elected Pope Benedict XVI.

2006
Berlusconi loses power by the narrowest of margins to a centre-left coalition led by Romano Prodi.

Rome on Film

I talian cinema was born in Rome in 1905. The country's first feature, *La Presa di Roma* – a dramatic tale of the city's incorporation into Italy in 1870 – marked the beginning of the Eternal City's enduring love affair with celluloid. It remains the heart of Italian cinema.

The silent era was dominated by historical spectaculars, epitomised by Giovanni Pastrone's kidnap drama set in the Punic Wars, *Cabiria* (1914). The success of these toga tales had industrialists and aristocrats queuing to finance Rome's burgeoning film industry.

The birth of Cinecittà

Mussolini saw film as the perfect propaganda vehicle for Fascism, and in a typical attempt to trump the Americans he built his own Hollywood-on-the-Tiber at Cinecittà, the largest film-making complex in Europe. Directors with the right ideological credentials were bankrolled by the regime, but created little of much merit. Nevertheless, some of Italy's greatest directors were meanwhile learning their trade at the studios, as second-unit directors or writers.

Neo-realism

The fall of Fascism marked the emergence of one of the world's great film movements: neo-realism. Stimulated by the desperate state of Italy at the end of the war and tired of escapist spectacle, the *neorealismo* auteurs set out to record the life of ordinary people.

At their forefront was Roberto Rossellini, who began shooting his masterwork, *Rome, Open City* (1945), on the devastated streets around Via Prenestina even before the German troops had left. It revolves around an extraordinary performance from Roman actress Anna Magnani, as a defiant matriarch.

The signature film of neo-realism was Vittorio de Sica's *Bicycle Thieves* (1948). The story of a man and his son in the Rome slums was a huge international success. De Sica bankrolled the film himself, and used non-professional actors. Other directors influenced by neo-realism included Federico Fellini and, in the 1960s, Pier Paolo Pasolini, whose subject matter was a Roman underworld of small-time thieves and desperate love. "We discovered our own country," said Fellini, "and its reality was so extraordinary we couldn't resist photographing it."

Fellini's devotion to Cinecittà made him the uncrowned king of the studios. He placed his adopted city under a microscope: *Roma* (1972) presented a fantastic vision of Rome, while *La Dolce Vita* (1960) satirised the idle rich who hung around the then glamorous Via Veneto, and left us the enduring image of Anita Ekberg cooling off in the Trevi Fountain.

Epics and comics

It's ironic that Mussolini's film city finally found fame with the Americans he was trying to outdo. In the 1950s good light, the pleasures of working in Italy and the renowned skills (but low costs) of its technicians brought Hollywood to Rome – turning Cinecittà into a household name for millions around the world.

For over a decade Cinecittà was synonymous with the epic – titles like *Quo Vadis* (1951) *Ben-Hur* (1959), Taylor and Burton's *Cleopatra* (1963) – but also made the film that launched a thousand tourist trips, *Roman Holiday* (1953). In its glory

years the studios produced over 1,000 films, employing hundreds of actors, extras, technicians and directors.

International productions brought added glamour to Cinecittà, but its bread and butter was Italian commercial movie-making. Italians have always loved their comedy stars. Each city has its home-town clown: Naples is forever linked with Totò and Massimo Troisi, while Florence has Roberto Benigni. When Rome's chief jester, Alberto Sordi, died in 2003, over 80,000 crammed the streets for his funeral; in a 50-year career he had appeared in over 100 films, including Fellini's 1953 classic *I Vitelloni*.

By the 1980s, though, Italian domestic film production was falling, as Hollywood movies filled Italian cinemas.

LEFT: Anita Ekberg exudes glamour and sex appeal in *La Dolce Vita*. **ABOVE LEFT:** neo-realist classic, *Bicycle Thieves*. **ABOVE:** poster for Cinecittà Burton and Taylor epic *Cleopatra*. **RIGHT:** taking a break on the set for big-budget HBO/BBC series, *Rome*.

Cinecittà's comeback

Television production replaced cinema as Cinecittà's everyday business. Home-grown comedies still play well in Italy, but in recent years there have only been fleeting glimpses of Rome in films shown outside the country. Turkish-born director Ferzan Ozpetek uses his adopted city in films like *La Finestra di Fronte* (The Window Opposite, 2003), set in the Ghetto.

But Rome's most acclaimed film-maker is Nanni Moretti, Italy's Woody Allen. The city is often centre stage in his films, notably *Caro Diario* (1994), where he scooters around the concrete suburbs in search of the essence of Rome. With a distinctively languid, ironic style, Moretti

returned to film-making in 2006 after a long gap with *Il Caimano* (The Caiman), an acid satire on the Italy of Silvio Berlusconi.

After years in the wilderness Cinecittà is back. Now that so many film sets are computer-generated, this is the best place in the world to find the skills and craftsmanship that can create real sets.

In 2002, Martin Scorsese reconstructed entire blocks of 19th-century New York here for *Gangs of New York*. This heralded a slew of international productions including Mel Gibson's *The Passion of Christ* (2004) and – recalling the scale of the old epics – the lavish HBO/BBC series *Rome*. Local film-makers can only hope this may pave the way for a new wave of international success for Italian cinema. ❏

ART AND ARCHITECTURE: THE CREATION OF A CITYSCAPE

Three great eras – the ancient city, the Renaissance and the Baroque – have largely defined Rome's visual identity, blending in an astonishingly harmonious mix, studded with masterpieces

Walking through Rome's Centro Storico, one is frequently amazed by the sheer size and grandeur of the buildings crammed into narrow, winding streets. At other times one might be struck by an exquisite fountain or façade that, although obviously the work of a major artist and worthy of being the pride of any other city, is ignored by the traffic and pedestrians rushing past.

Rome has the kind of beauty that provokes passionate responses. It has also been a centre of power throughout its 2,700-year history, home to ancient emperors, then popes, and even Mussolini. Every era has left its mark.

A visible past

Romans' indifference to their extraordinary surroundings is nothing new. Rightly or wrongly, they have been blamed for mistreating their architectural heritage since ancient times.

Every corner seems to have something worth stopping to look at: a shady courtyard with a bubbling fountain, a Baroque façade above a street market, an obelisk blocking traffic in a way no modern planner would allow.

Emperor Maxentius (AD 306–12) accused contemporaries of tearing down "magnificent old buildings" to get material for new houses. Pope

LEFT: the Temple of Antoninus and Faustina was converted to San Lorenzo in Miranda in the 1100s.
RIGHT: St Peter's dome from Castel Sant'Angelo.

Pius II (1458–64) shuddered at people burning marble monuments to obtain lime.

Goethe, visiting in the 1780s, complained that "what the barbarians left standing, modern architects have destroyed", and a century later the German historian Gregorovius thundered against the Piedmontese remodelling of the papal city. In the 20th century Alberto Moravia classified four-fifths of Rome "a disaster area of civic architecture". Yet these critics all stayed on in Rome, unable to desert it.

Locals' disregard has a natural explanation in overfamiliarity. Rome is a city standing on the shoulders of its predecessors, where layers of history run into each other. Materials have

First steps

Rome's first permanent civic buildings were erected in the Forum. Most of the area now called the Centro Storico was little-populated for centuries, and much of it kept empty as the Campus Martius, the training ground where Roman men kept themselves ever-ready for war. Wealthy families built villas on top of Rome's hills, especially the Palatine, Viminal and Esquiline, while the dip between them – only just west of the Forum – was the Subura, the great slum of ancient Rome.

Republican Rome, though, grew in a fairly haphazard fashion, with few of the monumental symmetries now associated with Roman cities, and little of the splendour its imperial role seemed to demand. Accordingly Julius Caesar was the first to set out on a programme to improve the city. Soon Rome was flaunting its wealth; under Caesar, 640 gladiators wore silver armour at the city's games.

Caesar's nephew the emperor Augustus (27 BC–AD 14) liked to boast that he had found Rome made of brick and left it of marble. The urbanisation of the Campus Martius began, and was divided into *rioni* – the zones of central Rome that still exist today. Large parts of the Imperial Fora also date from these years.

The capital of the world

With over 1 million people – a size not reached by any other city for nearly 2,000 years – Ancient Rome was closely packed, noisy and crowded. While the wealthy lived in elegant houses – relics of many of which have survived – the Roman masses lived in insanitary *insulae* or apartment blocks of mud-bricks and timber, and fires, house collapses and epidemics were common. The *insulae* grew so rapidly and rose so high that after the fire of AD 64 destroyed

been taken from older buildings to make new ones, and buildings adapted to suit changing needs. Medieval churches rise from the remains of ancient houses; a Renaissance palace balances on top of the Theatre of Marcellus, next to 20th-century apartments. Even if buildings disappear, their shapes remain. A key feature of Italian city life – the piazza – is a direct descendant of the ancient Forum.

THE FIRST FORUM

"Forum" is one of the most pervasive words the Romans have given to European languages. The marshy area below the Capitoline Hill was drained by Rome's Etruscan rulers as early as 600 BC, and served as a common space for every purpose – meeting up, buying and selling, settling disputes – and the site of the temple where the Vestal Virgins guarded the Sacred Flame, which ensured Rome's survival. Its grandeur grew with that of the city: around 180 BC the humblest market traders were driven out, and permanent law courts and trading halls were built. Later rulers added new Fora as monuments to themselves, but the original Forum remained the heart of the ancient city.

the city centre, a decree of Nero limited their height to 20 metres (60 ft).

In the wake of the fire, disagreement raged between those who wanted Rome's old alleys retained and Nero, who wanted broad avenues on which to display monuments to himself. As has gone down in legend, it was also rumoured that Nero had started the fire himself, to clear space for his vast palace, the Domus Aurea or Golden House. More practically, though, Nero forbade the use of wooden ceilings and insisted on the provision of water buckets in houses.

Little of Nero's constructions remains because they were destroyed by his successors Vespasian (69–79) and his sons Titus and Domitian. To win popularity and dissociate themselves from Nero they erected more democratic centres of enjoyment, among them the Colosseum, on land originally covered by Nero's private lake. Domitian's legacy was the stadium over which Piazza Navona was built.

One of Rome's greatest architects was Apol-

lodorus of Damascus, master builder of Emperor Trajan (98–117), responsible for Trajan's Forum and the semicircular market behind it – a revolutionary idea, regarded as one of the wonders of ancient Rome, and still astonishingly well-preserved. Trajan also built a massive bath complex, on another part of the land that was once part of the Domus Aurea.

Rome's emperors built on until their last

FAR LEFT: the triple arch of Septimius Severus and the Column of Phocas. ABOVE LEFT: the Colosseum. ABOVE: Trajan's Markets. RIGHT: Roman mosaic depicting actors.

ANCIENT ARCHETYPES

Around 55 BC Caesar's rival Pompey sponsored Rome's first permanent theatre, the Theatre of Pompey. Intended to offer sophisticated Greek-style theatre rather than the bloody spectacles ancient Romans usually enjoyed, it was so large the Senate often met there. The shape of the round building can still be seen behind Campo de' Fiori; Via di Grotta Pinta follows its curve. A few years later, Caesar built his own Basilica Giulia in the Forum. A combination of law court and trading centre, it consisted of a piazza surrounded by a double row of buildings, with shops on one side and mezzanine floors with embossed rounded arches, a style often copied in Renaissance architecture.

days – one of the last great monuments is the Arch of Constantine, completed only a few years before he left for Constantinople – but then centuries of construction came to a halt, and within decades much of the city was a ghost town. Few civic buildings survive from the centuries between the fall of the Empire and the Renaissance, but this was the time

The ruins of ancient Rome served later builders as a giant quarry for centuries, until many dwindled away to nothing.

when Rome's major churches were founded, often incorporating parts of pagan temples. Defensive towers were also built, like the Torre delle Milizie (1309), above Trajan's Market.

The great rebirth

A huge proportion of Rome's architectural gems date from the years between 1454 and 1670, when Rome was again one of Europe's great power centres, and at the heart of Renaissance and Baroque art and architecture.

The Renaissance – Rebirth – stemmed from a rediscovery of the ancient art and culture that had been abandoned after the Roman Empire fell in the 5th century. It began in Italy in the late 14th century and, over 150 years, swept across Europe, leading to fundamental changes in culture, intellectual life and the way people lived and saw their place in the world.

Christopher Columbus and Vasco da Gama discovered new countries and trade routes, and philosophers such as Erasmus reapplied the humanist philosophies of the ancients. While not yet questioning the supremacy of God, this attitude of enquiry encouraged a questioning of the dogma of the Catholic Church, which led ultimately to the birth of Protestantism.

In Italy, however, it was in art and architecture that the new movement was most visible – in the development of perspective, the more naturalistic presentation of subject matter and especially the human body, and the use of classical proportions and styles in building.

The Renaissance first developed in northern Italy, particularly Florence. Nevertheless, most great artists of the era came to Rome at some point, to study the classical lines of ancient relics, or carry out commissions for the popes.

Rome's own renaissance

In the mid-15th century, two factors aided the re-emergence of Rome as a cultural centre. First, the papacy of Nicholas V (1447–55) began a line of powerful popes with time, money and the desire to improve Rome's appearance. Secondly, the Italian League of 1455 ushered in a period of relative peace across Italy, leaving the popes free to occupy themselves with broader ambitions.

Many changes made in the ensuing 70 years still define the look of Rome today. Nicholas V believed Rome had to be made majestic again to be a worthy centre of the Christian world. Highly learned, he was a patron of artists, craftsmen and scholars: advised by the architect Alberti, he was also the first to propose that Constantine's Basilica of St Peter – which was threatening to fall down in any case – should be demolished and replaced with a giant new focus for the Church. This suggestion would not be fully taken up until 1506, by Pope Julius II (1503–13), and work would go on for 120 years, but over the decades the new St Peter's incorporated contributions from nearly all the greatest masters of Renaissance painting, sculpture and architecture.

These same masters left their mark elsewhere in Rome: Bramante, Julius II's first choice as architect of the basilica, had earlier built the lovely Tempietto beside the church of San Pietro in Montorio on the Gianicolo, revolutionary in its use of classical form and considered the first true Renaissance building in Rome. Raphael, a later director of works at St Peter's, painted frescoes that can be seen in the Vatican and Villa Farnesina, and Michelangelo, who aged over 70 designed St Peter's dome in the 1540s, had earlier painted the Sistine Chapel, sculpted the *Pietà* and, in 1536, designed the Campidoglio for Pope Paul III.

Artists continued to flock to Rome until the 1527 Sack, to work for the popes or the great families who vied for the papal throne – the Barberini, Borghese, Farnese, Pamphili and

FAR LEFT: the spectacular apse mosaics of Santa Maria in Trastevere. ABOVE CENTRE: fresco by Annibale Carracci in the Palazzo Farnese. LEFT: Michelangelo's staircase leading to the Campidoglio. ABOVE RIGHT: Bramante's Tempietto.

PAPAL STREET PLANS

The Renaissance popes changed the face of Rome in many other ways as well as in their individual buildings and great monuments. Sixtus IV (1471–84), patron of the Sistine Chapel, commissioned the Ponte Sisto or Sistine Bridge, the first new Tiber bridge in over 1,000 years. Leo X (1513–21) had Via di Ripetta created to link the Medici family palace and Porto di Ripetta, while another Medici pope, Clement VII (1523–34), commissioned Via del Babuino, thereby completing the *Tridente* or "Trident" of (today very fashionable) streets that, with Via del Corso, flow south from Piazza del Popolo.

streets built to link the city gates and improve access for pilgrims is still mostly intact: Via Felice (now Via Sistina, and other names) led straight to Santa Maria Maggiore and Santa Croce in Gerusalemme from Piazza del Popolo, one of four nodal points where obelisks were erected, with Santa Maria Maggiore, San Giovanni in Laterano and St Peter's.

City of the Baroque

In the latter part of the 16th century, creativity was curbed by papal decree, in response to the threat of Protestantism. The Council of Trent laid down guidelines for Church commissions: all art was to have an unmissable religious message. Realism was allowed, but there was to be no prettification, and emphasis had to be put on the suffering of martyrs to remind people of the infernal torments awaiting them if they offended the Church. Niccolò Pomarancio's gruesome frescoes of martyred saints in Santo Stefano Rotondo and Santi Nereo e Achilleo date from this time.

While the Renaissance was imported from Florence, Baroque style had its home in Rome. It may seem strange that the sombre images of the late 16th century should lead to the ornate Roman Baroque of the 17th, but both were provoked by the fear of Protestantism. Both sought to promote Catholicism, but while one used shock tactics, the other sought to dazzle.

Size and visual impact were the main themes explored in Baroque architecture: the aim of religious art and building was to exalt the greatness of the Church and create a foretaste of heaven, and to this end every kind of visual effect could be deployed. By the 1620s, extravagantly decorated churches with *trompe l'œil* ceiling paintings and gold-encrusted altars

others. From this time are churches such as Santa Maria del Popolo and Santa Maria della Pace, the *palazzi* on Via Giulia and of course great works of art, now mostly in the Vatican or the *palazzi* Barberini and Doria Pamphili.

Before and after the Sack, too, the popes left an indelible stamp on the layout of Rome *(see page 35)*. The greatest papal "planner" was Pope Sixtus V (1585–90). His network of

THE DEMON CARAVAGGIO

Caravaggio (1571–1610) was the greatest artist working in Rome at the end of the 16th century, but his fame lasted only a decade. Despite Counter-Reformation injunctions to show the realities of suffering, his dramatic lifelike figures and earthy details, his saints with dirty fingernails, did not meet with the approval of many art patrons used to the reverence of a Raphael or a Michelangelo, while many in the Church found such naturalism blasphemous.

Even more of a problem was his character: violent and argumentative, he had to flee Rome after killing a man in a brawl in 1606. Trouble followed him to Naples, Sicily and Malta, and it has never been clear how he died.

were thought more likely to keep people in the Catholic fold than portrayals of suffering. The basic form of these buildings might still owe much to classical models, but now everything was highly decorated with statuary and reliefs.

It was no accident Rome's first major Baroque churches were built for the new religious orders of the Counter-Reformation: the great Jesuit churches such as Il Gesù (1568–75)

The object of Baroque painting and building was to give the onlooker a vivid image of both the horrors of hell and – more frequently – the joys of heaven.

and Sant'Ignazio de Loyola (1626–50), and the initially less ornate Chiesa Nuova (1575–99) of the Oratorians, founded by St Filippo Neri, loved in Rome for giving charity to the poor.

FAR LEFT: grand stairway in the Palazzo Barberini.
TOP LEFT: fountain opposite the Pantheon (1575).
LEFT: *Bacchus* by Caravaggio. **ABOVE TOP:** Chiesa Nuova. **ABOVE:** ceiling of the Gesù. **RIGHT:** the Fountain of Neptune, Piazza Navona.

This was the age of Bernini and Borromini, whose façades grace streets and piazzas, and whose fountains and sculptures decorate Piazza Barberini and Piazza Navona, Ponte Sant'Angelo, Villa Borghese and the Vatican.

As well as exalting the Church, the Baroque could add grandeur to more earthly powers, and was eagerly taken up by great monarchs such as the Spanish Habsburgs or Louis XIV of France. Rome's great families were just as keen to demonstrate their wealth, by building massive city palaces and villas amid gardens. The Villa Borghese dates from this time, as do parts of Palazzo Doria Pamphili, Villa Doria Pamphili and the Palazzi di Montecitorio and Barberini. Once again artists flocked to Rome to study and find patrons among its great families. Velázquez, Rubens and Poussin all worked here, and left major works in Rome.

After about 1660, however, funding dried up, and the papacy and Roman aristocracy had to moderate their designs. No era since the Baroque has marked the city so deeply. The monuments of Bernini, Borromini and their contemporaries remain, stunning pieces of work that create a cityscape that is as Roman as the Colosseum and the Forum. ❏

BERNINI AND THE BAROQUE

The Roman Baroque style, perfected by Bernini, was the model for European Baroque

Gianlorenzo Bernini (1598–1680) was at the forefront of Roman Baroque, pioneering sublime and spectacular effects. Although more restrained than elsewhere in Europe, Roman Baroque is theatrical, bold, at times bombastic. Bernini's Rome is an open-air gallery of fountains and façades. Palaces and churches boast sweeping curves, majestic façades and theatrical vistas flanked by flights of steps. As a virtuoso architect and sculptor, Bernini worked in broad brushstrokes, with illusionistic verve. At ease with interiors and exteriors, he was a showman renowned for his theatricality and technical brilliance.

Bernini's style found favour with a succession of popes. Even St Peter's is, in part, a Bernini creation, graced by enfolding, keyhole-shaped colonnades. Other masterpieces include the witty design for an elephant to bear the obelisk of Santa Maria sopra Minerva and the graceful angels on Ponte Sant'Angelo. As for palaces, Palazzo Barberini (1629–33) heralded the Baroque style and was completed by Bernini, assisted by Borromini, who became his arch-rival *(see opposite)*.

ABOVE: having worked for decades on the interior of the basilica, Bernini was commissioned to redesign St Peter's Square (1656–67). The colonnaded arms of the elliptical piazza reach out to Catholics in a symbolic embrace from the Mother Church, according to Bernini.

LEFT: Bernini's Sant'Andrea al Quirinale (1658–70) is a subtle tour de force inspired by Michelangelo's architectural feats.

LEFT: Rome's loveliest Baroque square, Piazza Navona is home to three fountains and other works by rival architects Bernini and Borromini. In the foreground is Bernini's Fontana del Moro. His sumptuous fountains vie for attention with Borromini's church of Sant'Agnese, with its striking interplay of towers, domes and façade. **ABOVE:** Bernini's obelisk-carrying elephant outside Santa Maria sopra Minerva church. **LEFT:** *Apollo and Daphne*, which is displayed with other Bernini masterpieces in the Galleria Borghese. This is Bernini's most famous sculpture. The magnificent, youthful work shows the nymph fleeing from the sun god.

BELOW: in the church of Santa Maria della Vittoria is what many consider to be Bernini's sculptural masterpiece, *The Ecstasy of St Teresa*.

FRANCESCO BORROMINI

Borromini (1599–1667) made use of revolutionary, gravity-defying architectural forms. While Borromini lacked the confidence and all-round virtuosity of Bernini, his churches abound in visual trickery. His work is characterised by a sculptural quality, the alternation of convex and concave forms, and a conspicuous fondness for geometric designs as well as for subtle plays of light and shade.

San Carlo alle Quattro Fontane *(see page 120)* was Borromini's first solo commission. Based on an oval design, the ingenious church is notable for its illusionistic dome. The sinuous, seemingly swaying, walls inspired countless Baroque artists.

In his time Borromini's genius was not fully recognised, partly because of his temperament (he was a depressive who eventually committed suicide) and his rivalry with Bernini, but he is now considered one of the great masters of Baroque.

THE SHAPE OF MODERN ROME

In a city that is regularly compared to a giant museum,
the intrusion of modern streets, suburbs and rail lines
has just as often been condemned as vandalism.
Rome's survival, though, has always depended
on its ability to integrate past and future

So pervasive is the past in Rome – in the visual impact of Ancient Rome, the Renaissance and the Baroque – that it's easy to think this represents the whole city. And yet Rome has grown vastly since 1700, and has never ceased to grow, build and adapt.

By the time of the death of Bernini in 1680 the extraordinary impetus behind the creation of Baroque Rome had visibly fallen away. The Church continued to commission buildings and improvements in the 18th century, but on a far smaller scale. Stylistically, rococo flourishes were added to the Baroque, but most of the city's architects lived on the legacy of the past.

Nevertheless, two of Rome's most famous, and most popular, sights date from this time. The Spanish Steps, built to link the French church of Trinità dei Monti with Piazza di Spagna, were completed in 1726, while Nicola

The new Italian state set about the most rapid burst of new building seen in Rome since the days of the Empire.

Salvi's Trevi Fountain, designed for Pope Clement XII, was finished in 1762.

Modernity arrives

The changes brought by the 19th century were as much utilitarian as aesthetic. In 1856 Rome acquired its first railway line, to Frascati, and

in 1862 the first part of Stazione Termini was built. These few novelties in sleepy papal Rome, however, were as nothing compared to the transformation that came after the city's incorporation into a united Italy in 1870.

The new state's rulers were modernisers, but found in their new capital a decaying, archaic city impassable to modern communications. Some needs could be met by recycling: Bernini's Palazzo di Montecitorio became Italy's Chamber of Deputies. Other changes were far more drastic. All-new, wide, un-Roman-looking avenues were cut through to "open up" the old centre and connect it to an expanded Termini Station, such as Via Cavour,

LEFT: Richard Meier's new museum pavilion housing the ancient Ara Pacis altar. **RIGHT:** Rome is very well connected by rail to Italy and the rest of Europe.

Mussolini's Legacy

When we think of Roman architecture, we think mainly of Ancient Rome and the Renaissance, but Mussolini's Fascist regime of the 1920s and 1930s has left a powerful imprint on the city as well.

Whole areas of Rome are dominated by massive, conspicuous buildings with façades of white rectangular columns against a plain white or reddish-brown background, adorned with statues of naked athletes and grim-faced women holding ears of corn or bunches of grapes. This style even continued – shorn of its more obvious ideological symbols – after World War II, when Mussolini's regime had collapsed.

In contrast to Hitler, whose taste in art and architecture was always backward-looking, Mussolini liked to show he was in touch with 20th-century trends, and his regime recruited some of Italy's most innovative modern architects for its schemes, notably Marcello Piacentini and Angiolo Mazzoni. The style they came up with was a mix of austere Modernist functionalism and an evocation of Ancient Rome, with an added touch of the monumentalism that was a Fascist essential.

Some of the most striking examples are Piacentini's Città Universitaria, and the rebuilt Stazione Termini, begun by Mazzoni in 1937 but only completed (with major changes) in 1950. Another is the building south of the Circus Maximus now used by the United Nations Food and Agriculture

Organization, originally intended as the administrative hub of the African Empire of which Mussolini dreamed.

Some of Mussolini's projects involved not building but large-scale demolition. He wanted Italians to be more conscious of their Roman heritage, and so commissioned excavations of the Roman Fora. However, his interest was not academic, for he simultaneously destroyed a part of the Fora by driving Via dei Fori Imperiali through the middle of them, as a route to hold parades with the ancient ruins as an unbeatable backdrop. And the construction of Via della Conciliazione into the Vatican, a symbol of reconciliation between the Holy See and the Italian state, involved demolishing the Spina, one of Rome's most celebrated historic streets.

However, the most prominent examples of Fascist architecture can be seen at the Foro Italico (see page 196), and the area in south Rome known as EUR (pronounced ay-oor). The *Esposizione Universale di Roma* was to have been held in 1942, as a giant exhibition to mark 20 years of Fascist rule. The war prevented it from taking place, but building continued after 1945, and the EUR district is today a strange monument to Fascist taste (see page 216). ❏

LEFT: the Palazzo della Civiltà del Lavoro, EUR.
ABOVE: the Via dei Fori Imperiali.

Via Nazionale and Corso Vittorio Emanuele II. The new Italy wanted to add its own touches of grandeur to Rome to compete with those of the ancients and the popes, and did so in a bombastic style epitomised by the vast Vittorio Emanuele monument on Piazza Venezia.

Other developments included the creation of new residential areas such as that around Piazza Vittorio Emanuele (1886), and – one of the most positive – the building of the Lungotevere or Tiber embankment in the 1870s, which put a stop to Rome's disastrous floods.

20th-century transformations

These innovations were detested by lovers of Old Rome, but they effectively created Rome as a modern city, around its ancient core. And they enabled Rome to accommodate a flood of immigrants from rural Italy, which had been gaining momentum ever since Unification. In 1922 Rome had about 800,000 people; by the end of World War II it would have 1.8 million.

The idea of building self-contained estates on the edge of Rome, the Agro Romano, was first mooted in 1907. Expansion had started before 1922, with the Art Nouveau Coppedè Quarter for the wealthy in the north of the city, and the engaging Garbatella workers' quarter south of Testaccio. Then Mussolini ushered in his own dramatic changes, to build a city fit to be the seat of his intended empire *(see left)*.

He also decided Rome needed "living space and greatness", and began building the *borgate* (estates) of Prenestina, Pietralata and San Basilio. Depressing in form and materials, they soon became symbols of wretchedness.

Post-war, slums girdled Rome, while at the other end of the social scale the wealthy got planning permission to build on the Via Appia. Slum clearance began in 1976: older *borgate* were given lighting, power, mains water and bus routes, while others were replaced by supposedly exemplary new suburbs such as Tor Bella Monaca or Tor de' Cenci. However, these too developed the usual problems of poverty, poor services, unemployment and drugs.

Rome urgently needed to improve living standards and integrate its outer sprawl into the rest of the city by improving the inadequate transport system, but solutions to urban blight seemed lost in the tangle of local politics. Since 1993, though, under mayors Francesco Rutelli and Walter Veltroni, the city authorities have taken on a new prestige, and initiated impressive city-wide improvements in services and a swathe of new building. ❑

ABOVE: gateway in the Art Nouveau enclave known as the Quartiere Coppedè. **ABOVE RIGHT:** apartment block in Garbatella district, south of Testaccio.

Modern Rome's sprawling suburbs contain both urban disaster zones and charming, tree-lined experiments in city living.

MODERN ARCHITECTURE

In a city weighed down by its monumental past, some of the best-known modern architects are daring to make their mark

Modern architecture was a rarely seen phenomenon in Rome until a few years ago, when the state-of-the-art Auditorium by Genoese architect Renzo Piano, which opened in 2002, spawned a wave of major architectural projects by big-name architects. In the same year, a huge designer hotel opened near the station, one of the first completely new buildings in the historic centre in recent years.

Further out of town, the uplifting Jubilee

ABOVE: the striking white "sails" of Richard Meier's Jubilee Church. **LEFT:** Meier's more controversial Ara Pacis pavilion.

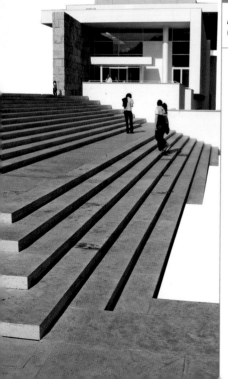

Church designed by superstar architect Richard Meier was a welcome addition to the unremarkable eastern suburb of Tor Tre Teste. Meier's design for the new pavilion housing the Ara Pacis, an ancient Roman altar, which opened in 2006, proved more controversial, but like it or loathe it, it's a major new landmark on the cityscape.

The biggest among Rome's many new arts centres *(see right)* is Anglo-Iraqi architect Zaha Hadid's new museum of contemporary art in the northern suburbs, slated to open in 2008, while in the southern EUR suburb a futuristic congress centre, a suspended, amorphous structure, is being built to a design by Massimiliano Fuksas.

Across the city, disused industrial buildings have been transformed. In the Marconi area, the vast Città del Gusto (City of Taste) complex in a remodelled granary is a beacon of culture and activity in an industrial wasteland, while Dutch architect Rem Koolhaas is converting an old food market on the southwest side of the city into a "City of Youth". As well as this wave of public building, there is a residential building boom. Rome's renaissance, it seems, is in full swing.

ABOVE: currently under construction, Zaha Hadid's contemporary art centre, MAXXI, will contain a complex network of interior and exterior spaces that will house two museums for the state collections of contemporary art and architecture.

NEW GALLERIES

The list of the city's innovative new spaces dedicated to the arts is impressive. Apart from Zaha Hadid's ambitious new museum *(see left)*, MACRO, Rome's contemporary art museum, is now spread over two sites, one a converted Peroni brewery, the other a converted slaughterhouse. An old power station is now home to the overspill of the Capitoline collection, while the stables of the hilltop Quirinal Palace have been converted into a clean, crisp space for high-profile exhibitions.

LEFT: the library of the ES hotel. This huge designer hotel near the station (on Via Filippo Turati) was one of the first completely new buildings in the historic centre in recent years. Owned by Radisson SAS, the slick establishment is an essay in minimalism. It has its own museum of 2nd-century ruins unearthed during construction.

RIGHT: Renzo Piano's Auditorium has three shell-like concert halls, built around an outdoor amphitheatre, and is set in parkland in the northern suburb of Flaminia.

ABOVE: part of the Capitoline Museums' vast collection of ancient statuary can now be viewed in the fabulous Centrale Montemartini museum, an imaginatively converted electrical power plant in Ostiense.

ABOVE: in the up-and-coming Testaccio neighbourhood, an old abbatoir on the edge of the Tiber has been converted into a site for cultural activities. Two of its pavilions have been given over to MACRO to house part of its contemporary art collection.

LEFT: the revamped Termini Station, one of the few successful pieces of post-war architecture in Rome, with its long, modernist façade in travertine stone, and graceful double curved roof.

PANINI

SANDWICHES

FOOD AND DRINK

Whether it's a long Sunday lunch or a stop-off for an ice cream on an evening stroll, eating in Rome is a very social activity – and one with 2,000 years of tradition, customs and ingenuity behind it

Culinary traditions run deep in Rome, reaching back to the ancient peoples who first populated the region. For centuries Romans have held firm against the influence of new ingredients, dishes and cooking techniques that have come as a result of Rome's contact with the rest of the world, as well as from the fads and fancies of the upper classes, emperors and popes.

The exotically spiced sauces, fancy game dishes and "delicacies" like fried parrots' tongues dressed with honey that delighted Roman emperors have faded into history, but something does remain from the high cuisine of the past: the unreserved pleasure with which Romans go to table. This is probably not the city to hunt down the top restaurants – few consider *la cucina romana* the best of Italy's regional cuisines – but Rome may well be one of Italy's most pleasurable cities in which to

Often, what might seem to be slow service is merely the Roman way of stretching a meal far into the night.

eat. Most restaurants plan on one seating per evening, so you will not be rushed, or pressured to leave. When in Rome, make a point of having a long, lingering meal – and have it in the open air, if the weather is good.

LEFT: fast food, Roman-style.
RIGHT: pizza is a Roman staple; there are more pizzerias in the city than restaurants.

La cucina romana

Quite a lot of the local cuisine involves offal, the so-called *quinto-quarto* (fifth quarter) of the animal. Long-time favourites include *rigatoni con pajata* (pasta with veal intestines) and *trippa alla romana* (tripe with tomato sauce, mint and pecorino), but you will find that most restaurants in the centre of town tend to avoid such specialities in favour of dishes from other parts of Italy that are more familiar to an international clientele, such as pasta with pesto sauce (from Genoa), risotto and polenta.

But you needn't eat innards to eat Roman. Every restaurant will have at least a few home-grown dishes, all sharing the frugality that marks the region's food, perhaps better called cooking than cuisine. Expensive restaurants offer adventurous dishes with long names, but the menu of a typical Roman establishment tells a less complicated story: *spaghetti alla carbonara* (with bacon, egg and pecorino cheese), *cacio e pepe* (with pecorino and black pepper) or *all'amatriciana* (with bacon or *guanciale*, cured pork jowl, and tomato), and *bucatini alla gricia* – Rome's own tube-shaped style of

pasta with *guanciale* – all share an undeniable simplicity. Pasta even makes its way into Roman soups: *pasta e ceci* (chickpea soup flavoured with rosemary) and *broccoli e arzilla* (clear soup of broccoli and skate). *Gnocchi alla romana* (potato dumplings in a meat sauce) are traditionally prepared on Thursday, while *baccalà* (salt cod) is served on Friday.

Nor is fish fussed over: clams tossed with spaghetti and olive oil become *spaghetti alle*

APERITIVO HOUR

The Milan-born tradition of an early-evening *aperitivo* accompanied by buffets of savoury munchies has exploded to epic scale in Rome. Gone are the days of humble olives and nuts; opulent spreads now top the counters of even the tiniest bars from around 6 to 8pm

each evening. Tramezzini sandwiches bursting with tuna, mozzarella and tomatoes, mini pizzas, omelette chunks and focaccia sandwiches left over

from lunch grilled to a crispy finish and sliced up in quarters. But this is only the beginning: fancier places offer pasta and rice dishes, salads, *bruschetta* and all manner of tempting *fritti* (deep-fried foods).

Most bars advertise their *aperitivo* as "Happy Hour", and offer drink specials as well. The classic Roman aperitif is bubbly Prosecco; Campari and soda is another best-seller. Otherwise opt for a glass of red or white wine, or the cocktail of your choice.

The establishments listed here represent a slice of Rome's ever-vibrant *aperitivo* scene.

Centrale Ristotheatre 6 Via Celsa, tel: 06-678 0501.
Fluid 46/47 Via del Governo Vecchio, tel: 06-683 2361.
Magnolia 4 Campo de' Fiori, tel: 06-683 09367.
Red 30 Via Pietro de Coubertin, tel: 06-806 91630.
Obikà 26 Via dei Prefetti, tel: 06-683 2630.
Friends 59 Via della Scrofa, tel: 06-6686 1416.
Doppio Zero 68 Via Ostiense, tel: 06-5730 1961.
Oppio Caffé 72 Via delle Terme di Tito, tel: 06-474 5262.

vongole, and *pesce azzurro* (fish from the sea) is baked in the oven *(al forno)* or cooked on the grill *(ai ferri* or *alla griglia)*. Two common meat dishes are *saltimbocca alla romana* (veal slices rolled with prosciutto and sage) and the arch-Roman *coda alla vaccinara* ("oxtail butcher's style", slow-braised in a garlic, pepper, tomato and celery sauce), but the meat to try is *abbacchio* (milk-fed lamb), which is usually roasted with herbs and garlic or served *alla scottadito* (as grilled chops).

Greens on the side

Save room for vegetables, which abound in Rome's markets all year long and are usually served simply prepared, often steamed or blanched and then briefly sautéed. November to April is the season for another Roman speciality, artichokes, which can be served many

Romans are the undisputed masters of the artichoke, which you can try prepared in several different traditional styles.

different ways. Among them are *carciofi alla giudea* ("Jewish-style" and so typical of the Ghetto – deep-fried) and *carciofi alla romana* (stuffed with garlic and mint, and stewed).

A typical winter salad is *puntarelle*, made by shredding the stalks of locally grown chicory and serving them with a lemon-anchovy dressing. Summer brings roasted peppers, aubergines and courgettes (zucchini) served in a variety of ways, and large tomatoes stuffed with herbs and rice, while in spring you'll see asparagus and *fave con pecorino* (raw broad beans with pecorino cheese).

Many Italians like to have just one main dish and finish a meal with a piece of fruit, then a coffee. Accordingly, appetisers and desserts get little attention in most Rome restaurants. A few common starters are melon or figs with prosciutto and *fiori di zucca* (deep-fried zucchini flowers filled with mozzarella and anchovies). Popular desserts are *torta di ricotta* (ricotta tart), *panna cotta* (eggless, firm creamy custard with a fruit sauce) and *tiramisù* (coffee trifle).

Find your wine

The local wines that still dominate the wine selections of most Roman restaurants – those from Frascati are the best-known – are nowadays much better than they used to be, but still pale in comparison with wines produced in other parts of Italy, which are now at last widely available in the capital. For a good wine, it's usually better to bypass the house wine and choose a non-local label.

FAR LEFT: chef at Ristorarte, one of a new generation of restaurants serving modern Roman cuisine. **LEFT ABOVE:** Roman pasta specialities; tomato and mozzarella salad. **ABOVE:** preparing an *aperitivo*. **ABOVE RIGHT:** artichokes are a Roman favourite.

Italians rarely drink without eating, but stopping by a bar for an early-evening aperitif with an (often sizeable) snack has lately become one of fashionable Rome's biggest fads. Wine bars *(enoteche)* are also very popular: they have much better wine selections than most restaurants, and offer a great alternative to a restaurant meal, with a relaxed, easy-going atmosphere. Choose from usually about a dozen wines available by the glass (or from more than a thousand different labels by the bottle), and a great selection of high-quality cheeses, salami and other cured meats and smoked fish, as well as soups and salads, quiches and gratins, and sometimes scrumptious home-made desserts.

Roman pizza

The Neapolitans are credited with inventing pizza, but Romans eat their fair share. There are more *pizzerie* than restaurants in town, and Romans have their own version of this staple dish: whereas a big Neapolitan pizza is made with a thick, softish dough and has a raised rim, a *pizza romana* is plate-sized, and rolled very thin and flat. Both kinds must be baked in a wood-burning stove *(forno a legna)*. A night out at a pizzeria (few are open for lunch) is a quintessential Roman experience.

ICE CREAM HEAVEN: ROME'S STAR *GELATERIE*

Romans have enjoyed ice cream since ancient times: Nero ate ice transported all the way from Vesuvius, mixed with fruit topping. Modern Rome has no shortage of fine parlours, and locals like nothing better than an evening *passeggiata* accompanied by a fresh *gelato*.

Many Roman bars and cafés sell ice cream, but don't be fooled – for the real thing, you must be more selective. Most of Rome's genuine artisan ice-cream makers have a long pedigree, and some are legendary. Here is a selection of the city's favourite *gelaterie*.

Gelateria del Teatro 22a Piazza San Simeone (Centro Storico). Hidden away, but worth finding, this newcomer is the pride and joy of Roman Stefano and his Peruvian wife. Their artisan ice cream uses fresh fruit bought daily from the market.

Il Gelato di San Crispino 42 Via della Panetteria (Fontana di Trevi), 56 Via Acaia (San Giovanni) and Collina Fleming (North Rome). Closed Tues. The cognoscenti consider this the cream of Rome's ice creamers. Tubs only (cones would interfere with the taste) and

flavours according to season. *Gelato* nirvana.

Giolitti 40 Via Uffici del Vicario (Piazza Montecitorio) and Casina dei Tre Laghi (EUR). Open daily. Grandma Bernardina established the Giolitti brand in 1890 by seating her eight *bambini* outside while they ate ice creams; when passers-by asked her how she managed to raise such beautiful children, she told them it was her milk products that did the magic. The modern bars overflow with different flavours.

Palazzo del Freddo di Giovanni Fassi 65–7 Via Principe Eugenio (Esquilino). Open summer noon–midnight, winter noon–9pm, closed Mon. The jazzy interior belies a tradition that dates back to 1890. Flavours are augmented by specialities such as the fruit or chocolate *pezzo duro*.

San Filippo 8–10 Via di San Filippo (Parioli). Closed Mon. Opened in 1947, this *gelateria* in the smart Parioli district has an unpromising exterior but icy delights await within. The selection may be limited but the quality isn't. Popular with politicians and actors.

I Tre Scalini 28–32 Piazza Navona (Centro Storico). Closed Wed. The home of the *tartufo* ice cream sits on Piazza Navona beckoning passers-by to try its famed chocolate truffle. Consider a *tartufo* takeaway to enjoy amid the buskers and fountains.

Vintage fashions

There's a well-rounded vintage scene, with most shops clustered along Via del Governo Vecchio, just off Piazza Navona. For an ultra Roman experience, spend the afternoon trying on 1970s leather jackets and boho dresses, and fuel up at one of the street's copious wine bars. Just around the corner on Via dei Coronari, the penchant for yesteryear continues, as the street is dotted with tiny antique shops.

When to hit the shops

Opening hours in Rome are a law unto themselves. What visitors find most surprising is the tendency for many shops to close for at least two hours at lunchtime and all of Monday morning. However, shopping hours in Italy are changing. In highly commercial and touristy areas such as the Tridente, Via del Corso, the Trevi Fountain and Via Nazionale, most shops, especially the chain stores, department stores and high-fashion boutiques, now operate a so-called *orario continuato* (continuous opening hours), sometimes called the not-quite-English *orario no-stop*, both of which mean they do not close at lunchtime, and may be open on Monday morning.

Sunday opening is another recent novelty. Again, it's mainly the big names, chain stores and department stores in touristy areas that open on a Sunday. Another thing to remember is that in July and August, as the heat starts to become oppressive, local and independent shops may close on Saturday afternoon, and most close for at least two weeks for their annual holiday.

GETTING AROUND

Getting from one area to another in Rome is easy. If you are staying in the city centre and are armed with a decent map, you can walk almost everywhere, and will definitely find it a more pleasant experience than trying to jam yourself onto one of the packed buses that chug through the traffic-choked city's central thoroughfares. Keep an eye out for the small electrical buses (116 is the favourite) that snake quietly through the city, however, as they can provide welcome relief for tired feet. For the more outlying areas there is usually a handy bus or a metro stop not too far away, to make it easier to carry your purchases home.

SHOPPING

When it comes to shopping, Rome does more than hold its own against its more famous northern rival, Milan. It has enough haute couture, chic boutiques, designer homeware and leatherware stores to satisfy the hungriest of style vultures

For years Rome has been vying with big brother Milan for status as a fashionista magnet. While history hawks and culture vultures perpetually head for the Eternal City, serious shopaholics are quick to name Milan as the hands-down fashion capital of Italy. Yet times are changing. Not only can Rome boast a thriving market for high-quality handcraftsmanship, in the face of sibling rivalry, Gucci, Prada, Armani and company have set up shop in the prestigious Piazza di Spagna area, and boutiques are springing up every which way.

Made in Rome

For the keen-eyed and eager shopper, there are unique purchases to be had, from that hand-cut leather jacket you've always dreamed of, to handwoven textiles and home-grown Roman designer wear. They may not be parad-

Now more than ever, Rome boasts a shopping scene for all tastes – from the seekers of chic to lovers of all things ornate and original.

ing the catwalks yet, but these unique up-and-comers are worth seeking out. In a city that refuses to leave behind the values of solid craftsmanship, so intrinsic to the "Made in Italy" mark, a savvy shopper will delight in the objects on offer.

LEFT: Via dei Condotti, designer-store central.
RIGHT: window shopping by the Spanish Steps.

Be aware that the big guns of Italy don't necessarily cost less on their own soil. Those with an eye on the major labels would be wise to peruse price tags at home before landing in the capital. The outlets outside of Rome are a bit of a trek, and not always worth the trip, so think twice about stocking up on your Prada, Fendi and Ferragamo.

The good news is that younger Roman labels like AVC (fabulous shoes) and Arsenale (a truly art gallery-esque women's boutique) are springing up right and left, paving the way for fresh Roman fashion.

For a rundown of the various neighbourhoods and where to buy what, *see pages 72–3.*

On the go

For Romans, *gelato* (ice cream) is not so much a dessert as an afternoon or after-dinner snack to accompany a leisurely stroll around town. Accordingly, *gelaterie* are never far away and stay open late. Other treats that can be picked up from street vendors all over town are roasted chestnuts in the autumn and winter, and refreshing *grattachecca* (shaved ice with syrup) and watermelon wedges in summer.

Romans often stop at the local bar a couple of times a day, first for a breakfast of espresso or cappuccino and a *cornetto* (the Italian version of the croissant), then another espresso and perhaps a snack, such as a *panino* or *tramezzino* (small sandwiches) later in the day.

Pizza a taglio (by the slice) is also easy to find. Thicker than pizzeria pizza and topped with dozens of imaginative combinations, *pizza a taglio* is always sold by weight; an *etto* (100 grams) is a small portion. Many of the

same shops also sell *supplì* (fried balls of rice and mozzarella), a classic Roman snack.

The gastronomically curious may like to visit the Museo Nazionale delle Paste Alimentari (daily 9.30am–5.30pm, tel: 06-699 1120), on Piazza Scanderbeg near the Trevi Fountain, for fascinating displays of all kinds of pasta. But a visit to a good *alimentaria*, or

> Romans may love a leisurely meal, but stopping for slices of pizza, a few scoops of ice cream or a shot of fruit and crushed ice is also an essential part of any *passeggiata*.

grocery shop, is as rewarding as a trip to any museum. You will find regional products from all over the country, but the local cheese to try is *pecorino romano*, made from ewe's milk in big wheels, bathed in brine and aged for 18 months. A by-product is *ricotta di pecora*, brought in fresh from the farms and delicious on its own. A memorable sandwich can be made from *porchetta* (whole roasted pig, sliced to order), a speciality of the hill towns around Rome. ❑

LEFT ABOVE: Roscioli, a popular Roman deli. **LEFT BELOW:** *porchetta*, a speciality of the hilltowns. **ABOVE:** Romans like their sweets simple, fresh and preferably home-made. **ABOVE RIGHT:** an espresso, the way to start the day and end a meal

DESIGNER HIT LIST

There's no reason to ignore your inner fashion muse, but in the midst of a designer shop-a-thon, fashionistas may wish to keep the following tips in mind:

For bags it's **Prada**, **Fendi**, **Furla** and **Gucci.**

For shoes, **Costume National**, **Prada**, **Ferragamo**, **Bruno Magli** and **Tod's.**

RIGHT: in and around Piazza Vittorio (Rome's modest Chinatown near the station), ethnic clothing and accessories abound. The major Via Nazionale *(pictured right)* is the place to go for bags and shoes. Numerous stockists carry the best of this year's collections ranging in style and price.

Trussardi and **Armani** for jeans.

D&G and **Cavalli** for over-the-top, flash appeal.

BELOW: across the Tiber from the historic centre, Trastevere is bursting with knick-knack shops, artisans' workshops and some great jewellery stores. It is also the site of Porta Portese, the massive Sunday market selling just about anything *(see page 204).*

Valentino and **Laura Biagiotti** for evening allure.

And nothing beats a perfectly tailored **Armani** suit. Just ask half of Hollywood.

MARKETS IN ROME

Neighbourhood markets are an essential part of the Roman way of life and are full of local colour

Rome has about 150 official *mercati rionali* (neighbourhood markets) which run from Monday to Saturday, where there's generally an abundance of the freshest fruit and vegetables, as well as stalls selling meat, fish, cheeses, hams and spices, and others loaded with kitchenware, household linens, clothing and toys. Although supermarkets are competing hard, there are a number of reasons why the tradition of buying from markets will be hard to extinguish. In the city centre a lack of space dictates that the supermarkets that do exist are still comparatively small, and have no convenient parking spaces. Buying from markets is still often more convenient, both economically and in terms of location.

Also extremely important are the personalised service and human contact. Many older people value this highly, and will spend time chatting to stallholders and other customers as they make their purchases. Markets, especially flea markets, also offer the opportunity to do some bargaining. Whether you go to buy or to browse, Rome's markets are worth visiting for their atmosphere alone.

ABOVE: Rome's biggest flea market is Porta Portese, held on Via Portuense and adjacent streets between Piazza Porta Portese and Via Ettore Rolli.

BELOW: although supermarkets have sprung up all over Rome in recent years, most Romans still prefer to buy fresh produce from their local daily market.

THE HIGHLIGHTS

The best of Rome's many street markets are listed below. Most of the produce markets are open from Monday to Saturday, 7am–2pm. **Campo de' Fiori** (Centro Storico) is Rome's most characteristic fruit and vegetable market. **Mercato dei Fiori**, Via Trionfale (Prati). A huge wholesale flower market that is open to the public on Tuesday morning only. Just south of here, **Mercato Trionfale**, on Via Andrea Doria (Prati), is an enormous fenced-in market that sells all kinds of produce and more. **Mercato di San Cosimato**, Piazza di San Cosimato (Trastevere) is a small but popular fruit and vegetable market. **Nuovo Mercato Esquilino**, Via Ricasoli (Esquilino) is the most multicultural produce market, with exotic herbs and spices, yams, sweet potatoes and okra, and lots of other goods as well.

Smaller traditional markets can be found in Trastevere's **Piazza San Cosimato**, San Lorenzo's **Largo degli Osci** (few tourists, low prices) and **Piazza dell'Unità**.

Specialist markets, and those selling goods other than fresh produce, include:

Mercato delle Stampe (Largo della Fontanelle Borghese, Centro Storico; Mon–Sat 8am–sunset), which sells prints and second-hand or antiquarian books.

Mercato di Via Sannio (Piazza San Giovanni in Laterano, San Giovanni; Mon–Fri 8am–2pm, Sat 8am–5pm) sells new and second-hand clothes; the occasional vintage gem can be found here for a bargain price.

Porta Portese (Trastevere; Sun 7am–2pm). This is the best flea market in Rome. Skill is required to get a real bargain, but it's great fun. Hang onto your bags and look out for pickpockets.

The **Soffitta Sotto i Portici** market (Piazza Augusto Imperatore, under the porticoes; first and third Sun of every month, except Aug, 9am–sunset) is an antiques and collectors' market.

Borghetto Flaminio (Piazza della Marina, north of Piazza del Popolo; Sun 10am–7pm; closed Aug). All the stallholders here are private individuals, selling heirlooms and clothing, so there is a wide range in quality and price. There's a small admission charge.

ABOVE: the city's best-known food market is Campo de' Fiori. Here you will find everything from upmarket stalls selling exotic fruits and rare herbs at exorbitant prices to stalls where fresher-than-fresh produce on show is grown by the farmer who is serving you.

BELOW: another classic Roman market is held on Via Sannio, just behind the Basilica of San Giovanni in Laterano. This is the place to come for jeans, leather jackets, sports gear and shoes. There are also several stalls selling retro and second-hand clothes.

CENTRAL ROME

TOP SIGHTS

Vatican Museums
page 141

Piazza Navona
page 158

Pantheon
page 154

Campo de' Fiori
page 170

Capitoline Hill
page 89

TRIDENTE
main map
126

THE VATICAN AND PRATI
main map
138

PIAZZA NAVONA
main map
152

CAMPO DE' FIORI
main map
152

C.

TRASTEVERE AND THE GIANICOLO
main map
202

AVENTIN
TESTAC
main m
212

**VIA VENETO AND
BORGHESE, and NORTH ROME**
main maps 186 and 190

Villa Borghese
page 188

QUIRINALE
main map 118

Spanish Steps
page 129

**MONTI AND
ESQUILINO**
main map
230

Trevi Fountain
page 117

**ANCIENT
ROME**
main maps
100 and 110

**CELIO AND
SAN GIOVANNI**
main map
222

Forum
page 100

APPIAN WAY
main map
240

Colosseum
page 111

8 4

Rome

0 _____ 500 m
0 _____ 500 yds

N

P.za Cinque
Giornate

Villa Ruffo

Lepanto

Flaminio

MONTE
PINCIO

P.le
degli Eroi

Via della Giuliana

Circonval. Trionale

Via di
S. Maria
d. Grazie

Viale Giulio Cesare

Viale delle Milizie

Via S. Pellico

Viale Angelico

Via S. Vespasiano

Via Ottaviano Barletta

Via della Milizie

Via Lepanto

Via M.

Via Michelangelo

Lgt. A. da Brescia

Via Flaminia

P.le
Flaminio

Lgt. in Augusta

P.za del
Popolo

Popolo

Casa di
Goethe

Via di Ripetta

Via del Corso

S. Vincenzo
d. Paoli

S. Gioacchino

Ottaviano-
San Pietro

SS. Rosario

Via F. Massimo

Via dei Gracchi

Via Cola di Rienzo

Colonna

Via Cicerone

PRATI

Boezio

Chiesa
Valdese

Ara
Pacis

S. Maria
d. Popolo

P.za del
Spag

Cas
Ke
She

Leone IV

Via Candia

Via Vaticano

Viale Vaticano

P.za del
Risorgimento

Via

Via Crescenzio

P.za
Cavour

Via V.
Colonna

Ponte
Cavour

Lgt. Marzio

Mausoleo
di Augusto

S. Carlo
al Corso

Palazzo
Borghese

Palazzo
Ruspoli

Pro

S. Lorenzo

Via del Corso

Via del

S.

GIARDINI

Pinacoteca Musei
Vaticani

VATICANI

Cappella
Sistina

Basilica di
San Pietro

Aula delle
Udienze Pontificie

Palazzo del
Sant'Uffizio

Borgo Pio

Palazzo
Giraud

San Pietro

P.za
Pio

Castel
Sant'Angelo

S. Maria in
Traspontina

Mausoleo
di Adriano

Ex Palazzo
di Giustizia

P.za
Tribunali

S. Antonio
d. Portoghesi

Palazzo
Montecitorio

Palazzo
Chigi

Gal
Alb

P.za Sor

Via del Corso

S. Maria in
Trastevere

Divi
Gregorio VII

Via Aurelia

Via d.
Cavalleggeri

L.go di P.
Cavalleggeri

S. Maria
alle Fornaci

S. Onofrio

Via delle Fornaci

Lgt. Castello

Ponte Vitt.
Em. II

S. Spirito
in Sassia

Ponte Pr.

P.za
Amedeo

P.za
d. Rovere

S. Giovanni
d. Fiorentini

Lgt. Tor di Nona

S.
Salvatore

S.
Simeone

Palazzo
Taverna

Palazzo
Gov. Vecchio

S. Agnese
in Agone

Navona

Cinque
Lune

Museo
Napoleonico

P.za
S. Agostino

Francesi

Palazzo
Madama

Pantheon

S. Luigi d.

P.za S.

S. Ivo

S. Andrea
d. Valle

Gesù

P.za
Colonna

S.
Ignazio

S. Maria
s. Minerva

Galleria
Doria Pamphilj

V. d. Plebiscito

Pal.
Venezia

P.

P.le
Garibaldi

VILLA
ABAMELEK

Via Aurelia Antica

Via della Cava Aurelia

Via Gregorio VII

Via delle Fornaci

Via Nuova d. Fornaci

Chiesa
dell'Annunziata

Villa
Lante

Carcere
Regina Coeli

S. Eligio

Palazzo
Corsini

Villa
Farnesina

Palazzo
Torlonia

Museo di
Roma in
Trastevere

Porta
S. Pancrazio

S. Maria in
Trastevere

Lgt. Gianicolense

Corso

Lgt. dei Tebaldi

Palazzo
Sacchetti

Chiesa
Nuova

Emanuele II

Pal. d.
Cancelleria

Campo
de' Fiori

Palazzo
Farnese

Palazzo
Spada

Lgt. Tebaldi

Via Giulia

Lgt. dei Vallati

P.za
Trilussa

S. Giovanni
d. Fiorentini

Emanuele II

Pal.
Braschi

Museo
Barracco

Area
Sacra

Via Arenula

Palazzo
Cenci

Palazzo
Mattei

Teatro di
Marcello

Crypta
Balbi

Palazzo
Balbi

Lgt. dei Cenci

Via del Teatro

Ponte
Garibaldi

I. Tiberina

S. Bartolomeo
all'Isola

Ponte
Cestio

Lgt. degli Anguillara

Lgt. del R. Sanzio

Ponte
Sisto

S. Cristogono

Palazzo S.
Congregaz.

P.za
Sidney
Sonnino

S. Cecilia in
Trastevere

S. Tempio
di Vesta

R I
Mor

VILLA
DORIA
PAMPHILI

Villa Doria
Pamphili

P.le
Aurelio

Via di Donna Olimpia

Via G. Ghisleri

Via Pio Foa

Via Fontelana

Via Vitellia

Il Vascello

P.za S.
Pancrazio

Viale delle Mura

Gianicolensi

Via G. Guinizzelli

Via G. Cavalcanti

Villa
Sciarra

S. Maria
Regina Pacis

P.za Ippolito
Nievo

Viale di Trastevere

Via Alessandro Poerio

Viale G. Manili

Via G.
Garibaldi

Via L. Manara

Via E.
Morosini

Palazzo
d. Esami

TRASTEVERE

S. Francesco
a Ripa

Via di Trastevere

Via G.
Induno

P.za Porta
Portese

Via Portuense

Viale di Trastevere

P.za Porta
Portese

Via Portuense

P.za
dell'Emporio

Lgt. Testaccio

Via
Giovanni Branca

Via
Nicola Galvani

Porto di Ripa Grande

S. Sat

S. Alessio

Priorato
di Malta

S. Anselmo

Lgt. Testaccio

TESTACCIO

Via B. Franklin

Monte
Testaccio

L.go Manlio
Gelsomini

Via Marmorata

Lgt. Aventino

MACRO al
Mattatoio

Ponte
Testaccio

P.ta S. Paolo

Piramide di
Caio Cestio

Piramide

Osti

Sta
S.

Recommended Restaurants, Bars & Cafés on page 91

THE CAPITOLINE HILL

The Capitoline Hill was the political power centre of the ancient world, beautified by Michelangelo's designs during the Renaissance and now home to the world's oldest museums. Close by, the Vittoriano monument overlooks traffic-clogged Piazza Venezia, linking the ancient world with our own

The Capitoline Hill started life as a fortified stronghold and later became the city's religious and political centre. As a 12th-century guidebook, *Mirabilia Romae (The Marvels of Rome)* stated: "The Capitol was the head of the world, where consuls and senators abode to govern the earth." At only 50 metres (150 ft), it may be the lowest of the city's seven hills, but Rome was founded at its feet. During the Renaissance, it was glorified with the Piazza Campidoglio, a harmonious square designed by Michelangelo, and second only to Piazza San Pietro in its architectural symmetry.

The twin crowns

In ancient times the hill looked quite different, with steep cliffs of porous tufa rock falling steeply on all sides of its twin crowns. On the southern crown, known as Campidoglio (the Capitol), stood the Tempio di Giove (Temple of Jupiter), which was the religious hub of the state. Originally the size of a football pitch, it was begun by the Etruscan kings and dedicated in 509 BC, the first year of the Republic. Behind its six-pillared, south-facing frontage a great anteroom led to the shrines of three great gods – Jupiter, Juno and Minerva. Every New Year's Day, the consuls were inaugurated in a formal ceremony on the Capitol.

The triumphal processions followed Via Sacra, the holy road, coming up the hill from the Forum. Remnants of the basalt paving of this street can be seen quite clearly from Via di Monte Tarpeo. Anyone guilty of treason was thrown from

Main attractions

SANTA MARIA IN ARACOELI
THE CAPITOLINE MUSEUMS
MAMERTINE PRISON
THE VITTORIANO MONUMENT
MUSEO DEL RISORGIMENTO
MUSEO DI PALAZZO VENEZIA

LEFT: Michelangelo's staircase leads to the Campidoglio, watched over by the twin gods, Castor (pictured) and Pollux.
RIGHT: Piazza Venezia viewed from the steps of the Vittoriano monument.

The spacious interior of Santa Maria in Aracoeli, and the stairway to its entrance (right).

BELOW: policing the Campidoglio.

Santa Maria in Aracoeli ❶

✉ Scala dell'Arca Capitolina 🕐 daily 9am–12.30pm, 3–6pm 💶 free
🚇 *see Musei Capitolini*

The site of the ancient Temple of Juno Moneta is now occupied by the church of Santa Maria in Aracoeli (St Mary of the Altar in the Sky). The church hides behind a 13th-century brick façade, but its origins go back much further, as its ancient columns testify. Records from AD 574 mention a church on this site. The present church was built by Franciscans in around 1250. The interior features an ornate coffered ceiling dating from 1572–5 and a striking Cosmatesque floor. This style of intricate, geometric polychrome patterns is named after Lorenzo Cosmati (1140–1210), its inventor. In the first chapel on the right are Renaissance frescoes by Pinturicchio from the life of St Bernard. The recent restoration of the Chapel of San Pasquale Baylon brought to

the Rupe Tarpea (Tarpeian Rock), the Capitol's southern precipice. The other crown of the hill housed the temple to Juno Moneta, the goddess who is supposed to have warned the Romans of an attack by Gauls in 390 BC by making her sacred geese honk. The mint also stood here, hence the word *moneta*, meaning money.

Capitoline Hill and Ancient Rome

light some beautiful 13th-century frescoes concealed behind 16th-century works. Steps lead down from the exit in the right transept to the level of the Piazza del Campidoglio.

PIAZZA DEL CAMPIDOGLIO

Between the hill's two peaks sits the **Piazza del Campidoglio** (Capitol Square). In ancient times it was the site of the Asylum, a sacred sanctuary that protected the persecuted, said to date back to the time of the founder of the city, Romulus. The magnificent square, its buildings and the broad staircase leading up to it were designed by Michelangelo for Pope Paul III, who wanted a majestic setting for the reception of the Holy Roman Emperor Charles V on his visit to Rome in 1536.

As it turned out, the square wasn't completed until the 17th century. Standing guard at the top of the **Cordonata**, as the staircase is known, are two imposing statues of Castor and Pollux. The piazza's centrepiece is a first-rate copy of an immense equestrian statue of Emperor Marcus Aurelius. The original is kept inside the Capitoline Museums.

Straight ahead is the **Palazzo Senatorio**. At the bottom of its double staircase is a fountain of Minerva flanked by two gigantic reclining statues representing the Nile (left with the Sphinx) and the Tiber (right with the she-wolf).

The Musei Capitolini ❷

✉ 1 Piazza del Campidoglio ☎ 06-8205 9127 🕐 Tue–Sun 9am–8pm 🎫 charge 🚌 30, 40, 44, 46, 60, 62, 63, 64, 70, 81, 84, 85, 87, 95, 117, 119, 160, 170, 175, 271, 492, 571, 628, 630, 715, 716, 780, 781, 810

The two grand *palazzi* on either side of the square – Palazzo Nuovo (New Palace) and Palazzo dei Conservatori (Conservators' Palace) – house the oldest public museums in the world. The **Musei Capitolini** are entered via the Palazzo dei Conservatori, on the right of Michelangelo's Cordonata. Together they contain a rich collection of ancient sculpture, and late Renaissance and Baroque art *(see pages 51–5)*.

The two palaces are connected via a passage lined with artefacts that runs underneath the square. From here you can visit the **Tabularium**, Rome's ancient archive (from 78 BC). It was built around the even older Temple of Veiovis, and rose four storeys high, with 10 arches opening onto the Forum, although all but three of them are now bricked up.

FOOD

Avoid the refreshment stands dotted around the major tourist sites unless you're absolutely desperate for a drink. They're overpriced and prey on thirsty tourists. If you don't want to be ripped off, it's worth stocking up on a supply of bottled mineral water from a grocery store (there's bound to be one near your hotel).

ABOVE LEFT: the she-wolf suckling Romulus and Remus. **BELOW:** fragments of a colossal statue of Constantine in the Palazzo dei Conservatori.

TIP

Some of the best views of the city can be seen from the cafés in the Palazzo dei Conservatori and the Vittoriano monument.

ABOVE RIGHT: tomb of the Unknown Soldier. **ABOVE:** admiring the view from the Tabularium. **BELOW:** the Vittoriano monument.

Memorable views across the Roman Forum can be had from here.

Mamertine Prison ❸

✉ 1 Clivo Argentario ⏰ daily summer 9am–7pm, winter 9am–5pm 💰 donation requested 🚇 *see Musei Capitolini*

A road winds its way down from the left of the Palazzo Senatorio to the church of San Giuseppe dei Falegnami and the **Carcere Mamertino**. Defeated kings and generals, having been paraded through the streets in their victor's triumphal march, were imprisoned here before being executed. A small chapel next to a spring commemorates St Peter, who is said to have been incarcerated here, and to have baptised his guards with water from a spring he miraculously created. From the prison, the road leads down to Via dei Fori Imperiali *(see page 97)*.

PIAZZA VENEZIA ❹

If all roads lead to Rome, then all roads in Rome seem to lead to Piazza Venezia, the hub of the city's road network since 1881. Some 800,000 Romans squeeze their cars through here every day, and it's not the best place to be during rush hour.

Il Vittoriano ❺

✉ Piazza Venezia ⏰ daily summer 9am–5.30pm, winter 9.30am–4.30pm 💰 free 🚇 *see Musei Capitolini*

Compared to the grace and majesty of the Campidoglio, Il Vittoriano that dominates the square, while undeniably impressive, is a bombastic structure. Romans refer to it irreverently as the typewriter, the wedding cake or even Rome's false teeth. In the 19th century, a whole swathe of medieval streets was razed to make way for this hulking white monument erected in honour of Victor Emmanuel II of Savoy, the first king of the newly unified Italy. However, entrance is free and visitors can climb the steps for wonderful views of the city and welcome refreshments in the outdoor café behind it *(see below)*.

Below the equestrian statue of Victor Emmanuel is the tomb of the Unknown Soldier flanked by perpetually burning flames and two armed guards. The monument also has a permanent museum complex. **The Museo del Risorgimento** recounts the history of the Risorgimento (literally "Resurrection"), a turbulent period of war and political wrangling that led to the reunification of Italy. However, few of the exhibits are labelled in English, and it's of limited appeal to those with only a passing interest in military history.

Around the back of the building, facing the Forum, is a space used for high-profile international exhibitions.

Palazzo Venezia ❻

✉ 118 Via del Plebiscito ☎ 06-6999 4319 ⓒ Tue–Sun 8.30am–7.30pm ⓖ charge ⓐ see Musei Capitolini

Although the Vittoriano is the most dominant, the Palazzo di Venezia is the most interesting building on this

square. Built by Cardinal Barbo in 1455 and enlarged when he became Pope Paul II, it was later handed over to the Venetian ambassadors and then the Austrians, until Mussolini decided it would make a perfect office and addressed the crowds from its balcony, the very balcony from which Pope Paul II watched the races along the Corso *(see page 127)*.

This palace now holds the **Museo di Palazzo Venezia**, with displays of medieval paintings, sculptures and artefacts, terracotta models (some by Bernini), ceramics, bronze sculptures, and glass, silver and ivory objects. The museum has a permanent collection of Renaissance arts and crafts, and also hosts regular exhibitions dedicated to national and international artists and art movements.

Behind the palace is the church of **San Marco** (8.30am–12.30pm and 4–7pm; closed Mon am and Wed pm), with a lovely mosaic in its 9th-century apse. Outside the church stands the buxom **statue of Madama Lucrezia**, one of Rome's so-called "Talking Statues" *(see page 160)*. ❏

Piazza Venezia is one of central Rome's busiest hubs. It is also a major bus terminus.

BEST RESTAURANTS, BARS & CAFÉS

The restaurants and bars in this area are very touristy and not really recommended, but we detail a few places worth visiting, as much for the views and atmosphere as for food and drink.

Restaurants

Vecchia Roma
🍽 18 Piazza Campitelli
☎ 06-686 4604 ⓒ L & D
Thur–Tue. €€€€ [p339, D1]
At Vecchia Roma you pay for the location, the ser-

vice and some of the city's finest outdoor seating. The classic dishes are usually good, although occasionally only competent, and the wine is excellent. It's expensive for what you get, but memorable.

Bars and Cafés

Caffè Capitolino (top of Palazzo dei Conservatori, adjacent to Piazza Campidoglio) has one of

the most panoramic views in Rome. Outdoor seating under elegant sunshades is expensive but delightful if it's not too hot. Inside, cafeteria-style service is cheaper. Open until 8pm in summer.

The **Ara Coelis Café** (behind the Vittoriano monument; also accessible from the Piazza del Campidoglio) is another great, if touristy, spot for a drink and affords fine views of the Forum and the Roman skyline.

Just off Piazza Venezia to the east is a former

theatre that attracts a thirty-something Roman crowd looking for a quirky night out. **Il Centrale Ristotheatre** (6 Via Celsa) has a bar with a lounge area and restaurant with live music, theatre or cabaret. From 7.30pm–midnight on Sundays you can have one drink and all you can eat from the buffet for a set price.

• • • • • • • • • •

Price includes dinner and a half-bottle of house wine.

€€€€ = €60 and up, €€€ = €40–60, €€ = €25–40, € = under €25.

PALAZZO DEI CONSERVATORI

The larger of the two Capitoline Museums has a varied collection of artworks, from ancient statues to Baroque paintings

Divided between two palaces on either side of the Campidoglio, the Capitoline Museum collection is the oldest public collection of classical sculpture in the world – the first exhibits were made over to the people of Rome by Sixtus IV in 1471. A visit to the museums begins in the Palazzo dei Conservatori (to the right of the Michelangelo staircase, as you face the equestrian statue of Marcus Aurelius), where the ticket office and cloakrooms are.

One of the most iconic exhibits here is the much-copied she-wolf wet-nursing Romulus and Remus, symbol of Rome. The wolf is Etruscan, dating from the 5th century BC, but the twins were added in the 15th century by Florentine artist Pollaiuolo. You can also get a good close-up view of the original equestrian statue of Marcus Aurelius (the one on the square is a copy) exhibited in an airy, skylit room. Other highlights include a graceful 1st-century BC figure of a boy removing a thorn from his foot, an earlier Venus, a fine collection of Renaissance and Baroque art, and fragments of a huge statue of Constantine.

The essentials

✉ *Piazza del Campidoglio; www.museicapitolini.org*

☎ 06-8205 9127

🕐 *Tue–Sun 9am–8pm*

💶 *charge*

🚌 30, 40, 44, 46, 60, 62, 63, 64, 70, 81, 84, 85, 87, 95, 117, 119, 160, 170, 175, 271, 492, 571, 628, 630, 715, 716, 780, 781, 810

ABOVE: detail from the vast frescoes decorating the Hall of the Orazie and Curiazi where the Public Council of Conservators convened. Painted by Mannerist Cavaliere d'Arpino (1595–1640), they illustrate the origins of Rome as told by the Roman historian Livy.

ABOVE: *The Rape of the Sabine Women* by Pietro da Cortona. He was a contemporary of Bernini, and together they pioneered a true Baroque style, as illustrated by the movement, richness of colour and theatricality of this painting. **BELOW:** this vivid portrait of Hannibal riding an elephant is central to the 15th-century murals that decorate the Hannibal Room which records the Punic Wars fought between Rome and arch-rival Carthage.

ABOVE: in the courtyard of the Palazzo dei Conservatori are the surreal fragments of a colossal statue of Constantine, which once stood in his basilica in the Forum. The gigantic marble head is 2 metres (6 ft) high. **RIGHT:** the celebrated bronze *Lo Spinario*, a delightful 1st-century BC statue of a boy plucking a thorn from his foot, inspired many Renaissance works. **BELOW:** sensual portrayal of St John the Baptist by Caravaggio.

ABOVE: the Palazzo dei Conservatori and Palazzo Nuovo are linked by an underground tunnel which leads to the Tabularium, the ancient Roman State Record Office, erected in 78 BC. It affords fine views of the Forum.

PALAZZO NUOVO

The smaller of the museum duo holds some of the finest examples of ancient Roman statuary in the city

An underground passageway lined with artefacts connects the Palazzo dei Conservatori with the Palazzo Nuovo, via the Tabularium *(see page 89)*, which offers an excellent view of the Forum. This second museum in the Capitoline duo is filled with row upon row of portrait busts of Roman emperors, but the first floor contains some exquisite examples of Roman statuary.

The most famous piece here is the *Dying Gaul*, a beautifully evocative statue of a fatally wounded warrior.

Other artworks worth singling out include the voluptuous *Capitoline Venus (pictured left)* and the red marble *Satyr Resting*, a copy of an original by Praxiteles. This is the statue which inspired Nathaniel Hawthorne's novel *The Marble Faun*. "It is impossible to gaze long at this stone image", wrote Hawthorn in the novel, "without conceiving a kindly sentiment towards it, as if its substance were warm to the touch, and imbued with actual life."

More earthly subjects on display include a drunken woman and children with various animals.

Look out also for the Mosaic of the Doves from Hadrian's villa and the 2nd-century mosaic of theatre masks.

BELOW: in the courtyard of the Palazzo Nuovo is a fountain which incorporates a 1st-century BC statue of a river god. Known as "Marforio", this is one of Rome's famous "talking statues", to which placards containing satirical comments on the events of the day were attached during the Renaissance.

LEFT: Cupid and Psyche, a Roman copy of a Greek original portraying the god of love embracing the goddess of the soul.

BELOW LEFT: the *Capitoline Venus* is another Roman copy of a Hellenistic original, which Goethe considered the finest ancient statue in Rome. This sensual statue portrays the goddess of love and beauty rising from the water, modestly – but ineffectively – trying to cover her body. It's likely that such an accomplished sculpture decorated a prestigious imperial home.

BELOW: the Hall of the Emperors contains portrait busts of Roman emperors and their families, while the Hall of Philosophers includes busts of Socrates, Sophocles, Demosthenes, Euripides and Homer.

RIGHT: the poignant statue of the *Dying Gaul*, thought to be the statue of a gladiator – "butchered to make a Roman holiday" in Byron's words – was discovered with another equally moving statue, the *Galata Suicide*, now housed in the Palazzo Altemps *(see page 162)*.

RIGHT: interspersed among the busts displayed on the ground-floor rooms are a variety of funerary reliefs, plinths and sarcophagi, the most famous of which is the 3rd-century sarcophagus depicting scenes from the life of Achilles.

ABOVE: the central exhibit in the Hall of the Doves is the exquisitely crafted mosaic of drinking doves found in Hadrian's Villa at Tivoli. In the same room is another highly expressive 2nd-century mosaic of two Greek theatre masks, probably from an imperial villa on the Aventine Hill.

ABOVE: the centrepiece of the design for the Piazza del Campidoglio was the magnificent statue of Marcus Aurelius (now a copy; the original is in the museum). Michelangelo found the statue so lifelike that he stood before the horse and commanded it to walk.

Recommended Restaurants, Bars & Cafés on page 113

ANCIENT ROME

This chapter shows you some of the places where
Ancient Rome thrived, declined and eventually fell.
Here lie the remains of the Fora, the Palatine,
the Colosseum and Nero's Golden House

By 7.30 in the morning, a traffic jam usually blocks the intersection of Via Labicana and Via dei Fori Imperiali which leads to the Colosseum and the Appian Way. This boulevard, commissioned by Mussolini for the greater glory of the Fascist Empire, slices through the heart of Rome's ancient sites. Here, Nero built an artificial lake to grace his palace. Then the Flavians – in a bid to return the tyrant's palace to the people – built the Colosseum. The construction of Via dei Fori Imperiali in 1932 was a relatively recent attempt to use Ancient Rome's monuments to underwrite modern political ambition.

Bulldozers flattened one of the city's oldest medieval quarters to make way for the route, destroying ancient walls, imperial palaces, temples and arches, some dating from the 3rd century BC. Architects ignored the archaeological massacre. When *Il Duce* ordered the removal of a pile of stones near the Colosseum, nobody pointed out that they marked the Meta Sudans, an ancient spring. Ludwig Curtius, then director of the German Archaeological Institute, said: "It would have been easy while building the street to

excavate those parts of the Fora of Julius Caesar and of Trajan still lying underground, and to direct the road over them as a bridge, but the dictator, concerned only for his next demonstration of power, was in a hurry…"

Originally, Mussolini had hoped to excavate the Imperial Fora, which would have served as decoration alongside his new processional road, symbolically connecting his regime with the glory of Roman antiquity. If these plans had been followed, an

Main attractions
THE IMPERIAL FORA
THE FORO ROMANO
THE PALATINE HILL
CIRCUS MAXIMUS
THE COLOSSEUM
NERO'S GOLDEN HOUSE

LEFT: the Arch of Septimius Severus.
RIGHT: 21st-century senator and centurion.

The simplest way to reach the Forum is to take metro line B or one of the buses indicated to Colosseo or Piazza Venezia. From Trastevere, the Aventine or Villa Borghese take tram No. 3. The entrance to Trajan's Markets is only a 10-minute walk away from the Colosseum.

RIGHT: Julius Caesar.
BELOW: Via dei Fori Imperiali.

archaeological park would have extended from the excavated Forum area to the ruins of the Baths of Caracalla and on to Via Appia Antica. But the project was never realised and the road became a major thoroughfare. It is unlikely that the ruins beneath it will ever come to light.

THE IMPERIAL FORA ❼

✉ Via dei Fori Imperiali ☎ 06-679 7702/06-679 7786 ⓒ daily 9.30am–7.30pm ⓔ free ⓜ Colosseo 🚌 60, 63, 64, 70, 75, 84, 85, 87, 117, 170, 175, 186, 810, 850

The remains of the Fori Imperiali lie on either side and buried beneath the Via dei Fori Imperiali. As Rome grew in power, its population increased and the original Roman Forum was no longer big enough to serve the city's needs. The Imperial Fora were built by a succession of emperors from Caesar to Trajan.

The **Imperial Fora Visitor Center** ❹ is located on the Via dei Fori Imperiali between Via Cavour and the Colosseum metro stop. Inside you can

find background information on the site, a small exhibition space, a café, a bookshop and toilets.

Caesar's Forum ❷

On the south side of the Via are the remnants of Caesar's Forum (Foro di Cesare), the first Imperial Forum, built in 51 BC by Julius Caesar when the original became too small for Rome's increasing population. It was dedicated, still unfinished, in 46 BC and completed under Augustus (23 BC–AD 14). Following Hellenistic models, it was square and enclosed by pillars. On its western side stood the Temple of Venus Genetrix (look for three reconstructed columns), built because

Imperial Fora (Fori Imperiali)

Recommended Restaurants, Bars & Cafés on page 113

RA - PATATINE -
- CIAMBELLE

Caesar believed himself to be a descendant of the goddess.

Forum of Augustus ●

The Foro di Augusto across the street was built to celebrate the emperor's victory and revenge over the army of Cassius and Brutus, who had led the conspiracy to assassinate Julius Caesar, his adoptive father. In the centre stood the temple of the war god Mars Ultor (Mars the Avenger), and in the great apses of the square stood statues of the mythical ancestors of Augustus' family.

Trajan's Forum and Trajan's Markets

The **Foro di Traiano ●** was a massive complex of temples, libraries and markets, surrounded by colonnades,

that outdid the other Fora in size and splendour. It was designed in AD 106 by Apollodorus of Damascus, the best architect of his time. Building it meant removing a small hill between the Quirinal and the Capitol. To the northwest, it was bound by the vast Basilica Ulpia, which had five naves. In its western apse, the Atrium Libertatis, slaves were liberated.

Trajan also commissioned his architect to build the **Mercati di Traiano ●** (Trajan's Markets; entrance 94 Via IV Novembre; tel: 06-679 0048; closed until end 2007, thereafter Tue–Sun 9am–sunset; admission charge), the ancient equivalent of a multi-storey shopping mall. Its remains stand behind the Forum on the slopes of the Quirinal, between two libraries on Via IV Novembre. They reveal a complex system of streets on various levels, with shops, administrative offices and spaces reserved for the distribution of grain to the public.

While there is also a lower entrance, the upper one on Via IV Novembre offers the best view of this marvellously preserved testament to

TIP

Before working your way around the Forum and trying to make sense of the ruins, it's a good idea to get an overview of the site. The best vantage point for this is the Tabularium or the terrace behind the Capitol *(see page 89)*. You can also refer to the detailed map of the Roman Forum *on pages 100–1.*

ABOVE LEFT: refreshment stands are a familiar sight. **BELOW:** Trajan's Markets.

Trajan's Column.

Roman daily life. You'll first enter the Great Hall, which recently reopened after restoration. This was most likely the place for grain rations. From the adjoining terrace are good views down to the commercial spaces below, which would have held offices and shops. The nearby Via Biberatica, which judging from its name (*bibere* means "to drink" in Latin) once housed bars for thirsty shoppers and businessmen.

The magnificent **Colonna Traiana** ❼ (Trajan's Column) nearby was erected in AD 113 to celebrate Trajan's victory over the Dacians (inhabitants of today's Romania). The 40-metre (120-ft) column is beautifully decorated with a spiral frieze of bas-reliefs depicting various phases of the Dacian campaigns (AD 101–2 and 105). Originally the reliefs were brightly painted and would have been visible from the balconies of the libraries. In AD 177, a golden urn containing the

emperor's remains was buried under the column. The statue topping the column is of St Peter, commissioned by Pope Sixtus in 1587 to replace what was once a statue of Trajan.

THE FORO ROMANO ❽

✉ Via dei Fori Imperiali 🕻 06-3996 7700 🕐 daily summer 8.30am–7.15pm, winter 8.30am–4.30pm 💲 free 🚇 Colosseo 🚌 60, 63, 70, 75, 81, 84, 85, 87, 160, 175, 186, 628, 810, 850

The best place to begin a tour of the Foro Romano is at the main entrance on Via dei Fori Imperiali, roughly level with Via Cavour. Originally a marshy valley between the Capitoline and Palatine hills, the area was drained by the Cloaca Maxima, the great sewer, and the site became a marketplace that developed into the religious, political and commercial centre of Republican Rome.

Forum (Foro Romano)

By the time excavations began in the 18th century, most of the Forum was buried under rubble, and the place was known as Campo Vaccino (Cow Field), since it was used for grazing cattle.

Via Sacra

From the entrance a path leads down to the Via Sacra (the Sacred Way), the oldest street in Rome, which once ran through the Forum from the Arch of Titus up to the Capitoline. Triumphal processions of victorious generals in horse-drawn chariots parading their prisoners and spoils of war, and followed by their soldiers, would pass along the street to the Temple of Jupiter on the Capitol, where they

Even if you don't know any Latin, you'll be able to pick out familiar names carved into the stone in the Roman Forum.

LEFT: view of the Forum from the Palatine Hill.

Forum (Foro Romano)

The Via dei Fori Imperiali is closed to traffic on Sundays.

would make sacrifices to Jupiter, the supreme god.

Walking westwards in the direction of the Capitoline, to the right lie the remains of the **Basilica Aemilia** , a massive assembly hall for politicians, businessmen and traders dating from the 2nd century BC. It was rebuilt by Augustus after a fire, and then again after another fire in 410, when Alaric and his Goths invaded the city during the conquest of Rome. You can still see the stains left by coins burnt into the floor. Until 1500, most of the hall was still standing, but Bramante, Rome's chief architect during the High Renaissance, used some of it to build Palazzo Torlonia in the Borgo quarter. On the steps, you can see the remains

of a temple to Venus, nicknamed *Cloacina* because the small circular building marks the spot where the **Cloaca Maxima** (the city's main sewer, built in the 1st century BC) empties into the valley of the Forum.

Beyond the Basilica Aemilia is the **Curia** , the ancient Senate House that was the centre of political life in Republican Rome. In the Middle Ages, the Curia was consecrated as a church, but the current building, a replica of Diocletian's, dates from 1937. The bronze doors are copies of the originals, which were transferred in the 17th century to the Basilica of San Giovanni in Laterano *(see page 221)*. In the cavernous inner hall (30 metres/90 ft long, 20 metres/60 ft wide, 20 metres/60 ft high), the 300-strong Senate would gather to control the destiny of the Empire. In front of the Curia is the Comitium, where the Popular Assembly met.

Even older is the **Lapis Niger** (Black Stone), a pavement of black marble laid to mark a sacred spot; according to legend, the tomb of Romulus, Rome's mythical founder, lies here. The remains of a monument from the 6th century BC have been excavated from under the Lapis Niger, and, while they do not prove the existence of the grave, they are evidence that Romulus was already venerated in early Rome.

Arch of Septimius Severus ⓔ

Behind looms the imposing Arco di Settimio Severo. The triple arch is 25 metres (75 ft) wide, 10 metres (30 ft) deep and 20 metres (60 ft) high. It was built in AD 203 to celebrate the 10th anniversary of the emperor's ascent to the throne. The reliefs on the arch depict the victorious campaigns Septimius Severus and his two sons, Geta and Caracalla, fought against the Arabs and the Parthians (in present-day Iran). In earlier years, the arch was topped by a statue of the emperor in a four-horse chariot.

Later, Caracalla had his brother murdered in the arms of their mother and then placed him under *damnatio memoriae* (exile from memory) by ordering the deletion from monuments of all references to Geta and replacing them with laudatory titles

to himself. You can still see the chisel marks on the inscriptions, which were originally inlaid with metal.

Beside the arch is the **Umbilicus Urbis**, a navel-shaped piece of stone that marked the centre of the city. Here, too, stood the **Miliarum Aureum**, a gilded bronze milestone that marked the start (or end) of all the Imperial roads connecting the main towns of the Empire to Rome. Beside it stood the **Rostra**, the speaker's platform moved here from the Comitium by Julius Caesar. It was once decorated with the prows or beaks *(rostra)* of ships captured at the

During the Middle Ages, part of the Arch of Septimius Severus, which was half buried in rubble, was used to house a barber's shop.

ABOVE: 1st–2nd-century statue in the Curia, said to portray either Hadrian or Trajan. **BELOW:** Arch of Septimius Severus.

Roman Domus

On Clivio di Scauro, south of the Colosseum, and under the Basilica of Saints John and Paul on the Caelian Hill, 20 underground rooms dated between the 2nd and 4th centuries AD were recently reopened to the public after extensive restoration work. A series of residences and a private baths built in the 2nd century AD were transformed into a single, luxurious house *(domus)* a century later by a wealthy owner and decorated with frescoes. The Roman Domus is now open to tourists (tel: 06-7045 4544; www.caseromane.it; Thur–Mon 10am–1pm and 3–6pm; admission charge). Entrance to the site is allowed every 30 minutes. Book in advance if you want a guided tour.

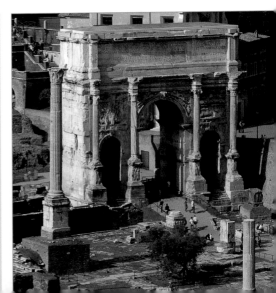

battle of Actium in 31 BC. Trophies from Cleopatra's fleet are reputed to have been displayed here as well.

Behind, to the right, are the remains of the **Tempio della Concordia** (Temple of Concord), a reconstruction by the Emperor Tiberius (AD 14–37) of the sanctuary erected to mark the peace accord between the patricians and plebians following the Class Wars of 367 BC.

Two temples

After their deaths, many emperors were automatically deified and had temples consecrated to them. All that remains of the **Temple of Vespasian** (AD 69–79), erected by his

RIGHT: Romans celebrating the Saturnalia.
BELOW: remains of the Temple of Saturn.

sons Titus and Domitian (both of whom later became emperors) are the three Corinthian columns that rise up behind the Rostra.

In the northwestern corner of the Forum stands the **Tempio di Saturno** (Temple of Saturn), which housed the Roman state treasury. All that remains of this, the most venerated temple of Republican Rome, consecrated in 498 BC, are eight Ionic columns on a podium. Saturn was god of agriculture and ruler of the mythical "Golden Age". Each year in December the festival of Saturnalia was celebrated *(see left)*.

Two columns

Heading eastwards now along the Via Sacra (with your back to the Capitol), to your left stands the Corinthian **Colonna di Foca** (the Column of Phocas), the most recent of the classical monuments in the Roman Forum. This column was erected in 608 by Smaragdus, the Byzantine exarch (governor) for Italy, in honour of the Eastern Emperor Phocas who donated the Pantheon to the Church. Next to it, a bronze

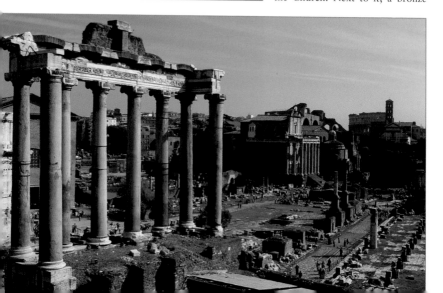

Recommended Restaurants, Bars & Cafés on page 113

inscription commemorates one of the sponsors of the paving of the Forum, L. Naevius Surdinus, in the 1st decade BC. A fig tree, an olive tree and a vine, which used to grow here, together with a statue of Marsyas, symbolised Roman justice.

Between the Column of Phocas and the Rostra is the base of the **Colonna Decennalia**, raised in AD 303 to celebrate 10 years of rule by the two emperors Diocletian and Maxentius. The relief on the base shows the *Souventaurilia*, the ceremonial state sacrifice of a boar, a ram and a bull.

Basilica Julia ❶

On the other side of the Via Sacra stood the **Basilica Giulia**. Started by Julius Caesar in 50 BC and completed by Augustus, it was originally the largest building in the Forum (101 metres/330 ft long and 49 metres/160 ft wide). All that remains of this two-storeyed, marble-faced structure are its pillared foundations. The basilica housed four courts of law, was the seat of the Roman office of weights and measures, and was a meeting place for bankers.

The Temple of Castor and Pollux ❶

Heading in the direction of the Colosseum, you'll come to the three surviving columns of the Tempio di Castore e Polluce, built in 448 BC to commemorate the decisive battle of Lake Regillus fought between Latins and Romans in 499 BC. The Romans believed victory was secured by the miraculous appearance of Castor and Pollux, Jupiter's twin sons, and built the temple in their honour. A block of marble from this temple was used by Michelangelo as the base for the equestrian statue of Marcus Aurelius he made for the Piazza del Campidoglio.

Behind the pillars is a small marble altar with reliefs of the heavenly twins, and the site of the **Lacus Juturnae** (Fountain of Juturna), the sacred well at which the Dioscuri (the collective name for Castor and Pollux) watered their horses after bringing news of the Roman victory.

On the other side of the temple, at the foot of the Palatine, is the oldest Christian structure in the Forum:

Dramatic remains of the Temple of Castor and Pollux.

BELOW LEFT: statue of Castor on Capitoline Hill. **BELOW:** the Emperor Vespasian by Peter Paul Rubens (1577–1640).

Vespasian

Emperor Vespasian was one of Imperial Rome's more successful rulers. His reign (AD 69–79) brought a welcome period of peace and prosperity to a city and an Empire in disarray following the death of Nero.

Vespasian put to shame the extravagances of Roman nobles by the simplicity of his own life. In order to restore state finances after the disastrous extravagances of Nero (AD 54–68), he renewed old taxes and instituted new ones; one such tax was levied on urine, which was collected from public urinals (it was a useful raw material for dyeing wool). When asked by one of his sons how he could make money with such a malodorous substance, he replied *"Pecunia non olet"* – money doesn't smell. These taxes helped finance the building of great public works, not least of which was the Colosseum.

Vestal Virgins had seats of honour in the circus and theatre and lived in luxury, but if they broke their vow of chastity, they were buried alive.

the church of **Santa Maria Antiqua** ❶ was built in AD 365 on the site of a temple to Augustus.

Temple of Caesar ❶

A path leads away from the church entrance back past the temple of Castor and Pollux to the Tempio di Cesare, which occupies the site where Caesar's corpse was cremated after his assassination on the Ides of March in 44 BC. So great was the grief of the people that they kept his funeral pyre burning for days. After the cremation, his ashes were washed with milk and wine, then buried. The temple was built on the site of the pyre by his adopted son, the emperor Augustus.

Behind the Temple of Caesar lie the remains of the walls of the **Regia**, the official residence of the Pontifex Maximus, the Chief Priest of Ancient Rome; the title is still held by the Pope today.

Temple of Vesta ❶

Directly opposite, 20 Corinthian columns surround the remains of the circular Tempio di Vesta, goddess of

the hearth and patron of the state. Here the Vestal Virgins kept the eternal flame of Rome burning and watched over the sacred image of Minerva (daughter of Jupiter and Juno), saved, according to legend, from blazing Troy by Aeneas. The Vestals entered divine service as young girls and lived a chaste life for at least 30 years in the **House of the Vestal Virgins**, the rectangular structure next to the temple, a once luxurious building.

Monumental temple

Back near the main entrance of the Forum, a broad flight of steps leads up to the **Tempio di Antonino e**

Faustina **O** (Temple of Antoninus and Faustina), built in AD 141 by the emperor in memory of his wife and converted to a church in the 12th century. It is the only Forum building that gives a real indication of just how monumental Roman temples were.

Basilica of Maxentius and Constantine **P**

The eastern half of the Forum is dominated by the Basilica di Massenzio e Constantino, a three-aisled basilica that was begun by Emperor Maxentius (303–12) and completed by his

successor, Constantine (306–30). Only the northern nave remains. The central nave was crossed by cruciform vaults, each resting on eight side pillars, one of which has been outside the church of Santa Maria Maggiore since 1613.

Numerous Renaissance architects are said to have used its apse and arches as models, the most famous being Michelangelo, who studied its hexagonal coffered arches when designing the dome of St Peter's.

In the western apse, a **Colossus of Constantine** was discovered in 1487. Bits of the huge statue, including head, feet and hands, can be seen in the courtyard of Palazzo dei Conservatori *(see page 92)*.

Temple and church

Next to the basilica is the circular **Tempio di Romolo O** (Temple of Romulus), dating from AD 309, which now forms the apse of the church of Santi Cosma e Damiano, converted in the 6th century. Beneath the temple are the remains of tiny rooms believed to have been part of a brothel.

FOOD

You can take a picnic into the Forum/ Palatine area. Officially, it's not allowed, but if you are discreet and tidy, there will be no problem.

LEFT: Temple of Antoninus and Faustina. **BELOW:** Basilica of Maxentius and Constantine.

With its colourful brickwork, the Romanesque belltower of the church of **Santa Francesca Romana** ⓡ will have caught your eye. The present building is 13th-century, though the façade was added in 1615. Francesca Romana is the patron saint of motorists, and on her festival day – 9 March – cars are parked as close as possible to the church to be blessed.

Arch of Titus ⓢ

Beyond the church, marking the end of the Via Sacra, stands the majestic Arco di Tito, the oldest triumphal arch in Rome, built by Domitian to celebrate the capture of Jerusalem in AD 70 by his brother Titus and father Vespasian. Reliefs inside the

arch show Titus in his chariot with Nike, goddess of victory, and the spoils of war, including a menorah, the ritual seven-branched candelabra, being carried in triumphal procession.

Temple of Venus and Rome ⓣ

Between the Arch of Titus and the Colosseum is the **Tempio di Venere e Roma**, originally built by Hadrian (AD 117–38) and rebuilt by Maxentius in 307 after a fire. At 110 by 53 metres (361 by 174 ft), it was the largest temple in Rome and comprised two shrines placed opposite one another, surrounded by pillared halls in the Greek style. It is well documented that Hadrian was an ardent admirer of Greek culture.

PALATINE HILL ⓽

✉ Palatine Hill ☏ 06-3996 7700
ⓒ daily summer 8.30am–7.15pm, winter 8.30am–4.30pm
ⓖ charge ⓜ Colosseo ⓑ 60, 75, 81, 84, 85, 87, 117, 175, 271, 571, 673, 810, 850

RIGHT: Farnese Pavilions on the Palatine.
BELOW: the Palatine Hill.

Recommended Restaurants, Bars & Cafés on page 113

From the Arch of Titus, the road goes up to the **Palatino**, where Rome's Imperial rulers lived in luxury. Legend holds that Romulus defeated his twin brother Remus on the Palatine Hill, and became the city's first ruler in 753 BC. Whatever the truth of this, archaeological remains do confirm the existence of a sheep-herding population whose simple homes were excavated on top of the hill. At the height of Roman opulence, the area offered a beautiful panorama of the city away from the chaos below, and expansive villas packed the area. It wasn't until the 16th century that Cardinal Farnese recognised the value of the land and purchased most of it.

Farnese Gardens

Paths and steps lead up to the **Orte Farnesiani** Ⓐ (Farnese Gardens).

These pleasure gardens were laid out in the 16th century for the cardinal, over the ruins of the Palace of Tiberius. They end at a viewing terrace with a fine panorama over the Forum. A subterranean vaulted passageway leads to the **Casa di Livia** Ⓑ (House of Livia; closed for restoration; *see right*).

In the southwest corner of the hill, excavations have revealed the oldest traces of a settlement in the city (8th century BC). The story goes that the Iron Age hut known as the **Capanna di Romolo** Ⓒ (Hut of Romulus) was the dwelling of a shepherd who raised Romulus and Remus, after they were suckled by the wolf in a nearby cave.

Domus Flavia and Domus Augustana

South of the gardens lay the **Domus Flavia** Ⓓ, built by Emperor Domitian, who is said to have lined his throne room with mirrors in order to see approaching enemies from any angle. The room with a pattern traced on its floor was the courtyard; behind that was the dining room, and the room to the right was

In 1860 excavations of the Casa di Livia revealed gloriously frescoed walls and elaborate mosaics. Some of these can be seen at the Palazzo Massimo (see page 233) and at the Capitoline Museum (see page 89).

ABOVE LEFT: Faustulus entrusting Romulus and Remus to his wife, Acca Larentia, c.1643.

An umbrella pine provides atmosphere but scant shade for the ruins of the Palatine Hill.

the *nymphaeum*, where diners retired for breaks during banquets.

Next to this palace was the **Domus Augustana E** (House of Augustus), private residence of the emperor; the oval building next to it, the vast outline of which can be clearly discerned, was a stadium built for the emperor's private games. To the south are the impressive ruins of the **Terme Severiane** (Baths of Septimius Severus).

Palatine Museum F

The tall grey building sandwiched between the Domus Flavia and the Domus Augustana is the Museo Palatino (www.pierreci.it; tel: 06-3996 7700; Mon–Sat 9am–1.30pm, 2.30–5pm). Inside is a fine collection of artefacts found during the course of excavations on the site.

CIRCUS MAXIMUS ⑩

The remains of the Palatine palaces overlook the Circo Massimo, one of the oldest Roman arenas. Not much of this 6th-century BC stadium remains, but you can make out the track, which was used mainly for chariot races. There are traces of seating to the south (the tower is a

Palatine (Palatino)

Foro Romano
Arco di Tito
Via Sacra
Colosseo

Via dei Foraggi
Tempio di Augusto
Teodoro
Casino Farnese
Palazzo di Caligola
Arco di Costantino

Via d. Fienelli
S. Teodoro
Victoriae
Clivus
Orti Farnesiani (Farnese Gardens) **A**
Vigna
Barberini
Palatinus
Clivus
Via

San
Capanna del Romolo (Hut of Romulus)
Tempio di Cibele (Temple of Cybele)
Casa di Livia (House of Livia) **B**
C
S. Bonaventura
di
V. Celio Vibenna

S. Giorgio in Velabro
Tempio di Apollo (Temple of Apollo)
Domus Flavia **D**
E Domus Augustana (House of Augustus)
Antiquarium
PARCO DEL CELIO

Via
Museo Palatino (Palatine Museum) **F**
Stadio
(Stadium)
San

S. Anastasia
Terme Severiane (Baths of Septimius Severus)
Gregorio

Via dei Ara Massimo di Ercole
Via
dei
Belvedere

Via dei Circo Massimo
Cerchi
Piazza di Porta Capena

0   100 m
0   100 yds
N
Circo Massimo (Circus Maximus)
Torre d. Molette
Porta Capena

Recommended Restaurants, Bars & Cafés on page 113

medieval addition). In its heyday the arena held around 300,000 spectators, and not only hosted chariot races, but also staged sea battles, which required the pumping of gallons of water into the stadium space.

THE COLOSSEUM ⓫

✉ Piazza del Colosseo 📞 06-3996 7700 🕐 daily 8.30am—one hour before sunset 📷 charge Ⓜ Colosseo 🚌 3, 60, 75, 81, 85, 87, 117, 175, 186, 204, 673, 810, 850

At the far end of the Roman Forum lie the remains of the majestic **Colosseum**, the most enduring

symbol of Ancient Rome. Its monumental grandeur and violent history have enthralled and appalled visitors for over 2,000 years. Work on its construction began in AD 72 under Vespasian, who decided to build it on the site of Nero's artificial lake, and was completed by his son Titus. The vast amphitheatre measured 190 metres (570 ft) long and 150 metres (450 ft) wide, had 80 entrances and could seat between 55,000 and 73,000 spectators. It opened in AD 80 with a three-month programme of games to satisfy a bloodthirsty audience. Christians fought lions, gladiators fought each other and wounded contestants lived or died according to the emperor's whim, expressed by the Imperial thumb, which pointed either up or down. Today, the walls of the various dungeons, cages and passageways, gruesome reminders of the centuries-long slaughter that took place here, can be seen through the caved-in floor of the arena.

The **Ludus Magnus**, the nearby training ground of the gladiators, was connected to the arena by a tunnel. The remains of seating for up to 3,000

Try and visit the Colosseum first thing in the morning, before the crowds build up.

LEFT: a reconstruction of the Colosseum.
BELOW: the defining image of Rome.

The Arco di Constantino, another triumphal arch built for the glory of the emperors.

ABOVE RIGHT: history lesson on site.
BELOW: *A Banquet in Nero's Palace,* by Henryk Sienkiewicz (1846–1916).

people shows how much the public liked to watch gladiators learning the tricks of their trade.

Gladiatorial combat was banned in AD 438, and over time the amphitheatre became a quarry supplying material for many of Rome's buildings, including Palazzo Venezia and St Peter's. In 1744, Benedict XIV consecrated the arena to the memory of Christian martyrs who died in it *(for more about the Colosseum, see pages 114–15).*

Between the Colosseum and the Palatine Hill is the **Arco di Constantino** (Arch of Constantine), built to commemorate Constantine I's victory over Maxentius at the Ponte Milvio in AD 312 *(see page 196).*

NERO'S GOLDEN HOUSE ⑫

✉ 1 Viale della Domus Aurea; www.pierreci.it ☎ 06-3996 7700
🕐 Tue–Fri 10am–4pm ⓒ charge, advance booking required
🚇 Colosseo 🚌 60, 75, 81, 85, 87, 117, 175, 186, 204, 673, 810, 850

A short walk uphill from the Colosseum is Nero's Golden House (Domus Aurea). Work began here in AD 64 immediately after a fire had devastated a large chunk of Rome.

Made up of a series of pavilions surrounded by a small artificial lake (on which the Colosseum now stands), pastures, woods and vineyards, it originally extended from the Palatine to the Caelian and Oppian hills. The enormous complex was filled with Greek statues and monumental fountains.

According to the Latin biographer Suetonius, its vestibule was large enough to contain a statue of Nero 40 metres (120 ft) high, and the house was covered in gold and decorated with precious gems and mother-of-pearl. There were dining rooms with ivory ceilings from which rotating panels showered guests with flowers, and fitted pipes sprinkled them with perfume. The palace had its own aqueducts to supply water for the fountains, and the baths could be filled with sea or sulphurous water, according to Nero's whim.

The main building was decorated with shiploads of plundered Greek works of art. But Nero did not have long to enjoy it. He committed suicide in AD 68 after he was condemned to death by the Senate.

Almost immediately the house began to be stripped, demolished or built on by his successors. In the early 16th century, frescoes belonging to the house were discovered by artists, including Raphael and Michelangelo, but no-one linked these cave-like rooms to the emperor's outrageous abode until centuries later.

Some 30 rooms are open to the public; many more are either off-limits or awaiting excavation. It is hard to get an idea of the opulence and size of the extraordinary 250-room mansion, built on an estate that covered a third of Ancient Rome; only the skylit Octagonal Hall gives any real idea of its former architectural grandeur. Visits are on a guided basis only, so be sure to book in advance. ❏

Enjoy a cocktail with a killer view of the illuminated Colosseum at the Hotel Gladiatori (www.hotelgladiatori.it; *see page 227*).

LEFT: fresco showing the birth of Adonis, from Nero's Golden House.

BEST RESTAURANTS, BARS AND CAFÉS

Restaurants

The overpriced tourist restaurants around the Colosseum should be avoided, but if you wander eastwards into the huddle of streets behind it you'll find some good neighbourhood eateries.

Forum Pizzeria

▨ 34–38 Via San Giovanni in Laterano 𝄞 06-7759 1158 🕲 L & D daily. €
[p340, B2]
A large pizzeria serving delicious, thick-crusted pizzas from a wood-fired oven.

Ristorante Mario's

▨ 9 Piazza del Grillo 𝄞 06-679 3725 🕲 L & D Tue–Sun. €–€€ [p339, E1]

Traditional Roman food (fish is their speciality) and a lovely pergola in the square outside, at affordable prices.

San Teodoro

▨ 49–51 Via dei Fienili 𝄞 06-678 0933 🕲 L & D Mon–Sat. €€€€ [p339, E2]
Located in a tranquil piazza, this elegant restaurant offers traditional food successfully updated and centred on seasonal availability. Staples are fish carpaccios and homemade pasta.

Bars and Cafés

A gay bar *(pictured right)* across from the Colosseum, **Coming Out**

(8 Via San Giovanni in Laterano) serves hot food until 2am; karaoke and a lively scene ensure a faithful following, not just from the gay community.

At **Oppio Caffè** (72 Via delle Terme di Tito) hi-tech meets classical Rome: plexiglass and video screens contrast with ancient brickwork. Outside seating provides stunning views of the Colosseum. Open all day; live music some nights.

● ● ● ● ● ● ● ● ● ● ● ●
Price includes dinner and a half-bottle of house wine.
€€€€ = €60 and up, €€€ = €40–60, €€ = €25–40, € = under €25.

THE GRIM GLORY OF THE COLOSSEUM

"While the Colosseum stands, Rome shall stand; when the Colosseum falls, Rome shall fall; when Rome falls the world shall fall"

The Colosseum is the city's most stirring sight, "a noble wreck in the ruinous perfection" in Byron's words. It was begun by Vespasian, inaugurated by his son Titus in AD 80, and completed by Domitian (AD 81–96). It could seat over 50,000 bloodthirsty spectators who revelled in the spectacle of gladiators fighting to the death. "Bread and circuses" was the judgement of Juvenal, the 1st-century poet, on the way the city's rulers kept the populace happy. With the fall of the Empire, the Colosseum fell into disuse. During the Renaissance, the ruins were plundered of their valuable travertine to build churches and palaces all over Rome.

Quarrying was only halted by Pope Benedict XIV in the 18th century and the site dedicated to Christian martyrs.

BELOW LEFT: the Gate of Life was reserved for victorious gladiators, while vanquished gladiators were sent to the Gate of Death, as depicted in this relief found at the Colosseum.
ABOVE TOP: Renaissance historians believed that ancient Roman arenas were sometimes flooded to stage mock naval battles, but there is scant evidence to suggest that such a display ever took place in the Colosseum.
BELOW: views from the higher tiers down to the arena show a maze of passageways normally hidden from view. The moveable wooden floor was covered in sand to soak up the blood. The subterranean section concealed the animal cages and sophisticated technical apparatus, from winches and mechanical lifts to ramps and trap doors.

The essentials

✉ *Piazza del Colosseo; www.pierreci.it* ☎ tel: 06-3996 7700 🕐 *daily 8.30am until one hour before sunset; ticket office shuts one hour before closing time* 💶 *charge* Ⓜ *Colosseo* 🚌 *3, 60, 75, 81, 85, 87, 117, 175, 186, 204, 673, 810, 850*

ENTERTAINMENT FOR THE MASSES

The Roman appetite for bloodshed was legendary, with the barbaric *munera*, or blood sports, introduced as a corrupt version of the Greek games. Although supremely public, the Colosseum was a stratified affair. The podium, set on the lowest tier, was reserved exclusively for the Emperor, senators, magistrates and Vestal Virgins. Above them sat the bourgeoisie, with the lower orders restricted to the top tier, and the populace on wooden seats in the very top rows. Shortly before the games began, the Emperor and his followers would enter the amphitheatre, and spectators would show their reverence by clapping, cheering, and chanting their sovereign's honorifics.

A trumpet call started the games and spectacles began with cries of "Hail to the Emperor, those about to die salute thee". If a gladiator tried to retreat into the underground chamber, he was pushed forward with whips and red-hot irons. The gladiators mostly fought to the death. A wounded man could beg for mercy by lifting a finger of his left hand. If the crowd waved handkerchiefs, he was saved. Thumbs down meant death. After the gladiators came the wild beasts, which were made to fight one another or human beings – armed or unarmed. The animals, mostly imported from Africa, included lions, elephants, giraffes, hyenas, hippos, wild horses and zebras.

On the arena's opening day, 5,000 animals were slaughtered. In AD 248, the millennium of the founding of Rome was celebrated by gladiatorial contests. Gladiatorial combat was banned in AD 404, while animal fights ended in the following century.

RIGHT: gladiators, named after the Roman sword, *gladius*, were mostly condemned criminals, prisoners of war or slaves. They were trained to fight then pitted against each other and against various exotic animals.

LEFT: men dressed in traditional Roman costumes stroll around the perimeter of the Colosseum – some indulge in light-hearted role-playing for the benefit of tourists, others will fleece you for a photo.

BELOW: school children learn the gory details of life in Ancient Rome with a history lesson in situ.

RIGHT: the Colosseum is Rome's top tourist sight, and when floodlit at night it creates a wonderful spectacle. It has been used as an arena for crowd-pulling concerts; Simon and Garfunkel played here on their 'Old Friends' tour.

Recommended Restaurants, Bars & Cafés on page 123

FONTANA DI TREVI AND QUIRINALE

The Quirinal, Rome's highest hill, is synonymous with
Italian politics. Its summit is crowned with the
President's official residence and at its foot,
hidden in the maze of narrow streets, is the
Trevi Fountain, one of Rome's most iconic sights

The Quirinal Hill, the highest of Rome's seven classical hills, is crowned by the Piazza del Quirinale and the imposing presidential palace. The square is somewhat austere, but the labyrinth of surrounding streets are well worth exploring.

Trevi Fountain ❶

A good place to begin a tour of the area is the Fontana di Trevi (Trevi Fountain), which rose to fame in Fellini's 1960 classic *La Dolce Vita* when blonde bombshell Anita Ekberg plunged provocatively into it for a midnight bathe. Nowadays, if you try to put a foot in the water, a whistle blast from the city police will stop you in your tracks. That, and a €500 fine.

However, no one will stop you from throwing a coin in the fountain (over your shoulder with your back to the fountain), an old custom said to ensure your return to the Eternal City. The steps around the fountain are always packed with tourists tossing coins, eating ice creams and taking endless photos.

The flamboyant rococo-style fountain was designed in 1762 by Nicola Salvi; "some sculptor of Bernini's

school gone absolutely mad in marble" was Nathaniel Hawthorne's assessment. Its central figure is the sea god Neptune standing astride a giant shell drawn by winged horses led by Tritons. One horse is placid, the other agitated, symbolising calm and stormy seas. In the niches on either side are statues of Health (right) and Abundance (left). Above the latter, a marble relief shows Agrippa commissioning the aqueduct in 19 BC, which still supplies the fountain to this day.

Main attractions

TREVI FOUNTAIN
ACCADEMIA DI SAN LUCA
PASTA MUSEUM
PALAZZO DEL QUIRINALE
SCUDERIE DEL QUIRINALE
SANT'ANDREA AL QUIRINALE
SAN CARLO ALLE QUATTRO FONTANE
BARBERINI PALACE
PIAZZA BARBERINI
PORTA PIA
SAN VITALE
PALAZZO ALLE ESPOSIZIONI
PALAZZO COLONNA

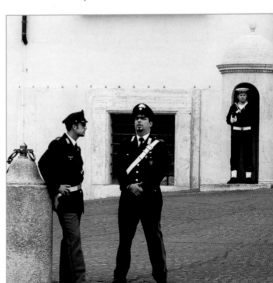

LEFT: the Trevi Fountain. **RIGHT:** guards outside the Quirinal Palace, official residence of the President of the Republic.

FOOD

With arguably the finest ice cream in town, the Gelateria San Crispino near the Trevi Fountain serves up original flavours made with all-natural ingredients. The signature flavour, Il Gelato di San Crispino, is a basic Italian *crema* made with wild Sardinian honey.

Accademia di San Luca ❷

✉ 77 Piazza dell'Accademia; www.accademiasanluca.it 📞 06-679 8850 🕐 Mon–Sat 10am–12.30pm ◎ free 🚇 Barberini 🚌 52, 53, 61, 62, 63, 71, 80, 81, 85, 95, 116, 117, 119, 160, 175, 492, 628, 630, 850

It's a five-minute walk from the fountain to the Galleria dell'Accademia di San Luca, Rome's school of art. The academy, named after St Luke, the patron saint of painters, was founded in 1577 to train artists in the Renaissance style. Bernini and Domenichino were former directors of this august institution.

The gallery, which has recently been extensively renovated, has a collection of portraits, drawings and landscapes of Rome spanning the centuries, including works by Titian, Guido Reni and Van Dyck.

There's also an impressive ramp, designed by Borromini, which spirals up to the top floors of the *palazzo*.

Free exhibits are held by art students, and the academy organises a prestigious architecture prize.

Pasta Museum ❸

✉ 117 Piazza Scanderbeg; www.pastainmuseum.com 📞 06-699 1120 🕐 daily 9.30am–5.30pm ◎ charge 🚇 Barberini 🚌 *see above*

Fontana di Trevi and Quirinale

The Museo Nazionale delle Paste Alimentari, which has been refurbished recently, explores the history of Italy's favourite food. Here you can learn about ancient grinding techniques, the rolling and cutting procedure, and a whole wealth of information about this Italian staple. The gift shop sells all kinds of pasta-related paraphernalia.

THE QUIRINAL

Follow Via San Vincenzo uphill from the Fontana di Trevi, then turn left into Via Dataria and take the steps up to Piazza del Quirinale. In the centre of the square are colossal statues of the heavenly twins, Castor and Pollux, with their horses. They came from Constantine's baths and were arranged around the obelisk (taken from Augustus' mausoleum) in the 18th century.

Palazzo del Quirinale ❹

✉ www.quirinale.it ☎ 06-46991
🕐 Sept–June Sun 8.30am–noon
(depending on state visits – check website) 💶 charge 🚇 Barberini
🚌 40, 60, 64, 70, 117, 170, 640

The square is dominated by the **Palazzo del Quirinale**, which was the summer palace of the popes until 1870, when it became the palace of the kings of the newly unified Italy. Since 1947, it has been the official residence of the President of the Republic. The oldest part of the palace is open to the public most Sunday mornings.

Scuderie del Quirinale ❺

✉ www.scuderiequirinale.it ☎ 06-3996 7500 🕐 daily 10am–8pm,
Fri–Sat until 10.30pm 💶 charge
🚇 Barberini 🚌 40, 60, 64, 70, 117, 170, 640

FOOD

A trip through the Pasta Museum will no doubt whet your appetite for a big plate of spaghetti. Nearby *spaghetteria* L'Archetto serves its scrumptious namesake 123 different ways, at 26 Via dell' Archetto, tel: 06-678 9064.

FAR LEFT: obelisk in the Piazza del Quirinale.
LEFT: all you need to know about pasta.
BELOW: the inauguration of Italy's new president, Giorgio Napolitano, in May 2006.

TIP

Not far from the Trevi Fountain, beneath the arthouse Trevi Cinema (which, incidentally, sometimes screens films in English), is the fascinating Area Archeologica del Vicus Caprinus (Thur–Sun 11am–3pm, Mon 4–7.30pm; admission charge). Here lie the remains of a 1st-century BC *caseggiato* – a communal Roman dwelling.

ABOVE RIGHT: park benches provide welcome shade.
BELOW: Piazza alle Quattro Fontane.

Part of the complex on the opposite side of the square, the former palace stables, or *scuderie*, have recently been converted into a bright and spacious two-level museum space, which hosts important exhibitions all year round. The stairs leading from the top floor back to the lobby have a glass wall which offers fine views of the city.

Across the square from the Quirinale Palace, the sugary-white **Palazzo della Consulta** houses Italy's supreme court. The structure was built atop the ruins of Constantine's baths.

BAROQUE MASTERPIECES

Via del Quirinale runs along the southeast flank of the palace and, on the opposite side, passes two pretty parks (dotted with shaded benches if you need a rest), and two Baroque churches. **Sant'Andrea al Quirinale ❻** (Wed–Mon 8am–noon and 4–7pm) is the work of Bernini, whose genius is demonstrated in the elliptical plan, gilded dome and stucco work. Light from the clerestory win-

dows illuminates the white-and-gold stucco work of the dome and the richly coloured inlaid marble of the walls and floor.

Further along is the tiny **San Carlo alle Quattro Fontane ❼** (Mon–Fri and Sun 10am–1pm and 3–6pm, Sat 10am–1pm) by Bernini's arch-rival, Borromini (1599–1667). It may be small (it is often referred to as San Carlino), but with its concave and convex surfaces it illustrates Borromini's ingenuity at creating the illusion of space in an awkwardly shaped site. His love for illusion and *trompe l'œil* is evident throughout the structure, most notably in the cloister, which is rectangular but appears octagonal.

Recommended Restaurants, Bars & Cafés on page 123

The church gets its name, Alle Quattro Fontane, from the four Baroque fountains at each corner of the busy crossroads, placed here in 1593, which represent the Tiber, the Nile, Diana and Juno. From here, the highest point of the Quirinal Hill, you can look down towards the Trinità dei Monti obelisk in one direction and the Santa Maria Maggiore obelisk in the other.

Barberini Palace **8**

✉ 18 Via Barberini, entrance on Via Quattro Fontane 📞 06-481 4591
🕒 Tue–Sun 9am–7pm 💲 charge
🚇 Barberini 🚌 52, 53, 61, 80, 95, 116, 119, 175, 492

From the Quirinal, Via delle Quattro Fontane leads to Palazzo Barberini, the family palace of Pope Urban VIII (1623–44), built by three of Rome's most prominent 17th-century architects, Bernini, Borromini and Maderno. It houses the **Galleria Nazionale d'Arte Antica**, which displays works from the early Renaissance to the late Baroque, including

Mental torment and genius often go hand in hand, as was the case for Borromini. The church of San Carlino was his first solo job, completed when the artist was just 35 years old. Borromini had hoped to be buried in the crypt's splendid funerary chapter, but his suicide put paid to that, and he was dumped in an unmarked grave at San Giovanni de' Fiorentini.

ABOVE LEFT: *La Fornarina* by Raphael.
LEFT: papal coat of arms on Sant'Andrea al Quirinale. **BELOW:** Fontana del Tritone on Piazza Barberini.

The Annunciation by Lippi, canvases by Caravaggio, Raphael's celebrated *La Fornarina*, a Tintoretto, Pietro di Cosimo's *Maddalena*, a portrait of Henry VIII by Holbein and a fine ceiling fresco by da Cortona. Parts of the palace are closed for restoration which is not due for completion until 2009, but the masterpieces are usually kept visible.

Bernini's fountains

In the **Piazza Barberini** ❾ are two Bernini fountains. The **Fontana del Tritone** (1632–7) features four dolphins supporting a shell on which the water-spouting Triton sits. The **Fontana delle Api** (Bee Fountain, 1641), on the north side of the square, features the ubiquitous bee, symbol of the powerful Barberini family. Running from the northwest of the piazza is Via Vittorio Veneto, the avenue rendered immortal in Fellini's film *La Dolce Vita* as the gathering place for the glitterati to see and be seen.

From here Via Barberini leads to Largo Santa Susanna and the church of **Santa Maria della Vittoria**, home to Bernini's *Ecstasy of St Teresa*, another masterpiece of Baroque sculpture *(see page 187)*.

The end of Via XX Settembre is marked by **Porta Pia**, Michelangelo's last architectural work, and an excellent example of the transition from High Rennassiance to Baroque architecture.

VIA NAZIONALE

Running parallel to Via del Quirinale is Via Nazionale (laid in 1870 when Rome gained its new status as capital), which links Piazza della Repubblica with the Imperial Fora. Towards the southern end are **San Vitale** ❿, built in the 5th century and restored in the 15th century, and the **Palazzo delle Esposizioni** ⓫ (194 Via Nazionale; tel: 06-489 411; currently closed for repairs and due to reopen end 2007).

This massive 19th-century building, designed by Pio Piacentini, houses a vibrant cultural centre, with an imaginative programme of art exhibitions and events.

Across the road are the impressive **Palazzo Koch**, headquarters of the Banca d'Italia, and the **Villa Aldobrandini**, behind which is a small public park (entrance on Via Mazzarino).

RIGHT: Porta Pia.
BELOW: interior of the Palazzo Colonna.

Recommended Restaurants, Bars & Cafés listed below

Palazzo Colonna ⓬

✉ 66 Piazza SS Apostoli, entrance on Via Pilotta; www.galleriacolonna.it
📞 06-678 4350 🕐 Sept–July Sat 9am–1pm 💶 charge 🚌 40, 60, 64, 70, 117, 170

Via Nazionale curves around into Via IV Novembre (leading to Piazza Venezia), passing Trajan's Markets and the Palazzo Colonna. The *palazzo* housed over 23 generations of the Colonna family, and represents a fascinating, if often juxtaposing, architectural panorama spanning four centuries (1300–1700). Inside is a charming art gallery, with richly vaulted, frescoed ceilings, one of which portrays Marcantonio Colonna's victory at the battle of Lepanto (1571). Artists represented here include Lorenzo Monoco, Veronese, Jacopo and Domenico Tintoretto, Pietro da Cortona and Guercino. Be sure to look out for Bronzino's gloriously sensuous *Venus and Cupid*, and Annibale Caracci's *Bean-Eater*, the gallery's most prized work.

From the palace, Via della Pilotta leads back to the Trevi Fountain. ❏

Via della Pilotta, overhung by four elegant bridges, connects the Palazzo Colonna with the gardens of Villa Colonna.

LEFT: street stall.
BELOW: News Café.

BEST RESTAURANTS, BARS AND CAFÉS

Restaurants

Al Presidente
🍴 95 Via in Arcione 📞 06-679 7342 🕐 L & D Tue–Sun. €€€ [p335, E3]
A family-run restaurant, with a lovely outdoor area. High-quality food and a good wine list, with a few selections to be had by the glass. A gem in this touristy area.

Le Tamerici
🍴 79 Vicolo Scavolino 📞 06-6920 0700 🕐 L & D Mon–Sat. €€€ [p335, E3]
Innovative, seasonal cuisine from an all-female team, with a minimalist decor providing dramatic contrast to the Baroque extravagance outside. This level of refinement, quality and service does not come cheap.

Vineria Il Chianti
🍴 81–82 Via del Lavatore 📞 06-678 7550 🕐 L & D Mon–Sat. €€ [p335, E3]
A buzzing, rustic locale with young staff and a Tuscan slant. Hearty soups, quiche with courgette flowers, wild boar fillet; pizzas in the evening and an appetising selection of cheeses served with honey or jam. Stays open late.

Bars and Cafés

Il Gelato di San Crispino (42 Via della

Panetteria; closed Tue) serves ice cream like no other. In a wide variety of flavours, it is served in paper cups, as cones affect the taste according to its creators.

The **News Café** (72 Via della Stamperia) takes its name from the racks of newspapers available for customers to read. A good all-day option for salads, soups and pastas.

In an anonymous gallery off the street is attractive, olde-worlde **Dagnino** (75 Via V. E. Orlando), a vast Sicilian pastry shop (try their speciality, the ricotta-stuffed *cannoli*) and *tavola calda* serving all-day sweet and savoury specialities.

• • • • • • • • • •
Price includes dinner and a half-bottle of house wine.
€€€€ = €60 and up,
€€€ = €40–60, €€ = €25–40, € = under €25.

Recommended Restaurants, Bars & Cafés on pages 134–5

PIAZZA DI SPAGNA AND TRIDENTE

The Spanish Steps provide a great spot for watching the world go by. Here, caricaturists sketch tourists, buskers play guitars, romantics pay homage to Keats and Shelley, backpackers sunbathe on the steps and shoppers crowd the windows of the elegant shops below. Off the Piazza di Spagna stretch the most fashionable shopping streets in Rome

The Tridente is a mecca for anyone interested in fashion, shopping or art; some tourists never stray from here. The area takes its name from the trio of streets built in the 16th century to relieve congestion in Rome's cramped medieval centre. Via del Corso, Via di Ripetta and Via del Babuino emanate like the prongs of a fork from the Piazza del Popolo, for centuries the main entrance to Rome for travellers coming from the north.

PIAZZA DEL POPOLO ❶

Piazza del Popolo is one of the most impressive squares in Rome. The paving was allegedly paid for by taxes levied on prostitutes, and the piazza was used for executions at one time. In the 19th century, the square was remodelled by Valadier, who created the oval form.

The most striking feature of this elegant square is the **obelisk**. Stolen from Egypt by Emperor Augustus, it once decorated the Circus Maximus, where it was used as a turning point during chariot races.

Standing at the ends of Via del Babuino and Via del Corso are two churches designed by Carlo Rainaldi

in the 1660s. Though they appear identical, one is octagonal and the other is dodecagonal. Stand between them for a good view down the Via del Corso to Piazza Venezia and the façade of the Vittoriano monument.

Santa Maria del Popolo ❷

✉ 12 Piazza del Popolo ☎ 06-361 0836 ◉ Mon–Sat 4–7pm, Sun 8am–7.30pm ◎ free ◪ Flaminio ▣ 88, 95, 117, 119, 490, 491, 495, 628, 926

Main attractions
PIAZZA DEL POPOLO
SANTA MARIA DEL POPOLO
THE CORSO
PIAZZA COLONNA
CASA DI GOETHE
SANTA MARIA IN VIA LATA
SAN LORENZO IN LUCINA
SPANISH STEPS
KEATS-SHELLEY HOUSE
VIA DEI CONDOTTI
ARA PACIS
MAUSOLEUM OF AUGUSTUS

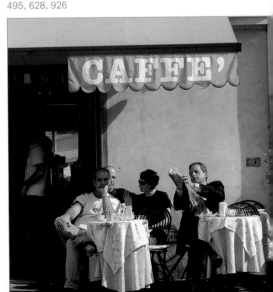

LEFT: the twin towers of Trinità dei Monti atop the Spanish Steps.
RIGHT: relaxing in the Piazza del Popolo.

One of the four lion fountains by Valadier (1823) that grace the Piazza del Popolo. In the background are Rainaldi's twin Baroque churches.

RIGHT: Santa Maria del Popolo.
BELOW: Caravaggio's *Conversion of St Paul.*

Across the piazza, by Porta Flaminia, is the church of Santa Maria del Popolo, built in 1472 over a pre-existing 11th-century chapel. According to legend, Emperor Nero was buried on the site by his spiteful lover, and 1,000 years later Pope Paschal II had the chapel constructed to rid the site of evil spirits.

The church was rebuilt in the late 15th century, and is packed with Renaissance masterpieces. The biggest attractions are the two paintings by Caravaggio, *The Conversion of St Paul* and *The Crucifixion of St Peter*, but also worth seeking out are the beautifully detailed frescoes by Pinturicchio, and Guillaume de Marcillat's exquisite stained glass inside the Bramante-designed apse.

The small Chigi chapel was designed by Raphael for influential banker Agostino Chigi, who commissioned numerous works of art and architecture, including the Villa Farnesina *(see page 205).* Mosaics in the dome depict God creating the solar system and Chigi's astrological chart. The chapel was completed by Bernini, who added two of his characteristic statues, one of Daniel and one of Habakkuk.

THE CORSO

The most important of the trio of streets that fan out from the Piazza del Popolo is **Via del Corso**, a long thoroughfare that links the square with the Piazza Venezia, another of Rome's central squares and one of its most terrifying traffic roundabouts. The name "Corso" dates

Piazza di Spagna and Tridente

Recommended Restaurants, Bars & Cafés on pages 134–5

and for the crippled. The German poet Goethe, who lived at No. 18 *(see page 128)*, described the races in his *Italian Journey*. They were finally banned at the end of the 19th century.

Piazza Colonna ❸

These days, the only people racing along the Corso are politicians being whisked at high speed to **Palazzo Chigi**, the prime minister's official residence, and the neighbouring **Palazzo Montecitorio**, the Chamber of Deputies, both on **Piazza Colonna**. This square marks the halfway point of the Via del Corso.

The southern half of the Corso between Piazza Colonna and Piazza Venezia is lined with stately palaces, most of which are banks, while the northern half, between Piazza Colonna and Piazza del Popolo, is a much more pedestrian-friendly shopping area. In the early evening and on Saturdays, Romans swarm into town to stroll up and down and window shop on this stretch of the Corso and the surrounding streets *(see shaded area on map opposite).*

from the 15th century, when Pope Paul II introduced horse racing *(corsi)* along its length. Pope Alexander VII straightened the road in the 16th century. The races were imitations of the ancient games (with all their atrocities), and it wasn't only horses that ran: there were races for prostitutes, for children, for Jews

TIP

Two spas in the vicinity will boost your flagging spirits after too much sightseeing or shopping. Try the Caribbean rejuvenation treatment at the **Aveda Day Spa** (9 Rampa Mignanelli; tel: 06-6992 4257), or join the international jet set indulging themselves at the spa of the stylish **Hotel de Russie** (9 Via del Babuino; tel: 06-328 8881).

LEFT: reliefs on the Column of Marcus Aurelius.
BELOW: Via del Corso.

Rome has been called the city of obelisks – it has at least 13. Most were brought back by triumphant armies and erected in public places to show the power of the Empire, but some – such as the one at the top of the Spanish Steps – are Roman imitations of Egyptian originals.

Dominating the Piazza Colonna is the street's only classical relic, the 30-metre (90-ft) **Colonna di Marco Aurelio** (Column of Marcus Aurelius). It dates from AD 180, and the bas-relief around the shaft depicts the campaigns of Marcus Aurelius against the Germanic tribes and the Sarmatians. Stairs lead to the top, where the original statue of the emperor was replaced with one of the Apostle Paul in 1589.

Casa di Goethe ❹

✉ 18 Via del Corso; www. casadigoethe.it 📞 06-3265 0412 🕐 Tue–Sun 10am–6pm 💲 charge 🚇 Flaminio 🔲 see page 125

ABOVE RIGHT: café near San Marcello.
RIGHT: Goethe.
BELOW: the church of San Marcello.

Not far from the Piazza del Popolo is the apartment where German poet Goethe lived for two years in the late 18th century. He shared the house with painter Hans Tischbein, whose depictions of the poet are on display.

You can peruse the writer's journals and a room dedicated to all his works, either written in, or inspired by, the Eternal City. Among them are *Iphigenia*, *The Roman Elegies*, *Faust*, *The Roman Carnival* and *Italian Journey*.

Three churches

Further down the Via del Corso, in a small square to the west, is the 12th-century church of **San Lorenzo in Lucina** ❺ (16a Piazza San Lorenzo in Lucina; tel: 06-687 1494; daily 9am–7.30pm).

It contains some busts by Bernini, and a grill, rumoured to be the very spot where the martyr St Lawrence was burnt to death for his refusal to hand over Church riches to the Roman city government. When questioned as to the whereabouts of the wealth, he is said to have presented the poor, crippled, and homeless, declaring that they were the true treasures of the Church.

On the other side of the Corso from Piazza Colonna is **Santa Maria in Via Lata** ❻, which has an impressive façade by da Cortona. In a side street next to the church is one of Rome's "talking" fountains, the *facchino* (or water-bearer). In the days before freedom of speech, the *facchino* and other "talking statues"

were hung with satirical and subversive messages and fulfilled much the same function as a newspaper *(see page 160)*.

Another noteworthy church is **San Marcello al Corso** ❼ (Mon–Sat 7am–noon and 4–7pm, Sun 8.30am–noon and 4–7pm), further along the Corso towards Piazza Venezia, which has a Van Dyck crucifix in the sacristy (you need to ask to see it).

The palace on the right at the end of the Corso houses the **Galleria Doria Pamphilj** ❽, details of which are included in the Piazza Navona chapter *(see page 156)*. There are several splendid buildings in the city called Doria Pamphilj (also spelt Pamphili),

after one of the oldest aristocratic Roman families. One of their members, Giovanni Battista Pamphilj, became Pope Innocent X (1644–55). The current generation of the family still live in this *palazzo* and their private apartments are sometimes open for guided tours.

THE SPANISH STEPS ❾

The sweeping Spanish Steps combine with the twin towers of the church of Trinità dei Monti on top and the harmonious square with its bizarrely shaped fountain below to form one of the most distinctive of Roman scenes. **Piazza di Spagna** is so called because there has been a Spanish Embassy to the Holy See here since the 17th century. The French, meanwhile, owned the land around the convent of **Trinità dei Monti** at the top of the steps, and so they claimed the right to pass through the square and named part of it French Square.

This petty rivalry between the French and Spanish reached a climax with the building of the Spanish Steps. The original design was intended to sing the praises of the

FOOD

For a taste of old-fashioned English style in the heart of the capital, try Babington's Tea Rooms. The creaky wood floors, serious black-skirted staff and all-round austere feel are like a trip back in time. The teapots for €11 a person will bring you right back to the present day, and one of the world's most pricey piazzas; 23 Piazza di Spagna, tel: 06-678 6027.

LEFT: a Fiat 500, the ultimate city car, on the Via del Corso. **BELOW:** Spanish Steps.

Byron, who had claimed that Rome was the city of his soul, was disappointed to find it "pestilent with English". His fellow Romantic poet Shelley was equally disturbed by the Brits abroad: "The manners of the rich English are wholly insupportable, and they assume pretences which they would not venture upon in their own country."

French monarchy, and there was to have been a huge equestrian statue of Louis XIV. However, the Pope was against this idea, so when the architect de Sanctis finally started building the steps in the 18th century, the only reference made to France was the little fleur-de-lis on the pedestals.

The cascade of the Spanish Steps is perennially crowded with visitors. In spring, the crowds share the steps with pots of blossoming azaleas. The centrepiece of the square at the bottom of the steps is the fountain by Pietro Bernini, who was aided in its construction by his more famous son, Gian Lorenzo. The so-called **Barcaccia** is a half-sunken boat fed by water from the ancient aqueduct *Aqua Virgo*.

The English ghetto

RIGHT: Caffè Greco.
BELOW LEFT: *Shelley in the Baths of Caracalla*, by Joseph Severn. **BELOW RIGHT:** Keats-Shelley House.

The Grand Tourists of the 18th century, most of whom were English aristocrats, stayed in this area on their visits to Rome (it came to be known as the English ghetto). In the 19th century many illustrious artists, writers and musicians followed in

their footsteps: Keats, Tennyson, Stendhal, Balzac, Wagner and Liszt among them.

Keats-Shelley House

✉ 26 Piazza di Spagna; www.keats-shelley-house.org 📞 06-678 4235
🕐 Mon–Fri 9am–1pm, Sat 11am–2pm
💲 charge 🚇 Spagna 🚌 117, 119

In 1820, Keats spent the last few months of his life in a small room overlooking the Spanish Steps; he

Grand Tourists

The term "Grand Tour" first appeared in 1670 in Richard Lassels's *Voyage through Italy*, when the British priest and traveller declared that "young lords" must visit Italy and France to educate themselves in the culture of antiquity. In the following centuries Italy's great cities became the main stops on a secular pilgrimage of English aristocrats and aspiring gentlemen wishing to complete their education. For the Romans, this procession of "Sirs" and "Miladies" represented an opportunity to cash in. Houses were rented out in the fashionable districts of Rome on the Corso and Piazza di Spagna, and tea shops (such as Babington's), hotels and cafés sprung up. With the arrival of mass transport in the middle of the 1800s travel became cheaper and safer; many writers, including Byron and Shelley, felt that the Grand Tour was de rigueur. The dalliances and foibles of these British in Italy became the subject for literary satire in the novels of E.M. Forster and Henry James, many of which have been dramatised for cinema.

Recommended Restaurants, Bars & Cafés on pages 134–5

died of consumption there in 1821, aged just 25. In 1906, the house was bought by an Anglo-American association and turned into a museum and library dedicated to Keats and his fellow Romantics who had made Rome their home. The Keats-Shelley House has an intriguing collection of personal objects and documents relating to the lives of Shelley and Byron, but the main focus is on Keats – his prints, paintings, books and death mask are on display.

SHOPPING STREETS

The former artistic enclave is now the haunt of big spenders and wishful window shoppers who come to flex their credit cards in its elegant and expensive shops. The area between Piazza di Spagna and Via del Corso is for dedicated fashionistas. Elegant **Via dei Condotti** ⓫ is designer-label heaven.

This street, plus the parallel **Via Borgognona** and **Via Frattina**, which are linked by the equally sumptuous **Via Bocca di Leone**, are home to all the top fashion outlets. **Via del Babuino** is lined with interesting design and antique shops. Parallel to this is **Via Margutta**, a pretty, narrow street (once home to Federico Fellini), with artists' studios, galleries and workshops. Twice a year (May and September/October), the street holds a special art show dedicated to the works of local painters. Matching the expensive shops in this area are some of the best hotels in Rome.

Towards the end of Via dei Condotti is the world-famous tourist trap **Caffè Greco**, said to have been opened by a Greek merchant in 1760. The great and the good down the centuries have frequented this café, including Baudelaire, Wagner, Taine, Liszt, Stendhal, Goethe, Byron, Keats and Shelley.

Rome's most opulent shopping street is Via dei Condotti, which starts at the Spanish Steps. The designer shops – Armani, Bulgari, Gucci, Prada among them – feature dazzling window displays and even more dazzling prices.

LEFT AND BELOW: shopping around the Spanish Steps.

Roman Fashion

Many glamorous and highly sought-after couturiers are based in Rome

While most of the Italian fashion business is centred on Milan, there are a handful of top designers who have made their base in Rome. The most famous of these is undoubtedly Valentino, who opened his Roman studio in 1959 and has enjoyed success ever since. His high-profile clients have included Sophia Loren, Audrey Hepburn and Jackie Kennedy, and his glamorous evening-wear is a constant winner at the Oscar awards ceremony.

Laura Biagiotti and Fendi are also big names in the world of international fashion who started in Rome. The former, who has been dubbed the "queen of cashmere", creates luxurious knitwear (coats included), silk separates and loose-fitting, feminine dresses. The designer is said to test-drive her designs personally for comfort. Her headquarters and home are located just outside Rome in the 15th-century castle of Marco Simone, a former medieval fortress. The four towers of the castle form the famous Biagiotti logo.

The second of the two, Fendi, is a company created by a married couple and their five daughters. They first set up their flagship shop on Via Borgognona on the site of a former cinema in the early 1950s. Today, half a century on, the shop is one of the largest in the area and sells beautiful bags, shoes, luggage and ready-to-wear clothes.

Two other legendary names are worth checking out: Fontana and Capucci. The heyday of the Sorelle Fontana (Fontana Sisters) is associated with the glamorous *Dolce Vita* of the 1950s and 1960s, when droves of aristocratic women and just about all the successful foreign actresses in Rome visited their atelier. You can see their ultra-classic, elegant clothes at Via della Fontanella di Borghese. Roberto Capucci also emerged during the 1950s and is best-known for the sculptural quality of his garments that look as good off as on the body. His work has been shown in important design museums in Italy, Vienna, Munich and Paris, and he has a boutique/atelier on Via Gregoriana.

More recently, the young Gai Mattiolo has been making his mark both at home and abroad. He has his own-name boutique in the ultra-swanky Via Borgognona, and many more in cities throughout the world. Adriana V. Campanile is the new favourite for shoe fanatics, and her designs are modern and stylish, and easily pass for pricier Piazza di Spagna luxuries.

Of course, just about all the other well-known Italian designers, among them Versace, Armani and Trussardi, have shops in Rome as well, mostly around Via Condotti. However, visitors who cannot afford top designer names should not be put off; there are plenty of boutiques selling clothes with far less frightening price tags. Remember, too, that Italy produces stunning shoes, bags and leather accessories, and a wide selection can be found in the city's shops. ❑

LEFT: a trademark Laura Biagiotti white suit.

Recommended Restaurants, Bars & Cafés on pages 134–5

The third road in the trident of streets, **Via di Ripetta** (*ripa* means river bank: a reminder that there was once a harbour here, back when ships still plied the Tiber) connects Piazza del Popolo to the Vatican, via the Mausoleum of Augustus and the Ara Pacis, two ancient monuments dating from the time of Augustus.

Ara Pacis ⑫

✉ Lungotevere in Augusta, www. arapacis.it 📞 06-8205 9127
🕐 Tue–Sun 9am–7pm 💶 charge
🚇 Flaminio 🚌 81, 117, 119, 224, 628, 913, 926

The **Ara Pacis**, a finely carved sacrificial altar built in 13 BC to commemorate the era of peace (*pax romana*) that followed Augustus' victories in Gaul and Spain, was painstakingly pieced together by archaeologists from original and reconstructed fragments, and erected in its current location by Mussolini in 1938. The altar is enclosed by a white marble screen decorated with reliefs illustrating mythological and allegorical scenes.

After years of neglect and botched restorations, the altar is now the principal exhibit in a new museum complex, designed amid great controversy by US architect Richard Meier. Inaugurated in 2006, his striking glass-and-travertine design is the only work of modern architecture in the historic centre of Rome, and as such has provoked strong reactions *(see right)*.

Mausoleum of Augustus ⑬

Behind the altar is the **Mausoleo di Augusto**, built between 28 and 23 BC, long before it was intended for use. The first person buried here was Augustus' nephew Marcellus, then Augustus himself in AD 14. It's hard to believe now that this overgrown ruin was one of the most magnificent sights in Rome, covered as it was with marble pillars and statues. ❏

Critics of Richard Meier's Ara Pacis Museum have likened it variously to a petrol station, a pizzeria and a giant coffin. Vittorio Sgarbi, a celebrity art critic and former Deputy Culture Minister, publicly set fire to a model of the building, and recently declared it "an indecent cesspit by a useless architect".

ABOVE: Mausoleo di Augusto.
BELOW: Ara Pacis.

BEST RESTAURANTS, BARS AND CAFÉS

Restaurants

Price includes dinner and a half-bottle of house wine:
€ = under €25
€€ = €25–40
€€€ = €40–60
€€€€ = more than €60

Al 34

✉ 34 Via Mario dei Fiori
☎ 06-679 5091 ⏰ L & D
Tue–Sun. €€ [p335, E3]
The service is fast, the prices honest, the atmosphere lively and the food classical Italian. Sample the *tonnarelli al granciporro* (pasta with crab) or the fresh fish *misto* (a mix of different fish), and the home-made Neapolitan *caprese* cake, *semifreddo al torroncino* (nougat ice-cream dessert) or pear and chocolate tart.

La Baguette

✉ 24–25 Via Tomacelli
☎ 06-6880 7727 ⏰ B, Br, L & D Tue–Sun, D only Mon. €–€€ [p335, D3]
The first Italian branch of a popular Belgian chain. Ideal for breakfast (exquisite croissants) or later, when large salads, quiches and open sandwiches made with fresh stone-ground bread can be washed down with organic wines, teas and fruit juices around large wooden tables. A terrace a couple of doors down is a major bonus in summer.

Dal Bolognese

✉ 1–2 Piazza del Popolo
☎ 06-361 1426 ⏰ L & D
Tue–Sun. €€€–€€€€
[p335, D2]
On the theatrical Piazza del Popolo, this smart restaurant with paintings on the wall, uniformed waiters and couches on which to sip your *aperitivo* serves good-quality staples from the Emilia Romagna region to a loyal clientele of politicians, film producers and assorted artists and celebrities. Closed three weeks Aug.

Da Gino

✉ 4 Vicolo Rosini ☎ 06-687 3434 ⏰ L & D Mon–Sat. €€ [p335, D3]
Vaulted ceilings and frescoes adorn this trattoria, where affordable Roman specialities are served following the traditional weekly calendar, which means fish on Tuesday and Friday. For dessert, home-made *crostate* (tarts) and a legendary *tiramisù*. No credit cards. Closed Aug.

'Gusto

✉ 9 Piazza Augusto Imperatore ☎ 06-322 6273
⏰ L & D daily, Br Sat and Sun. Restaurant €€–€€€, pizzeria €–€€ [p335, D2]
'Gusto is an empire: a pizzeria downstairs, an upmarket restaurant upstairs, a wine bar on the other side, an *osteria* next to that. There's even a well-stocked cookery store attached. The service is fast and friendly, and the general standard is high. An added feature is the outdoor seating most of the year under impressively austere 1930s porticoes that line the square. Booking advisable. Open late.

Hostaria dell'Orso

✉ 25c Via dei Soldati
☎ 06-6830 1192 ⏰ D only Mon–Sat. €€€€
[p335, D3]
Milanese superstar chef Gualtiero Marchesi is at the helm of the exclusive Hostaria dell'Orso in a *palazzo* that has been an inn since medieval times. Now a posh but hip restaurant-cum-piano bar-cum-disco, it has an expensive take on Italian haute cuisine which can be ordered à la carte or from four different set-price menus (*menù degustazione*).

Il Margutta RistorArte

✉ 118 Via Margutta ☎ 06-3265 0577 ⏰ L & D daily. €€–€€€ [p335, E2]
This is one of Rome's oldest vegetarian restaurants and offers refined contemporary Italian cuisine and walls filled with modern art, echoing its location in the artsy Via Margutta. At lunch there is a set-price buffet, and there's a good brunch on Sunday.

Matricianella

✉ 3–4 Via del Leone ☎ 06-683 2100 ⏰ L & D Mon–Sat. €€ [p335, D3]
Traditional Roman food in a cheerful setting. To start, try their crispy *fritto vegetale* (fried vegetables) and then, if you are a carnivore, the fettuccine with chicken liver and minced beef is a good bet. Closed three weeks Aug.

Nino

✉ 11 Via Borgognona
☎ 06-679 5676 ⏰ L & D Mon–Sat. €€–€€€
[p335, E3]
A cordial setting where genuine Tuscan food has been consumed for over 70 years. Sample the leek soufflé, wild boar with polenta, and pappardelle with hare sauce. The wine list is well thought out and has a good selection of half-bottles. At the upper end of this price scale, and well worth it. Closed Aug.

L'Osteria

✉ 16 Via della Frezza
☎ 06-322 6273 ⏰ L & D daily. €€ [p335, D2]
Informal but chic, and further proof that anything the 'Gusto team (*see above*) does turns to gold. Furniture and

ABOVE: Il Margutta RistorArte.

details have some 1930s touches, and the menu is a skilful combination of the traditional and the ultra-contemporary, with 400 cheeses, cured meats, deep-fried delicacies, omelettes, soups and good main courses. All served with hearty home-made bread and excellent wines by the glass or bottle from a selection of 1,700 labels.

Otello alla Concordia
81 Via della Croce 06-679 1178 L & D Mon–Sat. € [p335, E2] Authentically Roman food (*rigatoni all'amatriciana*, lamb and *tiramisù*) and fresh fish served in a room overlooking a pretty little courtyard, used in summer. Book ahead.

PizzaRé
14 Via di Ripetta 06-3211468 L & D daily. € [p335, D2] For a simple pizza after a heavy day's spending in the Spanish Steps' clothing mecca, try PizzaRé, maker of the thick and crusty Neapolitan

variety. Set-price menus including pasta and grilled meats at lunchtime. Pizzas at reduced price on Monday evenings.

Porto Maltese
7 Salita di San Sebastianello 06-678 0546 L & D Tue–Sun. €€–€€€ [p335, E2] Trendy bar and restaurant with a friendly atmosphere. Waiters can be seen heading to and from a large open aquarium at the front, full of wriggling eel, crabs and lobsters. Alternatively, choose from a more sedate fish counter at the back.

Taverna Ripetta
158 Via di Ripetta 06-6880 2979 L & D Mon–Sat. €€ [p335, D2] Romantic and atmospheric, this restaurant is perfect for lunch as well as dinner. The menu incorporates pasta, meat and fish. Try the gnocchi with basil and cherry tomatoes, and the outstanding *semifreddo* for dessert. Open late.

Bars and Cafés

One of the most appealing wine bars in the area is the **Enoteca Antica di Via della Croce** (76b Via della Croce). It's cosy in winter in its cellar-like interior, and delightful in summer if you can nab one of the few outdoor tables. You can just drink wine, chosen from their lengthy wine list, or you can eat here too.

Two other buzzing venues are the wine bar in the excellent **'Gusto** complex (9 Piazza Augusto Imperatore, *see previous page*), and a new ultra-modern rival pizzeria-restaurant-café-bar called **Recafè** (36 Piazza Augusto Imperatore).

Buccone (19 Via di Ripetta) existed long before wine bars became fashionable, and it is a joy just to take in the sheer authenticity of this high-ceilinged, old-fashioned emporium crammed with bottles of wine and regional specialities.

Old-fashioned, artsy hang-out **Café Notegen** (159 Via del Babuino) still has plenty of charm, although it is looking a little worse for wear these days. The all-day opening and affable manner are endearing.

There are a number of other historic cafés in this area. Long-time rivals **Canova** (16 Piazza del Popolo) and **Rosati** (5 Piazza del Popolo) face each other across the grand expanse of Piazza del Popolo. Both are good, but Rosati wins hands down for ambience. Furthermore, its cakes are mouth-watering, and the cocktails are a cut above the usual.

The large **Gran Caffè La Caffettiera** (61 Via Margutta) is in a former 17th-century theatre in the Via Margutta. It's a little pricey, but let the frescoes and Art Nouveau details wash over you, and you'll soon feel refreshed and relaxed about the prices.

The beautiful **Antico Caffè Greco** (86 Via Condotti) with its marble tables and red-velvet chairs is frequented mostly by tourists, but the bar out the front makes the most delicious coffee. Drink it standing at the bar, as it's much cheaper than when you are sitting at a table.

For the ultimate view of Rome, climb up the Spanish Steps and turn left to **Ciampini al Café du Jardin** (Viale Trinità dei Monti), open only in summer, where you can have light meals and cocktails as the sun sets on the Eternal City.

Recommended Restaurants, Bars & Cafés on page 145

THE VATICAN AND PRATI

The Vatican City is a shrine to the power and
extravagance of the Catholic Church through
the ages, and to its extraordinary artistic taste

Main attractions
ST PETER'S SQUARE
ST PETER'S BASILICA
THE VATICAN MUSEUMS
THE SISTINE CHAPEL
CASTEL SANT'ANGELO
THE BORGO
PRATI

The fabulous wealth and extravagance of the Catholic Church
through the ages is celebrated
without restraint in the Vatican State.
The immense basilica of St Peter's,
with its dome by Michelangelo and
an interior sumptuously bedecked
with Bernini's glistening creations, is
impressive enough. Then there are
the Vatican Museums, mile upon
mile of rooms and corridors containing historic treasures, and, of
course, the Sistine Chapel.

Covering a total area of little more
than 40 hectares (100 acres), Vatican
City is by far the world's smallest
independent sovereign entity. The
Lateran Treaty of 1929, concluded
between Pope Pius XI and Mussolini,
established its territorial limits. The
Vatican has its own stamps, currency, media, railway and police
force – the Swiss Guards. The city is
roughly trapezoidal in shape,
bounded by medieval walls on all
sides except on the corner, where the
opening of St Peter's Square marks
the border with Rome.

ST PETER'S SQUARE

Piazza San Pietro ❶ was laid out by
Bernini in 1656–67 for Pope Alexander VII. Its double-colonnaded wings

symbolise the outstretched arms of
Mother Church, embracing and protecting the congregation. The piazza
itself is keyhole-shaped, echoing St
Peter's role as holder of the keys to
heaven. In the centre are fountains
by Maderno and della Fontana, and
an Egyptian obelisk, brought to
Rome by Emperor Caligula in AD
37. Between the obelisk and each
fountain is a round marble slab,
from where the spectator obtains the
illusion that each colonnade has only
a single row of columns.

LEFT: St Peter's Square. **RIGHT:** view of
the keyhole-shaped square from the dome.

St Peter's Basilica ②

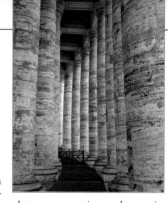

✉ Piazza San Pietro; www.vaticano.va
📞 06-6988 1662 🕐 daily 7am–7pm,
until 6pm in winter (no bare legs or
shoulders) 🎫 free for the basilica;
charge for dome and sacristy
🚇 Ottaviano-San Pietro 🚌 19, 23,
32, 34, 46, 49, 62, 64, 81, 492,
913, 990, 991, 999

*Michelangelo is said to
have made his mark on
the less spiritual side of
the Vatican as well.
Word has it that the
master designed the
blue-, yellow- and red-
striped uniforms (the
colours of the Medici
popes) of the Vatican's
famous Swiss Guards.
The uniforms have not
changed since the
corps was instituted in
the 16th century.*

At the end of the square, above a
triple flight of steps, stands the **Basilica di San Pietro**, an undeniably
impressive structure, but an unfortu-
nate mixture of conflicting architectural styles. Built on the site of St
Peter's martyrdom in AD 67 during
Nero's persecutions of the Christians,
the original Constantinian church
was of typical basilican form – a
Latin cross with a nave, side aisles
and a transept. It was lavishly decorated with mosaics, paintings and statuary, but became so dilapidated that
rebuilding became unavoidable.

In 1506, Julius II decided on a com-

plete reconstruction and commissioned Bramante, whose plan for the
new basilica was a Greek cross sur-
mounted by a gigantic dome. On
Bramante's death in 1514, the four
central piers and the arches of the
dome had been completed. Raphael
(d. 1520) then took over, and was
followed by Sangallo (d. 1546); both
men bowed to the clergy's wish for
greater capacity by designing a nave
and altering the ground-plan to that
of a Latin cross.

In 1546, however, before this could

Vatican and Prati

Recommended Restaurants, Bars & Cafés on page 145

be realised, the 72-year-old Michelangelo was summoned by Pope Paul III. He expressed his preference for the original Greek cross and central dome of Bramante; seeing the Pantheon as unambitious, though, he developed his own version of Brunelleschi's Florentine cupola, and substituted Bramante's piers with new ones of tremendous strength. The entire plan was realised after Michelangelo died in 1564; construction work was continued until 1590, when Pope Paul V decided that the Latin cross was more appropriate, demanding a nave.

Maderno extended Michelangelo's building to give it its current

form, adding the portico in 1614. The building was consecrated in 1626, 1,300 years after the construction of the original basilica. Seen from the square, Maderno's portico robs Michelangelo's dome of much of its power, though from a distance the cityscape is still dominated by the cupola.

St Peter's treasures

As you pass into the **portico**, the statue of Constantine on the left is by Bernini. Look up, opposite the 15th-century bronze central doors, to see a restored remnant of the original 13th-century mosaic, *La Navicella*, by Giotto. Inside the basilica, turn right for *La Pietà*, Michelangelo's remarkable statue of the Madonna and dead Christ, which he sculpted in 1499 when only 25. Mary is seated on a rock (the rock of St Peter) holding Christ's lifeless body, her face filled with sorrow. It is an incredibly moving work and the only one Michelangelo ever signed.

Halfway down the nave the 13th-century statue of St Peter by Arnolfo di Cambio is so widely venerated

St Peter's is the longest basilica in the world. The nave is the size of two football fields and the baldacchino is as high as a nine-storey building. The church has 21 altars, 14 chapels, 9 domes and capacity for 60,000 peope.

FAR LEFT: a curve of Bernini's colonnade in Piazza San Pietro. **LEFT:** Michelangelo's *Pietà*. **BELOW:** Mass on St Peter's Square.

Papal Audiences

Papal audiences are held in the Vatican on Wednesday at 10.30am, except in the height of summer, when they are at his summer residence at Castelgandolfo outside Rome. Apply for free tickets in writing to the Prefettura della Casa Pontifica, 00120 Città del Vaticano, or go to the office on the preceding Monday or Tuesday (it's through the bronze door watched over by Swiss Guards, to the right of the basilica). For more information, tel: 06-6988 4857. The Pope comes to a window above the piazza on Sunday at noon to give the traditional angelus blessing.

ABOVE: Pope Julius II ordering Bramante, Michelangelo and Raphael to construct the Vatican and St Peter's, by Vernet. **BELOW:** the Vatican Gardens.

that its foot, kissed by devout pilgrims for over seven centuries, is almost worn away.

In the centre of the basilica, directly under the dome is Bernini's **baldacchino** (1633), commissioned by the Barberini Pope Urban VIII. This huge bronze canopy (the largest free-standing bronze structure in the world) rises 26 metres (66 ft) over the holiest part of the church, the legendary tomb of St Peter. The twisted columns are replicas of the ones that Christ apparently leant against in the Temple of Solomon. It was cast from metal stripped from the Pantheon's dome, leading locals to quip, "What the Barbarians didn't do, the Barberini did." Bernini added the vine leaves and the bees, symbols of the Barberini coat of arms.

To the right of the baldacchino, stairs lead down to the **grottoes** (daily 7am–7pm, until 6pm in winter; free) containing the tombs of several popes, including that of the recently deceased Pope John Paul II.

On the apse wall, framed by the baldacchino, is another Bernini creation, the **Cattedra di San Pietro** (1665), a gilded bronze throne said to have been the episcopal chair of St Peter. It is supported by statues of the four fathers of the Church, and above it angels and putti surround a halo of gilt stucco with a key to heaven and the dove of the Holy Spirit.

Don't miss the ghoulish **tomb of Alexander VII**, another of Bernini's patrons, to the left of the transept. Just above the door is Bernini's last work, representing a skeletal allegory of death clutching an hourglass, reminding us that death comes to us all. The draped skeleton is surrounded by four statues representing Justice, Truth, Prudence and Chastity.

The dome

The entrance to the **dome** (daily 8am–6pm; until 5pm in winter;

Recommended Restaurants, Bars & Cafés on page 145

closed during ceremonies; admission charge) is on the right of the portico. The long climb to the top (there are 320 steps from where the lift stops) is rewarded by extensive views across the city.

The **Vatican Gardens** can be seen from the dome, but if you want a closer look you will have to book in advance *(see tip opposite)*.

THE VATICAN MUSEUMS ❸

✉ 100 Viale Vaticano; www. vaticano.va 📞 06-6988 4947/4676 🕐 summer Mon–Fri 8.45am–4.45pm, Sat and last Sun of month 8.45am–1.45pm, winter Mon–Sat and last Sun 8.45am–1.45pm; last admission 90 minutes before closing; closed Catholic holidays; no bare legs or shoulders 💶 charge; last Sunday in the month is free 🚇 Ottaviano-San Pietro, Cipro-Museo Vaticano 🚌 19, 23, 32, 34, 49, 62, 64, 81, 492, 913, 990, 991, 999

The Vatican Museums are a good 15-minute walk from St Peter's Square; just follow the walls north until you

reach the entrance. Expect a long queue, especially at weekends and on the last Sunday of the month, when the place gets mobbed as admission is free. To help visitors out, the museum authorities have devised four routes lasting from 1½ to 5 hours. All, including the shortest, take in the Sistine Chapel.

There are 10 collections in all, plus the papal apartments, but the undisputed highlights are the Sistine Chapel and the Raphael Rooms. Because different visitors have different tastes and because of the vast amount of exhibits contained in the museums, no single route is described here; only the main highlights. You'll find plenty of detailed information at the entrance.

Vatican post box. The Vatican has its own stamps, currency, radio station, newspaper and police force.

LEFT: detail from *The Creation of Adam,* on the Sistine ceiling.
BELOW: Giuseppe Momo's magnificent helicoidal staircase (1932).

Statue of Apoxyomenos, the Greek representation of an athlete. This is a 1st-century AD *Roman copy of a Greek original.*

BELOW: *Dispute from the Stanza della Segnatura, one of the Raphael Rooms.*

Sistine Chapel

No visit to the Vatican is complete without a look inside the Sistine Chapel. The walls, depicting scenes from the lives of Christ and Moses, were painted by some of the greatest masters of the Renaissance: Botticelli, Perugino, Ghirlandaio and Signorelli. It is Michelangelo's sublime frescoes, however, which have made the chapel universally famous (*see pages 148–9*).

The Raphael Rooms

The Stanze di Raffaello are four rooms decorated by Raphael in the 16th century at the request of Pope Nicholas V. The first room, the **Sala di Constantino**, was the last to be painted and, since Raphael was on his deathbed, is mainly the work of his pupils. The frescoes depict scenes from the life of Constantine.

The **Stanza di Eliodoro** was decorated in the years 1512–14. The subject matter alludes to events in Pope Julius II's life. *Expulsion of Heliodorus*, with angels chasing a thief out of the temple, refers to Julius's success in expelling the enemy from Italy.

The next room, **Stanza della Segnatura**, was where the Pope's council met to sign official decrees. The frescoes (1509–11) mix pagan and Christian themes. In the *School of Athens* fresco, representing the triumph of philosophical truth, Raphael portrays ancient characters with the features of contemporary heroes. The bearded figure of Plato in the centre is da Vinci; Bramante appears as Euclid in the foreground, and the thoughtful figure of Heraclites on the steps is Michelangelo. The *Parnassus* fresco, representing poetic beauty, features Homer, Virgil, Ovid, Dante and Boccaccio.

The last room, the **Stanza dell' Incendio di Borgo**, takes its name from the fresco depicting a terrible fire in the Borgo in 847, miraculously extinguished by Leo IV making the sign of the cross. This room was painted after the first half of Michelangelo's Sistine ceiling was uncovered, and direct influences can be seen in the monumentality of the figures.

For information on the other Vatican collections, *see Treasures of the Vatican, pages 146–7*.

Papal Insignia

Wherever you see a coat of arms with the crossed keys of St Peter topped with the triple crown, you know the building, sculpture or painting on which it appears was a papal commission. Each papal dynasty had its own insignia. Red balls signify the Medici popes, for example, while bees represent the Barberini, the greatest patrons of the Baroque. The Barberini bees can be spotted all over Rome, from Triton's Fountain to the baldacchino in St Peter's *(below)*. Other interesting papal symbols to look out for include dragons, doves, fleur-de-lis, cypress and olive trees, stars and hills.

Castel Sant'Angelo ❹

✉ 50 Lungotevere Castello; www.
castelsantangelo.com ☎ 06-3996
7600 ☺ Tue–Sun 9am–8pm
ⓔ charge 🚇 Lepanto 🚌 23, 34, 49,
62, 64, 80, 87, 492, 926, 990

Castel Sant'Angelo is approached
from across the Tiber by means of
the delightful **Ponte Sant'Angelo**, a
pedestrian bridge adorned with
statues of saints Peter and Paul and
10 angels sculpted by Bernini and his
students *(see page 54)*. Construction
of the castle began in AD 123, and
16 years later it became Hadrian's
mausoleum. It has since been a
fortress, a prison and the popes'
hiding place in times of trouble,

thanks to the *passetto*, the corridor
that connects the Vatican Palace
with the castle. The castle houses
artefacts from all periods of Roman
history, and many of the rooms,
such as the Sala Paolina painted by
del Vaga in 1544, are beautifully
frescoed.

The papal chambers and other
rooms are accessible via the spiral
ramp inside, which is still in an excellent state of preservation. At the top
of the ramp are the terraces and café,
both with superb views of the Dome
of St Peter's and the rest of Rome. (It
was from this parapet that Puccini's
heroine, Tosca, plunged to her
death.) The gigantic bronze statue of
the Archangel Michael that crowns
the citadel was placed here in 1753.

KIDS

If you're travelling with
children, the Castel
Sant'Angelo, with its
ramparts, trapdoors,
prison chambers,
drawbridges and
cannonballs galore, will
keep them amused.

ABOVE LEFT: view of
St Peter's from Castel
Sant'Angelo. **LEFT:**
Bernini's angels on
Ponte Sant'Angelo.
BELOW: Castel
Sant' Angelo from
the pedestrian
Sant'Angelo bridge.

Map on page 138

SHOP

Another feature of Prati is its markets. The wholesale flower market at 45 Via Trionfale has blooms and plants at give-away prices. Essentially a trade market, it is open to the public on Tuesday mornings. Nearby Mercato Trionfale is one of the city's largest, and runs along both sides of Via Andrea Doria. Here you'll find fresh produce, as well as clothing and housewares. There's also a superb covered market with a vast range of fruit, vegetables, meats, cheeses and bread, at Piazza dell'Unità.

BELOW: view of the Prati neighbourhood.

THE BORGO

If you've energy left after visiting St Peter's and the Vatican Museums, wander the warren of pedestrian streets just east of the Vatican. The first pilgrims to St Peter's were housed in hostels here, and the area is still a colony of international pilgrims today.

The relaxed charm of this atmospheric neighbourhood will soothe your tired feet as you meander along its medieval lanes and admire its ancient, ivy-clad *palazzi*. The quarter was formerly known as the Città Leonina, after Leo IV who built the fortified walls and connected the Vatican to Castel Sant' Angelo by an overhead passageway. Unfortunately a large part of the Borgo and its olde-worlde atmosphere were destroyed when Mussolini decided that St Peter's needed a more grandiose approach and tore the area in two with the Via della Conciliazione, which ruins the effect of Bernini's piazza, but allows for a full view of St Peter's.

South of the boulevard is **Borgo Santo Spirito**. The church of **Santo Spirito in Sassia ❺**, built for the Saxons in 689, was rebuilt in the 16th century. Next door, the **Ospedale Santo Spirito ❻** was set up by Pope Innocent III in the 13th century as an orphanage for unwanted babies. Within the hospital is the small **Museo Storico Nazionale dell'Arte Sanitaria** (3 Lungotevere in Sassia; tel: 06-678 7864; 10am–noon Mon, Wed, Fri), with an array of medical paraphernalia, and two beautifully frescoed wards.

PRATI

North of the Vatican lies the elegant residential area of Prati. Until the late 19th century, Prati was characterised by vast vineyards and gardens, hence the name, which means "meadows". The quarter was built in its present shape in response to an urgent need to expand the city after it was proclaimed capital of the newly unified nation in 1870.

Its strategic position just outside the Vatican walls makes this district convenient for sightseeing and shopping. Prati may lack the medieval charm of the Centro Storico, but if you want to get a deeper understanding of the real fabric and rhythm of everyday Roman life, then venturing into this neighbourhood is a great way to start.

Prati is easily reached on metro line A (get off at Lepanto, Ottaviano-San Pietro or Cipro-Musei Vaticani), or one of the many bus routes that terminate at Piazza del Risorgimento.

Most of the shops are concentrated around the Via Cola di Rienzo and Via Ottaviano, around Piazza Mazzini, which is laid out in a large star-shaped plan, and Piazza Cavour, immediately recognisable by its towering palms. Facing Piazza Cavour, with its rear towards the west bank of the Tiber, is the colossal **Palazzo di Giustizia** (Palace of Justice), dubbed *il palazzaccio* (the big, ugly building). Its riverfront façade is crowned with a bronze chariot and fronted by statues of the great men of Italian law. ❑

BEST RESTAURANTS, BARS AND CAFÉS

Restaurants

Price includes dinner and a half-bottle of house wine:

€ = under €25
€€ = €25–40
€€€ = €40–60
€€€€ = more than €60

La Cava

21 Via Attilio Regolo
06-321 5532
L Mon–Fri, D Mon–Sat.
€€ [p334, C2]
With its stark but stylish interior decorated with Travertine marble and keen young waiting staff this is a good place to go with a group. The dishes are modern Mediterranean, and sometimes a little too inventive for their own good, but mostly the chef pulls them off.

Clok

21 Via Vittorio Colonna
06-320 0230 L only Mon, L & D Tue–Fri, D only Sat, Sun. €–€€ [p335, D3]
One of a trendy new breed of pizzeria-cum-restaurant-cum-wine bar with big windows and minimalist design. You eat downstairs and chill out upstairs in a room with low seating, cushions and candles. Pizzas range from traditional to original (gorgonzola and apple).

Dante Taberna de' Gracchi

266 Via dei Gracchi
06-321 3126 L & D
Tue–Sat, D only Mon.
€€–€€€ [p334, B2]
A relaxing pastel-coloured interior and classic cuisine based mostly on fresh fish, and a different soup every day. Choose a fine wine from an endless list.

Il Matriciano

55 Via dei Gracchi
06-321 3040 L & D Sun–Fri in summer and Thur–Tue in winter. €–€€ [p334, B2]
Just around the corner from St Peter's, this restaurant has served genuine local food for over 90 years. Its signature dish is an excellent spaghetti all' amatriciana (spaghetti with tomato, onion and cured pork sauce).

La Pergola dei Cavalieri Hilton

101 Via A. Cadlolo, Monte Mario 06-3509 2152
D only Tue–Sat. €€€€
[off map p334, A1]
German superstar chef Heinz Beck has made this a place worth making a detour for. Enviable views, attentive staff and ultra-refined food (pictured right).

Osteria dell'Angelo

32 Via G. Bettolo 06-372 9470 L Tue–Fri, D Mon–Sat. €–€€ [p334, B2]
This neighbourhood trattoria with a fixed-price evening menu including house wine is always packed to the gills. Try the fritti to begin with and then a flavourful version of the Roman standard tonnarelli cacio e pepe (pasta with pecorino and pepper). Booking advisable. No credit cards.

Siciliainbocca

26 Via Faà di Bruno
06-3735 8400 L & D Mon–Sat. €€ [p334, B1]
Come here for a cheerful ambience and good Sicilian food seasoned with the island's flavours: lemons, olives, capers and plenty of sunshine. Their classic ricotta-filled cassata is excellent.

Taverna Angelica

6 Piazza Capponi 06-687 4514 L & D Sun, D only Mon–Sat. €€
[p334, B3]
Massimo Pinardi's restaurant has only been around a few years, but it quickly earned a reputation for high-quality food. Try smoked goose breast with celery, apple and walnuts, pasta with fennel and anchovy, or grilled swordfish with pesto.

Zen

243 Via degli Scipioni
06-321 3420 L & D Tue–Fri & Sun, D only Sat.
€€–€€€ [p334, C2]
High-standard, fresh Japanese food is Zen's strong point. Pick your dishes as they roll past you on the city's first sushi and sashimi conveyor belt, or order the tempura and other heftier dishes à la carte. Closed two weeks Aug.

Bars and Cafés

Pellacchia (103 Via Cola di Rienzo) makes its own ice cream on the premises and is deservedly famous. On an otherwise residential street **Antonini** (19–29 Via G. Sabotino) makes the kind of cakes you bring to dinner parties when you want to impress; perfect for an aperitif. **Bar Bar** (17 Via Ovidio, www.barbar.it) is the first so-called lounge bar in the city; its infinitely long bar counter and sleek furniture give it a New York vibe.

TREASURES OF THE VATICAN

Sensory overload, known as "Stendhal's Syndrome", is a natural response to the Vatican's endless artistic riches

The Vatican Museums house one of the biggest and most important art collections in the world. They merit a lifetime's study, but for those who have only a few hours, there are some sights that simply should not be missed.

The Sistine Chapel *(see pages 148–9)* with Michelangelo's marvelous ceiling, and the four Raphael Rooms *(see page 142)* are the star attractions. The Museo Pio-Clementino contains some of the greatest sculptures of antiquity *(see opposite)*. The Pinacoteca picture gallery houses an extensive collection of paintings from Byzantine times to the present, with works by Giotto, Bellini, Titian, da Vinci, Raphael, Caravaggio and many others.

The Vatican Library contains a priceless collection of illuminated manuscripts and early printed books. The Chapel of St Nicholas has some exquisite frescoes by Fra Angelico; and

frescoes by Pinturicchio can be seen in the Borgia Apartment.

More recent artwork is not neglected, either, and the Modern Religious Art Collection, adjoining the apartment, displays works by Paul Klee, Francis Bacon, Max Ernst and Henri Matisse, among others.

The Etruscan Museum, meanwhile, contains many artefacts found in tombs of the mysterious pre-Roman civilisation *(see pages 273–4 for more on the Etruscans)*.

The Gregoriano Profano Museum houses finds from the Baths of Caracalla, on the old Via Appia.

The essentials

✉ *100 Viale Vaticano; www.vaticano.va*
📞 *06-6988 4947/4676*
🕐 *summer Mon–Fri 8.45am–4.45pm, Sat and last Sun of month 8.45am–1.45pm, winter Mon–Sat and last Sun 8.45am–1.45pm* 💰 *charge*
🚇 *Ottaviano-San Pietro, Cipro-Museo Vaticano* 🚌 *19, 23, 32, 34, 49, 62, 64, 81, 492, 913, 990, 991, 999*

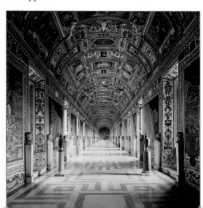

CLASSICAL MASTERPIECES

The Museo Pio-Clementino houses some of the greatest sculptures of Greek and Roman antiquity. In the Octagonal Courtyard of the Belvedere are three master-pieces of classical art: the *Atleta Apoxyomenos*, a 1st-century AD copy of a 4th-century BC bronze, depicts an athlete washing himself

after the exertions of a hard-run race. The beautiful *Apollo del Belvedere*, which depicts the Greek sun god, is another copy of a Greek original, which once stood on the Agora in Athens. The action-packed *Laocoön* (pictured above) a 1st-century BC copy of a 3rd-century BC bronze sculpture, was found near Nero's Golden House by the Colosseum. The marble statue depicts a Trojan priest of Apollo and his two sons struggling with two writhing sea serpents.

The remainder of the sculpture gallery is divided up into sections. The Hall of the Greek Cross (Sala a Croce Greca) houses porphyry sarcophagi of Emperor Constantine's mother and daughter. The Circular Hall (Sala Rotonda) has a huge gilded bronze statue of Hercules and a colossal head of Jupiter of Otricoli, a Roman copy of the Greek original. In the Hall of the Muses (Sala delle Muse) there are statues of Apollo and the Muses; in the centre, the *Belvedere Torso* (1st century BC) is a Greek work that was admired greatly by Raphael and Michelangelo.

The Animal Room (Sala degli Animali) is worth visiting for its remarkable animal statues by Antonio Franzoni (1734–1818), inspired by Roman originals. The Gallery of Statues (Galleria delle Statue) has more Roman copies of Greek originals; and for the Mask Room (Gabinetto delle Maschere), intricate 2nd-century AD mosaics of theatrical masks have been brought from Hadrian's Villa at Tivoli, just outside Rome.

ABOVE (MAIN PICTURE): Borgia Pope Alexander VI (1492–1503) occupied six apartments in the Vatican Palaces and had them decorated by Pinturicchio and his pupils. The frescoes portraying scenes from the lives of the saints, with Lucrezia Borgia in the guise of St Catherine, is the undisputed highlight.

ABOVE: detail from Raphael's *School of Athens* (1510–11) showing Plato and Aristotle with students including Michelangelo (with his famous boots on), who considered Raphael an arch-rival. In the Raphael Rooms.

LEFT: Galleria delle Carte Geographiche (Gallery of Maps): this superb barrel-vaulted gallery is frescoed with maps of Italy. Most were designed by a 16th-century monk.

RIGHT: Known as the *Mars of Todi*, this 5th-century BC bronze is one of the highlights of the Etruscan art collection.

SISTINE CHAPEL

The dynamism of the figures and mastery of colour and light still astonish visitors, as they did Michelangelo's contemporaries

The Sistine Chapel was built by Sixtus IV in 1473–81 as the official private chapel of the popes. It was also used for the conclaves by which a new Pope is elected, a function the chapel preserves today. Michelangelo was engaged to paint the ceiling by Pope Julius II in 1508. He worked single-handedly, lying on his back, for four years (1508–12). When the work was finally unveiled, it set the seal on his reputation as the greatest living artist.

The ceiling depicts scenes from Genesis, starting with God dividing light from dark and ending with the drunkenness of Noah. The sides show the ancestors of Christ and, on marble thrones, the prophets and the classical sybils who prophesised Christ's coming. Above these are the *ignudi*, nude figures holding up festoons with papal symbols and medallions. In the four corners are scenes of salvation, including the dramatic hanging of Haman, and Judith swiping off Holofernes's head.

Critics cannot agree if the ceiling is a neo-Platonic statement or a theological programme devised with the help of religious experts, including, perhaps, Julius II.

ABOVE: *The Fall of Man.* One of the nine ceiling panels depicting stories of the Creation, the Fall and Noah. The panels (painted in reverse order) are as follows: 1) Separation of Light and Darkness 2) Creation of Sun, Moon and Planets 3) Separation of Land and Sea 4) Creation of Adam 5) Creation of Eve 6) the Fall, and Expulsion from Paradise 7) the Sacrifice of Noah 8) the Flood 9) the Drunkenness of Noah.

THE LAST JUDGEMENT

Some critics say the overall theme of the Sistine Chapel is salvation, reaching its climax in the Last Judgement fresco on the end wall (painted by Michelangelo between 1535 and 1541). It depicts a harrowing image of the souls of the dead rising up to face the wrath of God. The good are promoted to heaven, while the damned are cast down into hell. The figure of St Bartholomew is depicted to the right of the beardless Christ, carrying his flayed skin in his left hand. The tragic face depicted on it is Michelangelo's self-portrait; his pained expression reflected the spiritual crisis he was going through and his contemporaries' lack of comprehension.

The fresco aroused violent controversy. The nudity of the figures was criticised as indecent, but Michelangelo's patron, Paul III, was overwhelmed by the work, truly appreciating its greatness. Some of his successors were not so enlightened. In 1564, Pope Paul IV, in a fit of prudery, ordered drapery to be painted over some of the nude figures.

RIGHT: towards the centre of the ceiling you will be able to make out the outstretched finger of the *Creation of Adam*, the Sistine Chapel's most iconic image.

FAR LEFT: *The Adoration of the Golden Calf*, by Cosimo Rosselli (1439–1507).

TOP LEFT: *The Purification of the Leper and the Temptation of Christ*, detail of two women in the crowd, by Botticelli (1481).

BELOW: the other paintings in the Sistine Chapel have been understandably overshadowed by Michelangelo's work. But the earlier frescoes on the lower walls illustrating scenes from the lives of Moses and Christ are worthy of more than a passing glance. They include works by Pinturicchio, Botticelli, Luca Signorelli and Perugino, who painted the fresco *Giving of the Keys to Saint Peter* pictured below (1481).

Recommended Restaurants, Bars & Cafés on pages 166–7

PIAZZA NAVONA AND THE PANTHEON

The Pantheon has stood in the heart of Rome for almost 2,000 years, while Piazza Navona is built on the foundations of a Roman stadium. Today this compact section of the Centro Storico is filled with Baroque buildings and churches, along with picturesque alfresco cafés

he area loosely referred to as the Centro Storico (the Historic Centre) is contained between the great bend of the Tiber to the west and the Via del Corso to the east. In ancient times, the area centred on the Campus Martius (Field of Mars), an army training ground dedicated to the Roman god of war which lay outside the *Pomerium*, the sacred boundary of the city. It was here, in front of the nearby Temple of Apollo (three pillars of which can still be seen next to the Teatro di Marcello), that generals returning from their military campaigns reported to the Senate.

As building space around the central Fora became scarce, the city gradually spread beyond the ancient walls and out towards the Tiber. By Imperial times the old Campus Martius had all but disappeared, and the area was filled with theatres, baths, porticoes and arenas, and dotted with verdant public parks. All that is left to remind us of the existence of the Field of Mars is an elegant little square and street called Piazza and Via di Campo Marzio.

Rome's population shrank in the Middle Ages due to devastating plagues and the relocation of the Empire's capital to Constantinople. Those who remained moved towards the Tiber. The river was good for defence purposes, for water, which there was no access to further inland because so many of the ancient aqueducts had been destroyed, and because it provided a transport route safe from highway bandits. The river current also turned floating mills, which were tied up between the banks.

The ruins in the area also provided building materials for new

Main attractions

THE PANTHEON
SANTA MARIA SOPRA MINERVA
GALLERIA DORIA PAMPHILJ
SAN LUIGI DEI FRANCESI
GOVERNMENT BUILDINGS
PIAZZA NAVONA
PALAZZO ALTEMPS
SANT'IVO
PIAZZA DI PASQUINO
MUSEO DI ROMA
PONTE SANT'ANGELO
VIA DEI CORONARI

LEFT: Piazza Navona.
RIGHT: Piazza della Rotonda.

Piazza Navona and the Pantheon, Campo de Fiori and the Ghetto

Recommended Restaurants, Bars & Cafés on pages 166–7

houses, churches and papal complexes. Some were used as forts or – as with the Pantheon – as churches. Almost all the major medieval, Renaissance and Baroque buildings in the Centro Storico are either expressions of an increasingly powerful Church, or reflect the intense competition for power and prestige among Rome's rich and aristocratic families.

But the Historic Centre has more to offer than churches and palaces. Its tangle of streets and alleys has been the home of the craft guilds since medieval times when these quarters were full of *botteghe* (workshops). The types of trade may have changed, but trade is still the lifeblood of the district. In and around Via dei Coronari and Via dell'Orso there are antique shops and fairs, while Piazza della Fontanella Borghese is the site of a print market.

One of the most interesting streets is Via dei Cestari (connecting the Pantheon and Largo Argentina). It is lined with shops selling religious raiments and equipment for the Catholic priesthood. Many façades incorporate old guild signs or pieces of ancient marble.

SHOP

There are countless curiosity shops clustered on Via del Pantheon, Via Maddalena, Via dei Pastini (where pasta of all sorts was once sold) and the side streets flanking Piazza di Pietra.

AROUND PIAZZA DELLA ROTONDA

The Piazza della Rotonda is one of the busiest squares in the city. Lined with cafés and with an obelisk at its centre, this quaint but small square can barely accommodate the throngs of tourists that pour into it to see the Pantheon. It's worth trying to beat the crowds by getting here as early as you can.

LEFT AND BELOW: street scenes.

The Pantheon ❶

✉ Piazza della Rotonda ☎ 06-6830 0230 ⏱ Mon–Sat 8.30am–7.30pm, Sun 9am–6pm € free 🚌 30, 40, 46, 62, 63, 64, 70, 81, 87, 116, 186, 204, 492, 628, 810

One of the most memorable and impressive of Rome's many architectural marvels is the Pantheon (Basilica di Santa Maria ad Martyres), the best-preserved ancient building in Rome. Originally built as a temple to all the gods, its subsequent conversion into a church in 609 saved it from being torn down. Only 15 metres (45 ft) above sea level, the Pantheon is now the lowest point in Rome. The ditch around it shows just how much the rubble has raised

Rome over the centuries: in ancient times one looked up to the Pantheon, not down.

As the inscription over the portico informs us, the statesman Marcus Agrippa, son-in-law of Augustus, built the original Pantheon in 27 BC in honour of the victory over Antony and Cleopatra at Actium. Agrippa's building, however, was severely damaged by fire in AD 80 and was completely rebuilt by Hadrian (AD 117–38), who has been credited as the building's architect, not just its patron.

The portico is stately and imposing: 16 massive Corinthian columns support a roof with a triangular pediment (the notches cut into the portico columns are said to have supported stalls for a fish and poultry market in the Middle Ages). The walls are 6 metres (20 ft) thick and the huge bronze doors 8 metres (24 ft) high. But the most striking aspect of the building is, of course, the dome *(see box below)*.

The Pantheon contains the tombs of painters and kings. The marble floor is an 1873 restoration. Raphael (1483–1520) is buried here.

ABOVE: Bernini's marble elephant on Piazza Minerva supports a 6th-century obelisk.
BELOW RIGHT: detail of the Pantheon façade.

The Pantheon Dome

A perfect hemisphere, and a symbol of beauty and harmony, the Pantheon dome had a profound impact on the architects of the Renaissance, influencing Brunelleschi's cathedral in Florence and Michelangelo's design for the dome of St Peter's. The height of the dome is the same as its diameter: 43.3 metres (142 ft). The hole (oculus) in its centre is still the only source of light. On sunny days, a beam of light pours through the oculus and moves around the Pantheon's interior, illuminating the frescoes and tombs. Originally, the dome was covered in bronze, but the Byzantine emperor Constans II stripped the outer layer off and took it to Constantinople in 667. Almost 1,000 years later, in 1620, the Barberini Pope Urban VIII had the inner layer melted down to make cannons for Castel Sant'Angelo and Bernini's baldacchino in St Peter's. This act of papal vandalism inspired the quip that "What the Barbarians didn't do, the Barberini did".

Recommended Restaurants, Bars & Cafés on pages 166–7

Santa Maria sopra Minerva

Southeast of the Pantheon, **Santa Maria sopra Minerva ❷** (Mon–Sat 7am–7pm, Sun 8am–7pm) is the only truly Gothic church in Rome. It was built in the 8th century on the site of a temple of Minerva. Its present form dates from around 1280 when it was rebuilt by Dominicans. Its most striking feature is the beautiful, Giotto-blue vaulted ceiling.

The church houses the tombs of several popes and cardinals, and the relics of St Catherine of Siena (the patron saint of Italy who died in the Dominican convent here in 1380). The last chapel on the right is decorated with a fresco of *The Assumption* by Filippino Lippi. In the bottom section the portraits of two young boys represent two Medici princes, future popes Leo X and Clement VII. To the left of the altar stands a Michelangelo sculpture of Christ the Redeemer, whose nudity shocked the Church at the time. It was carved as a nude figure in Florence, then sent to Rome, where it was ineptly finished by pupils.

Outside, the jovial little **elephant statue** with an ancient Egyptian obelisk on its back was designed by Bernini in 1667.

On nearby Via del Pie' di Marmo (Street of the Marble Foot), set on a pedestal in a shadowy corner is the massive and very worn foot of an ancient Roman statue.

Beyond stands the church of **Sant' Ignazio** (daily 7.30am–12.30pm and 3–7.15pm), built between 1627 and 1685 to honour St Ignatius, founder of the Jesuit order. The interior is the usual Baroque combination of gold embellishments, marble and statuary, but the highlight is Andrea Pozzi's fantastic *trompe l'œil* views of heaven.

Vaulting in Santa Maria sopra Minerva, the only true Gothic church in Rome.

LEFT: liturgical vestment shop on Via dei Cestari, "Religious Row". **BELOW:** priestly parade.

TIP

The Palazzo Doria Pamphilj frequently hosts classical concerts, and keeps the gallery rooms open for concert-goers to visit during the performance interval. For up-to-date programme information visit www.doriapamphilj.it.

Just south of here (off the Via del Corso) is Piazza del Collegio Romano and the entrance to the Galleria Doria Pamphilj.

Galleria Doria Pamphilj ❸

✉ 2 Piazza del Collegio Romano; www.doriapamphilj.it 📞 06-679 7323 🕒 Fri–Wed 10am–5pm 💶 charge (free audioguide) 🚌 62, 63, 81, 85, 95, 117, 119, 1 0, 175

The Galleria Doria Pamphilj contains one of the best art collections in Rome, with over 400 paintings from the 15th to 18th centuries. The 17th-century palace was the residence of the once-powerful Doria Pamphilj dynasty (it is still the prop-

BELOW: Titian's *Salomé* in the Galleria Doria Pamphilj.

erty of the Pamphilj family, who live in the opposite wing). Every inch of wall space in the ornate State Apartments is taken up with paintings, in keeping with the interior fashions of the time. The finest room here is the 18th-century Gallery of Mirrors – a Versailles in miniature. The light pouring in from the windows on both sides is reflected in the mirrors and gold frames to dazzling effect. The gallery is lined with sculptures, and ceiling frescoes depict the Labours of Hercules.

The collection was begun by Pamphilj Pope Innocent X, who was crowned in 1644, and expanded by subsequent generations. One of the museum's prize possessions is the portrait of Innocent X by Velázquez (painted in 1649), with a penetrating gaze and a certain ruthlessness in his expression. It's a masterpiece of realism, but the Pope was not flattered by it, dismissing it with the complaint that it was "too true". Three hundred years later, Francis Bacon made a famous copy. Nearby is a bust of the Pope by Bernini.

Other important works include Titian's *Salomé* (one theory suggests that John the Baptist's head is a self portrait of Titian and Salomé that of a lover who rejected him), a double portrait by Raphael, and two masterpieces by a young Caravaggio – *Rest on the Flight to Egypt*, much lighter than the rest of his oeuvre, and the *Magdalene*.

Government buildings

Rome is still the centre of Italian government, and there are two important government offices in heavily guarded old *palazzi* in this area. Behind Piazza Colonna, **Palazzo di Montecitorio** ❹ is where the Chamber of Deputies has met since 1871. Before that, it was the Papal Tribunal of Justice. Bernini drew up plans for the building in 1650, and Carlo Fontana saw the design and building through to completion in 1697. Virtually all that remains of the 17th-century design is the convex curve of the façade – designed to make the building look even bigger than it is – and the rusticated columns.

The Egyptian obelisk in front of the *palazzo* dates from the 6th century BC. It was used by Emperor Augustus for an enormous sundial he laid out in 10 BC. The sundial was discovered in the crypt of the nearby church of San Lorenzo in Lucina.

Another ancient relic that was adapted to modern usage lies in the nearby Piazza di Pietra, east of Piazza della Rotonda. The **Palazzo della Borsa** (currently under restoration) takes its name from its one-time role as Rome's stock exchange. Prior to that, the building, with its 11 ancient columns, was a customs house, and originally, in the 2nd century AD, it was the Temple of Hadrian, which is how it is mostly referred to now.

The Senate has occupied the elegant **Palazzo Madama** ❺ (which is also being restored) between Piazza della Rotonda and Piazza Navona

since 1870. It was built for the Medici family in the early 16th century, and several of its members lived here before becoming Pope, including Leo X (1513–21) and Clement VII (1523–34). Catherine de' Medici lived here until she married Francis I of France in 1533.

The palace gets its name from the Habsburg Madama Margherita (1522–86), the illegitimate daughter of Emperor Charles V and the wife of Alessandro de' Medici.

Caravaggio chapel

Opposite is the Baroque church of **San Luigi dei Francesi** ❻ (7.30am–12.30 pm and 3.30–7pm, closed Thur pm), the French national church in Rome, built in 1589. It contains works by Giacomo della Porta and Domenico Fontana, but it is the three Caravaggio masterpieces in the Capella Contarelli, showing scenes from the life of St Matthew (*The Calling of St Matthew*, *The Martyrdom of St Matthew* and *St Matthew and the Angel* – painted between 1599 and 1602) that make a visit very worthwhile. These won-

The 6th-century BC Egyptian obelisk stands in front of the Palazzo di Monte-citorio, home to the lower house of government.

RIGHT:
Palazzo Madama, seat of the Senate.

Street artists and caricaturists make a good living from the regular flow of tourist traffic on Piazza Navona.

derful and moving paintings demonstrate Caravaggio's astounding mastery of light and dramatic realism. Have a euro handy to light the chapel up.

AROUND PIAZZA NAVONA

Piazza Navona ❼ is one of the most animated squares in Rome, invariably full of Romans and foreign visitors wandering among stalls set up by hopeful artists or relaxing with a coffee in one of the many bars, or stopping for a chat by its gushing fountains.

Piazza Navona was built over the remains of the emperor Domitian's ancient athletics stadium: the stand forms part of the foundations of the flanking houses, and you can see one of the original entrances just behind the north end of the square.

The stadium originally measured 50 by 275 metres (150 by 825 ft), with the seats rising to 35 metres (105 ft). It was used for athletic contests and horse races, and was probably still in use when the Goths invaded in the 5th century. However, the plundering of its fabric began under Con-

RIGHT: *St Matthew and the Angel* by Caravaggio.
BELOW: Piazza Navona.

stantius II (third son of Constantine the Great), who carried off works of art and decorative features in 356 to adorn his new residence in Constantinople, after the seat of the Empire had been moved there.

Recommended Restaurants, Bars & Cafés on pages 166–7

Three fountains

The piazza owes its Baroque appearance to the Pamphilj Pope, Innocent X (1644–55), who enlarged his family palace and commissioned the square's magnificent centrepiece, Bernini's **Fontana dei Quattro Fiumi** (Fountain of the Four Rivers). The rivers in question – the Danube, the Ganges, the Nile and the Plate – are represented by four huge allegorical figures who in turn represent the four continents Europe, Asia, Africa and America. The Nile is blindfolded because the source of the river was then still a mystery. Rising above the statues is an obelisk taken from the Circus of Maxentius. The obelisk is topped by the figure of a dove with an olive branch to show that this once pagan monument has been converted into a Christian one.

To the south of the square is the **Fontana del Moro** (Fountain of the Moor). Its central figure (which looks more like a Triton than a Moor) was designed by Bernini.

The **Fontana del Nettuno** (Fountain of Neptune) at the northern end was originally just a large basin. The sculptures were added in the 19th century to create symmetry.

Churches and palaces

Pope Innocent also commissioned the Borromini façade of **Sant' Agnese in Agone**. Here, it is said, the saint was pilloried and stood naked in the stocks until her hair miraculously grew to protect her modesty. Inside the church there are underground chambers where you can see the ruins of the stadium of Domitian, a Roman mosaic floor and medieval frescoes on the wall.

To the left of the church is **Palazzo Doria Pamphilj** (not to be confused

TIP

From December until early January, Piazza Navona hosts a colourful Christmas fair at which all sorts of decorations, toys, sweets and Baroque-style Nativity scenes are sold, culminating in a carnival on the night before Epiphany (6 January).

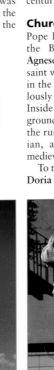

LEFT: fountain of Neptune. **BELOW LEFT:** one of the four allegorical figures in Bernini's Fountain of the Four Rivers. **BELOW:** Fountain of the Moor.

Talking Statues

Rome's "talking statues" were the mouthpiece of discontent in the city during the Renaissance

Rome's "talking statues" are a tradition born in the 1500s, when the citizens were governed directly by the Papacy. To avoid punishment they would secretly hang their caustic criticism, stinging epigrams and short satiric verses on a statue. This political dissidence often took place at night, the Romani enjoying a good laugh in the morning before the insults were removed by the authorities. The statues were sometimes draped with poems or jokes, but most often the postings were broadsides against the Vatican. The statues soon earned nicknames, the best-known being the Pasquino (Piazza di Pasquino, *see page 163*). This torso of a male figure, possibly from the 3rd century BC, is in such poor condition that it is hard to know who, or what, it represents. The roots of his nickname are recounted in a Roman legend saying he was "discovered" near a barber's shop or inn run by a Signore Pasquino.

The best-known "pasquinate" barb is a pun against Pope Urban VIII. This Pope from the Barberini family commanded Bernini to strip the ancient Roman bronze parts of the Pantheon to make the great baldacchino canopy for St Peter's altar. "*Quod non fecerunt barbari, fecerunt Barberini*" ("What the barbarians didn't do, the Barberini did") quipped Pasquino. This statuesque satire became so fervent that Pope Adrianus VI (1522–23) wanted Pasquino cast into the Tiber. The risk of ridicule for punishing a lump of stone saved the statue from the river bed – but severe laws were issued to stop the practice, and Pasquino was put under surveillance.

Marforio is known as Pasquino's friend. He and Pasquino were a bantering double act: one posing questions about politics and popes, the other retorting ironically. Marforio's statue – a reclining river god – is now in the Capitoline Museum; he was silenced when he was removed from the Roman Forum and placed in the museum by the Vatican for "safe keeping".

The Facchino (Porter) is a small fountain on Via Lata (just off the Via del Corso). Dressed in a typical porter's costume, nobody knows who made the statue – though it was once, wrongly, attributed to Michelangelo.

Madama Lucrezia sits on the corner of Piazza San Marco (next to Piazza Venezia). This marble is probably associated with the goddess Isis. Her nickname derives from a 15th-century Lucrezia who fell in love with the married king of Naples. Lucrezia came to Rome to ask the Pope to let the king divorce, but permission was denied. When the king died, Lucrezia moved to Rome – living near the Piazza San Marco.

The statue of the Babuino (Baboon) gives the Via del Babuino its name. This diminutive statue of Silenus (the ancient Greek woodland satyr) reclines on a fountain outside the church of St Athanasius. His wicked grin and his grubby brown torso make him one of the best-known of the talking statues – which became known collectively as *il Congresso degli Arguti* (the Shrewd Congress).

Until very recently the Babuino was still opining, with modern Romans venting their spleen in graffito and messages on the wall behind him. In a strange echo of past political censorship, the "messages" on the wall were recently cleaned up. But don't expect him to be quiet for long. ❏

ABOVE: Marforio, Pasquino's friend. **LEFT:** the marble torso on Piazza Pasquino is still festooned with comments on the events of the day.

with the Galleria Doria Pamphilj), designed by Rainaldi in the mid-17th century. It now houses the Brazilian Embassy.

Just off the square is the church of **Santa Maria della Pace** ❽ (Mon and Fri 10am–4pm, Tue–Thur 9am–noon), which was rebuilt in 1482 and then restored in 1656, when the convex, Baroque façade was added. The church contains Raphael's frescoes of *The Four Sybils*.

The nearby **Santa Maria dell' Anima** (daily 9am–1pm and 3–7pm) is the German-speaking church of Rome and was founded in 1500, although the present building was heavily restored in the 19th century. Apart from a Romano altarpiece, most of the works of art inside are by pupils and followers of Caravaggio, Michelangelo and Raphael.

Palazzo Altemps ❾

✉ 48 Piazza di Sant'Apollinare (nr Piazza Navona) ☎ 06-3996 7700 ⏰ Tue–Sun 9am–7.45pm ⊚ charge (combination ticket valid for three days includes Palazzo Massimo alle Terme, the Baths of Diocletian and Crypta Balbi) 🚌 30, 40, 46, 62, 64, 70, 81, 87, 116, 492, 571, 628, 916

Just north of Piazza Navona, Palazzo Altemps is one of the four sites of the Museo Nazionale Romano which holds the state collection of ancient treasures; the rest of the collection is split between Palazzo Massimo alle Terme, the Terme di Diocleziano, and the Crypta Balbi *(see page 173)*.

Full of tranquil rooms set around a central courtyard, this airy museum contains many treasures of classical statuary and art, most of which come from the priceless collection amassed by Cardinal Ludovisi. The prize exhibit is the Ludovisi Throne, a dec-

Remedies for the sweet of tooth and fractious children. Gumdrops in this tempting display are poetically named "tears of love".

LEFT: the Ludovisi Throne. **BELOW:** courtyard of the Palazzo Altemps.

FOOD

Avoid the overpriced cafés on the Piazza Navona. For a glass of wine and plate of cheese, cold cuts, pâté or any combination of snacks and salads, the Cul de Sac wine bar on Piazza di Pasquino is a good place to know about.

orative Greek sculpture, thought to date from the 5th century BC, which Mussolini sold to Hitler in 1938, and which is now believed to be one of a pair. Upstairs, the vaulting of the loggia is intricately painted with a vine-covered pergola full of winged putti, flowers, fruits and exotic birds, inspired by the flora and fauna imported by the explorers of the New World. It is lined with busts of the 12 Caesars.

RIGHT: Sant'Ivo.
BELOW: hidden courtyard of the Centro Storico.

Other masterpieces here include an incredibly well-preserved carved sarcophagus from the 3rd century and the moving *Galata Suicide*, said to have been commissioned by Julius Caesar, purchased by the cardinal at the same time as the *Dying Gaul*, now in the Capitoline Museum *(see page 94)*.

The *palazzo* also contains many frescoes and bas-reliefs, a private chapel, and parts of the ancient Roman houses on which its foundations can be seen.

East of Piazza Navona, on the parallel Corso del Rinascimento, is the **Palazzo della Sapienza**, which housed the headquarters of Rome's oldest university, La Sapienza, until it moved to the Stazione Termini area in 1935. It is now home of the State Archives. In the square is Borromini's **Sant'Ivo** ❿ (Sun 9am–noon only), a Roman Baroque church with a striking, white, spiralling bell-tower and unusual façade. On the main altar is a 1661 canvas by da Cortona showing St Ivo and other saints surrounded by angels.

Piazza di Pasquino

Off the southern end of Piazza Navona is **Piazza di Pasquino ⓫**. The mutilated marble torso leaning against the wall is thought to date from the 3rd century BC. It was found in Piazza Navona and brought here in the 15th century when it became one of Rome's "talking statues".

There were several of these across the city. At night, discontented citizens would express their disgust with the status quo by pinning criticisms to these statues. The penalty for this was death, regardless of rank and including clerics, but there is no record of the penalty being carried out *(see page 160)*.

The statue leans against a wall of the **Palazzo Braschi**, one of the last papal palaces built in Rome, in the 18th century. The *palazzo* is home to the newly renovated Museo di Roma.

Museo di Roma ⓬

✉ 10 Piazza San Pantaleo; www.museodiroma.comune.roma.it ☎ 06-8205 9127 ◷ Tue–Sun 9am–7pm ◉ charge ⬛ as for Palazzo Altemps

The Palazzo Braschi was built by Cosimo Morelli in the closing years of the 18th century as a papal residence for Pius VI (the chapel and staircase are by Valadier). It houses a sizeable collection of art and artefacts which document the daily life of Roman nobility from medieval times to the beginning of the 20th century.

Part of the collection is housed in the Museo di Roma in Trastevere, and the rest is shown in rotation. Most interesting among the paintings, which are of more historic than artistic value, is the series illustrating Roman festivities and processions.

Palazzo Massimo alle Colonne, next door to the Braschi, was designed in 1536 by Baldassare Peruzzi for the

Fine stucco-work allegory of Spring in the Palazzo Braschi.

BELOW: *The Puppet Theatre*, by Achille Pinelli (1809–41), in the Museo di Roma.

Massimo family, who occupy it to this day. The building is screened by a fine curved portico of Doric columns visible from the Via del Paradiso. Behind the palace, in Piazza de' Massimi, is an ancient column that may have come from the remains of Domitian's stadium.

AROUND CORSO VITTORIO EMANUELE II

Towards the Tiber end of the Corso Vittorio Emanuele II stands the 16th-century **Chiesa Nuova** , built for San Filippo Neri, founder of a great spiritual order. St Philip had wished the interior to be plain, but in the centuries after his death his disciples commissioned da Cortona to paint the magnificent frescoes that decorate the vault, apse and dome. Among the church's other treasures are three altarpieces by Rubens.

Next to the church is the **Oratorio dei Filippini**, built by Borromini between 1637 and 1662 as a place of worship for St Philip Neri's fraternity. St Philip was a strong believer in the spiritual benefit of music and instituted the musical gatherings that

later became known as oratorios. The building now houses the Capitoline Historical Archives. Its façade (badly in need of a good clean) was inspired by "the human body with open arms so as to embrace everyone who enters".

In **Piazza della Chiesa Nuova** is a 17th-century fountain that came from the Campo de' Fiori. On the rim of its basin is the inscription: *Ama Dio e non fallire – Fa del bene e lascia dire* (Love God and don't fail – Do good and make sure people talk about it).

TIP

For nearly a century, La Mostra dell'Antiquariato, a twice-yearly antiques market, has been held on Via dei Coronari. Every May and October dealers literally roll out the red carpet along the street and stay open for late-night shopping, while torches and candles light the way.

ABOVE RIGHT: on Via del Pellegrino.
BELOW: delivery for an antique shop on Via dei Coronari.
BELOW RIGHT: waiting for customers.

The nearby **Palazzo del Governo Vecchio** was the residence of the governor of Rome from 1624 until the mid-18th century.

The embankment

A little further west along Corso Vittorio Emanuele II is the **Palazzo del Banco di Santo Spirito**. Its façade (1520s) is by Antonio da Sangallo the Younger. From here, Via Banco di Santo Spirito leads to the lovely **Ponte Sant'Angelo ⓮**. The three central arches were part of the bridge Hadrian built in AD 136 to link his mausoleum – now the Castel Sant' Angelo *(see page 143)* – to the centre of the city. Most of the present bridge dates from the 17th century, but it was altered in the late 19th century to accommodate the new Tiber embankment. The glorious angels along the parapet were designed by Bernini in the 1660s.

At the southern end of the next bridge upriver, Ponte Umberto I, is the **Museo Napoleonico ⓯** (tel: 06-6880 6286; Tue–Sun 9am–7pm; admission charge). Among the Bonaparte family memorabilia is a cast of

the right breast of Napoleon's sister, Pauline, made by Canova in 1805, when he started work on the reclining nude in the Galleria Borghese *(see page 192).*

The nearby **Via dell'Orso** used to be lined with inns and was a favourite haunt of courtesans. Today, the area is better-known for its antique shops, interspersed with classy boutiques selling modern designer furniture. The **Via dei Coronari ⓰** is packed with some of the best antiques and fine-arts shops in Rome. ❑

The eye-rolling, ecstatic expressions of Bernini's ten angels on the Ponte Sant'Angelo have earned them the nickname "the breezy maniacs".

LEFT AND BELOW:
The traffic-free Ponte Sant' Angelo is Rome's loveliest bridge.

BEST RESTAURANTS, BARS AND CAFÉS

Restaurants

Price includes dinner and a half-bottle of house wine:
€ = under €25
€€ = €25–40
€€€ = €40–60
€€€€ = more than €60

L'Altro Mastai

✉ 53 Via G. Giraud ☎ 06-6830 1296 ⏰ D only Tue–Sat. €€€€ [p335, C4]
This gourmet restaurant specialising in Mediterranean haute cuisine is a firm favourite amongst the city's foodies. The chef, Fabio Baldassare, trained with Heinz Beck of the superlative La Pergola restaurant *(see page 145)*. The dishes can be sensational, but at an average cost of €100 a head expectations are not always met. Closed Aug.

Da Baffetto

✉ 114 Via del Governo Vecchio ☎ 06-686 1617 ⏰ D only daily. € [p335, C4]
One of the city's legendary pizzerias. Not the best pizza in town, but almost, its typically thin base is always on the right side of crusty. Service is brisk and the turnaround is fast, but if you go early or late, it is more relaxed. Be prepared to queue as no bookings are taken. No frills, no tablecloths, no credit cards. Closed two weeks Aug.

Il Bicchiere di Mastai

✉ 52 Via dei Banchi Nuovi ☎ 06-6819 2228 ⏰ L & D daily. €€ [p335, C4]
The right venue for a light (but not necessarily cheap) and memorable meal. Swordfish *carpaccio* with mango and sea bass *carpaccio* with a lemon vinaigrette sauce may be on the menu. For dessert try the ricotta served with plums marinated in armagnac.

Casa Bleve

✉ 48–49 Via del Teatro Valle ☎ 06-686 5970 ⏰ L & D Tue–Sat. €–€€ [p335, D4]
Casa Bleve is set against the stunning backdrop of the restored Palazzo Medici Lante della Rovere. An enormous semicircular counter is laden with all kinds of cold meats, salads and cheeses. Beyond, there's seating in a large, atmospherically lit room. With an exceptional wine list, this is a high-level *enoteca* worth seeking out. Closed three weeks Aug.

Convivio Troiani

✉ 31 Vicolo dei Soldati ☎ 06-686 9432 ⏰ D only Mon–Sat, L by request for groups of 8 and over. €€€€ [p335, D3]
Run by three brothers, Il Convivio is one of the city's foremost gastronomic temples.

Equal emphasis is placed on vegetable, fish and meat options, but they are always combined with something unexpected. Three elegant rooms and well-trained staff make for a truly rounded gourmet experience.

Cul de Sac

✉ 73 Piazza di Pasquino ☎ 06-6880 1094 ⏰ L & D daily. €–€€ [p335, D4]
One of the best-stocked wine bars in Rome. Space may be tight, but the atmosphere, prices and array of cheeses, cold meats, Middle Eastern-influenced snacks, hearty soups and salads all hit the right spot. It gets packed, so be prepared to queue as bookings aren't taken. Open late.

Il Fico

✉ 49 Via di Monte Giordano ☎ 06-687 5568 ⏰ L & D daily, in winter D only Mon. €€ [p335, C4]
This friendly eatery is very reasonably priced for its location, a stone's throw from Piazza Navona. All dishes are made with fresh seasonal ingredients. Try the pasta with mussels, pecorino cheese and cherry tomatoes.

Fortunato al Pantheon

✉ 55 Via del Pantheon ☎ 06-679 2788 ⏰ L & D Mon–Sat. €€–€€€ [p335, D4]
A place for those who don't want to take risks but want to eat well and be served quickly and efficiently. People keep coming back for the simple classical dishes, such as spinach and ricotta ravioli cooked with butter and sage, grilled squid or veal served with rocket.

Maccheroni

✉ 44 Piazza delle Coppelle ☎ 06-6830 7895. ⏰ L & D daily. €€ [p335, D3]
A lively trattoria with several rooms and some outdoor tables. It attracts a youngish clientele drawn by fair prices and competent, typical cuisine.

Myosotis

✉ 3–5 Vicolo della Vaccarella ☎ 06-686 5554 ⏰ L & D Tue–Sat, D only Mon. €€ [p335, D3]
A discreet, high-level restaurant with an exemplary wine list. A gourmet experience at an affordable price.

O' Pazzariello

✉ 19 Via Banco di Santo Spirito ☎ 06-6819 2641 ⏰ D only Tue–Fri, L & D Thur–Sun. € [p334, C4]

ABOVE RIGHT: Giolitti ice-cream parlour.

With an exhibitionist pizza-cook and *simpatico* waiting-staff, this is a sure bet for a fun and affordable evening. The pizzas are thick-crusted and range from small to gigantic.

Osteria dell'Ingegno

✉ 45 Piazza di Pietra
☎ 06-678 0662 ⏱ L & D
Mon–Sat. €€ [p335, E4]
Much frequented by politicians due to its location near parliament, this modern *osteria* specialises in light, inventive dishes. The sweets are home-made and the wines well chosen.

L'Osteria di Memmo

✉ 22 Via dei Soldati
☎ 06-6813 5112 ⏱ L & D
Mon–Sat. €€–€€€
[p335, D3]
In an old *palazzo*, three elegant rooms have been made over in modern minimalist style. The menu is creative, though first courses are a bit hit and miss. However, the main courses, desserts and wines compensate for any shortcomings.

Riccioli Café

✉ 13 Via delle Coppelle
☎ 06-6821 0313 ⏱ B, Br,
L & D daily (10–2am).
€–€€€ [p335, D3]
Riccioli Café was the first oyster bar in the city and serves sushi and sashimi, all beautifully displayed on wooden counters. It's one of the buzziest bars in the area at *aperitivo* hour.

La Rosetta

✉ 8 Via della Rosetta ☎ 06-686 1002 ⏱ L & D Mon–Sat. €€€€ [p335, D4]
One of the best seafood restaurants in Rome, where the produce is guaranteed to have been caught that morning and prepared by an experienced chef. But unless you go for the "working lunch" or a set-price *degustazione* (tasting) menu, your bill is likely to tip the €100-a-head mark for a full meal.

Da Tonino

✉ 18 Via del Governo
Vecchio ☎ No phone
⏱ L & D Mon–Sat. €
[p335, C4]

As the weekend queues testify, this is one of Rome's best-loved eateries. Stark lighting, basic decor and excellent local food, served in generous portions and at fair prices. Thursday is fresh gnocchi and tripe night; Friday is fish and *pasta e ceci* (pasta and chickpeas) night. No credit cards.

Vecchia Locanda

✉ 2 Vicolo Sinibaldi ☎ 06-6880 2831 ⏱ D only
Mon–Sat. €€ [p335, D4]
In a pedestrianised alleyway, this rustic restaurant offers decent if a little unadventurous food. A nice touch is that you can choose which home-made pasta to go with which home-made sauce.

Bars and Cafés

For a genteel snack lunch or tea with home-made cake, head to the delightful **Caffè Novecento** (12 Via del Governo Vecchio) not far from Piazza Navona.

A good glass of wine can be had in the friendly and reasonably priced **I Spiriti** (5 Via Sant'Eustachio), which stocks 250 labels and spills out onto a piazza.

The **Tazza D'Oro** (84 Via degli Orfani) serves some of the tastiest coffee in town. Standing room only.

For ice cream, **Giolitti** (40 Via Uffici del Vicario) has been scooping dozens of flavours since 1900. There is an olde-worlde dining room inside. **Cremeria Monteforte** (22 Via della Rotonda) makes some of the tastiest and best-quality ice cream in Rome. The flavours are relatively few, but choosing is still difficult as they are all equally tantalising. Mini-cones are available to try a flavour out before committing to a whole ice cream.

La Caffettiera (65 Piazza di Pietra) is a smart café where you can enjoy Neapolitan goodies.

Le Coppelle (52 Piazza delle Coppelle) has a central location and a great line in cocktails. Outdoor seating in summer, and a cosmopolitan vibe.

Recommended Restaurants, Bars & Cafés on pages 181–3

CAMPO DE' FIORI AND THE GHETTO

People have lived and worked in this picturesque part of Rome since the Middle Ages. The tangle of cobbled streets and alleys lead to the vibrant Campo de' Fiori market square and beyond into Europe's longest-surviving Jewish community

The southern part of Rome's Centro Storico is a triangle of tightly packed streets between the Corso Vittorio Emanuele II, Via Arenula and the river, with the lively little market square of Campo de' Fiori at its hub. In ancient times, this area was part of the Field of Mars (Campus Martius), a main training ground for the Roman army *(see page 151)*, until Julius Caesar's reign when the moneyed citizens of Imperial Rome moved in and built great complexes and theatres. By the Middle Ages, the area was a warren of small, dark, narrow streets, with the eastern side occupied by the Ghetto, lively now but a poignant reminder of the Jewish community's suffering.

In 1880, the rulers of a newly unified Italy set about putting their mark on the city and built the Corso Vittorio over the ancient tract of Via Trionfale and the winding, medieval Via Papale, destroying beautifully proportioned Renaissance squares and buildings in the process.

The resulting avenue had none of the grandeur that was intended, and today it's a traffic-choked thoroughfare that disrupts the beauty and harmony of the medieval streets around it.

AROUND CORSO VITTORIO EMANUELE II

Set off down the Corso from the Ponte Vittorio Emanuele, then turn right into **Via dei Banchi Vecchi**, leaving the busy avenue behind. At No. 22 is the fanciful façade of **Palazzo dei Pupazzi**, built in 1504 and decorated with elaborate stucco designs by Mazzoni. This street leads to **Via del Pellegrino**, which winds past artisans' workshops, bookshops and antique dealers to **Palazzo della Cancelleria** ⑰, a splendid Renaissance

Main attractions

CAMPO DE' FIORI MARKET
MUSEO BARRACCO
AREA SACRA
IL GESÙ
CRYPTA BALBI
PIAZZA MATTEI
JEWISH GHETTO
THE SYNAGOGUE AND MUSEUM
PORTICO D'OTTAVIA
PALAZZO CENCI
PALAZZO SPADA
PIAZZA FARNESE
TIBER ISLAND
SANTA MARIA IN COSMEDIN
THEATRE OF MARCELLUS

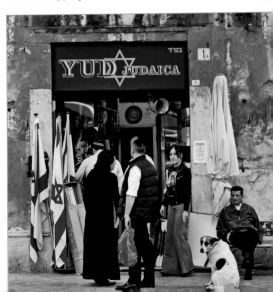

LEFT: Campo de' Fiori produce market.
RIGHT: Jewish quarter.

ABOVE RIGHT AND BELOW: flowers, produce, T-shirts and other novelty items for sale at Campo de' Fiori.

palace built between 1485 and 1527. The architect is unknown but the beautiful courtyard is attributed to Bramante, who also modified the adjoining 4th-century basilica of **San Lorenzo in Damaso**. Bramante had a reputation for destroying medieval monuments (the ancient St Peter's basilica is a prime example), which earned him the nickname *Maestro Ruinante* (Master Ruiner).

The palace was built for Cardinal Raffaele Riario, who is said to have financed it from the proceeds of one night's gambling, before being confiscated by the Pope and used as the Apostolic Chancery. It is not usually open to the public (it is still Vatican property), but is occasionally used as a venue for classical concerts.

Campo de' Fiori ⓲

South of the Cancelleria is the lively **Campo de' Fiori** (Field of Flowers), so named because it used to be a meadow that sloped down towards the Tiber. It has been the site of a produce market for centuries and was one of the liveliest areas of medieval and Renaissance Rome,

when cardinals and pilgrims would rub shoulders with fishmongers, vegetable-sellers and prostitutes.

The Campo de' Fiori is the most secular of Roman squares, for although it is as old as Rome itself, it has never been dedicated to any cult and to this day is free of churches. Its present aspect dates from the end of the 15th century, when the whole area was reshaped. It was surrounded by inns for pilgrims and travellers (there are still plenty of hotels in the area if you don't mind the noise). During the Renaissance, some of these hotels were the homes of successful courtesans, Vannozza Catanei, mistress of the Borgia Pope Alexander VI, among them. On the corner of the square and Via del Pellegrino you can see her shield, which she had decorated with her own coat of arms and those of her husband and lover.

Today, the Campo flourishes, thanks to a perfectly balanced infrastructure. It has everything from a butcher's and a baker's shop to clothes boutiques, a cinema and a bustling morning food market. At night, the Campo plays host to hundreds of Romans and visitors who frequent the bars and restaurants or simply hang out under the statue of Bruno, sipping beers until late into the night. Then the Campo has only a few hours to breathe before the market traders arrive to set up their stalls at the crack of dawn.

The streets around Campo de' Fiori still retain the names of trades originally practised in them. Via dei Baullari, the luggage-makers, leads to Piazza Farnese; Via dei Giubbonari, named after the sellers and makers of *gipponi* or bodices, is still lined with clothes shops, which are among some of the cheapest in town.

TIP

Via dei Cappellari was where the hat-makers congregated, but is now full of furniture restorers, gilders and carpenters practising their trade out on the street.

Museo Barracco ⑲

✉ 166 Corso Vittorio Emanuele; www.museobarracco.it
☎ 06-6880 6848 ⓒ Tue–Sun 9am–7pm ⓖ charge 🚌 30, 40, 46, 62, 64, 70, 81, 87, 116, 492, 628

LEFT: selecting the best at Campo de' Fiori.
BELOW: Roscioli Alimentari, for gourmet food.

Antique sculptures on display at the refurbished Museo Barracco.

Turning back up Via dei Baullari to Corso Vittorio, you reach **Palazzo Farnese** in Piazza San Pantaleo. Built for a French prelate, Thomas Leroy, in 1523 and decorated with fleurs-de-lis, this elegant Renaissance palace is now home to the Museo Barracco, a prestigious collection of antique sculpture. Artworks include Assyrian bas-reliefs, Attic vases, rare examples of Cypriot art and exceptional Phoenician, Etruscan and Roman pieces. It's easy to see why Giovanni Barracco, who spent his life collecting these masterpieces, called ancient sculpture "the mother of all the arts".

Further along Corso Vittorio, the magnificent church of **Sant' Andrea della Valle** ⑳ (9.45–11am; 4.30–6.15pm) has the second-largest dome in Rome after St Peter's. Its design is largely by Maderno, with frescoes by Lanfranco and Domenichino. The church is the setting for Act I of Puccini's much-loved opera, *Tosca.*

The church stands over some of the remains of the **Teatro di Pompeo**, a huge complex that spread from Campo de' Fiori to the temples at Largo Argentina. It was built in 55 BC as part of a plan to introduce some culture to Rome, but the Romans preferred the blood-and-guts entertainment of gladiators, fake battles and animal fights. You can ask one of the priests to take you downstairs for a look.

Next to the theatre was the **Curia Pompeia** where Julius Caesar was stabbed to death on the Ides of March (15 March), 44 BC. Remains of the theatre have been discovered in the cellars of the surrounding houses, and are visible at the Da Pancrazio and Da Costanzo restaurants, and in the breakfast room of Hotel Teatro di Pompeo, for those in the mood to eat or sleep amid famous ruins.

Largo di Torre Argentina

Next stop on Corso Vittorio is Largo di Torre Argentina, one of the busiest crossroads in the city and a major bus interchange. Its architecture – *palazzi*, banks and insurance companies – isn't very exciting. Only **Teatro Argentina**, a state-funded theatre and official home of the Teatro di Roma, radiates any atmosphere.

The Cat Women of Rome

The city's stray cat population numbers in the hundreds of thousands. Originally said to have boarded Rome-bound ships from Egypt, the felines made themselves at home among the ancient monuments. Since the excavation of the **Area Sacra** in 1929, stray cats have been taking refuge in the protected area below street level, sunning themselves amid the ruins at Largo di Torre Argentina. As their numbers grew, volunteer cat caretakers, referred to as *gattare* (cat women) fed and cared for the cats until an official sanctuary was established in 1993. The organisation receives donations and support from all over the world, and has even established a cat adoption agency. Visit the centre for more information and a look at some of Rome's oldest residents. Largo di Torre Argentina; www.romancats.de; tel: 06-454 2540; open daily noon– 6pm.

The real attractions lie in the middle of the square, several metres underground. During attempts to improve the road system in the 1920s, archaeologists excavated four temples (street levels in ancient times were some 10 metres/30 ft below today's level). The **Area Sacra** ㉑ dates from Republican times, around the 3rd and 4th centuries BC. It is not known to which gods the temples were consecrated, so they are known simply as temples A, B, C and D. Some of the remains, inhabited by Rome's many stray cats *(see opposite)*, can be seen from above.

East of the square is the large church of the **Gesù** ㉒ (7am–12.45pm and 4–8pm), more properly called Santissimo Nome di Gesù. Built between 1568 and 1584 with funds provided by the rich and powerful Cardinal Alessandro Farnese, it was Rome's first Jesuit church. The flamboyance of its design and decoration look forward to the Baroque churches of the next century. The founder of the Jesuit order, St Ignatius Loyola, is buried in the opulent Cappella di Sant'Ignazio di Loyola, built by Andrea del Pozzo in 1696. Above the chapel's altar is a statue of the saint, framed by gilded lapis lazuli columns.

Crypta Balbi ㉓

✉ 31 Via delle Botteghe Oscure
☎ 06-678 0167 ⊙ Tue–Sun 9am–7.30pm ⊚ charge ⊟ 46, 62, 70, 87, 186, 492, 571, 810, 916

Not far from the Gesù church is the Crypta Balbi, one of the four homes of the Museo Nazionale Romano collection *(see page 161)*. This huge courtyard, originally annexed to a theatre built for Augustus at the end of the 1st century AD, was excavated in 1981 and forms the basis for the fascinating Crypta Balbi Museum, inaugurated in 2000.

The museum combines state-of-the-art technology with the preservation and interpretation of archaeological finds on the site itself, tracing the development of Roman society from antiquity to modern times. The ruins beneath the structure can be visited once an hour (on the hour) for short periods, and reveal the expansive lobby of the theatre, built by Cornelius Balbus, a friend of Augustus.

Piazza Mattei ㉔

Just south of here is the cosy little **Piazza Mattei**, with a funky bar, a couple of trendy boutiques and one of Rome's most delightful fountains as

Ceiling detail in the Gesù church.

LEFT: Fontana delle Tartarughe.
BELOW: Crypta Balbi.

The Ghetto is a great place to find that unique hybrid, Roman-Jewish food, and other non-Italian delicacies. Try the kosher fast food and falafel at Mkosher, 64–5 Via Santa Maria del Pianto; dunk your blinis in a cup of Prince Vladimir tea at the Russian Tea Room, 7/9 Via dei Falegnami. Or if it's bagels, muffins and chocolate-chip cookies you're after, head for La DolceRoma bakery, an Austrian-owned spot at 20b Via del Portico d'Ottavia.

ABOVE: water pump in the Ghetto.
BELOW LEFT AND RIGHT: snapshots of the Jewish Ghetto.

its centrepiece. The **Fontana delle Tartarughe** (Tortoise Fountain) was sculpted by Taddeo Landini in 1585 and depicts four youths gently pushing four tortoises towards the water above. The tiny bronze turtles were added later, possibly by Bernini. **Palazzo Mattei** opposite houses the Emeroteca music academy.

JEWISH GHETTO

The Ghetto lies in the area between Largo Argentina, the river, Via Arenula and Teatro di Marcello. The first wave of Jewish settlers came in the 2nd century BC, and thrived

peacefully here until Titus' victory over Jerusalem in AD 70, after which their status changed from free men to slaves (the Colosseum workforce was largely made up of Jewish slaves).

In the centuries that followed, their fortunes and status fluctuated. In the Middle Ages the Jewish population enjoyed relative freedom, and were generally appreciated for their financial and medical skills. But then in 1555, Pope Paul IV's zero-tolerance policy culminated in a papal bull ordering the confinement of the Jewish population into an enclosed area around the Portico d'Ottavia, which became known from then on as the Ghetto. The area was surrounded by high walls with doors that were locked from the outside at night.

The walls of the Ghetto were destroyed in the revolutionary year of 1848. When Rome fell to King Emmanuel's troops in 1870, ending papal dominion over the city, the Jews were finally given the same rights as other Italian citizens. But persecution resumed with the outbreak of World War II, when the Fascist regime deported thousands of Jews to Nazi concentration camps.

Today, the area retains its Jewish heritage, and the streets are dotted with kosher shops and restaurants.

The Synagogue ㉕

✉ Tempio Maggiore, Lungotevere Cenci; museum: www.museoebraico. roma.it ☎ 06-6840 0661 ⏰ Sun–Thur 10am–5pm, June–Sept until 7pm ⊙ charge 🚌 30, 40, 46, 62, 63, 64, 70, 81, 87, 186, 204, 271, 492, 571, 628, 630, 780

The Synagogue, consecrated in 1904, was built to a great height to send a message to the Vatican across the Tiber. On 13 April 1986, Pope John Paul II and Rabbi Elio Toaff held a historic meeting here marking the first time that a bishop of Rome had prayed in a Jewish house of worship.

Attached to the Synagogue (make sure you carry some form of ID, as security is strict) is the **Museum of Jewish Culture**. Reopened in 2006 after careful renovations, the museum recounts the story of Rome's Jewish population through art, relics and a documentary film. Six new exhibition spaces contain treasures from the community, including Renaissance-era embroidery, stunning ritual items and original marble blocks from some of the *Cinque Scole*, Rome's five ancient synagogues.

Portico d'Ottavia ㉖

The church of **Sant'Angelo in Pescheria** (currently being restored), where Jews were once forced to attend penitential services, was built on the ruins of the Portico d'Ottavia, originally the entrance to a colonnaded walkway erected in 147 BC by Augustus to display statues captured from Greece. It was dedicated to his sister, Octavia, the abandoned wife of Mark Antony. In the Middle Ages, the ruin was used as a covered

fish market – above the arch of the portico, there is a Latin inscription demanding that all the fish exceeding the length marked have to be decapitated and their heads given to Conservatori (this was the preferred part for making fish soup).

Via del Portico d'Ottavia still has several medieval houses. At the end (No. 1) is **Casa di Lorenzo Manilo** (not open to the public). Lorenzo Manilo had this house built in 1468 and adorned it with a classical plaque. The Latin inscription dating the building employs the ancient Roman calendar that used the founding of Rome as its starting point. According to this, the year 1468 was 2221. Original Roman reliefs are embedded in the façades, as well as a fragment of an ancient sarcophagus.

TOWARDS PIAZZA FARNESE

A short distance west of here is the **Palazzo Cenci** ㉗, the family palace of the infamous Beatrice Cenci, who attracted sympathy for killing her brutal father, but was nevertheless condemned to death for witchcraft

The shop on the corner of Via del Portico d'Ottavia is a famous Jewish bakery specialising in a ricotta and black cherry torte. Ask for a slice of torta di ricotta e visciole. The tiny Forno del Ghetto is technically open Mon–Thur 8am–8pm, but the goodies are often gone by noon.

BELOW: in the narrow streets of the Ghetto.

TIP

The best way to get a glimpse of the magnificent frescoed ceilings of Palazzo Farnese is to walk by just after sundown, while people are still inside, and lights are on. If you're en route to dinner in the area it's worth a look.

and murder, and beheaded on Ponte Sant'Angelo in 1599. Only parts of the original medieval building remain. The present façade and details are Baroque. Note the architectural quirk of an indented balcony on the front facing Via Arenula.

Crossing back over Via Arenula, Via degli Specchi leads to **Palazzo Monte di Pietà**, which was set up as a pawnshop in the 16th century and is still used as an auction house, open to the public every morning. From here, turn left and then right into Via Capo di Ferro.

Palazzo Spada ㉘

✉ 3 Via Capo di Ferro; www.galleria borghese.it 📞 06-687 4896
🕒 Tue–Sun 8.30am–7.30pm
🎫 charge 🚌 23, 30, 40, 46, 62, 63, 64, 70, 81, 116, 280, 492, 571, 628, 630, 780, 916

The large building on your left, with the façade covered in stucco reliefs by Mazzoni, is Palazzo Spada. The Spada family bought the palace in 1632 and Borromini restored it, adding the ingenious corridor to the courtyard. Borromini raised the floor and shortened the columns to create a false sense of perspective, making the corridor appear much longer than it actually is. At the end, a statue was placed against a painted garden backdrop. The statue is less than 1 metre (3 ft) tall but from afar it seems to be life-size.

The *palazzo* is also home to the **Galleria Spada**, which has a fine collection of paintings, including work by masters including Rubens, Domenichino, Guercino, Tintoretto, Reni and Artemisia.

ABOVE RIGHT:
Palazzo Spada.
BELOW: Piazza Farnese.

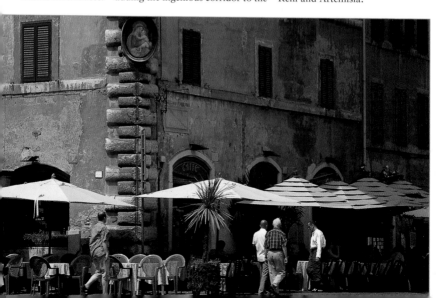

Piazza Farnese ㉙

The end of the street opens into Piazza Farnese, linked by a short street back to Campo de' Fiori. Its twin fountains incorporate two huge basins from the Baths of Caracalla *(see page 227)*. You'll want to linger in this picturesque square, and there's an inviting (if overpriced) bar where you can stop for refreshment.

The **Palazzo Farnese**, a masterpiece of High Renaissance architecture, was commissioned by Cardinal Alessandro Farnese in 1517 but only completed in 1589. The palace cost so much that for a while even the Farnese finances were strained. The original designs were by da Sangallo, but Michelangelo took over the work. When he died, Vignola and della Porta finished it off. Annibale Caracci frescoed the main salon over the central doorway. In 1874 Palazzo Farnese became the French Embassy, and it is now open to the public only on special occasions.

Via Giulia

Near the palace is Via Giulia, named after Pope Julius II who commis-sioned it as a monument to the Apostolic Church. When Bramante began work on it in 1508, the intention was to make it Rome's most important thoroughfare, connecting the Vatican with Ponte Sisto and the Ripa Grande harbour, and thus the centre of papal Rome. The centre-piece of the street was to be the Palazzo dei Tribunali, but the building failed to get beyond the foundations stage.

The street became a prestigious address, and many high profile people lived in its sumptuous palaces, including Antonio da Sangallo, Raphael and Benvenuto Cellini. The parties in Via Giulia were among the best in Rome, and on one occasion wine gushed from the Mascherone Fountain for three full days.

All this is hard to believe now, as the street is quiet and lined with expensive antique shops and art galleries. The elegant arch crossing the street was designed by Michelangelo and was intended to connect Palazzo Farnese with the Villa Farnesina across the Tiber, but the bridge was never built.

Mascherone Fountain, Via Giulia.

BELOW LEFT:
Michelangelo's arch, part of an uncompleted bridge on Via Giulia.
BELOW:
Piazza Farnese.

TIP

If you're not too squeamish, pay a visit to the Criminology Museum (29 Via del Gonfalone; tel: 06-6830 0234; open Wed–Sun 9am–1pm and 2.30–6.30pm). It displays articles relating to some of Italy's most sensational crimes, the clues and evidence used to incriminate the culprits, and the gruesome instruments used to extract confessions and punish the guilty.

RIGHT: resident Tiber Island dog. **BELOW:** boat on the Tiber. **BELOW RIGHT:** a stroll on the river bank.

Next to the arch stands the church of **Santa Maria dell'Orazione e Morte** (Mass on Sun 6pm), which was redesigned by Ferdinand Fuga (1733). Fuga was a member of the Compagna della Buona Morte, an association whose purpose was to give a decent burial to the poor. Grotesque and macabre arabesques of human bones – children's skulls, collarbones, ribs – decorate the walls of the crypt. The walls and the ceiling are covered with reliefs and mosaics.

Adjacent to the church is **Palazzo Falconieri** ⓿, which was modernised by Borromini for the Falcone family and is framed by two falcons' heads on female torsos. It is now the Hungarian Academy, and occasionally opens for exhibitions and concerts.

Off Via Giulia, in Via Sant'Eligio, is the beautiful little 16th-century church of **Sant'Eligio degli Orefici** ⓿ (Mon–Fri 9.30am–1pm), designed by Raphael, with a dome by Peruzzi.

A little further along the street, past the derelict church of **San Filippo**, is the fortified building of the **Carceri Nuove** (New Prison), built in 1655 to replace the gruesome prisons of Tor

di Nona and the nearby torture chambers of the Savella family, who until then were the papal gaolers.

Continuing past the Palazzo dei Tribunali, you come to several important Renaissance *palazzi*, including da Sangallo the Younger's palace at No. 66 and one of Raphael's houses at No. 85. The street ends with the church of **San Giovanni dei Fiorentini** ⓷ (daily 7.30am–1pm and 4–7pm; art collection closed in July and August), built in various stages by Sansovino, da Sangallo the Younger, della Porta and Maderno. The façade was added in the 18th century. Inside, there is a delightful sculpture of St John by the

Boat Trips on the Tiber

Rome was slow to catch on to the tourist potential of the Tiber, but in 2003 a river service was launched. A fleet of steamboats, led by the flagship *Rea Silvia* (christened after the mother of Romulus and Remus, mythical founders of Rome) started sailing the Tiber between the Duca D'Aosta Bridge and Ponte Marconi in Trastevere.

A number of services are available, including pleasure trips with on-board commentary, night-time cruises with dinner on board, cruises to Ostia Antica and a hop-on €1-a-trip boat. These services run Wednesday to Sunday, except the hop-on boats which run daily (11am–5.30pm).

Boarding points are the following: Ponte Duca d'Aosta, Ponte Risorgimento, Ponte Cavour, Ponte Sant'Angelo, Ponte Sisto, Calata degli Anguillara and Ponte Marconi.

For information and bookings, tel: 06-9774 5496; www.batelli diroma.it.

Sicilian Mino del Reame over the sacristy door, and an impressive apse altar by Borromini with a marble group, the *Baptism of Christ*, by Antonio Raggi. Both Borromini and Maderno are buried in the church.

TIBER ISLAND �33

The Isola Tiberina is a pretty island in the middle of the Tiber. It has long been associated with healing. Legend has it that in 293 BC the Romans asked the Greeks, and their god Aesculapius in particular, for help overcoming a plague. They were sent a shipful of snakes, whose venom was used to cure ailments. The plague was defeated and a temple to Aesculapius duly erected. The church of **San Bartolomeo** was built on the ruins of this temple in the 10th century. The island is also the site of the Fatebenefratelli (the "do-good-brothers") hospital founded in 1548.

The two bridges linking Isola Tiberina to the shore are among the oldest structures still in use in Rome. The **Ponte Fabricio** (leading to the north bank) was built in 62 BC by the civil engineer Lucius Fabricius, and there's an inscription to prove it. The **Ponte Cestio** was built in 42 BC by Lucius Cestius and restored in AD 370. The central arch is all that remains from that date; the rest is a late 19th-century reconstruction. This bridge leads into the heart of Trastevere.

Off the eastern end of the island are the remains of Rome's first stone bridge (142 BC), known as the **Ponte Rotto** (Broken Bridge). Most of what remains is from a 1575 reconstruction by Gregory XIII, the rest of which was washed away in 1598. The modern bridge behind it, **Ponte Palatino**, is sometimes called the English Bridge, because it is the only stretch of road in Rome on which cars are driven on the left.

Monument to St Bartholomew, whose relics are housed in the church of San Bartolomeo on Tiber Island.

ABOVE LEFT: ruins of Ponte Rotto.
BELOW: Tiber Island, a picturesque route to Trastevere.

Legend has it that if you tell a lie while your hand is in the Bocca della Verità, or Mouth of Truth, it will be bitten off. In a famous scene in Sidney Pollack's 1953 classic Roman Holiday, *Gregory Peck fooled Audrey Hepburn into believing – for a minute – he'd lost his hand to the statue.*

BELOW: Piazza Santa Maria in Cosmedin.

Santa Maria in Cosmedin ㉔

✉ 18 Piazza Bocca della Verità
📞 06-678 1419 🕐 daily
9.30am–5.50pm 💶 free 🚌 23, 44, 63, 81, 95, 160, 170, 628, 715, 716, 781

Back on the mainland, east of the bridge, is the **Piazza della Bocca della Verità**, once the site of the Forum Boarium, the cattle market of Ancient Rome. The square is named after the Bocca della Verità *(see left)*, which is in the portico of the church of Santa Maria in Cosmedin. First built in the 6th century, with additions made throughout the centuries, the church is a lovely mixture of early Christian, medieval and Romanesque design. The floors were replaced with stunning Cosmati pavements, and a belltower was erected in the 12th century. You'll find a Roman bathtub on the altar, used for baptisms, and an 8th-century mosaic in the sacristy. The name Cosmedin is Greek (it means "splendid decoration"), and Rome's oldest Greek Christian community has been worshipping here since the 700s.

Temples of Hercules and Portunus

In the piazza are two well-preserved Republican-era temples. The round one was recently restored and determined by archaeologists to be the oldest marble structure in the city, built in the 1st century BC to Hercules. The nearby square temple is dedicated to Portunus, the god of harbours, which makes good sense considering the vicinity of the Tiber.

Theatre of Marcellus ㉟

What looks like a smaller version of the Colosseum attached to a Renaissance *palazzo* is in fact the remains of the Teatro di Marcello. The once-glorious performance space was completed under the reign of Emperor Augustus, who named if after his nephew Marcellus. In its heyday, the 20,000-seat theatre flaunted three tiers, each supported with a different style of column, from the basic Doric to the extravagant Corinthian, and the top level, which has collapsed, was adorned with decorative theatre masks. Call 06-6710 3819 for a guided tour. ❏

BEST RESTAURANTS, BARS AND CAFÉS

Restaurants

Price includes dinner and a half-bottle of house wine:

€ = under €25
€€ = €25–40
€€€ = €40–60
€€€€ = more than €60

Antica Trattoria Polese

🖾 40 Piazza Sforza Cesarini
📞 06-686 1709 🍴 L & D
Wed–Mon. €€ [p335, C4]
Less packed than its rowdier neighbour Da Luigi, Polese has the better outdoor seating in a small piazza off Corso Vittorio, and a more refined Roman menu based on what is available at the market that morning. In the evening, pizza is also on the menu.

Il Bacaro

🖾 27 Via degli Spagnoli
📞 06-687 2554
🍴 D only Mon–Sat. €€
[p335, D3]
Located in a small, quiet street behind the Pantheon, the Bacaro oozes charm, and is perfect for a romantic soirée. Its cobbled stone and trellised outdoor area, and tiny internal room are much sought after, so booking is essential.

La Bottega del Vino di Anacleto Bleve

🖾 9a Via Santa Maria del
Pianto 📞 06-686 5970
🍴 Tue–Sat L only. €
[p339, D1]

A quintessentially Roman *enoteca* (wine bar) whose buffet is loaded with dozens of delicacies such as smoked swordfish, salmon rolls, *sformati* (flans) and cod carpaccio. Locals come here for the good food, well-chosen wine list and the *simpatia* of its husband-and-wife owners, Tina and Anacleto. *Aperitivo* hour starts at 6.30pm and the *enoteca* closes at 8pm.

Ditirambo

🖾 74 Piazza della
Cancelleria 📞 06-687
1626 🍴 L & D Tue–Sun, D
only Mon. €€ [p339, C1]
The atmosphere is busy but convivial. The varied menu includes numerous and unusually creative vegetarian options, such as ricotta flan with raw artichokes and a pomegranate vinaigrette, and wholemeal pasta with red onions and pecorino cheese. There are many good cuts of meat and plentiful fish dishes. The desserts are home-made, fresh and heavenly; the wine list is extensive and the waiters happy to tell you all about it. Closed three weeks in Aug.

Ar Galletto

🖾 102 Piazza Farnese
📞 06-686 1714 🍴 L & D
Mon–Sat. €–€€ [p339, C1]
A simple trattoria with

Roman classics such as *spaghetti alla carbonara*, *abbacchio* (lamb) and *involtini* (meat rolls). The view of Michelangelo's Palazzo Farnese and Bernini's two fountains is unforgettable.

Da Giggetto al Portico d'Ottavia

🖾 22 Via del Portico
D'Ottavia 📞 06-686 1105
🍴 L & D Tue–Sun. €€
[p339, D1]
It may be very popular with tourists, but don't let that put you off. The standards are reliably high as they take their Roman-Jewish cooking very seriously here, and the service is equally efficient and pleasantly old-fashioned. Try one of

five menus, all of which usually include *carciofi alla giudia* (deep-fried whole artichokes), stuffed courgette flowers or salted cod fillets.

Il Gonfalone

🖾 7 Via del Gonfalone
📞 06-6880 1269 🍴 L & D
Mon–Sat, L only Sun. €€
[p334, C4]
This restaurant with lovely outdoor seating is an understated gourmet experience. Vegetarians, fish-lovers and meat-eaters are equally well served. The cuisine style is a nouvelle take on Mediterranean. There's a bar and lounge area downstairs where people drink and dance until the small hours.

Price includes dinner and a half-bottle of house wine:

€ = under €25
€€ = €25–40
€€€ = €40–60
€€€€ = more than €60

Hosteria del Pesce

🖂 32 Via di Monserrato
☎ 06-686 5617 ⊙ D only
Mon–Sat. €€€–€€€€
[p338, C1]
The scrubbed wood and streamlined interior set the tone for this quality restaurant which happily lives up to its pretensions. Hosteria del Pesce serves only the freshest fish, either raw or cooked, and the white-only wine list is judiciously composed.

Da Luigi

🖂 23–24 Piazza Sforza Cesarini ☎ 06-686 5946
⊙ L & D Tue–Sun. €€
[p335, C4]

Traditional (and therefore heavy) Roman fare at this always-packed venue on a small square off Corso Vittorio Emanuele. There's a pleasant breeze and a convivial atmosphere on the outdoor patio. Frequented by tourists and locals alike.

Il Pagliaccio

🖂 129a Via dei Banchi Vecchi ☎ 06-6880 6471
⊙ L & D Wed–Sat, D only Mon and Tue. €€€ [p335, C4]
This smart restaurant has a limited but creative menu with an emphasis on beautiful presentation and quality ingredients. It's expensive but, as its regular customers agree, well worth it.

Der Pallaro

🖂 15 Largo del Pallaro
☎ 06-6880 1488 ⊙ L & D

Tue–Sun. € [p339, C1]
This quintessentially Roman trattoria is owned by the jovial Fazi couple and is a reliable favourite for those with big appetites and smaller budgets. There is no menu, but for about €20 (house wine and water included) you are served several courses that will leave you more than satisfied. Unsophisticated but tasty; the artichokes are excellent and the desserts home-made. No fish. Open past midnight. No credit cards.

Dal Pompiere

🖂 38 Via S. Maria dei Calderari ☎ 06-686 8377
⊙ L & D Mon–Sat.
€€–€€€ [p339, D1]
Waistcoated waiters dance attendance on customers in the wood-panelled and frescoed rooms of this fine restaurant occupying the first floor of the Palazzo Cenci. The food is Roman-Jewish and consistently good – which means the tables are consistently full.

Renato e Luisa

🖂 25 Via dei Barbieri
☎ 06-686 9660 ⊙ D only
Tue–Sun. €–€€ [p339, D1]
A reliable and affordable trattoria in a rustic, simple setting, serving classic dishes accompanied by good house wines. You could start with fettuccine with pachino tomatoes and buffalo ricotta, followed by turkey cooked with rosemary and honey, rounded off with a perfect crème brûlée.

Roscioli

🖂 21 Via dei Giubbonari
☎ 06-687 5287 ⊙ L & D
Mon–Sat. €€ [p339, C1]
This family-run deli-cum-restaurant receives rave reviews for its authentic produce and inventive food combinations, such as their signature dish, *tonnarelli* with grouper fish, pistachios and fennel seeds. Cheerful, pleasant atmosphere.

Il Sanpietrino

🖂 15 Piazza Costaguti
☎ 06-6880 9595
⊙ D only Mon–Sat. €€€
[p339, D1]
Located in the former

LEFT: Da Giggetto al Portico d'Ottavia.
ABOVE RIGHT: Roscioli.

stables of a fabulous 18th-century *palazzo*, Oscar di Mauro's acclaimed restaurant serves a mixture of Ghetto food and Roman dishes inspired by his grandmother, who has cooked for Pavarotti.

Sora Margherita
🍽 30 Piazza delle Cinque Scole   📞 06-687 4216   🕐 L & D Tue–Thur, D only Fri & Sat, summer open Mon D and closed Sat. € [p339, D1]
A small, basic trattoria in the heart of the former Jewish Ghetto, serving simple and hearty fare (much of it vegetarian) accompanied by bread from renowned Trastevere bakery La Renella. The sweets are home-made, and the highly palatable local wine is from Velletri outside Rome. No credit cards.

Taverna degli Amici
🍽 37 Piazza Margana   📞 06-6992 0637   🕐 L & D Tue–Sat. €€–€€€

[p339, D1]
A refined alfresco restaurant in an ivy-draped square of the Ghetto district. It serves subtly different versions of Roman classics as well as plenty of interesting vegetarian dishes.

Trattoria Moderna
🍽 16–17 Vicolo dei Chiodaroli   📞 06-6880 3423   🕐 L & D Mon–Sat. €€ [p339, D1]
A lively restaurant with appealing decor. The owners are experienced Roman restaurateurs, and the menu is classical Mediterranean with some modern touches.

Zio Ciro
🍽 1 Via della Pace   📞 06-686 4802   🕐 D only daily. € [p335, D4]
Succulent, Neapolitan-style, thick-crusted pizzas (the Roman ones have thinner bases) and a range of pasta dishes and salads. Excellent value by Roman standards. Outdoor seating.

Bars and Cafés

Zi' Fenizia (64 Via Santa Maria del Pianto) has been declared the best takeaway pizzeria in the city by Gambero Rosso, Italy's answer to the Michelin guides. It's all kosher, and their signature pizza topping is a tasty combination of anchovy and endives.

Il Goccetto (14 Via dei Banchi Vecchi) has been serving good wines and even better cheeses for over two decades in this medieval bishop's palace with frescoed ceilings. Some 800 different labels are available for sale, of which about 40 can be tasted by the glass.

Award-winning ice-cream maker **Alberto Pica** (12 Via della Seggiola) has been making *gelato* all his life and is rather better at it than most. People travel from all over Rome to enjoy his superlative ice creams.

For a hot or cold drink, or an innovative cocktail any time of the day or night (until 2am), head to the modern **Lot 87** (87 Via del Pellegrino), just off Campo de' Fiori. Feel free to nurse a drink for as long as you like as you sit browsing the papers or magazines kept in the racks by the door.

A kitsch but quintessentially Roman place, **Jonathan's Angels** (16 Via della Fossa) is bright and full of colour, and filled with quirky memorabilia, including dozens of portraits of the owner with his children. It also boasts the most memorable loos in town, complete with their own fountain.

Sciam (56 Via del Pellegrino) is a laid-back Middle Eastern tea room with a tempting selection of sweet and savoury dishes. You may even be tempted to take a puff of the aromatic hookah pipes. Open until 2am.

Wine Time (15 Piazza Pasquale Paoli) is a buzzing oasis of good wine and good humour. You can sit at the counter or at tables, your drinks accompanied by delicious cheeses, salads and desserts. Just across the river from Castel Sant'Angelo.

BELOW: walking the dog on Via Veneto.
ABOVE RIGHT: *The Archangel Michael Slaying the Devil* by Guido Reni.

At the southern end of the Via Veneto, this Baroque church also goes by the name of I Cappuccini (The Capuchins). The Capuchin friars broke away from the Franciscans in 1525, but still emulate the humble lifestyle of their patron saint, dressing in a simple brown robe with a cord belt, and sandals without socks. This church has been the home of the Capuchin order in Rome since 1631.

It has two noteworthy paintings: *The Archangel Michael Slaying the Devil* by Guido Reni and *St Paul's Sight Being Restored*, by Pietro da Cortona. But the main draw is in the crypt, which contains the bones and skulls of 4,000 Capuchin friars, ornately displayed *(see box on left)*.

Gardens of Sallust

The **Horti Sallustiani** (Gardens of Sallust) lie between Via Veneto and the Villa Borghese Gardens. Gaius Sallustius, a historian and profiteer who made enormous fortunes out of the campaigns of 40–30 BC, embellished his home with magnificent gardens. Soon hailed as one of the wonders of the world, they were quickly appropriated by the Empire. Vespasian and Titus preferred this part of Rome to the Palatine.

Fountains, pools and mosaic floors once drew awed visitors. Now the gardens lie 15 metres (45 ft) below street level, buried by the rubble from collapsed houses and the building activity of the 19th century.

Archaeological finds from the gardens include the obelisk at the top of the Spanish Steps and those on show as part of the collection of the Museo Nazionale Romano *(see page 233)*.

In the Middle Ages, the family of Ludovisi-Boncompagni injected new life into the by then unkempt gardens by planting 30 hectares (74 acres) of vineyards. They lasted until the property boom of the 1880s, which spelt their demolition. The Società Generale Immobiliare, backed mainly by German and French capital, made an irresistible offer to the Ludovisi princes, and the villa was split up. All that remains is the 16th-century **Casino dell'Aurora** in the gardens of the Swiss Cultural Institute.

Palazzo Margherita ❸

The other part of the gardens spared by developers is behind the American Embassy, which is housed in **Palazzo Margherita**, completed in 1890. One of the Ludovisi princes had this gigantic building constructed as a substitute for his lost garden, but his money ran out and he had to sell it to the Savoy royal family, who moved the queen mother in. It bears her name to this day.

SANTA MARIA DELLA VITTORIA ❹

✉ 17 Via XX Settembre ⏰ Mon–Sat 8.30am–noon, 3.30–6pm, Sun 3.30–6pm 🎫 free 🚇 Repubblica 🚌 16, 38, 60, 61, 62, 84, 86, 90, 92, 217, 360, 910

To the south of the *palazzo*, on the corner of Piazza San Bernardo and Via XX Settembre, stands the church of **Santa Maria della Vittoria**, begun by Carlo Maderno in 1605. It contains Bernini's famous Baroque Cornaro side-chapel, which uses natural lighting effects to highlight the *Ecstasy of St Teresa*, a sculpture of Teresa of Avila, one of the great saints of the Counter-Reformation, portrayed with open mouth and half-closed eyes at the climax of her vision of Christ. She described how an angel pierced her heart with a flaming golden arrow. It has prompted many writers and critics over the centuries to suggest that the love she is experiencing may not be entirely divine.

In its Dolce Vita heyday, the five-star Excelsior on Via Veneto played host to some of the most glamorous stars of the day. Many a tempestuous scene between hot-headed lovers Frank Sinatra and Ava Gardner was played out within its walls.

BELOW LEFT: Bernini's *Ecstasy of St Teresa.*

Bone Idols

Beneath the church of Santa Maria della Concezione is an extraordinary crypt which contains the bones of 4,000 monks. Many churches have charnel houses, but this arrangement of skeletal remains into intricate designs is unique. The crypt is full of unusual tableaux: brown-cowled skeletons bow to visitors over arches of hip bones and pelvises; an infant skeleton attached to the ceiling brandishes a scythe, surrounded by rosettes made from vertebrae; a large clock comprises finger and foot bones. And in case this is not enough to remind you of mortality, a sign ominously informs us that: "What you are now, we once were. What we are now, you shall someday be".

The origins of this death cult are unclear. The church says that when French Capuchin friars came to Rome they found a shortage of burial space and created this monument. There is also the legend of "a half-mad monk with time on his hands and a certain passion for tidiness." Whatever the motives, this is Rome's most artistic cemetery.

Eventually, in 1901, the state bought the villa and, two years later, gave it to the people. The Villa Borghese, along with the Pincio Gardens and the Villa Giulia, is now home to a handful of museums, a cinematic cultural centre and the city zoo.

The **Villa Borghese Gardens** are laid out over rolling hills with winding paths, little lakes, statues and pretty flower beds hidden here and there. On Sunday, the people of Rome take over the park. Every corner is full of picnicking families, strolling lovers, cyclists and joggers, squealing children at play, while their fathers sit with transistors pressed to their ears straining to hear commentary of the match of the day.

There are several entrances to the park, but the main one is at the top of Via Veneto, at Porta Pinciana.

VILLA BORGHESE

At the northern end of Via Veneto, outside the Porta Pinciana, is the **Villa Borghese**, which was founded at the beginning of the 17th century by Cardinal Scipione Borghese Caffarelli, a nephew of Pope Paul V. The family later extended their property by buying some nearby land, so that 100 years ago the park encompassed 75 hectares (190 acres), which the Borghese frequently opened to the public. Property developers cast a greedy eye on the villa in the late 19th century, and their plans provoked the first battle to save the Romans' traditional society promenade.

ABOVE: the Pincio Gardens. **BELOW:** family picnic in the park.

Carlo Bilotti Museum ❺

✉ Viale Fiorello La Guardia, Villa Borghese; www.museocarlobilotti.it
☎ 06-8205 9127 ⊙ Tue–Sun 9am–7pm ⓔ charge ⓡ Flaminio
🚌 95, 116, 490, 495

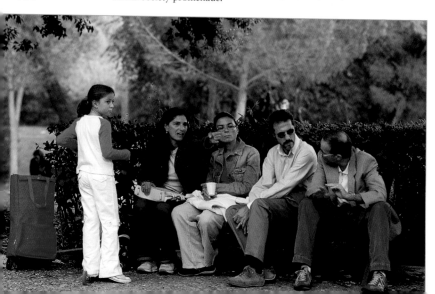

A wide *viale* leads downhill from the Porta Pinciana, passing the **Galoppatoio** (horse track) on the left and a statue of Goethe on the right. A little further ahead, the old orangery (Aranceria) has been restored and transformed into a museum containing a collection of works by Carlo Bilotti, an Italo-American collector who favoured modern art. The core of the collection is made up of 22 paintings and sculptures by Giorgio de Chirico. There is also a portrait of the larger-than-life arts patron Larry Rivers and one of his wife and daughter, the *Portrait of*

Tina and Lisa Bilotti (1981) by Andy Warhol. Other key works include *Summer* by Gino Severini and the large bronze *Cardinal* by Giacomo Manzù. The complex regularly houses important modern and contemporary art exhibitions.

Pincio Gardens ❻

From Piazzale Canestre walk down Viale delle Magnolie and head over the bridge, crossing busy Viale del Muro Torto below, into the **Pincio Gardens** at the southwest corner of the park. These formal gardens were designed by Valadier in the 19th century. Look out for the fanciful water clock and the **Casina Valadier**, once an elegant café visited by the intellectuals of the Roman *belle époque*. Nowadays, it is an expensive restaurant with a fabulous view from its terrace (www.casinavaladier.it; tel: 06-6992 2090; Tue–Sat 12.30am–3pm, 8pm–11pm, Sun lunch only).

Outside the restaurant is a stand full of bicycles and pedal-carts for hire – not a bad idea, especially if you plan on visiting the museums across the park. The romantic ter-

TIP

Just inside the park, on the other side of the Porta Pinciana, stands the new Casa del Cinema (www.casadelcinema.it). The lovely converted villa boasts several screening rooms (showing the occasional film in English), a book and DVD shop, and a cinema library containing scripts and movie stills. The CineCaffè (daily 9am–7pm), which serves drinks and light meals in an airy atmosphere, is an appealing place to add to your Villa Borghese itinerary.

LEFT: admiring the view from the Pincio Gardens. **BELOW:** Sunday activity.

North and Central Rome

V. Pietro
Via Sabino
Circonvallazione Salata
VILLA CHIGI
Via di Villa Chigi
Viale Libia
Viale Tripoli
Via Ascari
NOMENTANA
Piazza
Vescovio
Via Gargano
V. del Foro Italico

Moschea di Roma
(Rome Mosque)

V I L L A   A D A

Catacombe
di Priscilla **13**

S. Agnese
fuori le Mura **17**
V. di Santa
Mausoleo di
S. Costanza

SS. Martiri
Canadesi

Villa
Mirafiori

Villa
TORLONIA **16**

Villa
PAGANINI

Quartiere
Coppedè **14**

Villa
Albani

Museo d'Arte
Contemporanea
di Roma (MACRO) **15**

Corpus Domini

Ministero dei
Lavori Pubblici

Polizia

SALARIO

Villa Ada

Istituto Poligrafico
dello Stato

Mausoleo di
Lucilio Peto

Via Salaria

Piazza
Buenos
Aires

Via Piave

S. Roberto
Bellarmino

PARIOLI

Stazione
Campi
Sportivi

Stazione
Acqua
Acetosa

Piazza
delle Muse

Galleria
Borghese

Chiesa
Luterana

VILLA GIORI

SS. Cuore
Immacolato
di Maria

Stazione
Euclide

Museo
Africano

Museo
Zoologia

Bioparco

Galleria
Naz. d'Arte
Moderna

VILLA
BORGHESE

Villa Medici

VILLA
ELIA

PINCIANO

Accademia
Britannica

Tempio
d. Esculapio

Museo
Canonica

GIARDINO
DEL LAGO

Tempio
d. Diana

Villa Giori

Auditorium Parco
di Musica Pinsudski **19**

Palazzetto
dello Sport

Stadio
Flaminio

MAXXI **20**

VILLA
FLAMINIA

FLAMINIA

Museo Etrusco
di Villa Giulia

Explora II
Museo dei
Bambini

Villa Ruffo
Staz. Flaminio

Viale del
Muro Torto

S. Maria
d. Popolo

Casa di
Goethe

Museo
Henrik
Christian
Andersen

Corso di Francia

Ponte
Milvio

Istituto Storico
e di Cultura
dell'Arma
del Genio

Ministero
della Difesa

Porta del
Popolo

Ponte P. Nenni

Piazza
del
Popolo

Stadio d.
Farnesina

Ministero degli
Affari Esteri

Foro
Italico **18**

Rai
Auditorium

Stadio
Olimpico

Lungotevere Maresciallo Diaz

Piscina
Coperta

Ponte
Duca
d'Aosta

Lungotevere (Tiber)

Città
Giudiziaria

Ottaviano
S. Pietro

Via della Giuliana

0 ————— 500 m
0 ————— 500 yds

N

Recommended Restaurants, Bars & Cafés on page 197

race of the Pincio overlooks Piazza del Popolo and offers a splendid vantage point to view the city. It's a particularly delightful spot for an evening stroll.

Villa Medici ❼

Further down the Pincio hillside is the majestic **Villa Medici**. Rebuilt in the 16th century for the Crescenzi family, it was then passed to the Medicis, before being confiscated by Napoleon in 1803 and made the home of the French Academy. It is open for occasional exhibitions and concerts. There are also guided tours of the gardens on Saturday and Sunday morning (advance booking, tel: 06-67611).

Giardino del Lago ❽

Backtrack and cross the bridge to where a wide *viale* leads up to **Piazza di Siena** on the right. This oval track is the site of the International Horse Show in May – an important social and sporting event.

To the left is the pretty **Giardino del Lago**, with a tiny lake in the middle of which stands a reproduction of a Greek temple of Aesculapius. Rowing-boats can be hired for a brief paddle. Nearby, you will find the **Fountain of Fauns**, created in 1929 by Giovanni Nicolini.

Galleria Nazionale d'Arte Moderna ❾

✉ 131 Viale delle Belle Arti; www.museidiroma.com ☏ 06-3229 8451 ⏰ Tue–Fri, Sun 8.30am–

7.30pm, Sat 9am–11pm; ⓒ charge
🚌 3, 19, 231, 926

Two sloping ramps lead to Viale delle Belle Arti and the neoclassical façade of the Galleria Nazionale d'Arte Moderna. It has a permanent collection of 19th- and 20th-century pieces (dating until the 1960s) by Italian and foreign artists including de Chirico, Van Gogh, Modigliani, Degas, Cézanne, Courbet, Kandinsky, Mondrian, Klimt, Henry Moore and others. The gallery also frequently hosts travelling exhibitions of international importance. There is also a café and a reasonably priced restaurant.

Nearby **Museo Henrik Christian Andersen** (20 Via Pasquale Stanislao Mancini, Piazzale Flaminio; www.gnam.arti.beniculturali.it; tel: 06-321 9089; Tue–Fri 9am–7pm) is a branch of the GNAM, and offers a look at the Norwegian-American artist, whose bold, bronze statues of men in all their glory were not always so well received.

Next door, in the Piazza Winston Churchill, is the **Accademia Britannica**, designed by Lutyens and home to visiting scholars.

Entrance to the National Gallery of Modern Art, housing a collection of 19th- and 20th-century art, including a group of paintings by the Macchiaioli, Italy's answer to France's Impressionists.

ABOVE LEFT: the water clock.
BELOW: boating in the Giardino del Lago.

TIP

Add some romance to your jaunt in the park. Pick up a gourmet picnic-to-go from nearby Piazza di Spagna-area restaurant GiNa. Luxury packs come complete with chequered cloth, plates, flatware, wine-glasses, a bottle of your wine of choice, a thermos of espresso and, of course, a sumptuous meal. GiNa: 7a Via San Sebastionello; tel: 06-678 5201; www.ginaroma.com.

RIGHT: you can take a break at the Etruscan Museum café.
BELOW: intricately decorated Etruscan bronze from Palestrina.

Museo Etrusco di Villa Giulia ⑩

✉ 9 Piazzale di Villa Giulia ☎ 06-320 0562 ⏱ Tue–Sun 8.15am– 7.15pm
ⓒ charge 🚇 Flaminio
🚌 3, 19, 231, 926

To the west of the modern art gallery is Rome's Museum of Etruscan Art. It is housed in the Villa Giulia, a splendid late Renaissance palace built as a summer villa for Julius III between 1551 and 1553. The museum gives a unique insight into the life and art of

the enigmatic pre-Roman civilisation of the Etruscans. Among the many outstanding exhibits are the sweet 6th-century BC sarcophagus of a married couple – *degli Sposi* – from the excavations in Cerveteri, and a 6th-century bronze statue of Apollo of Veio. These and other pieces form one of the finest collections of Etruscan art in the world, rivalled only by that of the Vatican.

Some of the collection is on show in the restored, 16th-century Villa Poniatowski nearby. Once part of the Villa Giulia complex, it was renovated in the early 19th century by the Polish Prince Stanislao Poniatowski.

The zoo ⑪

✉ Piazzale del Giardino Zoologico; www.bioparco.it ☎ 06-360 8211
⏱ 7 Apr–30 Sept daily 9.30am–7pm, Oct–Nov 9.30am–6pm, rest of the year 9.30am–5pm ⓒ charge
🚇 Flaminio 🚌 bus: 52, 53, 217, 360, 910, 926; tram: 3, 19

The road leading uphill to the left ends at the entrance to the zoo, or Bioparco, its official eco-friendly name. In the past the zoo had a reputation for being neglected, but in recent years there have been some worthy and fairly successful attempts to phase out the caging of exotic animals and keep other specimens in more humane, purpose-built environments that more closely resemble their natural habitats.

Galleria Borghese ⑫

✉ 5 Piazzale Scipione Borghese; www.galleriaborghese.it ☎ 06-328101 ⏱ Tue–Sun 9am–7pm, controlled entry every two hours on the hour until 5pm, reservations advisable in high season ⓒ charge
🚌 5, 19, 52, 53, 88, 116, 119, 217, 910, 926

In the eastern corner of the park, one of the world's great private art collections is housed in the Casino Borghese, built as a summer home for the worldly, pleasure-loving Cardinal Scipione Borghese between 1613 and 1615. The cardinal was a great patron of the arts and laid the basis for the remarkable collection of paintings and sculptures on view today *(see pages 198–9).*

NORTHEAST OF THE CITY

To the northeast *(see map on page 190)*, **Via Salaria** crosses the suburbs and leads out to the Sabine Hills, and onward to the Adriatic coast. This old Roman road is named after the salt *(sale)* which was transported into Rome from the sea and through the hills. Just before the Salaria Bridge (1874) is the hill of Monte Antenne,

where the Sabine settlement of the Antemnae is said to have stood. It is here that the Romans, under Romulus, supposedly kidnapped the Sabine women to populate their growing empire. Via Salaria was an important street and, in the early years of Christianity, many churches and catacombs were built here.

Catacombe di Priscilla ⓭

✉ 430 Via Salaria; web.tiscali.it/catacombe-priscilla ☎ 06-8620 6272 ⏰ Feb–Dec Tue–Sun 8.30am–noon, 2.30–5pm 💶 charge 🚌 63, 86, 92, 310

Entered through the cloister of a Benedictine monastery, the 13-km (8-mile) network of catacombs evolved between the 1st century and 4th centuries. Seven early popes and numerous martyrs were buried here, hence the high-quality frescoes and stucco decorations. The catacombs extend under the park of Villa Ada, now the Egyptian Embassy but formerly Victor Emmanuel II's hunting lodge. It is surrounded by a beautiful park which is open to the public.

KIDS

If you've children in tow, two good places to know about are the zoo *(see page 192)* and the nearby Explora Museum (82 Via Flaminia; tel: 06-361 3776), a science museum full of interactive displays to keep them amused.

ABOVE LEFT: outside the zoo. **ABOVE:** the *Good Shepherd* mosaic in the Catacombe di Priscilla. **BELOW:** the Galleria Borghese.

TIP

On the other side of the Villa Ada is the chic residential area of Parioli, where the main attraction is Rome's first mosque. Built in 1992, it serves a Muslim population of 100,000 and is the largest mosque in Europe to date. Noted for its modern feel and contextual design, the mosque sits on over 3 hectares (7½ acres) of verdant park space, and its interior follows a forest motif. To reach the mosque, take the local Viterbo-bound train to Acqua Acetosa (Campi Sportivi).

RIGHT: decorated housefront in the Quartiere Coppedè.
BELOW: Villa Torlonia.

Quartiere Coppedè

To the east of Via Salaria, just off Piazza Buenos Aires, is the fashionable Quartiere Coppedè, a residential area named after a Florentine architect who designed many buildings here between 1921 and 1926, using Art Nouveau-inspired motifs. Of particular interest is Piazza Mincio, a square with an unusual fountain of frogs that Gabriele d'Annunzio described as "a genuine disgrace to Rome". Coppedè, whose buildings were the last notable architecture of pre-Fascist Rome, intended this square to show a harmony between the individual details of each house and the great tradition of Florentine craftsmanship.

MACRO

✉ 54 Via Reggio Emilia; www.macro.roma.museum ☎ 06-6710 70400 ☏ Tue–Sun 9am–7pm
ⓐ charge 🚌 3, 19, 36, 38, 60, 62, 80, 84, 490, 491, 495

At the beginning of Via Nomentana, set in a former Peroni brewery, is the Museo di Arte Contemporanea di Roma (MACRO). One of two sites (the other is in Testaccio, *see page 217*), it houses artworks by the key figures in Italian contemporary art.

The site is currently being expanded (hence the reduced entrance fee) and connected with glass walkways to other buildings behind it. The expanded venue will be ready in 2009. There is also a café and museum store on site.

Villa Torlonia

✉ 70 Via Nomentana; www.musei villatorlonia.it ☎ 06-8205 9127
☏ 1 Apr–30 Sept Tue–Sun 9am–7pm,

Recommended Restaurants, Bars & Cafés on page 197

Mar and Oct 9am–5.30pm, 1 Nov–28 Feb 9am–4.30pm ⓒ charge ⊟ 36, 60, 84, 90

Further east, on Via Nomentana, the Villa Torlonia was the last great villa built in Rome. In the early 19th century, the aristocratic Torlonia family contracted French architect Valadier to design the villa, which had a small lake, guesthouse, sports field and Temple of Saturn. The splendid three-storey residence, the Casino Nobile, was Mussolini's home from 1924 until 1943 (his rent was 1 lira a month). It was then occupied by Allied Forces, who used it as a military command base, but after the war it was left to disintegrate.

Following 50 years of neglect the palace has been restored to something of its former glory, and was opened to visitors in 2006. The rooms are lavishly decorated – the chandeliered ballroom is the grandest – though furnishings are sparse, as so much was looted or destroyed. You can also visit the network of bunkers Mussolini had built in case of air raids or gas attacks.

While you're in the Villa Torlonia grounds, the **Casina delle Civette** (Owl House) is also worth a visit. The Swiss chalet-style residence was built in 1840 and restored in the 1920s in the Art Nouveau style, with stained-glass windows featuring idyllic scenes of flora and fauna.

Sant'Agnese fuori le Mura ⑰

✉ 349 Via Nomentana; www.santagnese.net ☎ 06-861 0840 ⓒ church: daily 7.30am–noon, 4–7.30pm, catacombs and mausoleum: Tue–Sat 9am–noon, 4–6pm ⓒ charge for catacombs ⊟ 30, 60, 84, 90, 93

Continuing down Via Nomentana, you come to Sant'Agnese fuori le Mura, an important early Christian church built over the site of the tomb of St Agnes (martyred in AD 304) in the mid-4th century by Princess Costantina, daughter of the Emperor Constantine. It was rebuilt by Pope Honorius I in the 7th century. The relics of St Agnes are housed in the high altar. Every 21 January, the saint's day, two lambs are blessed and shorn to make woollen robes for the Pope.

The adjoining catacombs are remarkably well preserved. The nearby church of St Costanza, built as Constantina's own mausoleum, contains some interesting 4th-century mosaics depicting scenes of the *vendemmia* (grape harvest).

FLAMINIA

Northern Rome is connected to the city by the Via Flaminia, which begins at Piazza del Popolo and continues in a straight line all the way to the historic Ponte Milvio *(see below and page 196)*, a Roman footbridge which offers wonderful views of the Tiber. From here it's a short walk to the Foro Italico sports centre, one of the most intact examples of Fascist-era architecture in the city.

An old Peroni brewery is now home to Rome's contemporary art collection.

BELOW: lovers on Ponte Milvio.

The Love-Locks of Ponte Milvio

The ancient bridge of Ponte Milvio has become a pilgrimage site for lovers who seal their *amore* in a ritual of fixing a padlock to the third lamp-post on the north side, turning their back to the river, and throwing the key into the Tiber. The love-lock tradition originated in 1992, with the publication of Federico Moccia's romantic novel *Tre Metri Sopra il Cielo* (Three Metres above the Sky). The book found favour with Rome's youngsters, who identified with the Romeo-and-Juliet story of teenagers from different backgrounds falling in love. The protagonists' lock-and-key ritual in the novel spawned hundreds of real-life imitators. In 2004 the book was made into a successful film, and Ponte Milvio's lamp-post is now covered with multicoloured chains and locks bearing the names of the *innamorati*. With space running short on the original lamp stand, lovers wanting to pledge have enlisted other posts on the bridge.

Ponte Milvio is one of Rome's oldest bridges. Dating back to 2 BC, it is one of only three bridges that stood in the ancient city. It was the site of the great battle between rivals for the Imperial crown: Constantine and Maxentius. On the eve of the battle in AD 312 Constantine had a vision of Christ, and converted to Christianity. He went on to win the battle and turn the Roman Empire to Christianity.

ABOVE RIGHT: concert hall in the Auditorium.
BELOW: a modern Olympian at the Foro Italico.

Foro Italico ⓲

The Foro Italico sports complex was designed for Mussolini in the late 1920s by prominent architect Enrico del Debbio. This district was formerly dominated by the **Stadio dei Marmi**, built in the style of a Greek stadium and surrounded by 60 marble figures of athletes in heroic poses. Today, it is dwarfed by the **Stadio Olimpico**, the huge football and athletics stadium immediately behind it, with capacity for 80,000 spectators. This is where the opening ceremony of the 1960 Olympics took place, and, when the World Cup was held here in 1990, the stadium was extended into the Monte Mario behind it.

The stadium now hosts football matches most Sundays during the season, and is the venue for much passion and excitement – and also, unfortunately, violence when the two home teams, AS Roma and SS Lazio, come together in a derby.

The Foreign Ministry, the Farnesina, stands on an empty patch east of the stadium, with Viale Macchia di Farnesina running behind it.

The Auditorium ⓳

✉ 15 Viale Pietro de Coubertin; www.auditorium.com 📞 06-8024 1281 🚇 Flaminio, then tram 2 🚌 53, 217, 231, 910

Back on the south side of the Tiber, just north of the Parioli district and east of Flaminio, is the largest arts complex of its kind in Europe. The state-of-the-art Auditorium-Parco della Musica designed by Genoese architect Renzo Piano opened in 2002. The huge venue is set in open parkland, with a 7,600-seat capacity spread over three concert halls, and a large outdoor amphitheatre. It even incorporates a ruined Roman villa, unearthed during construction. The "city of music" offers an excellent programme of international music and dance. See the website for up-to-date details.

MAXXI ⓴

✉ 2 Via G. Reni; www.maxxi museo.org 📞 06-321 0181 🕐 Tue–Sun 11am–7pm (for exhibitions) 💶 free 🚇 Flaminio, then tram 2 🚌 19, 53, 217, 225, 910

Just across Via Flaminia, west of the auditorium, the Museo Nazionale delle Arti del XXI Secolo (MAXXI) is taking shape. The impressive new centre for contemporary arts and architecture, designed by Zaha Hadid, is not due for completion until the end of 2008, but if you want to visit, small temporary exhibitions are held in a dedicated space throughout the year. ❑

BEST RESTAURANTS, BARS AND CAFÉS

Restaurants

Price includes dinner and a half-bottle of house wine:

€ = under €25
€€ = €25–40
€€€ = €40–60
€€€€ = more than €60

Cantina Cantarini

☒ 12 Piazza Sallustio
☏ 06-474 3341 ⊙ L & D
Mon–Sat. €€ [p336, B2]
A high-quality family-run trattoria where the price is still right. Dishes are meat-based the first part of the week, fish-based Thur–Sat.

Casina Valadier

☒ Pincio Gardens, Villa Borghese ☏ 06-6992 2090
⊙ L & D Tue–Sat, L only Sun.
€€–€€€ [off map p336, A1]
The service can be indifferent and the quality of the food is not necessarily reflected in the price,

but you might be prepared to risk it just to enjoy the location (pictured below).

Al Ceppo

☒ 2 Via Panama, Parioli
☏ 06-841 9696 ⊙ L & D
Tue–Sun. €€–€€€
[off map p336, A1]
A class act with impeccable and imaginative food, a vast wine list and home-made sweets.

Girarrosto Fiorentino

☒ 46 Via Sicilia ☏ 06-4288 0660 ⊙ L & D daily.
€€–€€€ [p336, A2]
An island of reliability in a sea of tacky venues. The service is faultless, and wall-hangings give it a pleasantly dated look. All the classic Roman dishes are on offer, along with some Florentine specialities, including wonderful T-bone steaks.

L'Ortica

☒ 573 Via Flaminia Vecchia
☏ 06-338709 ⊙ D only
Mon–Sat, L only Sun. €€€
[off map p335, D1]
Something of a trek from Villa Borghese, towards the Stadio Olimpico, foodies will nevertheless find L'Ortica worth the effort: delicious Neapolitan specialities are the order of the day here, with the Sfizi di Napoli platter – gourmet bite-sized treats – a great introduction to the region's famous cuisine. There's a lovely terrace, open in summer.

Papà Baccus

☒ 36 Via Toscana ☏ 06-4274 2808 ⊙ L & D
Mon–Fri, D only Sat. €€€
[p336, A2]
Renowned for its attentive service and Tuscan

cuisine. Meat features heavily, but there are also fish and vegetarian options.

La Terrazza dell'Eden

☒ 49 Via Ludovisi ☏ 06-478121 ⊙ L & D daily.
€€€€ [p336, A2]
One of the capital's top restaurants, with a panoramic terrace that's as much of a draw as the food; try the risotto with melted taleggio and aubergine. The extensive wine list (650 bottles to choose from) is another mark in its favour.

Bars and Cafés

The recently revamped **Doney** (145 Via Veneto) harks back to *Dolce Vita* glamour. A good bet for everything from breakfast to dinner, cocktails and aperitifs.

Caffè delle Arti (73 Via Gramsci) in the Villa Borghese's National Gallery of Modern Art is touted as the finest museum café in Italy. It has a beautiful terrace

and a fine interior. The restaurant is open in the evenings, and also serves Sunday brunch.

ReD (12 Viale Pietro de Coubertin). The Auditorium's designer restaurant-bar is all sweeping lines and elegant aesthetics, with red the predominant colour. Stop by for one of the city's chic-est cocktails.

GALLERIA BORGHESE

Legacy of an art-loving cardinal, this is one of the finest collections of paintings and statuary in Rome

The Galleria Borghese is housed in an early 17th-century *palazzina* built for Cardinal Scipione Borghese. The cardinal was a great patron of the arts and laid the basis for the remarkable collection of paintings and sculptures on view today. Between 1801 and 1809 the sculpture collection was severely depleted, when more than 500 pieces were sold to Napoleon; these now make up the Borghese Collection of the Louvre in Paris. But there are still some marvellous pieces on show.

The cardinal was an early patron of Bernini, and the villa contains some of his best work, including his dramatic statue of *David*, caught just as he is about to release his slingshot *(above)*, *Apollo and Daphne* and *Pluto and Persephone*.

Scipione was one of the few cardinals to appreciate Caravaggio, and the collection includes several of his paintings, alongside works by other great Italian masters including Raphael, Correggio, Titian, Perugino, Lotto, Domenichino, Giorgione, Dossi and Bassano, as well as by Rubens and Cranach, among others.

TOP: Titian's *Sacred and Profane Love, c.*1515, made for an aristocratic wedding, is loaded with symbolism. **ABOVE:** Raphael's celebrated *Deposition*, 1507.

RIGHT: *David and Goliath*, by Caravaggio, 1606. The head of Goliath is a self-portrait, said to be a sign of contrition by the artist for the murder he had recently commited.

The essentials

✉ *5 Piazzale del Museo Borghese; www.galleria borghese.it*

☏ *06-841 6542*

🕐 *Tue–Sun 9am–7pm; entrance every two hours on the hour until 5pm; visits limited to two hours*

💶 *charge*

🚌 *5, 19, 52, 53, 88, 116, 119, 217, 910, 926*

THE PATRON'S PALACE

The Casino Borghese was built as a summer house for the pleasure-loving cardinal Scipione Borghese between 1613 and 1615. As a close associate of the Pope, he entertained many high-profile guests in his *palazzina*. The ancient statuary and the building itself, modelled on the classical villa, recalled the glories of Imperial Rome, and with the precious art collections on display, were a forceful demonstration of the cardinal's power.

In his will, he stated that the villa and grounds should never be separated. In 1902, the entire Villa Borghese estate was bought by Umberto I of Italy and presented by him to the city.

ABOVE: the gleaming Galleria Borghese is made of creamy white travertine which reflects the light.

LEFT: one of the highlights of the collection is the sensual statue of Pauline Bonaparte by Canova. The 19th-century femme fatale, whose conquests in the bedroom matched her brother's on the battlefield, was appropriately sculpted as Venus Victrix. When asked how she could possibly have posed so scantily dressed, she replied, "The studio was heated."

RIGHT: *Venus and Cupid with a Honeycomb*, by German painter Lucas Cranach the Elder (1531).

Recommended Restaurants, Bars & Cafés on pages 208–9

TRASTEVERE AND THE GIANICOLO

Rome's traditional working-class district "across the Tiber" has always stood apart from the rest of the city. Although it is now the gentrified turf of bourgeois Romans and expats, Trastevere retains a special charm. Rising behind it, the Gianicolo hill offers some of the best views of the city

cross the river *(trans Tiberim)* from the Centro Storico lies Trastevere. The area has a long history as the residence of outsiders: in Roman times it was settled by sailors, foreign merchants and a large Jewish community which later moved across the river. Over time, Trastevere's separation from the rest of the city resulted in the development of its own customs, traditions and dialect.

For centuries, the Trasteverini considered themselves to be *i romani di Roma*: Rome's Romans – a cohort of proud working men and women who faced life with a quick-witted sardonic joy. The energy of life on the streets of *er core de Roma* – the heart of Rome – nurtured some of the city's great artistic talent. The actor Alberto Sordi turned Trastevere's backstreets dialect into his comedy trademark. Inventor of the Spaghetti Western, Sergio Leone, grew up in Viale Glorioso, and his neighbourhood school was also the Alma Mater to filmmusic maestro Ennio Morricone.

But the old *Trasteverini* are a dying breed. After the war, the area's down-at-heel charm attracted gentrifying expats and middle-class Romans. Inhabitants with roots going back

generations departed for housing on Rome's periphery. The new *Trasteverini* are more likely to be artists, actors and film stars in residence, such as John Malkovich.

Fortunately, Trastevere has kept some of its idiosyncracies, even if many of the old *trattorie* and *osterie* have given way to pizzerias, pubs and trendy wine bars. During the day, it is left to its sleepy self: residents exercise dogs and do their daily shopping, while children play and the elderly sit outside their houses. In the evening,

Main attractions

SANTA MARIA IN TRASTEVERE
MUSEO DI ROMA IN TRASTEVERE
SAN FRANCESCO A RIPA
VILLA FARNESINA
PORTA PORTESE FLEA MARKET
SANTA CECILIA IN TRASTEVERE
PALAZZO CORSINI
ORTO BOTANICO
PIAZZALE GARIBALDI
BRAMANTE'S TEMPIETTO
VILLA PAMPHILI PARK

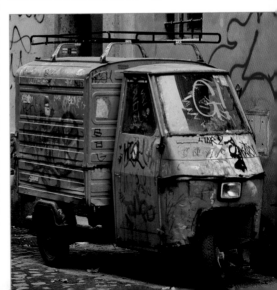

LEFT: the mellow shades of a Trastevere street. **RIGHT:** graffiti is inescapable in Rome and prolific in Trastevere.

PIAZZA SANTA MARIA IN TRASTEVERE

This cobbled square is the throbbing heart of the neighbourhood and is one of the most charming piazzas in Rome. There's a steady ebb and flow of tourists and locals whiling away their time in the cafés or sitting on the steps of the **fountain** (1692) around which musicians perform in summer.

the streets and squares are packed with locals and tourists, who flock here to eat, drink or stroll among stalls selling ethnic jewellery, and fortune-tellers shuffling their cards.

One major blot on this appealing landscape is the amount of graffiti scrawled across walls and doors. Also late-night drunk and disorderly behaviour, something until recently unheard of in Rome, is on the increase in and around the main square. Locals are campaigning hard for the mayor to address these social problems and for stronger policing in the area.

ABOVE: Santa Maria in Trastevere and a detail from the interior mosaic.

Santa Maria in Trastevere ❶

✉ Piazza Santa Maria in Trastevere
🕒 daily 7.30am–1pm, 4–7pm 💶 free
🚋 8, 780, H tram

The piazza is named after the basilica on its eastern side, one of the oldest churches in Rome and one of the first to be dedicated to the Virgin. It was traditionally founded in the 3rd century, and rebuilt in the 12th century, although the portico was added in 1702. The 12th- and 13th-century mosaics, both inside and outside the church, are spectacular, and it is worth

Trastevere and the Gianicolo

taking a pair of binoculars to enjoy their details. *The Life of the Virgin* series is by Cavallini (1291). Also worthy of note are the 21 granite columns which divide the nave from the aisles. These were taken from classical buildings including the Baths of Caracalla *(see page 227)*.

Museo di Roma in Trastevere ❷

✉ Piazza Sant'Egidio 📞 06-581 6563 🕒 Tue–Sun 10am–4pm 💶 free 🚌 8, 780, H tram

Northwest of the square, this small museum, housed in a beautifully restored Carmelite convent, is dedi-

cated to Roman folklore. The exhibition on the upper floor begins with a collection of watercolours by Ettore Roesler Franz (1845–1907), known as "Lost Rome". They present a rose-tinted Rome as it was before the urban restructuring of the 1870s, through romantic scenes of daily life in and around the Tiber.

At the far end of the floor is a series of life-size reconstructions of Roman life in the 18th century, and a room chock-full of objects from the studio of popular Trastevere poet Carlo Alberto Salustri (1871–1950), known as Trilussa (he is also remembered in a statue that graces the **Piazza Trilussa**).

The staircase features casts of the so-called "Talking Statues" *(see page 160)*. The ground floor of the museum is used for temporary exhibitions, often focusing on photography and new media.

The atmosphere is more brisk and businesslike in **Piazza San Cosimato** to the south, where the daily food market is surrounded by grocers, bars, restaurants and a hospital.

FOOD

Brush up on your bad language and visit La Parolaccia restaurant (3 Vicolo del Cinque; Mon–Sat), where food is served accompanied by bawdy language (the restaurant's name means swear word) and a brusque but entertaining Roman manner.

BELOW LEFT: busker on the main square.
BELOW: the façade of Santa Maria in Trastevere.

ABOVE: Piazza Sidney Sonnino. **BELOW:** Bernini's statue of *The Blessed Ludovica Albertoni*.

VIALE DI TRASTEVERE

Like every old quarter of Rome, Trastevere had to make sacrifices when the capital started expanding after 1870. Many historic buildings and streets were destroyed in order to make way for the **Viale di Trastevere**, a broad boulevard that cuts through the patchwork of Trastevere's little streets. At its northern end, on the banks of the Tiber, is **Piazza G.G. Belli** ❸, named after the much-loved 19th-century Roman dialect poet, Giuseppe Gioacchino Belli (1791–1863) whose statue stands here.

Behind Piazza Belli is **Piazza Sidney Sonnino** ❹. The Torre degli Anguillara, the last of many towers

that once guarded Trastevere, is marked with a plaque commemorating Dante's stay here in 1300. The nearby church of **San Crisogono** ❺ (daily 8.30am–6.30pm) was built over one of the oldest sites of Christian worship in Rome, dating from the 3rd century. The façade is a 17th-century copy of the medieval original. Inside are remains of a 5th-century basilica.

San Francesco a Ripa ❻

✉ Piazza di San Francesco d'Assisi
🕐 daily 7.30am–1pm, 4–7pm   💶 free
🚋 8, 780, H tram

On the south side of the Viale di Trastevere lies the church of San Francesco a Ripa. Dedicated to St Francis, who stayed in a convent near here, it contains a powerful late work by Bernini, the statue of *The Blessed Ludovica Albertoni*. From a wealthy family, she spent her fortune and ruined her health caring for the poor.

Renowned for her religious ecstasies, she became known as a miracle-worker and, it was said, had the gift of levitation. Her ecstatic expression is reminiscent of his more famous statue of St Teresa in Santa Maria della Vittoria *(see page 187)*.

Porta Portese

The church is not far from **Porta Portese**, a gateway built by Urban VIII on the site of the ancient Porta Portuensis. Rome's cheap and cheerful **flea market** ❼ is held here on Sunday mornings *(see opposite)*.

Santa Cecilia in Trastevere ❽

✉ 22 Piazza di Santa Cecilia   🕐 daily 10am–12.30pm, 4–6.30pm, crypt: Mon–Sat 10.15am–12.15pm, Sun 11.30am–12.30pm   💶 free
🚋 8, 780, H tram

Nestling in a quiet and secluded part of Trastevere, this church is dedicated

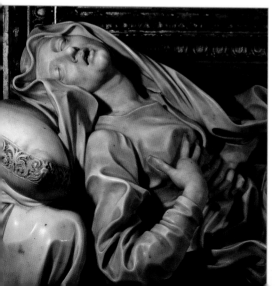

to the martyr St Cecilia, traditionally regarded as the inventor of the organ and the patron saint of music. Condemned to death for her faith in 230, she was to have been executed by means of suffocation, but when this failed, an executioner was despatched to behead her. She survived three strokes of the axe, living for a further three days and converting 400 pagans before she finally died. In 1599, her tomb was opened and her body, in a semi-foetal position, was found in a miraculous state of preservation. The artist, Maderno, made a beautiful statue of the saint which can be seen beneath the high altar.

VIA DELLA LUNGARA

Via della Scala leads from Piazza Sant'Egidio to the **Porta Settimiana**, a gate erected by Emperor Septimius Severus and replaced by Pope Alexander VI in 1498. From here Via Garibaldi climbs to the Gianicolo *(see page 206)*. This route was used in the Middle Ages by pilgrims en route to the Vatican, before the building of the "*retifili*" – the long, straight roads built by the Renaissance popes. The longest of these is Via della Lungara, laid out in the early 16th century to connect Trastevere with the Borgo. It's a short walk from the Porta Settimiana along Via della Lungara to the Villa Farnesina, a Trastevere gem.

Villa Farnesina ❾

✉ 230 Via della Lungara ☎ 06-680 27268 ⏰ Mon–Sat 9.30am–1pm 💶 charge 🚌 125

This sumptuous villa was built between 1508 and 1511 for the fabulously wealthy papal banker, Agostino Chigi. Renowned for his lavish banquets, Chigi was also a noted patron of the arts and had his

SHOP

Rome's most famous flea market is Porta Portese *(see opposite)*, held on Sunday 7am– 2pm on Via Portuense and adjacent streets between Via Ettore Rolli and Porta Portese. Go early if you want to get the bargains and avoid the crowds.

LEFT: Villa Farnesina. **ABOVE:** puppets for sale at Porta Portese. **BELOW:** detail from Raphael's *Triumph of Galatea*.

KIDS

The Piazza Garibaldi is home to a puppet theatre. It opens daily at 4pm, and has entertained children for decades. Please give generously, as it survives on donations from the public.

the 115 goes up the Gianicolo hill.

BELOW RIGHT:
Piazzale Garibaldi.

villa decorated with a series of beautiful frescoes by some of the best artists of the time. The highlights of the downstairs rooms are Raphael's sensual *Triumph of Galatea* and *Three Graces*. Upstairs is a fine *trompe l'œil* depicting contemporary views of Rome by Peruzzi, and Sodoma's magnificent *Wedding of Roxanne and Alexander*.

Palazzo Corsini ⓿

✉ 10 Via della Lungara; www.galleri aborghese.it/corsini 📞 06-688 02323 🕒 Tue–Fri 9.30am–1.50pm, entrance at allotted times of 9.30, 11.30 and 12.30, Sat–Sun 8.30am–1.50pm 💰 charge 🚌 125

Built in the 15th century for a wealthy cardinal, this *palazzo* opposite the Villa Farnesina now houses part of the **Galleria Nazionale d'Arte Antica** collection, which includes works by Fra Angelico, Rubens, Van Dyck, Caravaggio and Luca Giordano, whose *Christ among the Doctors* is one of the collection's key works. (The rest of the collection is in Palazzo Barberini, *see page 121*).

Orto Botanico ⓫

✉ 23a Via Corsini 📞 06-686 4193 🕒 Mon–Sat 9.30am–6.30pm in summer, until 5.30pm in winter 💰 charge 🚌 125

Originally part of the Corsini palace grounds, the botanical gardens are now open to the public. There are about 7,000 plants on display, including a scented garden for the blind and a collection of medicinal herbs. On the slopes up to the Gianicolo is a series of tiered fountains.

THE GIANICOLO

The Gianicolo (Janiculum hill) is climbed from Trastevere via the long and winding Via Garibaldi. The hill was the site of one of Italy's decisive battles for independence, when in 1849 Garibaldi and his army defeated French troops sent to restore papal rule. At noon, a cannon blast sounds to commemorate the struggle for liberation.

Piazzale Garibaldi ⓬

You can either walk or hop on a bus (115 or 870) up the hill to Piazzale

Bramante's Tempietto

When the centre of the Renaissance shifted from northern Italy to Rome at the end of the 15th century, the atmosphere of the Eternal City gave the architects of the day fresh impetus to rediscover the styles and motifs of antiquity. Donato Bramante had learnt his trade in the north and moved to Rome in 1499. His Tempietto di San Pietro in Montorio (1502) is the first monument of the High Renaissance style. It possesses a gravity all of its own – not surprising, considering its location: it marks the spot that was believed to be the site of St Peter's crucifixion. On closer inspection, you will notice there is very little surface decoration, and the colonnade is also unadorned. Too small to fit a congregation (5 metres/ 15 ft in diameter), the circular temple supports a classical entablature, which lends further weight and severity. These features, combined with the perfect classical proportions, make the Tempietto a brilliant homage to antiquity.

Garibaldi. The broad square is dominated by an **equestrian monument** to the freedom-fighter, while further north is another for his wife, the intrepid Anita, represented as an Amazon. Views from the terrace are magnificent.

Via Garibaldi

If you're catching the bus up to the Piazzale it's worth jumping off on the way up at the church of **San Pietro in Montorio**, with works by Vasari, del Piombo and Bernini, but most importantly **Bramante's Tempietto** ⓭ (Tue–Sun 9.30am–12.30pm, 2–4pm; free), one of the gems of the Renaissance *(see box left)*. During the bloody fighting that took place in 1849, the wounded were brought into the church, which was right next to the battlefield. A commemorative plaque on the outside of the church, with a French cannonball stuck to it, marks the event.

A little further uphill stands the **Fontana dell'Acqua Paola**, a fountain commissioned in 1612 by Pope Paul V to grace the end of an ancient aqueduct built by Trajan.

FURTHER AFIELD

Southwest of Trastevere lies the green and well-heeled **Monteverde Vecchio** residential zone, built in the late 19th and early 20th centuries. This is one of the most desirable places in Rome to live. Here also is the vast **Villa Pamphili park** ⓮ (entrance on Via di San Pancrazio; dawn–dusk; bus 115, 870, 710 to Piazzale Aurelio), the largest green space in Rome, with undulating terrain, fields, picturesque walkways, pine forests, fountains, lakes and gardens, as well as an ice rink and pony hire.

The basilica of **San Pancrazio** (Piazza San Pancrazio; daily 8.30am–12.30pm; bus 75) was founded in the 6th century on the burial site of a young Roman martyr, who was beheaded for his faith in 304. Underneath the church are the **catacombs of San Pancrazio** (Mon–Fri 10am–noon, 4–6pm; admission charge).

Not far to the east is another, far smaller but beautifully designed park and house, the **Villa Sciarra** ⓯ (35 Via Calandrelli; 9am–dusk; bus 75, 44). The park boasts botanical plants and statues of mythological figures. ❏

Opposite the church of San Pietro in Montorio, a striking white monument is Mussolini's tribute to the heroes of the Risorgimento (1848–70). On it is written the slogan "Roma o morte" (Rome or death), Garibaldi's famous war-cry uttered on this spot.

BELOW sunset view from Piazzale Garibaldi.

BEST RESTAURANTS, BARS AND CAFÉS

Restaurants

Price includes dinner and a half-bottle of house wine:
€ = under €25
€€ = €25–40
€€€ = €40–60
€€€€ = more than €60

Alberto Ciarla
✉ 40 Piazza San Cosimato
☎ 06-581 8668 ◷ D only Mon–Sat. €€€€ [p338, C2]
Friendly staff, sophisticated decor and six set-price gourmet fish menus or à la carte. One of the top fish restaurants in the city, but it's not cheap. Reserve.

Antica Pesa
✉ 18 Via Garibaldi
☎ 06-580 9236 ◷ L & D Mon–Sat. €€€ [p338, C2]

This historic Trastevere restaurant serves up all the usual Roman classics, along with some surprises: try the ravioli with white truffles, or steak with strawberries and balsamic vinegar. Booking advised.

Antico Arco
✉ 7 Piazzale Aurelio ☎ 06-581 5274 ◷ D only Mon–Sat. €€€ [p338, B2]
Excellent restaurant on the Gianicolo hill; some traditional dishes, some more innovative. The speciality is risotto with a Piedmontese cheese. Closed two weeks Aug.

Asinocotto
✉ 48 Via dei Vascellari
☎ 06-589 8985 ◷ D only

Tue–Sat, L & D Sun. €€€ [p339, D2]
Small, typical Trastevere trattoria offering refined and creative cuisine (gnocchi with peppers and mint, veal liver in raspberry vinegar). Gay-friendly and gay-owned.

Checco er Carettiere
✉ 10–13 Via Benedetta
☎ 06-580 0985 ◷ L & D daily. €€–€€€ [p338, C1]
A pleasant outdoors section and a steadfast Roman menu of fish and meat make this a sure bet. Sweets and ice cream are home-made.

Il Ciak
✉ 21 Vicolo del Cinque
☎ 06-589 4774 ◷ D only Tue–Thur, L & D Fri–Sun. €€ [p338, C2]
Game hanging in the windows testifies that this is a meat-eating venue. Dishes based on hearty Tuscan recipes and served with the house Chianti.

La Cornucopia
✉ 18 Piazza in Piscinula
☎ 06-580 0380
◷ L & D Wed–Mon. €€ [p339, D2]
Specialising in fish dishes, this restaurant's other selling point is its lovely garden, which is a pleasant place for dinner in the summer months.

Enoteca Ferrara
✉ 41 Piazza Trilussa
☎ 06-5833 3920 ◷ D only daily. €€–€€€ [p339, C1]
Minimalist decor and creative menu (with organic ingredients), comprehensive wine selection (850 labels). Light snacks or full meals. Reservations essential at weekends.

La Fraschetta
✉ 134 Via S. Francesco a Ripa ☎ 06-581 6012 ◷ D only Mon–Sat. € [p339, C2]
Simple pizzeria and trattoria menu served with house wine in a jovial atmosphere.

Alle Fratte di Trastevere
✉ 49–50 Via delle Fratte di Trastevere ☎ 06-583 5775 ◷ L & D Mon, Tue, Thur–Sat, L only Sun. €€ [p339, C2]
A family-run, authentic Trastevere trattoria serving up Roman dishes with Neapolitan touches; try the oven-roast sea bream. In summer, request one of the few outside tables.

Glass Hostaria
✉ 58 Vicolo del Cinque
☎ 06-5833 5903 ◷ D only Tue–Sat. €€€ [p338, C2]
An ultra-modern newcomer to traditional Trastevere, Glass offers creative Italian cuisine and attentive service. Though the cutting-edge

LEFT: Trastevere has a wide choice of pizzerias.

design won't be to everyone's taste, it does make a change from Trastevere's predominantly red-checked-tablecloth, trattoria decor.

Jaipur

🍽 56 Via di San Francesco a Ripa 📞 06-580 3992 🍷 L & D Tue–Sun, D only Mon. €€ [p339, C2]

If you just can't face another pizza, Jaipur is one of the city's best Indian restaurants, with friendly service and a great selection of tandoori dishes. Particularly strong on vegetarian options.

Le Mani in Pasta

🍽 37 Via de' Genovesi 📞 06-581 6017 🍷 L & D Tue–Sat. €€ [p339, D2]

Inviting and friendly restaurant serving meat and fish carpaccios; home-made pastas are cooked in myriad different ways. No menu, but the prices are reasonable. Booking advised. Closed three weeks Aug.

Panattoni

🍽 53 Viale Trastevere 📞 06-580 0919 🍷 D only Thur–Tue. € [p339, D2]

Not the most inspiring of interiors, but a Rome classic for its thin crusty pizzas, large antipasti buffet, low prices and its quicker-than-lightning, brusque Roman service.

Paris

🍽 7a Piazza San Calisto 📞 06-581 5378 🍷 L & D Tue–Sat; L only Sun. €€€ [p339, C2]

Elegant, slightly dated decor and reliably excellent traditional Roman-Jewish cuisine characterise Paris: golden deep-fried vegetables and *coda alla vaccinara* (braised oxtail with tomatoes, celery and white wine). Small outdoor eating area. Closed three weeks Aug.

Dar Poeta

🍽 45–46 Vicolo del Bologna 📞 06-588 0516 🍷 D only daily. € [p338, C2]

Pizzas made with a blend of yeast-free flours which creates an incomparably fluffy base. Tasty toppings. No reservations.

Rivadestra

🍽 7 Via della Penitenza 📞 06-6830 7053 🍷 D only Mon–Sat. €€–€€€ [p338, B1]

This recently opened "concept restaurant" bases its menu round fresh, seasonal ingredients. Predominantly Roman flavours are spiced up with the odd Oriental touch.

Spirito Divino

🍽 31a/b Via de' Genovesi 📞 06-589 6689 🍷 D only Mon–Sat. €€ [p339, D2]

History permeates this restaurant which stands atop the remains of a synagogue and an ancient Roman house. Classic dishes, many based on recipes used in Ancient Rome. The wine list is international and has won plaudits.

Trattoria degli Amici

🍽 5 Piazza Sant'Egidio 📞 06-580 6033 🍷 D only Mon–Sat. €€ [p338, C2]

This restaurant gives work experience to mentally and physically handicapped people. There's a friendly atmosphere, hearty Roman cooking and great value for money. Popular so book ahead. Closed Aug.

Da Vittorio

🍽 14a Via di San Cosimato 📞 06-580 0353 🍷 D only Mon–Sat. € [p339, C2]

One of Trastevere's most popular pizzerias, Da Vittorio serves up delicious Neapolitan-style pizza; try the house special Vittorio, with a classic topping of mozzarella, tomato and basil. Great atmosphere and good value.

Bars and Cafés

The perfect place for a pre-dinner cocktail or a post-dinner drink is **Ombre Rosse** (12 Piazza Sant'Egidio). In a scenic piazza, it has a lively atmosphere and is open all day every day (except Sunday morning).

Trasté (76 Via della Lungaretta) has low seats and tables and lots of cushions, and serves all kinds of teas, fruit- and milk-shakes and alcoholic beverages.

Freni e Frizioni (4–6 Via del Politeama) is a buzzy bar open for breakfast, lunch and dinner, but is most popular for aperitifs in the early evening, when the crowds spill out onto the piazza outside.

Bar San Calisto (3–4 Piazza San Calisto) is small and plain but nevertheless pulls in an incredibly mixed crowd.

Its chocolate ice cream and hot chocolate in winter are deservedly famous.

Stardust (4 Vicolo de' Renzi) is open late, and attracts an arty, trendy crowd.

The ever-popular **Friends Art Café** (34 Piazza Trilussa), open all day long until late at night, is a good place for a quick bite or an expertly mixed cocktail.

On the scenic Gianicolo hill, the **Caffè del Gianicolo** (5 Piazzale Aurelio) is a simple bar where light snacks and fruit-shakes can be consumed indoors and out.

The best-priced café in lovely Piazza Santa Maria is **Caffè di Marzio** (15 Piazza Santa Maria in Trastevere). Friendly staff and excellent opportunities for people-watching.

Recommended Restaurants, Bars & Cafés on pages 218–19

AVENTINO AND TESTACCIO

The most southerly of Rome's hills, the Aventine
has always been a tranquil and sought-after
residential area. It is also home to a number of
religious shrines. Testaccio, once a busy
working river port, is still one of the city's most
down-to-earth and genuinely Roman districts

The Aventine Hill is now one of
the most desirable places in
Rome to live, a tranquil oasis
conveniently close to the city centre.
Considered the "Sacred Mount" in
ancient times, it is the site of pagan
temples and of some of Rome's earliest Christian churches.

For centuries, the Aventine lay
outside the city walls. It remained
virtually uninhabited until 494 BC
when the plebeians retreated here to
organise the first general strikes
against patrician rule. During the
latter years of the Republic, it was
the residence of foreign merchants
and nouveau riche plebeians.

By the Imperial era, the hill had
moved right up the social scale. The
aristocracy moved in and built magnificent temples and luxury villas on
it. In subsequent centuries, several
churches were built on the ancient
sacred sites. Today, the Aventine
remains a well-to-do neighbourhood.

THE AVENTINE HILL

High on the hill is the **Parco Savello**,
the gardens once surrounding the
12th-century residence of the noble
Savello family. Today the park is a
peaceful destination for walks or

picnics, lined with orange trees and
overlooking the river towards the
Vatican.

Santa Sabina and Sant'Alessio ❶

✉ Piazza Pietro d'Illiria ⒸⒹaily
7am–12.30pm, 3.30–7pm €free
🚌 81, 122, 160, 175, 628, 715

The gardens flank the early Christian
basilica of Santa Sabina, skilfully
restored to its near-original state in
1936. It was built in the 5th century

Main attractions
SANTA SABINA
PIAZZA DEI CAVALIERI DI MALTA
PIRAMIDE DI CAIO CESTIO
PROTESTANT CEMETERY
TESTACCIO
MATTATOIO
CENTRALE MONTEMARTINI
GARBATELLA
SAN PAOLO FUORI LE MURA
EUR

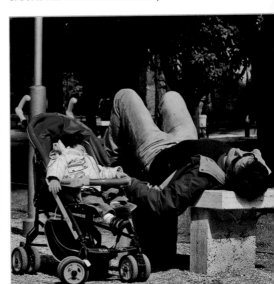

LEFT: the Pyramid of Caius Cestius – a
touch of Egypt in the heart of Rome.
RIGHT: siesta time in the Parco Savello.

A Maltese cross in Piranesi's Piazza dei Cavalieri di Malta.

by a priest from Dalmatia, Peter of Illyria, on the site of the house of a martyred Roman matron called Sabina. The broad nave is lined with elegant Corinthian columns, relics of a temple which once stood here. The west door, made of cypress wood, is as old as the church; its carved panels depict biblical scenes, including the earliest known representation of the Crucifixion.

Next door, the church of **Sant' Alessio** has a fine Romanesque *campanile* (belltower). A pretty courtyard leads into a Baroque interior with a gilt-covered relic of a stair-

case, beneath which St Alexis is said to have lived and died.

The Knights of Malta

From here, Via Santa Sabina leads into **Piazza dei Cavalieri di Malta ❷**. The square is named after the ancient chivalric order founded in 1080 as the Hospitallers of St John to run a hospital for pilgrims in Jerusalem.

Aventino, Testaccio and Garbatella

Recommended Restaurants, Bars & Cafés on pages 218–19

The Hospitallers became a powerful military order, based in Malta until they were expelled by Napoleon in 1798. The Knights of Malta have been based in Rome ever since.

The square was designed by the 18th-century engraver Piranesi and has heraldic symbols containing allusions to the military prowess of the knights. Piranesi was also responsible for the monumental gate to the **Priorato di Malta**, the residence of the Grand Master of the order.

Santa Prisca and San Saba

Down the hill and to the northeast is the church of **Santa Prisca** ❸ (11 Via di Santa Prisca; daily 7am–noon 4.30–6.30pm), said to occupy the site of a 3rd-century house belonging to Prisca and Aquila, who invited St Peter to dine here. Beneath the church are the remains of a *mithraeum*, a grotto to the ancient god Mithras.

Further down the hill you come to the Viale Aventino, which divides the main Aventine Hill from the smaller one known as *Il Piccolo Aventino*. On the right are remnants of the city walls dating from the 4th century BC.

Across Piazza Albani, Via San Saba leads to the pretty 10th-century church of **San Saba** ❹ (20 Piazza G. Bernini; daily 8am–noon 4–9pm), founded in the 7th century by exiled Palestinian monks. A selection of ancient sculptural fragments is displayed in its portico, and the interior has some Cosmatesque work and remains of a 13th-century fresco of St Nicolas.

This door leads to the gardens of the Priorato di Malta. Peek through the keyhole for an unusual view of the dome of St Peter's framed by a tree-lined avenue.

LEFT: in conversation outside Sant'Alessio. **BELOW:** view of the Tiber from the Parco Savello.

The ashes of Romantic poet Shelley are in the Protestant Cemetery. He drowned off the coast of Viareggio and was cremated in the presence of Lord Byron. His heart, however, was snatched from the pyre and was buried alongside Mary Shelley in an English churchyard.

ABOVE: Porta San Paolo and the Piramide di Caio Cestio. **BELOW:** the moving inscription on Keats's tomb.

PIRAMIDE

Originally called the Porta Ostiense, because it marked the beginning of the road to Ostia, **Porta San Paolo** ❺ is one of the best-preserved of the ancient city gates. It was renamed after St Paul who entered Rome through it. Impressive though the gateway is, it is overshadowed by the **Piramide di Caio Cestio** ❻, the tomb of a vainglorious Roman officer, Gaius Cestius, buried here in 12 BC.

Protestant Cemetery ❼

✉ 6 Via Caio Cestio; www.protestant cemetery.it ☎ 06-574 1900
🕐 Mon–Sat 9am–5pm 💶 free
🚇 Piramide 🚌 3, 23, 30, 60, 75, 175, 280

Adjoining the pyramid is Rome's **Cimitero Acattolico**, known in English as the Protestant Cemetery. Romantic poets Shelley and John Keats (who died in a house overlooking the Spanish Steps), and the son of the German writer Goethe are buried here. The cemetery is perhaps more properly regarded as the burial place of non-Catholics rather than just foreigners, and it also contains the graves of a number of prominent Italians, including Antonio Gramsci, founder of the Italian Communist Party.

TESTACCIO

Testaccio, the area west of Porta San Paolo, doesn't feature on most tourist itineraries, but it's worth a visit if you want to experience a genuine Roman working-class district, before it goes the way of Trastevere and trendification changes its character for good.

By the Middle Ages Testaccio had largely been abandoned, and wasn't developed into a residential area until the end of the 19th century when rows of low-cost tenement blocks with internal courtyards were built to house the workers. Many of these so-called *case popolari* are still rent-controlled working class residences, though the influx of a new generation of more moneyed residents drawn to the fashionable district is driving property prices up.

Testaccio is now one of the most culturally active areas in Rome, with theatres, a cinema, a music school and some of the liveliest nightlife in town. Many of the old wine cellars have been transformed into clubs and late-night bars.

Piazza Testaccio ❽

Despite its ongoing gentrification, Testaccio still retains something of an authentic working-class appeal. The boisterous daily produce market in Piazza Testaccio is a testimony to this.

To the south lies **Via Galvani**, home to some trendy minimalist restaurants

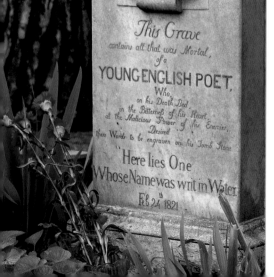

This Grave
contains all that was Mortal,
of a
YOUNG ENGLISH POET,
Who,
on his Death Bed,
in the Bitterness of his Heart,
at the Malicious Power of his Enemies,
Desired
these Words to be engraven on his Tomb Stone
"Here lies One
Whose Name was writ in Water."
Feb 24th 1821

serving fusion cuisine. Galvani leads to Monte Testaccio, which is bounded by **Via di Monte Testaccio**, an uninhabited, quasi-rural lane that is best visited at night when its clubs, bars and restaurants, housed in unlikely looking warehouses and low buildings, really get going.

Monte Testaccio ❾

The heart of the district is the 35-metre (105-ft) high Monte Testaccio, or "Hill of Shards", which gets its name from the broken bits of amphorae that can be found here. Testaccio was basically an ancient landfill site. The amphorae used to transport oil and wine were dumped here once their contents had been unloaded in the warehouses of the

Republican port which lined the Tiber between Ponte Testaccio and Ponte Aventino. Today the mound is closed to the public, but you can arrange guided visits through the Comune di Roma Archaeological Tourism (tel: 06-6710 3819). Views of the Tiber valley from the top are splendid.

MATTATOIO

Between Monte Testaccio and the river lies the Mattatoio, the city's former slaughterhouse dating from 1891, when the cattle market was moved here from Piazza del Popolo. For decades, the Mattatoio was the main source of revenue for Testaccio, but in 1975 it was pensioned off when a modern "meat centre" was built outside the city. Today, the buildings house exhibition spaces, the university's architecture department and other art-related activities. Part of the complex is occupied by a contemporary art gallery *(see page 61)*.

Another section is home to **Villaggio Globale** (entrance on Lungotevere Testaccio; tel: 06-575 7233), an alternative arts venue with live music acts, drawing a young, punky crowd.

TIP

Several of the clubs and restaurants built into Monte Testaccio offer a view of the amphorae shards at their lower levels. One of the finest displays can be seen in the back room of Ketum Bar (24 Via Galvani; www.ketumbar.it; tel: 06-5730 5338). The oriental-inspired fusion restaurant and bar attracts a hip crowd, and the food is a welcome break from everyday Italian.

LEFT: posters advertising local gigs and events. **BELOW:** Testaccio market.

EUR

The stark district was Mussolini's attempt to build a city fit for Fascists. Today it is a sought-after residential neighbourhood

The rather clumsy acronym EUR stands for the Esposizione Universale di Roma (Universal Exhibition of Rome), which was to have been held in 1942 to mark the 20th anniversary of Mussolini's accession, but because of the war it never took place. The slightly hilly site, south of San Paolo, was intended to form an impressive entrance to a new town extending all the way to Ostia. But by the time the Fascist regime was over, only two palaces on either side of Via Cristoforo Colombo had been built.

A start had been made on **Palazzo della Civiltà del Lavoro** (Palace of the Civilisation of Labour), popularly known as the "square Colosseum". Piacentini's plans for the new town combined monumental grandeur and a repetitive motif: square pillars, square ground plans and square roofs. The buildings radiate a cold beauty that is all the more striking because, in the city's centre, nothing is

rarer than a straight line. After the war, Mussolini-style architecture gave way first to glass façades and reinforced concrete, and then to post-modernism. The result is a largely unplanned mishmash of styles.

But it is not all modern. There is a reminder of Ancient Rome in the form of the **Abbazia delle Tre Fontane**, the 8th-century abbey on the northeast slope of the EUR hill, reached by a path from the sports ground on Via delle Tre Fontane. This is where St Paul was reputedly beheaded (see page 218).

Museums are EUR's main attraction. The **Museo Nazionale Preistorico-Etnografico Luigi Pigorini** (www.pigorini.arti.beniculturali.it; Tues, Thur–Sat 9am–2pm, Wed, Sun 9am–8pm; admission charge) on Piazza Marconi has a large collection of prehistoric artefacts. Next to it, the **Museo Nazionale delle Arti e Tradizioni Popolari** (www.popolari.arti.beniculturali.it; Tue–Fri 9am–6pm, until 8pm Sat–Sun) presents a lively portrayal of Rome's social history (though everything is labelled in Italian).

Opposite the **Museo dell'Alto Medioevo** (Tue–Sat 9am–2pm) houses valuable medieval collections. But the most interesting of all is the **Museo della Civiltà Romana** (10 Piazza G. Agnelli; www.museociviltaromano.it; Tues–Sun 9am–2pm), which chronicles every aspect of life in Ancient Rome.

For those with children who need appeasing, the amusement park here is worth knowing about: **Luneur** (Via delle Tre Fontane, www.luneur.it; opening times vary, see website). Another good place for cooling off is the open-air **swimming pool** (Viale America, 20, www.piscinadellerose.it).

The quickest way to reach EUR is by metro on the B line, but there are many bus services from the city centre. ❑

LEFT: Palazzo della Civiltà del Lavoro, symbol of EUR.
ABOVE: macho Mussolini statuary.

MACRO al Mattatoio ⑩

✉ 4 Piazza Orazio Giustiniani, www.macro.roma.museum ☎ 06-6710 70400 🕐 Tue–Sun 4pm–midnight 🎫 free 🚇 Piramide 🚌 bus: 23, 30, 75, 95, 280,673, 716 tram: 3

This is one of two sites occupied by the Museo d'Arte Contemporanea di Roma (The other main site is in the process of expansion, *see page 194*). The Mattatoio gallery hosts impressive art shows and installations, often in collaboration with the big guns on the contemporary art scene, including MoMA and PS1.

SOUTH OF THE CENTRE

First impressions of Ostiense, a former industrial district south of Testaccio, are not favourable. But for those interested in discovering the face of modern Rome, it's worth delving beneath the grubby surface of this up-and-coming young area. Bars, restaurants and clubs are mushrooming in the streets around Via Ostiense.

Rome's former wholesale food market, the vast Mercati Generali ⑪ is undergoing a Covent Garden-style make-over led by Dutch architect Rem Koolhaas, who is transforming the area into a state-of-the-art shopping and leisure district with shops, boutiques, cafés and galleries.

Centrale Montemartini ⑫

✉ 106 Via Ostiense; www.centrale montemartini.org ☎ 06-574 8042 🕐 Tue–Sun 9am–7pm 🎫 charge 🚇 Garbatella 🚌 23, 271, 769

Just a 10-minute walk from the Piramide di Caio Cestio is Ostiense's main attraction. What began as a temporary solution to the over-crowding of the Capitoline Museums has become a delightful landmark museum. Four hundred pieces of Roman sculpture are on permanent display in a converted electricity power plant. The juxtaposition of statues with machinery, tubes and furnaces make this a highly unusual venue, well worth a detour.

Garbatella

On the other side of Via Ostiense is the vibrant working-class neighbourhood of Garbatella (Metro B Garbatella, exit left side), worth visiting both for its old-Rome authenticity and for the architecture. The area was conceived and constructed in the 1920s during the post-WWI building boom. First intended for city workers and immigrants, the quarter was modelled on the English "garden city", which laid out two or three-storey buildings in plots with plentiful gardens and gathering space, in the hopes that newcomers to the city

Rome's team colours: the inhabitants of Testaccio are said to be the most loyal supporters of the Roma football team.

LEFT: street art in Ostiense. **BELOW:** Centrale Montemartini.

San Paolo fuori le Mura ⑭

✉ 186 Via Ostiense 📞 06-541 0341
🕐 daily 7am–7pm 🎟 free 🚇 San
Paolo 🚌 23, 128, 271, 670, 707,
761, 766, 769, 770

St Paul was martyred in AD 67 at Aquae Salviae, about 3 km (2 miles) from San Paolo fuori le Mura. Legend relates that when he was beheaded, after having converted one of Nero's favourite concubines, milk instead of blood flowed from his veins.

ABOVE: Cinema-Teatro Palladium.

would thrive among their Roman neighbours in communal harmony. The architects in charge of the project, Sabbatini and Giovannoni, added character to what might otherwise have been run-of-the-mill housing projects, with balconies, chimneys, floral embellishments and arches.

Piazza Bartolomeo Romana ⑬, one of the neighbourhood's most characteristic squares, is home to the **Cinema-Teatro Palladium** (www.teatro-palladium.it; tel: 06-5706 7779). Today the arts centre stages international music and dance performances, and participates in the prestigious multimedia RomaEuropa Festival (www.romaeuropa.net).

In an unappealing site between Via Guglielmo Marconi and the Tiber stands San Paolo fuori le Mura, one of Rome's four patriarchal basilicas.

Built on the site of St Paul's tomb, it was once the most glorious church in Rome, but first it was sacked by Saracens, then in 1823 almost completely destroyed by a fire. It may have lost much of its ancient splendour, but it's impressive nonetheless. Remnants of the original basilica include a set of doors dating back to the 11th century, engraved with stories from the Bible, and a Gothic tabernacle by Arnolfo di Cambio, rising over the high altar.

The 13th-century mosaic in the apse depicting Christ and Saints Peter, Paul, Andrew and Luke, was the work of Venetian craftsmen sent to Rome by the Doge. The cloisters are among the most beautiful in Rome. ❏

BEST RESTAURANTS, BARS AND CAFÉS

Restaurants

Price includes dinner and a half-bottle of house wine:
€ = under €25
€€ = €25–40
€€€ = €40–60
€€€€ = more than €60

Addo' Masto 2

✉ 43 Via G. Bove 📞 06-574 6372 🍽 L & D Tue–Sun. €–€€ [p339, E4, off map] Though their speciality is Neapolitan-style pizza, the family that owns this restaurant near Ostiense

Station also offer a range of well-executed fish and seafood dishes.

Agustarello

✉ 100 Via G. Branca 📞 06-574 6585 🍽 L & D Mon–Sat. €€ [p339, D4] This restaurant specialises in cooking with the "poor" ingredients that this area – one of the city's most authentic – is famous for: *coda alla vaccinara* (oxtail in a tomato-based stew), tripe and the like.

Desserts are similarly traditional; the ricotta tart is a must-try.

Le Bistrot

✉ 160 Via delle Sette Chiese 📞 06-512 8991 🍽 D only daily. €€–€€€ [p339, E4, off map] A little way from Testaccio in villagey Garbatella, this cosy restaurant offers a variety of vegetarian dishes; the menu is split between pasta and dishes with a French slant.

Checchino dal 1887

✉ 30 Via di Monte Testaccio 📞 06-574 6318 🍽 L & D Tue–Sat. €€€ [p339, D4] Typical Roman cuisine, excellently prepared. Known throughout the city. Booking advisable. Closed Aug.

Doc

c9 Via Beniamino Franklin 📞 06-574 4236 🍽 D only Mon–Sat. €€ [p339, C4] A refined but informal interior sets the tone for this small restaurant specialising in fish, though meat-eaters and vegetarians are well catered for.

Estrobar

20 Via P. Matteucci
06-5728 9141 D only daily. €€€ [p339, D4]
This classy restaurant within the designer Abitart hotel has an arty theme. Exhibitions of young artists' work provide a suitable backdrop for the sophisticated menu. There's also a tasting menu, and an extensive wine list.

Da Felice

29 Via Mastro Giorgio
06-574 6800 L & D Mon–Sat, L only Sun. €€ [p339, D4]
A Testaccio institution, this bustling restaurant serves up classics of Roman cuisine such as roast lamb with rosemary potatoes. Closed three weeks Aug.

Ketumbar

24 Via Galvani 06-5730 5338 D only daily. €€–€€€ [p339, D4]
Sleek, minimalist interior. Sushi, nasi goreng and braised tuna fillets with parmesan wafers. Music gets louder as the evening wears on.

The Kitchen

3m Via dei Conciatori
06-574 1505 L & D Mon–Sat. €€ [p339, E4, off map]
A slick, designer-style restaurant, as befits its location in trendy

Ostiense, The Kitchen offers creative Italian cuisine with a slight difference: the kitchen is open, so diners can watch their meals being prepared.

Manali

108 Viale Avignoni 06-8992 7741 D only Mon–Sat. €€ [p339, D4, off map]
This pleasant, airy restaurant near the lake in EUR offers creative Mediterranean cooking, using seasonal ingredients. Home-made desserts include a delicious white chocolate mousse *cannolo*.

Maybe

23 Piazza Marconi
06-4544 8247 L & D Tue–Fri, D only Sat & Sun, L only Mon. €€€ [p339, D4, off map]
Situated in a rather stark modern building typical of EUR architecture, ultra-modern Maybe benefits from a vast terrace whose tables are lit by candles in the summer. The cuisine is classic Mediterranean with a modern twist; try the seafood and porcini mushroom ravioli.

Da Oio a Casa Mia

43 Via Galvani 06-578 2680 L & D Mon–Sat. €€ [p339, D4]
Well-made Roman specialities (pasta classics and lots of meat- and offal-based dishes) in a friendly neighbourhood trattoria.

Pecorino

64 Via Galvani 06-5725 0539 L & D Tue–Sun. €€€ [p339, D4]
Modern and inviting restaurant that does classic *cucina romana*, with an emphasis on meat dishes.

Remo

44 Piazza S. Maria Liberatrice 06-574 6270 D only Mon–Sat. € [p339, D4]
One of the best pizzerias in the area, with good starters. No booking.

Tallusa

11 Via Beniamino Franklin No phone L & D daily. € [p339, C4]
A great budget option, with delicious takeaway meze served with pitta bread.

Tuttifrutti

3a Via Luca della Robbia 06-575 7902 D only Mon–Sat. € [p339, D4]
Hidden down a

ABOVE: Estrobar at the Abitart hotel.

side street, Tuttifrutti is a friendly, charming restaurant. The menu changes on a daily basis but always contains Italian classics such as *cacio e pepe* pasta and baked lamb. Closed two weeks Aug.

Bars and Cafés

Oasi della Birra (38 Piazza Testaccio) is a popular meeting spot for young Romans, with a choice of more than 500 beers from all over the world.

For an espresso, cappuccino or light lunch head to trendy **Il Seme e la Foglia** (18 Via Galvani).

Doppio Zero (68 Via Ostiense) is a chic new

café which offers light meals and snacks, as well as a selection of delicious cakes at teatime.

For more of the latter, try also **Andreotti** (54b Via Ostiense), a historic *pasticceria*, where they'll not only serve you a perfect cappuccino, but also beautifully wrap up any pastries you want to take with you.

CELIO AND SAN GIOVANNI

The Lateran, on the eastern extremity of the Caelian Hill, was the centre of the Catholic Church until the Papacy was transferred to the Vatican in the 14th century. Slightly off the beaten track, this area is packed with striking ancient monuments and churches steeped in history

When the Lateran Palace was the seat and residence of the popes (from the 4th century until the papacy's temporary move to Avignon in 1309), the Lateran was the centre of the Catholic Church. On the return of the papacy to Rome in 1377, the Pope's official residence was moved to the Vatican, but the Lateran remained an important centre for the Church – popes were still crowned here until 1870.

PIAZZA DI SAN GIOVANNI

At the heart of the Lateran district is **Piazza di San Giovanni**, flanked by the **Palazzo Lateranense** (Lateran Palace; closed to public). The original papal residence, founded in the 4th century, was damaged by fire and fell into ruin. In 1586, Pope Sixtus V commissioned Domenico Fontana to build a new palace as a papal summer residence, though it was never used as such. Fontana's Baroque palace now houses the offices of the diocese of Rome (of which the Pope is bishop). It was the site of the historic meeting that led to the 1929 Lateran Treaty, which established the current boundaries of the Vatican and stabilised its relationship with the Italian state.

San Giovanni in Laterano ❶

✉ 4 Piazza San Giovanni in Laterano
☎ 06-6988 6433 ⏰ daily 7am–6.30pm 🎟 free 🚇 San Giovanni
🚌 3, 16, 81, 85, 87, 117, 186, 218, 590, 650, 714, 810, 850

Next to the palace stands the mighty **San Giovanni in Laterano**, the "mother of all churches" and the first Christian basilica in Rome, founded by Constantine the Great. The church has stood here since 313, but it has burnt down twice and

Main attractions

SAN GIOVANNI IN LATERANO
SCALA SANTA
SANTI QUATTRO CORONATI
SAN CLEMENTE
PARCO DEL CELIO
SANTA MARIA IN DOMNICA
SANTI GIOVANNI E PAULO
THE BATHS OF CARACALLA

LEFT: Baths of Caracalla.
RIGHT: Palazzo Lateranense.

been rebuilt several times. As a result, it is a mixture of styles from the exquisite 4th-century baptistry to the majestic Baroque interior.

The east façade, through which you enter, is the work of Alessandro Galilei (1732–5), but Fontana designed the north façade when he was rebuilding the Lateran Palace.

The central doorway has the original bronze doors taken from the Roman Curia of the Forum. The façade is crowned by 15 huge statues of Christ and the Apostles, visible for miles around. Most of the marble-clad interior is the result of remodelling by Borromini (1646), but some of the works of art and church furnishings are far older. They include a fragment of fresco attributed to Giotto (1300) and a 14th-century Gothic baldacchino from which only the Pope is allowed to celebrate Mass. The nave's gilded wooden ceiling was completed in 1567. Other features of note include

The ancient bronze doors of San Giovanni in Laterano.

ABOVE RIGHT:
the gilded wooden ceiling of San Giovanni in Laterano.

the Baroque frescoes and reliefs of the transept, and the peaceful 13th-century cloisters *(see margin, right)*.

The Baptistery

The **Battistero Lateranense** (Baptistery; daily 8am–12pm and 4–7pm; free) was part of the original complex, built by Constantine around 320; it was rebuilt in its present octagonal shape in the 5th century. In the earliest days of Christianity, all Christians were baptised here. The chapels of San Giovanni Evangelista (St John the Evanglist) and Santi Rufina e Secunda (the original

Celio and San Giovanni

entrance) contain a series of exquisite 5th-century mosaics.

Standing 30 metres (100 ft) high, the **obelisk** on the square is the tallest and oldest in Rome; it honours the Pharaoh Tutmes III and once stood in the Circus Maximus.

Scala Santa ❷

✉ Piazza San Giovanni in Laterano
🕒 Apr–Sept daily 6.30am–noon, 3–6.15pm, Mass at 6pm, Oct–Mar 3.30–6.45pm 💶 free 🚇 San Giovanni 🗺 *see page 221*

Across the street from the Lateran Palace is the entrance to the Scala Santa, said to be the stairs that Christ ascended when he was tried by Pontius Pilate. Brought to Rome from Jerusalem by Constantine's mother, Helena, they are protected under a layer of wood, but you still have to mount them on your knees, and the devout (who arrive in bus loads) do so slowly, stopping on each of the 28 steps to pray.

You can cheat and walk up one of the side staircases to the **Sancta Sanctorum** (Holy of Holies; tel: 06-772 6641; Mon–Sat 7am–noon and 3.30–4.30pm; admission charge), where there is a painting of Christ – said to be the work of St Luke and an angel.

Santi Quattro Coronati ❸

✉ 20 Via dei SS Quattro 🕒 daily 9am–noon, 4.30–6pm 💶 free
🚌 85, 87, 117, 571, 810, 850

Originally part of the fortress that protected the Lateran Palace, the "Four Crowned Saints" belongs to a community of silent Augustine nuns.

TIP

The cloisters (daily 9am–6pm) of San Giovanni in Laterano are a high spot of any tour of the basilica. Completed around 1230, they are the work of father-and-son team Jacopo and Pietro Vassalletto, supreme masters of the Cosmatesque school of mosaic work. Note how the columns are inlaid with chips of coloured glass and marble, which were plundered from ancient remains.

LEFT: Santi Quattro Coronati. **BELOW:** penitent pilgrims climb the Scala Santa on their knees.

Cross, which she found at the same time as the Scala Santa.

San Clemente ❹

✉ Via dei SS Quattro; www.basilica sanclemente.com 📞 06-774 0021
🕐 Mon–Sat 9am–12.30pm, 3–6pm, Sun noon–6pm 💶 free; excavations admission charge 🚇 Colosseo 🚌 60, 75, 85, 87, 117, 571, 810, 850

The present church, built over the remains of a much larger 4th-century edifice, dates from the 11th century.

You can ring a bell and ask a kind-hearted nun to give you the key so you can see into the beautiful 12th-century cloisters, with slender columns and a fountain, or to the **Chapel of San Silvestro**. This 13th-century chapel contains an endearing fresco illustrating the conversion of Constantine to Christianity by St Sylvester (who was Pope at the time). You can see the emperor suffering from what looks like the advanced stages of a skin disease, then travelling to Rome to be cured by the Pope. A mosaic depicts St Helena's discovery of the True

ABOVE: San Clemente. **BELOW:** sculpture depicting the birth of Mithras. **BELOW RIGHT:** the ceiling of San Clemente.

The basilica of **San Clemente** is one of Rome's most fascinating churches, with some of the finest mosaics and frescoes in the city. Run by an order of Irish Dominicans, it is in fact two churches, one built on top of the other, beneath which there lie still earlier remains. The present church dating from the 12th century is built in basilica form with three naves divided by ancient columns. In the apse is a beautifully detailed mosaic depicting the cross as the Tree of Life nourishing all living things. Against a background of brilliant gold, the crucified Christ is depicted in jewel-like blues, reds and greens.

In the **Chapel of St Catherine** are some lovely early Renaissance fres-

Mithras

Mithraism was a mystery religion which came from the Eastern Mediterranean in the 2nd century BC and was practised throughout the Roman Empire from the 1st century BC to the 5th century AD. It is difficult to unravel the exact workings and beliefs of Mithraism as the rituals were the secret of its exclusively male members. It was particularly popular with the army, with followers of the cult enduring severe ordeals, involving heat, cold and hunger. One ritual involved being locked in a coffin for several hours. Worship took place in a temple or *mithraeum* – a cave constructed to resemble Mithras' birthplace.

One extraordinary aspect of Mithras is the similarity with the life of Christ. Mithras' birth was over the winter solstice, he became a travelling teacher who performed miracles, had 12 disciples, was called the Good Shepherd and the Messiah, had a last supper, was buried in a tomb, rose three days later on Sunday, and was celebrated once a year in the spring.

Recommended Restaurants, Bars & Cafés on page 227

coes of the life of St Catherine of Alexandria by Masolino (1383–1447) and Masaccio (1401–28). You can see Catherine praying while the wheel to which she was strapped and tortured to death is prepared.

To the right nave a staircase leads down to a 4th-century church, with fine 11th-century frescoes of miracles being performed by St Clement, the fourth pope.

Temple of Mithras

An ancient stairway leads deeper underground to a Roman alley and a maze of damp corridors and eerie chambers. Down here is the earliest religious structure on the site, a 2nd-century **Temple of Mithras**, dedicated to the Persian god whose cult spread to Rome *(see box opposite)*.

THE CELIO

The Celio (Caelian Hill), incorporated into the city in 7 BC when the defeated citizens of the rebellious city of Alba lived there, is one of the seven classical hills of Rome. Today it's home to Villa Celimontana, surrounded by a pleasant park.

Parco del Celio ⑤

Sprinkled with ancient ruins and some fine early medieval churches, Villa Celimontana was once a vineyard, and was bought by the Mattei family in the 16th century, who turned it into gardens and an art gallery. The villa is now a public park – a calm and safe sanctuary of greenery and birdsong in a chaotic city. There are two entrances; the main gateway is on Piazza della Navicella.

A short driveway leads to the villa building, which is now the home of the Italian Geographical Society. To the left of the building are some winding pathways, a pristine lawn, and views over southern Rome and the Baths of Caracalla. To the right of the main building is a charming sloping area planted with trees and offering plenty of picnic spots. The park is often home to art exhibitions and special events; in the summer a series of evening jazz concerts is held here.

On the southeastern edge of the park is the 5th-century church of **Santo Stefano Rotondo** ⑥ (tel: 06-421199; Tue–Sat 9.30am–12.30pm

In the Parco del Celio is a children's playground, with pony rides available.

BELOW: scouts picnic in the Parco del Celio.

The ancient Arco di Dolabella was incorporated into Nero's aqueduct.

and 3–5pm; bus no. 117), one of the few remaining circular churches in the city. The soft natural light that filters through its windows reveals gruesome 16th-century frescoes of martyred saints by Pomarancio.

Santa Maria in Domnica ❼

✉ 10 Via della Navicella ☎ 06-700 1519 ◷ 8.30am–12.30pm, 4.30–7pm 🚌 81, 673

On the other side of Via della Navicella is the 9th-century church of Santa Maria in Domnica. In the apse is a magnificent mosaic of the Virgin and Child surrounded by saints and angels in a garden of paradise – the man on his knees at the Virgin's feet is Pope Paschal I, who commissioned the mosaic.

Turn left outside the church to reach Via di San Paolo della Croce, which is straddled by the dramatic 1st-century **Arco di Dolabella** ❽, part of Nero's great aqueduct *(see page 113)*. Next to the arch, the gateway of **San Tommaso in Formis** is decorated with a 13th-century mosaic

showing Christ with two freed slaves, one black and one white.

Santi Giovanni e Paolo ❾

✉ 13 Piazza Santi Giovanni e Paolo ☎ 06-700 5745 ◷ daily 8.30am–noon, 3.30–6pm ◉ free 🚇 Circo Massimo 🚌 60, 75, 81, 175, 673

The Via di San Paolo della Croce leads to the church of Santi Giovanni e Paolo. The first church here was built in the 4th century, but the present one is mainly 12th-century, with an early 18th-century interior. The 13th-century belltower was built into the remains of a temple of Claudius. The church also gives access to the

ABOVE RIGHT: mosaic of Virgin and Child with Pope Paschal I in the church of Santa Maria in Domnica. **BELOW:** the Baths of Caracalla.

remains of houses dating back to the 1st century AD (13 Via Chiavio di Scauro; Thur–Mon 10am–1pm and 3–6pm; admission charge).

San Gregorio Magno ❿

✉ 1 Piazza di San Gregorio Magno
☎ 06-700 8227 ⓒ daily
8.30am–12.30pm, 3–6.30pm ⓔ free
🚇 Circo Massimo 🚌 60, 75, 81,
175, 271, 673

Another noteworthy church in this area is the 17th-century **San Gregorio Magno**. Founded by St Gregory in the 6th century, the church is run by Benedictine monks. Inside, the medieval chapels of Santa Barbara and Sant'Andrea are of particular interest, the latter with frescoes by Guido Reni and Domenichino. The chapel of St Sylvia dates from the 17th century.

The Baths of Caracalla ⓫

✉ 52 Viale delle Terme di Caracalla;
www.pierreci.it ☎ 06-3996 7700
ⓒ Tue–Sun 9am until one hour before dusk, Mon 9am–2pm ⓔ charge
🚇 Circo Massimo 🚌 160, 628

In AD 212 these were the most luxurious baths of Rome and the city's largest until the completion of the Baths of Diocletian a century later. In their heyday, these baths could accommodate 1,600 people. Visitors could enjoy the use of libraries and lecture rooms, a gymnasium and a stadium, quite apart from the complex of saunas and pools.

The interior was sumptuously decorated with marble, gilding and mosaics. The unearthed statues are now scattered among various collections, but the buildings are still impressive, their vaults rising 30 metres (100 ft). ❏

TIP

The remains of the *caldarium* (hot room) in the Terme di Caracalla are used to stage an annual outdoor opera and ballet festival in July and August.

LEFT: fragments of mosaic are scattered around the Baths of Caracalla.

BEST RESTAURANTS, BARS & CAFÉS

Restaurants

Crab
✉ 2 Via Capo d'Africa
☎ 06-7720 3636 ⓒ L & D
Tue–Sat, D only Mon. €€€
[p340, B2]
A reputable but expensive seafood restaurant with the best oysters in town, as well as every kind of crustacean and mollusc imaginable.

Isidoro
✉ 59a Via San Giovanni in
Laterano ☎ 06-700 8266

ⓒ L & D Sun–Fri, D only Sat.
€–€€ [p340, B2]
Fifty pasta first courses, mostly suitable for vegetarians, although on Fridays many of them are fish-oriented. You can ask to try several different varieties of pasta on one plate.

La Tana dei Golosi
✉ 220 Via San Giovanni in
Laterano ☎ 06-7720 3202
ⓒ L & D Mon–Sat. €€
[p340, B2]
A different regional Italian cuisine is featured every two months. High-quality and often organic ingredients and a refined ambience. Fixed-price cheaper lunch menu.

Ai Tre Scalini
✉ 30 Via dei SS Quattro
☎ 06-709 6309 ⓒ L & D
Tue–Sun. €€ [p340, B2]
Modern, inviting decor and convenient for the Colosseum. Equally strong on meat, fish and pasta. If it's too hot outside, try one of the naturally cool rooms on the lower level.

Bars and Cafés

Sitting at the rooftop bar of **Hotel Gladiatori** (125 Via Labicana) gives you an unparalleled view of the Colosseum; a charming place for an atmospheric aperitivo.

The lively **Shamrock** (26d Via Capo d'Africa) offers Guinness on tap and reasonable pub food.

● ● ● ● ● ● ● ● ● ● ● ●
Price includes dinner and a half-bottle of house wine.
€€€€ = €60 and up,
€€€ = €40–60, **€€** =
€25–40, **€** = under €25.

MONTI AND ESQUILINO

This sprawling area centres on the Esquiline and Viminal hills that lie between the Colosseum and Stazione Termini. Wander the streets of bohemian Monti and multicultural Esquilino, take in the artworks and mosaics of their many fine churches, and visit a stunning collection of Roman antiquities

In ancient times Monte Esquilino, the largest of Rome's seven hills, was the site of communal burials for slaves and executed prisoners. Emperor Augustus transformed the area into an aristocratic residential zone with palatial villas and idyllic gardens. Maecenas, a rich bon vivant and Augustus' lifelong friend, built himself a luxury villa on the hill, and Virgil and Horace also had homes here. Nero built his magnificent Domus Aurea *(see page 112)* on the Oppian Hill (Colle Oppio), which was later incorporated into the foundations of Trajan's Baths. Pope Sixtus V's magnificent villa stood on the site of what is now Termini Station. While the wealthy lived in luxury on the breezy summit, the foot of the hill was occupied by the slums of the densely populated Suburra district.

Many of the ancient palaces and villas of the area were cleared or built over to make way for the boulevards flanked by stately *palazzi* built after Unification in 1870.

MONTI

These days traffic thunders along Via Nazionale and Via Cavour, two characterless thoroughfares intersecting the area, but between the lower end of them is a cluster of pretty, narrow, cobbled streets lined with bars, restaurants and boutiques, which make up the heart of the trendy bohemian Monti district. To the east, centred around the faded splendour of Piazza Vittorio, lies the Esquilino quarter, now the capital's prime multicultural district, with many shops and restaurants owned and run by North Africans, Indians and Chinese.

The western side of the Esquiline Hill known as Rione Monti or simply

Main attractions

SANTA MARIA MAGGIORE
SANTA PRASSEDE
SAN PIETRO IN VINCOLI
MUSEO NAZIONALE D'ARTE ORIENTALE
TERME DI DIOCLEZIANO
PALAZZO MASSIMO ALLE TERME
STAZIONE TERMINI
SANTA CROCE IN GERUSALEMME
SAN LORENZO
SAN LORENZO FUORI LE MURA

LEFT: streets of Monti.
RIGHT: Termini Station.

TIP

If you are in the area on 5 August, head for Santa Maria Maggiore, where the Festa della Madonna delle Neve is celebrated. Thousands of white flower petals cascade down from the roof of the church, commemorating the legendary snowfall on the Esquiline Hill.

called Monti, is now a lively district popular with artists, artisans and boutique-owners, and has a number of notable churches.

Santa Maria Maggiore ❶

✉ Piazza Santa Maria Maggiore; www.vatican.va 📞 06-483 195 🕐 daily 7am–7pm 🎫 free 🚇 Termini 🚌 C3, 16, 70, 71, 360, 649

According to legend, in August of AD 352, following a vision of the Virgin Mary, Pope Liberius witnessed a snowfall on the summit of the Esquiline Hill. To commemorate the miracle he built the basilica of Santa Maria Maggiore.

The church is the only one of the four patriarchal basilicas in Rome to have retained its paleo-Christian structures. The 18th-century Baroque façade gives no indication of the building's true antiquity, but step inside and its venerable origins become apparent.

The striking gilded coffered ceiling and elaborate chapels are 16th- and 17th-century additions, but the mosaics that decorate the triumphal arch and the panels high up on the nave walls are the original 5th-century ones. To the right of the main altar is the burial place of Bernini, Rome's Baroque genius.

Santa Prassede ❷

✉ 9 Via Santa Prassede 📞 06-488 2456 🕐 daily 7.30am–noon, 4–6pm 🎫 free 🚇 Termini 🚌 C3, 16, 70, 71, 360, 649

South of Santa Maria Maggiore lies **Santa Prassede**, built by Pope Paschal I in the 9th century. He commissioned mosaic-workers from Byzantium to decorate the apse, the triumphal arch and the chapel of San Zeno, reintroducing an art that had not been practised in Rome for three centuries – with stunning results.

Monti and Esquilino

Recommended Restaurants, Bars & Cafés on pages 236–7

San Pietro in Vincoli ❸

✉ 4 Piazza di San Pietro in Vincoli
📞 06-488 2865 🕐 daily 8am–
12.20pm, 3–8pm 💶 free
🚇 Cavour 🚌 C3, 16, 70, 71, 75, 84, 117

From Piazza dell'Esquilino, in front of Santa Maria Maggiore, the busy Via Cavour descends the hill towards the Forum. Halfway down, a steep flight of steps leads to Via delle Sette Sale and San Pietro in Vincoli.

The church of St Peter in Chains was founded in the 5th century as a shrine for the chains said to have bound St Peter during his imprisonment in Jerusalem. They are preserved in a bronze-and-crystal reliquary beneath the high altar. Over the centuries the church was rebuilt and restored many times, but the ancient Doric columns lining the nave remained. The church is also home to Michelangelo's monumental *Moses*, part of the unfinished tomb that the artist was preparing for Pope Julius II.

Offbeat Monti

The cobblestone streets between Via Cavour and Via Panisperna are lined with artisans' shops, funky clothes shops, cool bars and ethnic restaurants. This area retains traces of its medieval past, as well as an intimate villagey atmosphere. Here you'll find some of the most interesting boutiques and workshops in town.

Just off Via Panisperna is the beautifully restored Piazza degli Zingari, where gypsy *(zingari)* caravans

once congregated. From the square, Via Urbana leads to the church of **Santa Pudenziana** ❹ (9am–noon and 3–6pm), built over a house where St Peter allegedly stayed. Dating from the 4th century, its apse is decorated with one of the earliest known Christian mosaics.

OPPIO

The **Oppian Hill**, site of Nero's legendary Golden House – the **Domus Aurea** ❺ *(see page 112)*, is now an ill-kempt park strewn with rubbish and home to lots of stray cats, but there are some lovely views of the Colosseum from up here, and it's pleasant to get away from the bustle of the city. Cutting through this area is the busy Via Merulana.

Museo Nazionale d'Arte Orientale ❻

✉ 249 Via Merulana 📞 06-4697 4801/2 🕐 Mon, Wed, Fri and Sat 8.30am–2pm except 1st and 3rd Mon of month, Tue, Thur and Sun 8.30am–7.30pm
💶 charge 🚇 Vittorio E 🚌 C3, 16, 714

Steep steps link San Pietro in Vincoli with Via Cavour.

LEFT: bar in Monti.
BELOW: Santa Maria Maggiore.

TIP

The Museo Nazionale Romano's collection of classical Roman art and statuary is contained in four different sites: the Terme di Diocleziano and Palazzo Massimo alle Terme near the station, Palazzo Altemps by Piazza Navona and Crypta Balbi near the Jewish Ghetto. A museum card, valid for seven days, covers all four sites.

ABOVE RIGHT: Santa Pudenziana. **BELOW:** boutique in Monti.

The 19th-century Palazzo Brancaccio houses the Museum of Oriental Art, a small but impressive collection ranging from 6,000-year-old Middle Eastern pottery to 18th-century Tibetan fans and ancient artefacts from the Swat culture in Pakistan. The museum also includes sections on Nepal, India, China, Japan, Korea and southeast Asia. In the gardens are remains of Nero's water cistern, the Sette Sale, built for his private house and used to feed Trajan's Baths.

Further along Via Merulana is the **Auditorio di Mecenate** ❼ (visits must be booked in advance on tel: 06-6710 3819; admission charge), dating from 30 BC and believed to be the *nymphaeum* of Maecenas' villa. Inside are the remains of frescoes depicting garden scenes, birds and small figures.

Follow Viale del Monte Oppio downhill to the 8th-century **San Martino ai Monti** ❽ (7am–noon and 4–7pm), a damp, dark church dotted with mosaic remnants and classical statuary.

ESQUILINO

In many cities the area around the main train station is scruffy and insalubrious, and Rome is no exception to this, with Termini Station surrounded by shabby apartments and run-down hotels. The city council claims that Esquilino is undergoing a "renaissance", which may not be evident as yet, but it certainly deserves one as there is plenty to see.

Terme di Diocleziano ❾

✉ 79 Via Enrico de Nicola; www.archeorm.arti.beniculturali.it
☎ 06-3996 7700 ⒸBdaily 9am–1.30pm, 2.30–5pm ⓒ charge
🚇 Termini 🚌 36, 40, 64, 170

At the northern end of Piazza della Repubblica are the remains of the Baths of Diocletian, one of the four sites of the Museo Nazionale Romano. Early in the 4th century, these baths – then the largest and most beautiful of the city's 900 bathhouses – were a buzzing centre of social activity. They fell into ruin after the aqueduct that fed them was destroyed by invading Goths.

In the 16th century, the church of **Santa Maria degli Angeli** (www.santamariadegliangeli roma.it; tel: 06-488 0812) was built inside the *tepidarium* (warm bath) to a design by Michelangelo. The interior exploits the massive vaulting of the ancient building to dramatic effect. Highlights include a painting by Domenichino of the *Martyrdom of St Sebastian* and an elaborate timepiece on the nave floor.

The splendid **Aula Ottagona** (Octagonal Hall; Tue–Sat 9am–2pm, Sun 9am–1pm; free) round the corner is an integral part of the immense structure of the baths in which are displayed sculptures from the museum collection.

Palazzo Massimo alle Terme ⑩

✉ 1 Largo di Villa Peretti ☎ 06-480 201 ⓒ Tue–Sun 9am–7.45pm ⓐ charge ⓡ Termini ⓑ all buses to Termini

On Piazza dei Cinquecento is the imposing Palazzo Massimo alle Terme, the main site of the Museo Nazionale Romano's museum quartet, where you'll find the most important part of its vast collection of Roman antiquities. There's a stunning array of statuary on the ground floor from the Republican Age (2nd–1st century BC) to the late Imperial Age (4th century AD), but best of all are the splendid floor mosaics and wall paintings from the houses of wealthy Romans, seen at their best in the delicate frescoes

from the Villa di Livia, the house of Augustus' wife that once stood on the Via Flaminia. The frescoes decorated the dining room and depict a garden paradise.

Stazione Termini ⑪

On the other side of the piazza is one of the few successful pieces of post-war architecture, the graceful ticket hall of **Stazione Termini**, designed by Angiolo Mazzoni. Its undulating roof echoes the remains of the Servian Walls which are visible through long glass windows. Uncovered during the building of the first station in 1867, they are believed to date from the reign of Servius Tullius (6th century BC).

Aula Ottagona houses some exquisite pieces of early Roman sculpture.

LEFT: mosaic detail in the Palazzo Massimo alle Terme.
BELOW: Terme di Diocleziano.

FOOD

The monks and friars at the church of Santa Croce in Gerusalemme run a small kiosk that sells jam, honey and excellent chocolates.

The revamped station now offers a vast selection of services including a shopping centre, an excellent art gallery (by platform 24), a gym, restaurants, a post office, a church and a medical centre.

Towards Porta Maggiore

Directly south of the station is **Piazza Vittorio Emanuele II ⑫**. Built in the late 19th century to accommodate government ministries, it features one of the longest colonnades in Europe. A food market runs off the piazza on Via Ricasoli (Mon–Sat 7am–3pm).

Several blocks east is the church of **Santa Bibiana ⑬** (154 Via Giolitti; 8.30–10.30am and 4.30–7.30pm). Small enough to seem like a private chapel, it is one of Bernini's first architectural projects.

Heading south on Via Giolitti, you pass the romantic remains of the 4th-century **Tempio di Minerva Medica**, a landmark if you arrive by train. To the southeast is **Porta Maggiore ⑭**, a wonderfully preserved 1st-century gate which also served as an aqueduct. You can still see the channels that carried the water. In 1917, a 1st-century underground basilica was discovered here (tel: 06-699 0110 or ask at a tourist information point to arrange a visit).

Santa Croce in Gerusalemme ⑮

✉ 12 Piazza Santa Croce in Gerusalemme 📞 06-701 4769
🕐 daily 7am–12.30pm, 2.30–6.30pm
💶 charge 🚌 81, 85, 87, 571, 649, tram 3, 5, 14

South of Porta Maggiore, along Via Eleniana, is the splendid white façade of Santa Croce in Gerusalemme, which was established in AD 320 by St Helena, Emperor Constantine's mother, to house fragments of the True Cross and other relics that she acquired on a visit to the Holy Land.

Next door, the **Museo Nazionale degli Strumenti Musicali** (www.museostrumentimusicali.it; admission charge; Tue–Sun 8.30am–7.30pm) has some 3,000 pieces documenting musical history from antiquity to the 19th century.

Surrounding the church and the museum are the remains of the 3rd-century **Anfiteatro Castrense**. The section along Via Castrense is particularly well preserved.

ABOVE: interior of Stazione Termini.
BELOW: bust of Marcus Aurelius.

EASTERN SUBURBS

East of the railway tracks, beyond the ancient Porta Tiburtina, lies the densely populated area of **San Lorenzo**, known as the student area of Rome. Built to house workers in the 1880s, but with few amenities or public services, the area has a reputation for being a focus for left-wing unrest. Today it is one of the city's liveliest districts, its streets – named after Italic and Etruscan tribes – filled with restaurants, artisans' workshops and cultural diversity.

Nearby is the Città Universitaria, one of Europe's biggest universities, which was constructed in the 1930s in typical Fascist style: big, white and imposing.

San Lorenzo fuori le Mura ⓰

✉ 3 Piazzale del Verano ☎ 06-491 511 🕒 daily 7.30am–12.30pm, 3–7pm 🎫 free 🚌 bus: 71, 492, 649, tram: 3, 19

The area takes its name from the ancient basilica of San Lorenzo fuori le Mura (St Lawrence outside the Walls), which stands at the entrance to the vast Verano cemetery. One of Rome's first Christian places of worship, the basilica is made up of two churches joined together.

The raised apse is the nave of the Constantinian church erected in 330 (rebuilt in the 6th century with beautiful Corinthian columns); the 5th-century basilica next door forms the present nave. The two were joined together in the 8th century. The interior is decorated with early mosaics and some beautiful Cosmatesque work. To the right is the entrance to the pretty 12th-century cloister and underneath lies a labyrinth of catacombs. The church was badly bombed in World War II, but was soon restored to its former glory. ❑

Artists' studios rub shoulders with cheap and cheerful restaurants in the student quarter of San Lorenzo.

LEFT: urban expression in San Lorenzo.
BELOW: Richard Meier's Jubilee Church.

Tor Tre Teste

Rome's isolated eastern suburb of Tor Tre Teste has a church designed by Richard Meier which was inaugurated in 2003. The **Chiesa di Dio Padre Misericordioso** (www.diopadremisericordioso.it; 7.30am–12.30pm and 3.30–7.30pm) on Via Francesco Tovaglieri stands somewhat incongruously but majestically in the centre of a triangular site, with a public park on one side and several 10-storey apartment blocks on the others. Its three striking white shells of graduated height curve up and over the main body of the church. The stark white of the walls, a Meier trademark, creates a sensation of space and light, enhanced and amplified by the dizzying array of skylights and the walls of glass.

BEST RESTAURANTS, BARS AND CAFÉS

Restaurants

Price includes dinner and a half-bottle of house wine:

€ = under €25
€€ = €25–40
€€€ = €40–60
€€€€ = more than €60

Africa

✉ 26 Via Gaeta 📞 06-494 1077 🕐 L & D Tue–Sun. €
[p336, B3]
Stewed dishes from Ethiopia and Eritrea which you scoop up with flat bread. Some vegetarian options.

Agata e Romeo

✉ 45 Via Carlo Alberto 📞 06-446 6115 🕐 L & D Mon–Fri. €€€€ [p340, B1]
Despite their weekend closing and the fact that the kitchen shuts down at 10.30pm, this is still one of the city's best dining experiences. Highly creative dishes (for example, Irish cod served in four different ways and trench-seasoned cheese soufflé with pear sauce). Huge wine selection from its renowned cellar. Booking essential.

Gli Angeletti

✉ 3 Via Angeletto 📞 06-474 3374 🕐 D only daily. €€ [p340, A1]
Enjoying a great location, overlooking a picture-postcard piazza, Gli Angeletti serves up tasty dishes such as tagliolini with red onion, pancetta and balsamic vinegar, and duck breast in a marsala sauce.

Arancia Blu

✉ 55–65 Via dei Latini, San Lorenzo 📞 06-445 4105 🕐 D only Mon–Sat, L & D Sun. €€ [p337, D4]
An upmarket vegetarian restaurant which offers consistently tasty food, using the freshest produce.

Alle Carrette

✉ 14 Vicolo delle Carrette 📞 06-679 2770 🕐 D only Tue–Sun. € [p340, A1]
Here, tucked away in a little side street close to the Forum, is what many consider the best pizzeria in the area. There's a beer tavern feel to it and some outdoor seating.

Cavour 313

✉ 313 Via Cavour 📞 06-678 5496 🕐 L & D Mon–Sat, D only Sun. €–€€ [p340, A1]
This attractive *enoteca* has an impressive 500 bottles on its wine list and friendly staff who are happy to advise on which of their platters of cheeses and cold meats pairs best with your chosen vintage.

F.I.S.H.

✉ 16 Via dei Serpenti 📞 06-4782 4962 🕐 L & D Tue–Sun. €€€ [p340, A1]
A trendy fusion and sushi restaurant done up in hi-tech style. The menu is fish-based only and divided into four sections – oriental,

oceanic, Mediterranean and sushi/sashimi. The results are mostly very good. Limited dessert options, but that's not what people come here for. At the lower end of this price scale.

Formula Uno
🖃 13 Via degli Equi, San Lorenzo 🕿 06-445 3866 🕒 D only Mon–Sat. € [p337, D4]
Genuine buffalo mozzarella on the pizzas makes this a cut above most pizzerias, and the fried *baccalà* (salt cod) is excellent.

Da Franco ar Vicoletto
🖃 1–2 Via dei Falisci, San Lorenzo 🕿 06-495 7675 🕒 L & D Tue–Sun. € [p337, D4]
A real neighbourhood trattoria with no frills, just lots of good and fishy food. Pick the set-price menu and the waiters will bring out dish after dish of seafood served with pasta or salad, or simply grilled, roasted or fried.

Il Guru
🖃 4 Via Cimarra 🕿 06-474 4110 🕒 L & D Mon–Sat. €€ [p336, A4]
To satisfy your need for something not pizza or pasta-based go to Guru, one of the most welcoming Indian restaurants in town. Choose various dishes from the classic tandoori

LEFT: Zest at the Radisson SAS es. Hotel.

or curry options or one of three fixed menus – vegetarian, fish, meat.

Hang Zhou
🖃 33c Via San Martino ai Monti 🕿 06-487 2732 🕒 L & D daily. € [p340, B1]
One of the better of the many Chinese restaurants in Rome, Hang Zhou offers a fixed menu or à la carte. Particularly good are the steam-cooked vegetable ravioli and the chicken with ginseng. The fried ice cream is delicious. Closed three weeks Aug.

Hasekura
🖃 27 Via dei Serpenti 🕿 06-483648 🕒 L & D Mon–Sat. €€€ [p336, A4]
A small, streamlined interior makes a classic Japanese setting for sushi, sashimi and tempura. At lunchtime you can choose from one of many *degustazione* menus priced at €15–35.

Hostaria degli Artisti
🖃 6 Via G. Sommeiller 🕿 06-701 8148 🕒 L & D Mon–Sat, L only Sun. €€ [p341, D2]
In an anonymous part of town where there are few shops or restaurants you will find this delightful trattoria, a temple to the cuisine of Campania. Run by a husband-and-wife team who have given it their own unique slant. Flavours of anchovy, buffalo mozzarella and fish and seafood dominate an enjoyable experience. Neapolitan

music on Friday and Saturday nights.

La Piazzetta
🖃 23a Vicolo del Buon Consiglio 🕿 06-699 1640 🕒 L & D Mon–Sat. €€ [p339, E1]
A popular and cosy restaurant which, due to its small size, can get very packed. Fish and large portions of perfectly cooked pasta are polished off with enthusiasm, and the in-house puddings are excellent. Some seating in the medieval lane outside in summer.

Tram Tram
🖃 44 Via dei Reti, San Lorenzo 🕿 06-490416 🕒 L & D Tue–Sun. €€ [p337, D4]
A small, cosy trattoria. Pugliese specialities such as linguine with squid and porcini.

Bars and Cafés

Il Palazzo del Freddo di Giovanni Fassi (65–7 Via Principe Eugenio) is a Roman institution. Its huge, kitsch interior is filled with locals day and night (it's open until midnight) queuing to get their hands on some of the tastiest ice creams in the city. Their speciality is *gelato al riso* (rice ice cream). Sublime.

For a decidedly more contemporary experience, which is worlds away from the multi-

Trattoria Monti
🖃 13a Via San Vito 🕿 06-446 6573 🕒 L & D Tue–Sat. €€ [p336, B4]
The owners are from the Marches region and the menu reflects this: home-made vegetable lasagne, chicken or rabbit in *potacchio* (with tomato, onion, garlic and rose-mary), roast turkey with balsamic vinegar. There is fish on Friday, and the menu changes almost daily in this long and narrow, elegant trattoria. Closed three weeks Aug.

Uno e Bino
🖃 58 Via degli Equi, San Lorenzo 🕿 06-446 0702 🕒 D only Tue–Sun. €€ [p337, D4]
Although surrounded by the college bars of San Lorenzo, this small restaurant offers an out-standing and affordable gourmet experience.

cultural area in which it stands, try the rooftop chill-out bar of the luxury **Radisson SAS es. Hotel** (171 Via Filippo Turati). Here you can sip a cocktail as you lounge on leather sofas and look out onto the streamlined spectacle of Termini Station below.

Friendly **Vineria Monti DOC** (93 Via Giovanni Lanza) is a great local *enoteca* which serves hot and cold light meals.

Recommended Restaurants & Bars on page 243

THE APPIAN WAY

Just outside the city walls, the "Queen of Roads" begun in 312 BC was an important part of Christian Rome. The old Appian Way is home to ancient monuments, catacombs and dramatic ruins.

R omes's first great military road, the Via Appia Antica, initially led to Capua 200 km (124 miles) away; by 191 BC it extended to Brindisi, the main port for Greece and the Eastern Empire, and was known as the *regina varium*, "Queen of Roads". As Roman law prohibited burial within the city walls, the Appian Way became lined with tombs, vaults and mausoleums. Later it became the site of the first catacombs built by the early Christians.

Although the Appian Way has suffered greatly throughout the centuries, with many of the monuments reduced to rubble, there is still lots to see, and it is a wonderful area to spend a day. You can hire bikes from the visitors' centre *(see box on page 241)*.

TO PORTA SAN SEBASTIANO

Once part of the Appian Way, the Via di Porta San Sebastiano passes through the **Parco degli Scipioni ❶**. At No. 9 is the **Sepolcro degli Scipioni** (closed for restoration work), the mausoleum of the powerful Scipio family. The first family member entombed here was L. Cornelius Scipio, a consul in 298 BC. By the middle of the 2nd century BC, the square tomb was full and an annexe was dug adjacent to it.

Nearby is the 1st-century AD Columbarium of **Pomponio Hylas** (also closed to visitors), which stored the cremated remains of those too poor to build their own tombs. Rich Romans often had *columbaria* built for their freedmen, but this was probably a commercial venture in which people bought a slot.

To go inside, make an appointment at the Museo delle Mura.

Main attractions

MUSEO DELLE MURA
VIA APPIA ANTICA
DOMINE QUO VADIS
FOSSE ARDEATINE
CATACOMBS
CIRCUS OF MAXENTIUS
TOMB OF CECILIA METELLA

LEFT: Claudio aqueduct.
RIGHT: fresco detail of the Last Supper in the catacombs of St Domitilla, 2nd century AD.

Appian Way

Museo delle Mura ➋

☏ 06-7047 5284 ◷ Tue–Sun 9am–2pm Ⓒ charge 🚌 118

Porta San Sebastiano is the largest and best-preserved of the gateways in the Aurelian Wall, and inside, the Museo delle Mura gives a detailed account of the building of the walls, once almost 20 km (12 miles) long with 381 towers. In AD 403, their height was doubled – to 12 metres (40 ft). They were then 3.5 metres (12 ft) thick and had 18 gates. Older buildings were incorporated into the walls.

A walk along the top gives some idea of the view the Imperial legionaries had as they watched for barbarian armies. Today, however, there are concrete blocks in every direction, except towards Via Appia, where the Campagna is almost in its original state.

When the Via Appia was extended outside the city walls to Capua, it followed an existing route to the Alban Hills and was the major campaign path for the conquest of southern Italy. In 190 BC it was extended via Benevento to Brindisi,

Recommended Restaurants & Bars on page 243

connecting Rome with the eastern Mediterranean. When the Empire fell, the road decayed and was not used again until the time of Pius VI.

VIA APPIA ANTICA

Beyond the gate is Via Appia Antica. The first part, with the main monuments and sights, is not an entirely pleasant walk due to unrelenting traffic. About 1 km (½ mile) down, on the left, is the church of **Domine Quo Vadis** ❸ ("Lord, where are you going?"), where the Apostle Peter, after escaping from a Roman prison, is said to have met Jesus. Jesus replied to Peter's question: "To let myself be crucified a second time."

Jesus is said to have left his foot-

prints on the road and you can see them, preserved, inside the church.

To the left of the church is the little Via della Caffarella, which leads into the Caffarella valley, a lovely stretch of Roman countryside, scattered with ruins, sheep and farmhouses. If you take the right fork at Domine Quo Vadis and head along Via Ardeatina, you come to **Fosse Ardeatine** ❹ (174 Via Ardeatina; tel: 06-678 3114; Mon–Fri 8.15am–3.15pm, Sat–Sun until 4.45pm), a moving memorial to the 335 Italians who were murdered on 24 March 1944, in revenge for an ambush by Resistance fighters in which 32 Nazi soldiers were killed. The victims had nothing to do with the attack, but were rounded up, shot and buried in a mass grave. After the war, their bodies were retrieved and reburied in sarcophagi in the mausoleum.

Catacombs

On the way back to Via Appia are the **Catacombe di San Callisto** ❺ (daily 8.30am–noon and 2.30–5pm; see page 245). In the **Cripta dei Papi** (Crypt of the Popes), inscriptions of

The church of Domine Quo Vadis, built on the spot where St Peter is said to have met Jesus.

LEFT: Porta San Sebastiano. **ABOVE LEFT:** the Archeobus runs along the Appian Way. **BELOW:** the San Sebastiano catacombs are one of the most popular to visit.

Bikes and Buses

A hop-on hop-off minibus, the Archeobus, leaves daily from Termini Station and goes the length of the Appian Way (www.trambusopen.com; tel: 06-6840 901; daily departures every 40 mins 9.30am–4.50pm; ticket purchased on board or online, and valid all day).

Alternatively, you can hire a bike from the visitors' centre (www.parcoappia antica.org; 60 Via Appia Antica; tel: 06-5135 316; daily 9.30am–5.30pm; book ahead if in a group) or take a guided bike tour; the itinerary lasts about 2½ hours and winds through the Caffarella valley (daily) and along the Appian Way (Sundays and Bank Holidays). The best time to visit is on a Sunday or Bank Holiday, when traffic is restricted.

TIP

Signs and symbols in the catacombs:

Dove holding a twig – reconciliation between God and Man.

Anchor – sign of hope.

Fish – symbol of Christ (the initial letters of the Greek word for fish make the phrase "Jesus Christ, God's Son, Saviour").

Dolphin – coming to save the shipwrecked, Jesus the Saviour.

Jonah and the Whale – the Resurrection.

RIGHT: the colossal tomb of Cecilia Metella.
BELOW:
Circo di Massenzio.

at least 10 bishops of Rome from the 3rd and 4th centuries have been discovered. Among them is the first documented use of the title "Pope" for the bishop of Rome (from AD 298).

Also open to the public are the **Catacombe di San Sebastiano 6** (Mon–Sat 8.30am–noon and 2.30–5.30pm; *see page 245*), the first of the underground burial sites to be so called due to its proximity to a cave (from the Greek *kata*, near, and *kymbas*, cave), and the **Catacombe di Domitilla 7** (Wed–Mon 8.30am–noon and 2.30–5pm; *see page 245*), one of the largest catacombs in Rome. Contrary to popular belief, the catacombs were not used for worship, nor for hiding in during times of Christian persecution; the excavated rooms were used for simple funeral ceremonies.

Among the rows of shelves for the dead are a lot of little "tombs", used for the tragically high number of infant deaths, and some particularly large or imposing ones, usually belonging to martyrs who were reburied in Roman churches in the Middle Ages. Further along Via

Appia, at No. 119a, are the Jewish catacombs of Vigna Randanini. To visit them you need to seek permission from the Comunità Ebraica in Rome.

Circus of Maxentius 8

✉ 153 Via Appia Antica 📞 06-780 1324 🕐 Tue–Sat 9am–1pm
💶 free 🚌 660

Also worth seeing are the **Circo di Massenzio**, built by the Emperor Maxentius, and the **Mausoleo di Romolo**, both from around AD 310. The Circus was used for chariot races and could seat 10,000 spectators. Maxentius' Imperial palace, **Villa di Massenzio**, is nearby (opening times as above).

The tomb of Cecilia Metella **9**

✉ 161 Appia Antica, www.pierreci.it
☎ 06-780 2465 ⏰ daily 9am–4.30pm (closing time varies according to season) ⓖ charge ⬛ 660

The tomb of Cecilia Metella was built around 50 BC for the daughter of Quintus Metellus Creticus, conqueror of Crete. She was later the wife of Crassus, son of the famous member of the Triumvirate of Caesar's time. During the 14th century the tomb was incorporated into a fortress and crenallations added by the Caetani family, relatives of the Pope, who used to boost the family coffers by extracting tolls from passers-by.

After this, the Via Appia is far more rural, sparse and quiet, with overgrown ruins, fabulous gated modern villas and shady trees. Along the roadside are the remains of many tombs built by the great families of Rome. To the east, you can see the dramatic arches of the Claudio aqueduct, one of 11 that supplied Rome with water at the height of its power.

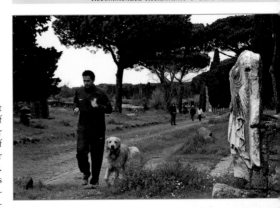

Beyond the crossing with Via Erode Attico, the remains in the farmland to the left are those of the 2nd-century AD **Villa dei Quintili** (1092 Via Appia Nuova; www.pierreci.it; Mon–Sat 9am–1.30pm and 2.30–5pm). If you look closely, you can see a *nymphaeum* and aqueduct arches. Finally, where the Via Appia joins the road that leads back to Via Appia Nuova is **Casale Rotondo**, a late 1st-century BC tomb, with fragments of relief stuck to its sides and a farmhouse and garden sitting on top. ❏

TOP AND ABOVE: on Sundays the Via Appia Antica is popular with runners and cyclists.

RESTAURANTS & BARS

Restaurants

L'Archeologia
✉ 139 Via Appia Antica
☎ 06-788 0494 ⓖ L & D
Wed–Mon. €€–€€€
Set in a 16th-century house with a beautiful outdoor area and ancient ruins on view. Fresh fish daily. Excellent wine cellar in an old catacomb.

Cecilia Metella
✉ 125–129 Via Appia Antica
☎ 06-513 6743 ⓖ L & D
Tue–Sun. €€–€€€

Just across from the catacombs of San Sebastiano, this could easily have been a tourist trap but isn't. Good cooking, and a delightful terrace.

Hostaria Antica Roma
✉ 87 Via Appia Antica
☎ 06-513 2888 ⓖ L & D
Tue–Sun. €€€
This charming restaurant's garden features ancient Roman ruins. Specialities include gnocchi with clams and a succulent beef fillet with truffles. A tasting menu of ancient recipes is available on Tuesdays and Thursdays.

Ar Montarozzo
✉ 4 Via Appia Antica
☎ 06-7720 8434 ⓖ L & D
Tue–Sun. €€€
A lovely restaurant with garden for alfresco eating and a predominantly fishy menu; try the risotto with asparagus tips and prawns. All the usual Roman classics are here, too, and there's an extensive wine list, with 300 bottles.

Bars

Bar Appia Antica (on the corner of Via Appia Antica and Via Cecilia Metella; closed Mon) is a good place for a restorative coffee and a snack before or after a brisk walk along the Appian Way's famous but sometimes wearying cobblestones.

• • • • • • • • • • •
Price includes dinner and a half-bottle of house wine.
€€€€ = €60 and up,
€€€ = €40–60, **€€** = €25–40, **€** = under €25.

RELICS OF THE CATACOMBS

"A desert of decay, sombre and desolate; and with a history in every stone that strews the ground" – Charles Dickens

For health reasons and habit, the Romans buried their dead outside the city walls; the Appian Way is lined with the tombs of Romans, Christians and Jews – and, for the less wealthy, catacombs, whose labyrinthine galleries contain niches *(loculi)* built into the tufa rock.

While Christian and Jewish practice was burial of the body, Romans believed in cremation, with the ashes buried in an urn. Christian bodies, embalmed or shrouded in linen, were placed on ledges in the walls, sealed beneath marble slabs on the floor or interred in family vaults *(cubicula)*.

The Christianisation of Rome led to the cult of the early martyrs, with pilgrimages and renewed interest in the catacombs. The frescoed interiors are adorned with Christian symbols or graffiti, from a dove, fish or anchor to acanthus leaves and vines. While some are mossy and mouldering, the weather-worn tombs make an impressive proclamation of faith. Today, the Via Appia is an inspired or desolate scene, depending on one's mood.

ABOVE: the Last Supper fresco in the catacombs of St Callistus. Founded around the middle of the 2nd century AD, they are part of a huge complex of galleries, 19 km (12 miles) long and more than 20 metres (66 ft) deep. Callistus was the deacon in charge of the cemetery; he was born a slave and became Pope before dying as a Christian martyr in 222. These catacombs were only discovered in 1850.
LEFT: skulls and fragments of engravings in the catacombs of St Callistus.

SUBTERRANEAN SCENE

Three of the largest Roman underground burial sites are to be found in the vicinity of the Appian Way:

• **Catacombe di San Callisto** (110 Via Appia Antica; tel: 06-5130 1580; daily 8.30am–noon and 2.30–5pm; admission charge; bus no. 218). Rome's first official Christian cemetery encloses the crypts of many early popes and saints.

• **Catacombe di San Sebastiano** (136 Via Appia Antica; tel: 06-785 0350; Mon–Sat 8.30am–noon and 2.30–5.30pm; admission charge; bus nos 118, 218, 660). Three exquisitely preserved mausoleums and miles of subterranean galleries over four levels.

• **Catacombe di Domitilla** (282 Via delle Sette Chiese; tel: 06-511 0342; Wed–Mon 8.30am–noon and 2.30–5pm; admission charge; bus nos 714, 218). One of the earliest images of Christ as the Good Shepherd features among its sublime frescoes.

The following are in the northeast of Rome:

• **Catacombe di Priscilla** (430 Via Salaria; tel: 06-8620 6272; Feb–Dec Tues–Sun 8.30am–noon and 2.30–5pm; admission charge; bus nos 86, 92, 63). In the 3rd and 4th centuries, these catacombs were the preferred resting place of the upper classes.

• **Catacombe di Sant'Agnese** (349 Via Nomentana; tel: 06-861 0840; Sun and religious holidays 4–6pm, Mon 9am–noon, Tues–Sat 9am–noon and 4–6pm; admission charge; bus nos 36, 60).

TOP RIGHT: this fresco, a particularly delicate tomb decoration, is in the catacombs dedicated to the Roman soldier who became a Christian martyr.

BELOW: underground Rome has more to offer than catacombs. This 1st-century Temple of Mithras, dedicated to a polytheistic Persian cult, lies below San Clemente. In a relief, Mithras is depicted slaying a bull, the symbol of fertility.

MAIN PICTURE: this chamber, called the Hypogeum, is part of an underground tomb or *ipogeo*. These were often frescoed, depicting pagan scenes such as funerary feasts or blood sacrifice. Henrik Ibsen enjoyed lying among the tombs.

ABOVE: many Jews converted to Christianity, but those who kept their faith were buried separately in the Jewish Catacombs.

Excursions from Rome

EXCURSIONS FROM ROME

All roads may lead to Rome, but it's worth considering going in the opposite direction to explore the fertile, hilly areas, Etruscan and Roman sites, and Renaissance villas and gardens, all within easy reach of the capital

Given that more than 20 million tourists pour into Rome each year, it's surprising that so few find their way into the Roman hinterland. The region of Lazio remains relatively unexplored, but has plenty to offer. As with any major metropolis, the area immediately around the capital doesn't instantly give way to a pastoral idyll. The shift from suburban sprawl and industrial development to rolling countryside is gradual. However, there are some delightfully picturesque pockets and landmarks to discover, all within easy reach of the city.

The Pope is not alone in choosing the gentle, wine-producing hills of the Castelli Romani south of Rome for his rural retreat. During the sweltering summers and at weekends Romans leave the capital in droves to indulge in the region's excellent food and wine – a favourite Italian pastime – lounge around its lakes and enjoy the scenery. Sun-seekers head for convenient Lido di Ostia, but the resort of Fregene, north of the Tiber, has more cachet. The most scenic stretches of beach, however, are a lengthier drive away at the southern end of the Lazio coast.

Ostia Antica, Hadrian's Villa and the Etruscan graves of Cerveteri draw romantics to their ruins. Lake Bracciano appeals to escapists, walkers, golfers and riders. Villa d'Este, with its pleasure palace and water gardens dominating the town of Tivoli, is a favourite spot for picnickers.

The chapters in this section cover the most popular day-trip destinations, though some places may tempt you into an overnight stay (recommended hotels are listed in the Travel Tips section at the back of this book).

Most of the destinations are accessible by bus or train, but a hire car will give you much more flexibility and enable you to explore Lazio's countryside and coast at your leisure. ❏

PRECEDING PAGES: the ruins of Hadrian's Teatro Marittimo, Villa Adriana.

OSTIA ANTICA

The evocative ruins of the Roman town of Ostia, surrounded by pines and flat coastal plains, make a good excursion from the dusty hustle and bustle of Rome. For a sun, sea and sand break, bypass the Lido di Ostia and head for Fregene or explore Lazio's more scenic southern beaches

According to legend, King Ancus Marcius founded a port town in the 7th century BC and named it **Ostia ❶** after the *ostium* or mouth of the Tiber. However, the archaeological evidence dates only to the second half of the 4th century BC, when fortifications were built around the town. Rome was very dependent on this one connection with the sea, because all its essential commodities – especially grain – were transported from Ostia along the **Via Ostiensis**. It also became the main base of the Roman fleet in around 300 BC, and by the Imperial era had become a major city, with a population of about 80,000.

Rome's dependence on Ostia was good news for the port's inhabitants. The trade of imported goods from the West and East brought the local population wealth and luxury. The town even had special status, with the male inhabitants being freed from military service. There was also money to be made from holidaymakers. On hot summer days, when the stone streets of Rome practically blazed, Romans fled to the seaside resort.

However, when Emperor Augustus transferred the Roman naval base to Misenium, Ostia felt the loss of the free-spending sailors and all the associated trade. For a while, it remained the unloading point for the grain ships and, in AD 41–54, Claudius had new docks built, but the beginning of the end of Ostia was already evident – the harbour was silting up. Not even a new harbour basin – now the airport of Fiumicino – that was dug on the orders of Trajan (AD 98–117) could stop this process. The coastline gradually moved west, and today Ostia is several kilometres from the sea.

Main attractions
OSTIA ANTICA
MEDIEVAL OSTIA
LIDO DI OSTIA
FREGENE
ANZIO AND NETTUNO

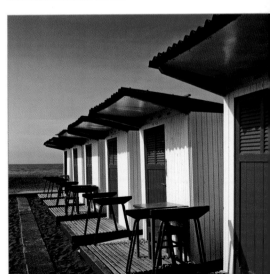

LEFT: the Capitolium Curia, Ostia Antica.
RIGHT: beach huts at the Lido di Ostia.

Part of the well-preserved mosaic in the Baths of Neptune.

Mass exodus

Ostia's prosperity peaked in the early 2nd century, but its decline was steady and relentless. Emperor Constantine's decision to move the capital of the Empire to Constantinople in the 4th century, continual pirate attacks and, in the early Middle Ages, the threat of Saracen invasions, meant that Ostia's population was forced to leave their homes. Soon, the only inhabitants left were malarial mosquitoes.

At that time, the coastline was about 4 km (2 miles) further inland than it is today. Luckily for archaeologists, the city was never repopulated, and it has been very well preserved under a bed of sand. Although the ruins were quarried for building materials in the Middle Ages, about two-thirds of the Roman town can now be seen, thanks to extensive archaeological excavation.

Since the 19th century, when excavations began under Popes Pius VII and Pius IX, this archaeological treasure house has been systematically laid bare. The better finds are on display in Rome's museums.

RIGHT: one of few statues left *in situ* – most of the finds are in museums.
BELOW: evocative ruin.

OSTIA ANTICA

✉ www.ostia-antica.org 📞 06-5365 8099 🕐 Tue–Sun Apr–Oct 8.30am–6pm, Nov–Mar 8.30am–4pm 🄴 charge 🚉 Ostia Antica/Scavi

Among the umbrella pines and wild flowers of the ancient site are the remarkably well-preserved remains of warehouses, shops, baths and barracks, temples and theatres. They give as good an insight into the everyday urban life of ancient Rome

Ostia Antica

Recommended Restaurants on page 255

as the Forum, or even Pompeii. From the entrance, visitors follow the **Decumanus Maximus A**, the same main road used by the Ancient Romans, which leads through the city centre. Worthwhile noting en route are the **Terme di Nettuno B** (Baths of Neptune), named after their glorious mosaic floor, and the **Teatro C** (Theatre), which warrants a visit for the splendid views offered by its upper tiers. Underneath these tiers there would have been taverns and shops. Beside the theatre, three large masks have been mounted on tufa columns – they were originally part of the Theatre's decoration. In summer months, the Theatre is used to stage plays and concerts.

Also well worth looking at are the stalls in the **Piazzale delle Corporazioni D** (Square of the Guilds), where lovely floor mosaics preserve the insignias of the various guilds, most of which were associated with the fitting and supplying of ships.

The Forum

The Decumanus Maximus leads to the **Foro E** (Forum), where citizens congregated and justice was dispensed by city officials, and the **Capitolium Curia F**, Ostia's largest temple, which was dedicated to Jupiter, Juno and Minerva. Beyond is the **Schola di Traianum G** (School of Trajan), formerly the headquarters of a guild of merchants, and the **Basilica Cristiana H** (Christian Basilica).

The workers of Ostia lived in *insulae*, Roman apartment blocks that were three or four storeys high. The **Casa di Diana I** (House of Diana), near the Forum, is one of the

The Pontine archipelago is a group of volcanic islands just off the coast of Lazio. Ponza is the largest and best-equipped with hotels and restaurants, and is a popular weekend getaway with Romans. A trip to this picture-postcard island is a relaxing way to round off a Roman holiday. There's a regular ferry service from Anzio, the nearest port to Rome, and the journey time is about 70 minutes. For more information visit www.ponza.com

ABOVE LEFT: one of a trio of theatrical masks.
BELOW: the Theatre, still used to stage occasional summer performances.

Lazio Beaches

Sunseekers should avoid Ostia and head instead for the cleaner beaches a little further afield

Lido di Ostia, just half an hour by train from Piramide metro station, and the surrounding beaches are the most popular, and locals start descending on them at weekends in their hundreds of thousands from late May or early June. This cannot be attributed to the cleanliness of the water or the charm of modern Ostia, but to its convenience as the nearest seaside resort to Rome and the fact that it is packed with *stabilimenti* – amenities, and a rather chaotic nightlife.

It is worth bearing in mind that Italian beaches are organised around *stabilimenti balneari*, bathing establishments, which increasingly offer far more than clean toilets, deckchairs, sunloungers and umbrellas for hire (for a daily fee). Since many holidaymakers spend their whole day there, the complexes have increased their services, and many now offer sporting equipment for hire, host children's activities, put on courses for adults and children, and have cafés which may include full-blown restaurants.

A more upmarket alternative to Lido di Ostia is **Fregene**, north of the Tiber, about 40 km (25 miles) west of Rome. Once the glamorous retreat of the *Dolce Vita* set, this appealing resort, backed by a pine wood and luxury villas, is fashionable again. It's an hour's journey by bus from the Lepanto metro station or by train from Termini to Maccarese, then bus to nearby Fregene.

Another alternative some 10 km (6 miles) south of Ostia is the sand dunes of **Capocotta**. A once-infamous nudist beach (a small, respectable and predominantly gay section, known as Il Buco, remains, just beyond the gates, going towards Torvaianica), it has totally cleaned up its act and is now run by a Rome City Council-backed consortium which offers free *stabilimenti*. Located behind several gates, which close at about 7.30pm, this stretch of coastline is clean, well kept and of some natural beauty, since it is located within the protected Parco del Litorale Romano. Take the Roma–Lido di Ostia train from Piramide metro station but get off at Cristoforo Colombo, the last stop. Here you can hire a bike and pedal down the coast, or wait for the "Mare 2" shuttle bus.

Further south, **Anzio** and **Nettuno** are two nostalgic port towns with hotels, restaurants, seafront cafés and boutiques. For a heady mix of antiquity and sunbathing, head to the beach at Villa di Nerone, to which you can walk or cycle with ease from the centre of Anzio, located under the town's lighthouse. Here you can sunbathe in full view of the remains of Nero's palace. Trains to Anzio and Nettuno leave regularly from Roma Termini.

For the first really clean water and large sandy beaches south of Rome you will have to go a bit further, to **Sabaudia** (direct buses leave from the EUR Fermi metro stop), or the ancient Roman port of **Sperlonga** (about halfway between Naples and Rome). ❑

ABOVE: bathing establishment in Ostia.
LEFT: the coast of southern Lazio.

smarter ones and is well preserved. It had a balcony on the second floor, its own private bathhouse and a central courtyard where there was a cistern to collect water.

An interesting insight into the sort of housing used by ancient Romans, it also incorporates a tavern on the ground floor, complete with a marble counter on which customers were served their sausages and hot wine (sweetened with honey), as well as ovens, storage facilities, and a beer garden for outdoor drinking.

The Museum

North of the Casa di Diana, a Renaissance building houses the **Museo ❶**. Originally built for storing salt from the nearby salt pans, today the excavation museum contains a collection of sculptures, tools, mosaics, sarcophagi and a variety of other finds from the site, which help to build a picture of daily life in Ostia.

MEDIEVAL OSTIA

Before heading either back to Rome or on to the beaches of Ostia, while here don't miss the opportunity to visit the medieval town of Ostia.

Developed around the ruins of Gregoriopolis, a fortified citadel built on the orders of Pope Gregory IV between 827 and 844, Ostia was a medieval village within defensive walls; its inhabitants worked in the nearby salt pans.

After it had been destroyed by invading forces in 1408, Martin V built a defensive tower against the barbarians and Saracens. This tower became the centre of a castle built by Pontelli later in the same century for the future Pope Julius II, then a cardinal. However, the attacks continued and, together with the silting-up of the river and a huge flood in the 16th century, drove the inhabitants away.

You can visit the **Castello di Giulio II** (16 Piazzale della Rocca; tel: 06-5635 8099; Tues–Sun 9am–1.30pm, also 2.30–4.30pm Tues and Thur; free) as the castle is now known. It has some interesting features, such as scarped curtain walls, which were innovative at the time, but became commonplace in the 16th century.

You can also see the fortress's museum, its church, Santa Aurea, and the Palazzo Episcopale, official residence of the bishop of Ostia. The latter houses some notable frescoes by Peruzzi. ❑

On the Decumanus Maximus.

LEFT:
fisherman in Anzio.

BEST RESTAURANTS

Ristorante Il Monumento	Lo Sbarco di Enea
✉ 8 Piazza Umberto I	✉ 675 Via dei Romagnoli
☎ 06-565 0021 ⏱ L & D	☎ 06-565 0034 ⏱ L & D
Tue–Sun. €€–€€€	Tue–Sun. €€€
Close to one of the entrances to the medieval *borgo* of Ostia Antica, this restaurant offers a great selection of fish dishes – the house special is spaghetti with shellfish and squid. Carnivores are well provided for with classic Italian dishes such as chicken with white wine, rosemary and garlic.	Right next to the entrance to the ruins, this reliable fish restaurant is perennially popular. The new pizzeria next door, under the same ownership, is a more economical option.

● ● ● ● ● ● ● ● ● ● ● ● ● ● ●
Price includes dinner and a half-bottle of wine. €€ = €25–40, €€€ = €40–60.

Recommended Restaurants & Bars on page 261

TIVOLI

Pressed against a hillside with commanding views of the plains below, this small workaday town was once home to Roman emperors and Renaissance aristocrats. The historic villas people flock to Tivoli to visit are testament to its glory days as a retreat for the rich

Tivoli is one of many towns set in the hills outside Rome that has long served as a getaway for Romans during the hot summer months. The town itself would be unremarkable, but for its famous villas and gardens which make it a popular attraction and a worthwhile day trip. The Renaissance Villa d'Este, of Tivoli fountains fame, and the Villa Gregoriana park are within the town, while the impressive remains of Hadrian's Villa are a couple of kilometres south of it. Tivoli is about 31 km (19 miles) east of Rome.

If you're driving, take the A24 Roma–L'Aquila motorway and exit at Tivoli e Castel Madama. Alternatively, trains for Tivoli depart from Stazione Tiburtina, or you can take a bus (journey time approximately 45 minutes) from Ponte Mammolo station on metro line B.

VILLA D'ESTE ❷

✉ 1 Piazza Trento, Tivoli; www.villadestetivoli.info ☎ 199-766 166
🕒 Tue–Sun 8.30am–1 hr before sunset
🎫 charge 🚉 Tivoli

The Villa d'Este – a UNESCO world heritage site – is a big tourist draw. The villa itself is worth a visit, with its beautiful frescoes, but the main reason people come here is to see the wonderful fountains and waterworks.

Originally a Benedictine convent, the building was converted into the Governor's Palace in the 13th century. In 1550, Cardinal Ippolito d'Este, son of Lucrezia Borgia and grandson of Pope Alexander VI, was elected governor. He immediately set about renovating the villa and its gardens, to turn it into something befitting his aspirations to the papacy. Ippolito commissioned Pirro Ligorio to design

Main attractions
VILLA D'ESTE
VILLA GREGORIANA
VILLA ADRIANA

LEFT: a fresco in the Villa d'Este.
RIGHT: oval fountain in the villa gardens.

The gardens

A walk through the terraced gardens, geometrically laid out with more than 500 fountains, is a delight. The first glimpse you get of the gardens is from the upper terrace, which offers a wonderful vista of the lawns, fountains and walkways that fan out from the central axis which runs down the hill. The café here is a good spot to relax and take in the view of the gardens and the valley below.

As you wend your way from top to bottom, the main fountains to look out for include the **Viale delle Cento Fontane** (Avenue of a Hundred Fountains), a row of close-set pipes that spray water into the air, which terminates at one end with the

TIP

On summer weekends, the Villa d'Este extends its opening times until midnight for visitors to enjoy the spectacle of the fountains beautifully floodlit. Visit the website for current dates.

ABOVE AND RIGHT: Avenue of a Hundred Fountains.
BELOW: view of the "Rometta" fountain and the plains below Tivoli.

the grounds. Ligorio, who had studied the nearby Hadrian's Villa, excavated the hillside, laid it out in terraces and built an aqueduct and underground canal fed by the river Aniene, to supply the extensive waterworks. The gardens took seven years to complete, and their beauty and ingenuity created the desired impact.

Ippolito d'Este never did make pope, but he did leave a memorial to himself in the fountains, which have delighted visitors for centuries and served to inspire waterworks all over Europe. After the decline of the Este family, the Habsburgs inherited the villa, but they were poor caretakers. After World War I, the Italian State took it over and began the long task of its restoration.

Fontana dell'Ovato (Oval Fountain) decorated with nymphs, and at the other with the **Rometta** (Little Rome), a minature representation of Roman landmarks. Halfway along is the **Fontana dei Draghi** (Fountain of Dragons), made in honour of Pope Gregory XIII, who was once a guest here, and whose papal insignia included a dragon.

One of the most inventive of these playful creations was the **Fontana dell'Organo Idraulico** (Fountain of the Hydraulic Organ), designed with an elaborate water-operated organ. Recently restored, it can be seen in operation every two hours from 10.30am. Notice the two upper reliefs portray Apollo and Orpheus playing the lyre and the violin. The **Fontana della Civetta e degli Uccelli** (Fountain of the Owl and the Birds) was another ingenious invention, designed to reproduce the screech of an owl and birdsong through water power (daily demonstrations every two hours from 10am).

One word of warning: avoid the temptation to drink or touch the water – it comes from the sewers.

PARCO DI VILLA GREGORIANA ③

✉ Largo Sant'Angelo; www.villa gregoriana.it ☎ 06-3996 7701 ⏰ Tue–Sun Mar and mid-Oct–end Nov 10am–2.30pm, Apr–mid-Oct 10am–6.30pm, Dec–Feb by appointment only ⓒ charge 🚌 Tivoli

Tivoli's watery attractions don't all flow in the Villa d'Este. The town is full of ancient remains of temples and other buildings – some (such as the Temple of Vesta) are extremely well preserved, while others have been incorporated into medieval churches.

Not far from the Temple of Vesta is the entrance to the newly restored Villa Gregoriana, a dramatic and steep wooded park set in a rocky gorge which was created in 1835 at the request of Pope Gregory XVI, whose aim was to avert frequent flooding of the town by diverting the flow of the River Aniene here.

Steep paths lead down to the villa's galleries, terraces and belvederes, from which visitors can admire the great waterfall and the nearby grottoes, both natural and artificial.

The 100-metre (300-ft) high Grande Cascata is fed by the River Aniene.

BELOW: the Tempio di Vesta overlooks the Parco Villa Gregoriana in the gorge below.

There is a café just outside the site of Hadrian's Villa, but you might want to consider packing a picnic. There are plenty of benches and shady spots amid the olive trees to sit and enjoy lunch amid the ruins.

ABOVE RIGHT:
archway in the thick boundary walls.
BELOW: the Canopus.

VILLA ADRIANA ❹

✉ Via Tiburtina, 6 km (4 miles) south-west of Tivoli ⏰ daily 9am–1 hr before sunset 🎟 charge 🚉 Tivoli and bus CAT no. 4 🚌 Cotral bus from Ponte Mammolo, direction Via Prenestina

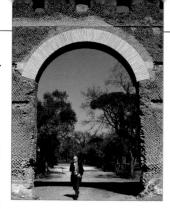

Even more impressive than the Villa d'Este are the ruins of Hadrian's Villa, the most magnificent country residence of Imperial times.

When Rome was flourishing, Tivoli (ancient Tibur), in the foothills of the Sabine Hills, was a favoured retreat for wealthy citizens. Among the frequent guests at their splendid villas were Horace, Catullus, Maecenas, Sallust and Emperor Trajan.

In AD 117, Hadrian started to build a luxurious refuge for himself at the foot of the hill on which Tivoli stands. The emperor was a skilled architect (he was the creator of the Pantheon), and his plan was to reconstruct the monuments that had most impressed him on his travels through the Empire, particularly in Greece and Egypt. Another innovation was his idea of scattering the individual buildings over the 60 hectares (148 acres) of the park, rather than grouping them in a central complex. All the buildings were connected by covered walkways and underground passages (cryptoportici), to protect against the weather.

Just before entering the ruins, take a look at the model reconstruction of the villa, which gives a good impression of the sheer scale and splendour of Hadrian's grand design.

Beautiful imitations

One of the most noteworthy structures is the colonnaded garden court, known as the **Pecile**, a reproduction of the Stoa Poikile Hadrian had seen

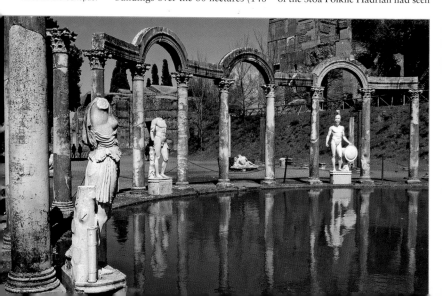

in Athens. The surrounding wall, 230 metres (760 ft) long, has survived on the north side, as has a basin in the centre. On the inner side stood a covered, pillared entrance.

One of the most outstanding buildings to survive is the **Teatro Marittimo** (Maritime Theatre), a circular building with a columned porch, inside which a circular moat surrounded an island that was reached by two wooden swing bridges. On the island stood a miniature villa where the emperor could relax in safety and privacy.

Between the Pecile and Maritime Theatre, the remains of a great dome that once covered the **Terme** (Baths) demonstrate the very high architec-

tural standards that were employed.

The most ambitious of Hadrian's replicas was the **Canopus**, a copy of the famous Temple of Serapis near Alexandria in Egypt; the 15-km (10-mile) canal, lined with luxury residences and statues, led from the River Nile to the Temple. Hadrian tried to imitate the scenario by creating a 119-metre (390-ft) long canal, by the side of which stood marble architraves and copies of Egyptian statues.

The southern bank was originally occupied by a copy of the Serapis shrine, but all that remains is a large niche in the rock and a big chunk of rock lying in the water basin.

Excavations of the villa, first carried out to obtain marble, have turned up more than 300 statues, as well as friezes, frescoes and mosaics. The museum near the Canopus displays various minor finds, but the majority of statues and other finds are now on display in museums throughout the world.

Hadrian didn't enjoy his Imperial palace for long – he died only four years after it was completed. ❏

Relaxing in the shade of the olive trees that line the Pecile basin.

LEFT: reclining statue near the Canopus.
BELOW: the terrace café at the Villa d'Este.

BEST RESTAURANTS AND BARS

Restaurants

Adriano

✉ 194 Via di Villa Adriana
☎ 0774-535028 🍴 L & D Mon–Sat, L only Sun. €€€
Located right next to the entrance to Hadrian's Villa, this restaurant has a large, shady terrace as well as a more formal indoor dining area. The creative menu might include dishes such as courgette-flower risotto and ricotta and spinach-

stuffed ravioli. Also has a few rooms.

Ristorante Sibilla

✉ 50 Via della Sibilla
☎ 0774-335281 🍴 L & D Tues–Sat, L only Sun. €€€
A few minutes from Piazza Garibaldi, Tivoli's central square, this historic restaurant has hosted popes, kings and emperors – but the charming staff are welcoming to all, and the menu of classic Italian dishes won't dis-

appoint. The shady terrace, with its views of nearby Villa Gregoriana, is a lovely spot in warm weather.

Bars

Admire the view of the Tivoli fountains and gardens from the café on the upper terrace of the Villa d'Este *(pictured right)*.

● ● ● ● ● ● ● ● ● ● ● ●
Price includes dinner and a half-bottle of house wine.
€€€€ = €60 and up,
€€€ = €40–60, **€€** = €25–40,
€ = under €25.

GREEN RETREATS

Lazio has many hidden gardens, both formal and wild. These peaceful retreats offer respite from the city's hustle and bustle

A trip out of the city in search of the region's little-explored gardens is a welcome antidote to a hectic sightseeing schedule and the weight of all that history. Options range from densely flowered oases such as the Giardini della Landriana and wild, medieval Ninfa, to wildlife sanctuaries such as the peaceful Oasi di Porto and fairytale gardens like the fountain-filled Villa d'Este and the Castello di Vignanello. Gardens generally open to the public from April to October, to coincide with the flowering season. Some gardens put on special events to showcase the plants in bloom; the most popular are the springtime flower shows at the Giardini della Landriana, which offer stunning displays of gardens in bloom, bursting with plants of every description.

All the gardens illustrated here are within easy reach of Rome, and make good day-trip destinations for those willing to hire a car and make a day of it; if you're reliant on public transport, Villa d'Este and the Oasi di Ninfa are just a short train ride away. A specialised Italian tour operator, Great Garden Tours, organises private visits and guided tours to some of Italy's most spectacular gardens, including those not normally open to the public (*see www.greatgardentours.com for details*).

ABOVE: GIARDINI DELLA LANDRIANA

These gardens, designed by English landscape architect Russell Page (1906–85), are distinctive for their orderly, geometric design: the grounds are divided into 30 "rooms" separated by hedges and paths. Don't miss the Valley of the Roses: hundreds of varieties bloom in romantic disarray across the hillside overlooking the lake, in beds bordered by thyme, lavender and clove pinks, interspersed with slim cypresses.

Open weekends and public holidays Apr–May 10am–noon and 3–6pm, first and third Sunday of June, July, September and October 10am–noon and 4–7pm. By car, take the Via Pontina out of Rome until the Campo di Carne exit. Follow Via Campo di Carne until you reach the gardens at No. 51.

LEFT: OASI DI NINFA

A bustling, prosperous city in medieval times, Ninfa was all but destroyed in a bloody civil war in 1382. Derelict for centuries, its ruins were restored and various botanical species planted in the 1920s. Ninfa has retained its otherworldly appeal: plants and trees grow unchecked amid the moss-covered parapets and crumbling towers – remnants of its medieval past.

Open April–October, the first Saturday and Sunday of the month. Take a regional train from Stazione Termini to Latina Scalo (30 min), then a taxi from the station for around €15.

RIGHT: VILLA D'ESTE

The grounds of the magnificent Villa d'Este in Tivoli are dotted with water features, from dramatic, gushing waterfalls to musical fountains, nymphaeums and grottoes. See it dramatically illuminated at night if you get the chance. *For more information see page 257.*

Open Tuesday–Sunday 8.30am–one hour before sunset; evening visits mid-June to mid–September Friday–Saturday 9pm–midnight. Take the train from Stazione Tiburtina to Tivoli; Villa d'Este is at 1 Piazza Trento, just off the main square.

LEFT: SAN LIBERATO

This magical garden lies 40 km (25 miles) north-west of Rome, overlooking Lake Bracciano. It is full of exotic specimens such as Japanese cherries and tulip trees, and has a delicate, manicured rose garden. Open April–October first and last Sunday of the month, November first and second Sunday. By car, take the GRA ring road out of Rome (exit 5, Cassia Veientana towards Viterbo). Take the Trevignano-Mazzano exit. At Trevignano take the Settevene-Palo road to Bracciano until you reach the gardens at No. 33.

LEFT: CASTELLO DI VIGNANELLO

This beautiful villa has been owned by the aristocratic Ruspoli family for centuries. Ottavia Orsini, an ancestor of the Ruspolis, can be credited with the garden's creation, widely regarded as one of the most beautiful Italian parterres. The perfectly rectangular space is subdivided by mixed hedges of bay, laurel and box; the boxes-within-boxes form patterns, tracing the initials of their creator in the central beds.

Open April–October Sundays and holidays, 10.30am–1.30pm and 3–6pm. Take the GRA ring road out of Rome (exit 5, Cassia Veientana towards Viterbo). At Monterosi take the Cimina road, then continue towards Vignanello, following signs to the castle.

LEFT: OASI DI PORTO

Surprisingly peaceful considering it's just over 1 km (½ mile) from Fiumicino Airport, this nature reserve is worthy of a visit. A vast lake makes an ideal habitat for migratory birds, and the surrounding parkland is dominated by imposing Roman pine trees, oaks and poplars. Guided tours by horse-drawn cart can be organised; call 06-588 0880 for details.

Open mid-October to mid-June, Thursday and Sunday 10am–4pm. From Rome, take the Roma–Fiumicino motorway, pass the airport exit and follow the viaduct towards Ostia. Take the first right to Fiumicino, then immediately left onto Via Portuense; the entrance to the Oasi is 3 km (2 miles) along the road.

Recommended Restaurants, Bars & Cafés on page 271

CASTELLI ROMANI

For a leisurely country drive through towns and villages famous for their food and wine, hire a car and tour this group of small towns southeast of Rome – a popular weekend retreat for the city's inhabitants

Rome

Southeast of Rome lie the Colli Albani, a group of volcanic hills which form a vast horseshoe shaped crater 60 km (37 miles) in circumference. Within this giant horseshoe are a number of smaller craters, two of which contain the beautiful lakes of Nemi and Albano. Thirteen towns in the Alban Hills are known collectively as the "Castelli Romani" (Roman Castles). The name stems from the fact that they evolved around the feudal castles of Roman patrician families who sought refuge here when anarchy ruled in Rome. The Castelli are best explored by car, though they can be reached by Cotral buses which depart from the car park at Anagnina station at the end of metro line A. Frascati is reached by car on Via Tuscolana; Castel Gandolfo, Albano and Ariccia by Via Appia Nuova. Lake Albano, Marino, Genzano and Nemi are reached by Via dei Laghi, which leaves Via Appia Nuovo just south of Ciampino Airport.

FRASCATI ⑤

Frascati, which takes its name from the thatch *(frasche)* used to roof its huts, turned from a small settlement into a town in 1197, when the ancient city of Tusculum was destroyed and its population settled here. During World War II, it was seat of the German High Command and suffered heavy damage from Allied bombing, which left much of the town destroyed. Many of its historic buildings, including several churches, were rebuilt after the war.

Frascati is the nearest of the Castelli Romani, only 21 km (13 miles) away from Rome. One of the best times to visit is in October,

Main attractions
FRASCATI
TUSCULUM
GROTTAFERRATA
ROCCA DI PAPA
MONTE CAVO
MARINO
CASTEL GANDOLFO
GENZANO
NEMI
OASI DI NINFA

LEFT: the Genzano flower festival.
RIGHT: spring blooms in the Oasis of Ninfa.

TIP

In June hydrangea producers come to Frascati from all over Italy to compete in the lovely hydrangea festival. July and August are also eventful with food and wine festivals, theatre performances and concerts, and a celebratory gathering of vineyard-owners and farm labourers.

ABOVE RIGHT: a flask of Frascati in a back-street cantina. **BELOW:** porchetta stand.

when the grape harvest begins; a *frasca di lauro*, a laurel twig, is displayed; the smoke of the first wood fires mixes with the sweet scents from the vineyards; and a fat, fresh *porchetta* (whole-roast pig stuffed with aromatic herbs, for which the region is known) lies on the counter of every *alimentari* (local grocery).

Wine and *porchetta*

The town's trademark is its wine – a light, quaffable wine with a faint, refreshing prickle – which is a product of the rich volcanic soil. In Italy, Frascati is drunk mostly by the *Frascatani* themselves. Much of the stuff on sale in supermarkets bears little relation to the drink served in the *cantine* (wine shops or bars), which ranges from pale to dark yellow.

Most of the exported wine comes from neighbouring towns and villages rather than Frascati itself, but the reason it is so poor is that most is based on the rather bland Trebbiano grape; only the better producers – Fontana Candida and Colli di Catone (especially Colle Gaio) – use Malvasia. For more information on

wine producers and wine tours and tastings in Frascati, visit the tourist office on Piazza Marconi.

Begin with a walk around town, starting at **Piazza San Pietro**. From here, go through the little *galleria* (walkway) next to the cinema to **Piazza del Mercato**, where there is a closed produce market and plenty of stalls where you can get a good sandwich bursting with *porchetta*. Go left past the market and you will find several wine shops and bars in **Via Regina Margherita** and further on in **Piazza del Olmo**, that allow customers to bring *cibo proprio* (their own food).

Frascati villas

Frascati is not only famous for its wine, but also for its palaces and gardens. Next to the bus station is the park of **Villa Torlonia**, originally part of a 16th-century estate that was bombed to the ground in World War II. Now only the gardens remain, and the striking Teatro delle Acque (Theatre of the Waters) fountain designed by Carlo Maderno.

Standing majestically above the town, with commanding views of the surrounding countryside and, on a clear day, Rome, is the **Villa Aldobrandini**. Built in 1602 for Pietro Aldobrandini, a nephew of Pope Clement VIII, the villa is still occupied by the Aldobrandini family and closed to the public, but you can

Recommended Restaurants, Bars & Cafés on page 271

visit the grounds (Mon–Fri 9am–1pm and 3–5pm, until 6pm in summer; permits are available from the tourist office on nearby Piazza Marconi; tel: 06-942 0331; free).

Back down on the main square, the former stables of the villa have been sensitively restored and converted by Massimiliano Fuksas into a fabulous exhibition space for high-profile art exhibitions. **Le Scuderie Aldobrandini** (6 Piazza Marconi; www.scuderiealdobrandini.it; tel: 06-9417195; Tue–Sun 10am–6pm, until 7pm on Sat) is also the new home for the Tuscolano Museum, displaying finds from the nearby ancient city of Tusculum.

TUSCULUM ⑥

About 5 km (3 miles) from the Villa Aldobrandini is the site of the ancient hilltown of Tusculum. The city of the Latins (founded, according to legend, by Telegonus, son of Circe and Ulysses) was a monarchy before it fell within Rome's sphere of influence in the 6th century BC.

Later, in 340 BC, the city participated in the revolt against the Romans. From the 10th to the 12th centuries, the counts of Tusculum ruled over it – as well as Rome. In 1191, the Romans destroyed the town as an act of revenge for its subjugation, and its inhabitants fled to Frascati. Few ruins remain, but the views from up here are splendid, and it's a nice spot for a picnic.

GROTTAFERRATA ⑦

It's only a few kilometres from Frascati to **Grottaferrata**, known for its Greek Orthodox abbey. The **Abbazia di San Nilo** (128 Corso del Popolo; www.abbaziagreca.it; tel: 06-945 9309; daily 6am–12.30pm and 3.30pm–sunset; free) was founded in 1004 by Nilus, a monk from Calabria

Aldobrandini's own organic Frascati is for sale on the premises.

LEFT: remains of the amphitheatre at Tusculum. **BELOW:** Villa Aldobrandini.

A shrine to the Virgin on Monte Cavo.

fleeing north to find a site safe from attack by Saracens. Under Byzantine rule, southern Italy had a large Greek minority, whose descendants survive today in a few remote areas.

The monastery was built on the remains of a sepulchre dating from the Republican era. The abbey church, **Santa Maria di Grottaferrata**, is decorated with some fine mosaics and has beautiful frescoes by Domenichino in the Cappella dei Santi Fondatori. On Sunday morning, Mass is celebrated according to the Greek Orthodox rite.

From here, you can see the cross atop the hill at **Rocca Priora** ❽, the highest town in the Castelli at 768 metres (2,520 ft), which is often covered in snow in winter.

ABOVE RIGHT:
entrance of the
Abbey of San Nilo,
Grottaferrata. **BELOW:**
detail of a fresco by
Domenichino, in the
chapel dedicated to
Saints Nilo and
Bartholemew.

ROCCA DI PAPA ❾

The town of **Rocca di Papa** ("The Pope's Rock") lies a few miles away, on the northern flank of the **Monte Cavo**, the highest peak of the Alban Hills (949 metres/3,114 ft). This attractive medieval town has a *quartiere bavarese*, named after the Bavarian mercenaries who were sta-

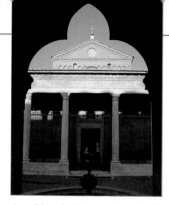

tioned here by Emperor Ludwig III in the 1320s. Rome is only a few miles away and yet the city, whose lights twinkle like glow worms below, couldn't seem more distant.

The wine of Monte Cavo is excellent, and a particularly delicious local speciality, the *sfogatelli* mushroom, is worth seeking out.

MONTE CAVO ❿

From Rocca di Papa, you may want to climb to the peak of **Monte Cavo**, following Via Sacra through the oak woods. The summit is a little disappointing because it is covered in hundreds of TV antennae. These stand over the remains of the ancient shrine of Jupiter, worshipped by the 47 federated Latin cities, and a more recent monastery. Despite the antennae, the view is fantastic.

MARINO ⑪

Marino, another of the Castelli Romani noted for its wine, holds a celebrated wine festival each October. The town's fountains flow with wine, and there's plenty of wine tasting, eating and parading through the streets. The main square, **Piazza Matteotti** (named after the Socialist leader murdered by Mussolini) is dominated by the Fountain of the Moors, built in honour of the *condottiere* (mercenary admiral) of the papal fleet, Marcantonio Colonna, victor of the sea battle of Lepanto in 1571.

The **Madonna del Rosario** church is well worth a visit. Built in 1713, it is the most beautiful rococo church in Lazio.

CASTEL GANDOLFO ⑫

The popes' summer residence at Castel Gandolfo is beautifully situated 400 metres/1,300 ft above the crater rim of Lago di Albano. This was the site of Alba Longa, the city founded by Aeneas. After a long struggle between Alba Longa and Rome, the latter won. Alba Longa was destroyed as a punishment for treachery, but the temples were spared. They are said to have occupied the exact spot of the papal villa.

The Holy See acquired Castel Gandolfo at the end of the 16th century, and in 1628 Pope Urban VIII commissioned Maderno to design a villa here. Completed by Bernini, the **Papal Palace** is linked by bridges and loggias to the other two pontifical villas, Villa Barberini and Villa Cybo. The gardens are closed to the public for security reasons. In summer, the Pope holds the angelus prayer at midday on Sunday on the **Loggia della Benedizione.**

Stendhal, Goethe and Gregoro-

vius all had a high opinion of Castel Gandolfo, and modern Romans love it, too, particularly because it is so close to **Lago di Albano** ⑬. The clean water of this volcanic lake invites boating and swimming, but in the middle, where it is 170 metres (558 ft) deep, there are dangerous currents. There is a delightful footpath, 10 km (6 miles) long, around the lake. On Sunday, it is as crowded as the seaside.

To the southwest of the lake, the supposed tombs of the Horatian and Curatian families can be seen in **Albano Laziale** on the right-hand side of Via Appia Nuova, if you are travelling in the direction of Ariccia. The local park has remains of the **Villa of Pompey.**

Ariccia ⑭ itself contains a number of works by Bernini. He restored the **Palazzo Chigi** (which can be visited by guided tour; www.palazzo chigiariccia.it; tel: 06-9330 053) and designed the church of Santa Maria dell'Assunzione and the pilgrim sanctuary of Santa Maria di Galloro. Like Frascati, the town is famous for its *porchetta.*

Swiss Guard on duty at the Papal Palace in Castel Gandolfo.

BELOW: Castel Gandolfo overlooking Lago di Albano.

Statue in the garden of Diana, Nemi.

GENZANO ⑮

Further along Via Appia Nuova, on the southeastern edge of the little crater-lake of Nemi, is the medieval town of Genzano, famous for its Flower Festival and its bread. The *Infiorata* takes place on the first Sunday after "Corpus Domini", usually in June, when the main street leading up to the church of **Santa Maria della Cima** is carpeted with holy pictures made from 5 tonnes of flower petals gathered by the townsfolk.

NEMI ⑯

BELOW: the lakeside town of Nemi.

Set on a spur of rock above the lake of the same name is Nemi, known for its *fragole di bosco* (wild strawberries) and the Strawberry Festival on the

first Sunday of June, when free fruit is distributed. This unspoilt little village, surrounded by woods, was once home to a sacred shrine to the goddess Diana, in whose honour Caligula built two huge, ornate barges. These were sunk by the emperor's enemies and were only raised in the 1920s, then destroyed when the building they were kept in caught fire during an Allied air raid in 1944.

The **Museo delle Navi Romane** (15 Via Diana; tel: 06-3996 7900; Mon–Sat 9am–1.30pm and 2.30–5pm; admission charge) displays one-fifth scale models of the Imperial boats, plus some of the decorative elements which survived and objects from Diana's sanctuary, the site of which can be visited on request.

OASIS OF NINFA ⑰

Southeast of the Castelli Romani, about 60 km (38 miles) from Rome, the Oasi di Ninfa is one of the most evocative places in Lazio. If you are in a hire car and in the vicinity, a visit to these medieval ruins overgrown with exotic plants is worth considering. *For more information, see page 263.* ❑

BEST RESTAURANTS, BARS AND CAFÉS

Price includes dinner and a half-bottle of house wine:
€ = under €25
€€ = €25–40
€€€ = €40–60
€€€€ = more than €60

CASTEL GANDOLFO
Ristorante Bucci
✉ 31 Via de Zecchini
☎ 06-932 3334 ☺ L & D
Thur–Tues. €€–€€€
With great views of Lake Castelgandolfo from its terrace, this family-run restaurant is strong on pasta dishes and meaty *secondi*.

FRASCATI
Da Una Cantina
✉ 8 Via Ottaviani ☎ 06-941 7379 ☺ D only
Mon–Sat, L only Sun. €–€€
In the heart of Frascati's Centro Storico. Chefs Mariella and Giacomo change the menu on a monthly basis according to what's in season; dishes are prepared using the freshest of ingredients. Excellent wine list. Booking advised.

GENZANO
Ristorante Pietrino e Renata
✉ 8 Via Cervi ☎ 06-939 1497 ☺ L & D Tue–Sun. €€
One of the best restaurants in the region, serving dishes made with seasonal ingredients. Specialties include zucchini flowers stuffed

with mozzarella, bean, barley, and black cabbage soup, papardelle with porcini mushrooms and fettuccine with chicken livers. Good wine list.

I Strilloni
✉ 33 Via G. Garibaldi
☎ 06-939 6519 ☺ L & D
daily. €€
Though mainly meat-based, in the tradition of the Castelli Romani, there are also a few fish-based dishes on the menu, such as fettuc-cine with scampi and ricotta. Attentive service.

GROTTAFERRATA
La Briciola
✉ 12 Via D'Annunzio ☎ 06-945 9338 ☺ L & D Tue–Sat,
L only Sun. €€€
A competent exponent of the hearty fare that the Castelli Romani hilltowns are known for: chickpea, barley-and-chestnut soup and lamb stew are typical dishes. Leave room for dessert, though: the pear and chocolate *millefoglie* is divine.

MARINO
Al Cantuccio
✉ 3 Via G. Carissimi ☎ 06-938 8906 ☺ L & D Tue–Sun.
€–€€
This friendly, family-run trattoria serves up excel-lent cooking at very rea-sonable prices; try the outstanding beef tagliata with rosemary. Tables are set up on the pretty terrace in summer.

Trattoria la Credenza
✉ 4 Via Cola di Rienzo
☎ 06-938 5105 ☺ L & D
Mon–Sat. €€€
Authentic Castelli cuisine such as *zuppa di baccalà e ceci* (salt-cod and chickpea stew), *coratella d'abbacchio* (lamb offal with artichokes) and *fagioli con le cotiche* (pork and beans). Good choice of wines.

NEMI
Il Castagnone
✉ Diana Park Hotel, 44 Via Nemorense ☎ 06-936 4041
☺ L & D daily. €€
This family-run hotel restaurant offers classic

Italian cuisine and great views over the lake in Nemi from the summer dining terrace.

ROCCA DI PAPA
La Longarina
✉ 1 Via dei Colli ☎ 06-949 5135 ☺ L & D Tues–Sun.
€€
Surrounded by wood-land, this restaurant is a tranquil place to sample the regional cuisine. Pasta dishes include the tasty fettuccine with porcini mushrooms and bacon, and meat is cooked on the grill in front of diners, with cuts generous enough to suit the hungriest of carni-vores. The crispy pizza, cooked in a wood-fired oven, is also tempting.

ABOVE AND BELOW: deep-fried lamb chops prepared by Il Castagnone's chef.

Recommended Restaurants & Bars on page 279

ETRUSCAN TOWNS

The Etruscans built a series of cities, founded leagues and painted frescoed tombs in northern Lazio more than 2,700 years ago. The remains of these cities make for a fascinating archaeological excursion

There are many Etruscan settlements in central Italy. This chapter highlights the most important ones in Lazio. Touring Etruria by car is probably the best way to take in the sites, though they can all be reached by train from either Trastevere, Ostiense or Termini stations in Rome, or on a COTRAL bus from certain metro stations (ask at the tourist office for details).

Anyone whose curiosity is aroused by this mysterious and once powerful ancient race will find the well-preserved ruins of these archaeological sites fascinating. Some historical background will enhance the experience and help decode the ruins as well as the collections of Etruscan artefacts displayed in many city museums.

Etruscan origins

In about 800 BC, Etruscans settled on the west coast where Tuscany and Lazio are today. The origins of the Etruscans still puzzle scholars, but wherever they came from, they were a highly civilised people who had a hearty appetite for life. Hundreds of Etruscan tombs have survived, many with wall paintings depicting dancing, dinner parties and music-making. Other paintings show battle and hunting scenes. The Etruscans were also extremely skilled craftsmen. Their speciality was metalworking. Italy was rich in minerals, and trade in metal goods soon became the basis of an active urban society. Cities sprang up where previously there had only been simple villages.

Each Etruscan city supported itself by trade. Eager to obtain luxury goods from the Greek colonists, the Etruscans developed overland routes to reach the Greek cities. These cut straight through Latium, the plain

Main attractions

VEIO
PALESTRINA
CERVETERI
TARQUINIA
VITERBO

LEFT: Il Palazzo Papale, the jewel of Viterbo. **RIGHT:** a fine Etruscan fresco.

The Apollo of Veio, a masterpiece of Etruscan art, whose knowing, mysterious smile bears some resemblance to that of Leonardo's Mona Lisa.

BELOW: the 2,000-year-old Nile Mosaic in the Palazzo Barberini, Palestrina.

south of the Tiber occupied by Italian natives called Latins. One of their trading posts on the route south was a Latin village called Rome, originally only a cluster of mud huts. Under the influence of the Etruscans the settlement flourished. They drained the swamp that became the Roman Forum and built grand palaces and roads.

For 300 years, Etruscan kings ruled Rome. But by the 5th century BC their power was fading. The last king, Tarquin the Proud, was driven out when the Romans opted for a Republic. After this the Etruscans stayed north of the Tiber and their influence declined.

VEIO ⓲

The Etruscan city closest to Rome, once the largest in southern Etruria, is Veio. Unlike other sites, where only tombs remain, the **Archaeological Area of Veio** (Località Isola Farnese, Via Riserva Campetti; tel: 06-3089 0116; Tues–Sun 8.30am–2pm, until 4pm Thur and Sat; admission charge), which lies within the protected Parco di Veio (www.parcodiveio.it), includes

parts of a swimming pool and the lower section of a temple. The striking Portonaccio sanctuary was located outside the city walls. Originally, it had a terracotta roof and was decorated with a series of larger-than-life statues of various gods. A block of tufa stone and an underground gallery are the only ruins left from this construction. The famous **statue of Apollo** *(pictured left)* dating from the 6th century BC was found in the temple dedicated to Minerva.

PALESTRINA ⓳

Ancient **Praeneste** (modern Palestrina) is one of the oldest towns of Latium (Lazio). According to myth, it was founded by Telegonus, son of Ulysses and Circe. The town was flourishing in the 8th century BC, but it wasn't until the 4th centuury that it became part of Rome. During the civil war between Marius and Sulla, Marius fled to Praeneste, which was besieged by Sulla's troops and eventually destroyed.

Sulla wanted to make amends and so ordered the reconstruction of the **sanctuary of Fortuna Primigenia**, the

Recommended Restaurants & Bars on page 279

mother of all gods. In the Middle Ages a new town rose on its ruins. In 1944 bombs destroyed part of the town, bringing the temple to light and prompting excavations.

The temple was one of the grandest of antiquity. It comprised a series of terraces on the slopes of Mount Ginestro connected by ramps. Adorned with statues and blazing with torches, the complex must have been an impressive sight, which could be seen from afar. The goddess Fortuna was worshipped in the upper part of the shrine. In the 16th century, a palace was built into this upper circle of the temple, occupied first by the patrician Colonna family and then by the Roman Barberini, who expanded it in the 1640s.

Museo Nazionale Archeologica di Palestrina

✉ 1 Piazza della Cortina 📞 06-3996 7900 🕐 daily 9am–8pm ⓒ charge

The Colonna-Barberini Palace now houses the Palestrina Museum, where countless busts and other local finds are on display, including the badly damaged remains of the statue of Fortuna. The Nile Mosaic on the top floor is the museum's prize exhibit. Dating from the 1st century BC, it shows, in detail, the Nile valley after the annual flood, a scene teeming with peasants, fishermen, priests, soldiers and animals.

Access to the excavated site (with a ticket bought from the museum) is

In the 17th century Praeneste changed its name to honour its most famous native son, Pierluigi di Palestrina, born here in 1525. His distinguished career as a composer included many years as an organist and choirmaster at St Peter's in Rome.

LEFT: Palestrina's 12th-century belltower. **BELOW:** the majestic entrance to the Palazzo Barberini which sits atop the site of Praeneste.

TIP

The best way to reach Cerveteri from Rome by public transport is to take the *regionale* (ie not an Inter-City or Eurostar) train to Pisa which stops at the town. Alternatively, a COTRAL bus leaves from Lepanto station on metro line A.

ABOVE RIGHT: the 6th-century BC sarcophagus of a married couple, discovered in Cerveteri, can be seen in the Villa Giulia Etruscan Museum in Rome.
BELOW: visiting the Cerveteri necropolis.

opposite the palace. The lower part of the shrine is buried beneath the old town of Palestrina which is enclosed within the temple's extensive walls. In the central **Piazza Regina Margherita** the Seminario incorporates the remains of the *area sacra*. Most archaeologists agree that this was the entrance to the **Oracle** – one of the most important of ancient times.

CERVETERI ⑳

Ancient remains, even older than those at Ostia, can be found near Cerveteri, where an Etruscan settlement called Kysry was established about 45 km (28 miles) northwest of Rome and only 6 km (4 miles) from the sea. In the 7th and 6th centuries BC, Kysry became one of the most powerful cities in Etruria, with a population of around 25,000. Revenue came mostly from rich ore deposits in the nearby Tolfa Hills, but there were also strong commercial ties with Hellenic lands, the influence of whose merchants made it the centre of a lively and sophisticated cultural life.

Kysry maintained good relations with its Roman neighbours. But even-

tually the barbaric strength of rising Rome wiped away what had been a refined and joyous civilisation. Under Roman rule the town became known as Caere. It grew steadily poorer, but was not abandoned until the Middle Ages, when the population then moved east to Ceri, renaming their abandoned town Caere Vetus, which evolved into Cerveteri.

Necropoli della Banditaccia

✉ Via della Necropoli della Banditaccia, 2 km (1¼ miles) from Cerveteri centre
☎ 06-994 0001 ⓒ Tue–Sun 8.30am–1 hour before sunset ⓔ charge

Nothing remains of the ancient town bar a few walls, but it is worth going to look at the excavation of Caere's necropolis on a hill, an atmospheric site with countless tombs carved into the soft tufa rock.

The oldest tombs (8th century BC) have a small circular well where the urns containing the ashes of the dead were placed. The first chamber-tombs, also cut into the stone and covered with rocky blocks and mounds *(tumuli)*, appeared as early as the 7th century BC. The noble Etruscans were either enclosed in great sarcophagi with their effigies on top, or laid out on stone beds in their chamber tombs. In the 6th and 5th centuries BC, the so-called cubic graves became common. These rectangular tombs were laid out in regular rows of streets, reflecting the social changes that had taken place in the city. By then, prosperity had spread to the lower classes and a

Recommended Restaurants & Bars on page 279

social levelling had taken place. From the 4th to the 1st century BC, the dead were buried in underground tombs called *hypogaea*, fairly plain by comparison to the earlier tombs.

The largest tomb in Cerveteri is the Tomba dei Rilievi *(see right)*. Other important tombs to look out for include the Tomba della Capanna, the Tomba dei Dolii, Tomba dei Letti e dei Sarcofagi, Tomba dei Vasi Greci, Tomba della Cornice and Tomba degli Scudi e delle Sedie.

Museo Nazionale Cerite

✉ Castello Ruspoli, Piazza Santa Maria ☎ 06-994 1354 ⏰ Tue–Sun 8.30am–7.30pm 💶 charge

Excavations of the tombs not already plundered (the Romans were the first collectors of Etruscan antiquities) revealed goods of gold, silver, ivory, bronze and ceramic. The vases show strong Greek influence as well as the excellent quality of Etruscan craftsmanship. Some of the objects found in the graves, including domestic implements, vases and terracotta lamps, are housed here in the 16th-

century Castello Orsini. However, finds from Cerveteri are scattered as far afield as the British Museum, the Louvre in Paris, the Vatican's Museo Gregoriano and the Villa Giulia in Rome, which includes the famous sarcophagus of the married couple, the Sarcofago degli Sposi.

TARQUINIA ㉑

The Etruscan town of Tarquinia stood on a hill northwest of the picturesque medieval town bearing the same name. The town existed as early as the 9th century, but by the 8th and 7th centuries BC it was a rich and powerful city and became an active commercial and industrial centre. Its political supremacy extended over a vast area inland as far as the Cimini Mountains and Bolsena Lake.

Necropoli dei Monterozzi

✉ Zona Archeologica Via Ripagretta ☎ 0766 856308 ⏰ Tue–Sun 8.30am–2pm winter, 8.30am–1 hr before sunset summer 💶 charge

The Necropolis di Tarquinia, together with that of Cerveteri, is the

Cerveteri's most impressive tomb is the Tomba dei Rilievi, which belonged to a wealthy family. Dating from the 4th century BC, it has space for 32 bodies and is decorated with coloured reliefs depicting weapons, tools, household implements, musical instruments and furnishings.

BELOW LEFT: the 7th-century Tomba della Cornice, Cerveteri. **BELOW:** balm container in the shape of a warrior on his horse.

Cities for the Dead

Every Etruscan town or village had another "city for the dead" built outside its walls. For the Etruscans, life in the next world was just as important as life on earth – perhaps even more so, judging by the fact that dead were buried in larger spaces than the living inhabited. The Etruscans believed not only in the everlasting soul but in the survival, in some shape or form, of the human body after death, so the tombs had to be suitably equipped for the deceased to carry on living in the next world in the way he or she had become accustomed to living on earth. Accordingly, the dead were supplied with food and jewellery and surrounded with all the things that they had loved most when alive – even household furniture, such as beds and chairs, were carved out of the rock, giving a detailed impression of Etruscan everyday life. The most stunning necropolis, the Necropoli della Tomba Banditaccia *(see above)* can be found at Cerveteri off the main Civitavecchia road.

TIP

If you are exploring the area north of Rome by car, consider a trip to Lago di Bracciano, famous for fishing and watersports. In Bracciano, the 15th-century Castello Orsini is worth visiting, but more idyllic is the medieval village of Anguillara on the southern shores of the lake.

ABOVE: Tarquinia Museum. **BELOW:** shopping on Via di San Lorenzo, Viterbo. **BELOW RIGHT:** a pork butcher in Viterbo.

most important Etruscan burial site. It stands on a hill south of the original town, occupying an area 5 km (3 miles) long by 1 km (⅔ mile) wide. Some tombs are painted with frescoes that are a precious document of Etruscan life, depicting banquets, dancing and musicians, athletics or gladiatorial fights, funeral processions, and even erotic scenes.

At any given time no more than 15 of the 6,000 tombs are accessible, as they are opened in rotation in an effort to preserve the delicate paintings. The Tomba della Caccia e della Pesca (530–20 BC), which shows some lively fishing and hunting scenes, and the Tomba del Cacciatore (the Tomb of the Hunter, 530–10 BC) are among the oldest. The Tomba delle Leonesse (Tomb of the Lionesses) shows a pronounced Greek influence.

One of the best-known is La Tomba dell'Orco (4th century BC), which depicts a banquet attended by the prominent Surinna family.

Museo Nazionale Tarquinense

✉ Palazzo Vitelleschi, Piazza Cavour
☎ 0766 856036 🕒 Tue–Sun 8.30am–7.30pm 🅰 charge

This museum in the atmospheric medieval town of Tarquinia houses one of the most important collections of Etruscan artefacts in Italy, most of which were discovered in the necropolis.

VITERBO ㉒

Viterbo's roots can be traced right back to the Etruscans. Crammed with medieval alleyways, porticoes, noble fountains and fine squares, alongside bustling streets lined with shops, cafés and restaurants, this characterful town, just 98 km (60 miles) from Rome, is ideal for a day trip. The most notable of its many historic buildings is the 13th-century **Palazzo Papale**, a favourite residence

TIP

Many of the most valuable finds from the sites covered in this chapter have been transferred to Rome. The most important Etruscan collections can be seen at the Villa Giulia (see page 192) and the Etruscan Museum in the Vatican (see page 146).

of the popes. On the same square the Romanesque **cathedral of San Lorenzo** was built on top of an Etruscan citadel. The shop-lined **Corso Italia** leads to the **Piazza del Plebiscito**, dominated by the town hall and governor's palace. To the east the medieval **San Pellegrino quarter**, a labyrinth of narrow alleyways, arches and hidden corners, is the most atmospheric part of town.

Just outside the city wall, east of the centre, the **Museo Civico** (Piazza Crispi; tel: 0761-348276; Tue–Sun 9am–7pm, until 6pm in winter) contains a collection of Etruscan finds such as sarcophagi with bas-reliefs, pottery urns and vases, and some bronze idols. There is also a small collection of paintings. Adjacent to the museum is the convent church of **Santa Maria della Verità**, worth visiting for its beautiful 13th-century cloister and the Mazzatosta chapel, frescoed by Lorenzo da Viterbo, a pupil of Piero della Francesca. ❑

LEFT: the Papal Palace.

RESTAURANTS AND BARS

CERVETERI

Antica Locanda le Ginestre

☒ 5 Piazza Santa Maria
☎ 06-994 0672 ☺ L & D
Tue–Sun. €€€
Set on a pretty square, conveniently located for exploring the Etruscan tombs, this restaurant offers great home-made pasta dishes, with mainly fishy *secondi*.

PALESTRINA

Lo Schiribizzo

☒ 14 Piazza Garibaldi
☎ 06-953 7705 ☺ L & D
Fri–Sun, D only Tue–Thur.
€–€€
This small trattoria serves both restaurant fare and pizza, but the latter, prepared in the view of diners and cooked in a wood-fired oven, are the main draw.

TARQUINIA

Arcadia

☒ 6 Via Mazzini ☎ 0766-855501 ☺ L & D Tue–Sun.
€€–€€€
This restaurant, right in the centre of historic Tarquinia, has a fish-based menu, an extensive wine list and charming staff. Closed Jan.

VITERBO

Enoteca La Torre

☒ 5 Via della Torre
☎ 0761-226467 ☺ L & D
Tue–Sat, L only Sun.
€€–€€€
Located within the medieval walls of Viterbo, this upmarket restaurant rediscovers ancient local recipes, but with a modern twist. There's also a tasting menu, with each dish paired with a different local wine. The wine bar under the same management next door serves lighter dishes, such as platters of cheese and cold meats, and the shop attached serves gourmet treats and wines and liqueurs of the region. Closed end July and Aug.

• • • • • • • • • •
Price includes dinner and a half-bottle of house wine.
€€€€ = €60 and up, €€€ = €40–60, €€ = €25–40, € = under €25.

INSIGHT GUIDES

ROME
Travel Tips

TRANSPORT

GETTING THERE AND GETTING AROUND

Rome is easy to get to, but less easy to get around. Planes and trains deliver tourists to the city from all over the world with speed, efficiency and regularity. On arrival, however, brace yourself for a chaotic transport system – the bus network is hard to get to grips with, the metro coverage inadequate and driving a nightmare. The good news is that most places of interest in the city centre are within walking distance. A good map and comfortable walking shoes will be your best investment.

ABOVE: an orange ATAC bus.

GETTING THERE

By Air

Scheduled flights from around the world land at the main airport, **Aeroporto Leonardo da Vinci** in Fiumicino (tel: 06-65951; www.adr.it), about 30 km (18 miles) southwest of Rome. The airport is served by most major national carriers, including Alitalia and British Airways. Along with several American carriers, Alitalia operates daily flights from New York and other US cities.

Charters fly in to **Ciampino Airport** (tel: 06-65951; www.adr.it), the city's second airport, about 15 km (9 miles) southeast of the city. Low-cost airlines easyJet and Ryanair are among many firms operating services to Ciampino *(for information on getting into the city from the airport, see pages 283–4).*

AIRLINES

Alitalia
Tel: 06-2222 (Rome)
Tel: 0870-544 8259 (UK)
Tel: 01800-223 5730 (USA)
www.alitalia.com
British Airways
Tel: 199-712266 (Italy)
Tel: 0870-850 9850 (UK)
Tel: 1-800-AIRWAYS (USA)
www.britishairways.com
Continental
Tel: 06-6605 3030 (Italy)
Tel: 0845 607 676 (UK)
Tel: 800-231 0856 (international destinations from USA)
www.continental.com

Delta
Tel: 848-780 376 (Italy)
Tel: 0845-600 0950 (UK)
Tel: 800-221 121 (USA)
www.delta.com
easyJet
Tel: 899-234589 (Italy)
Tel: 0871-244 2366 (UK)
www.easyjet.com
Ryanair
Tel: 899-678 910 (Italy)
Tel: 0871-246 0000 (UK)
www.ryanair.com

By Train

Rome is well served by rail connections to the majority of major European cities, and the national railway, **Ferrovie dello Stato**, is efficient and relatively inexpensive. There are several categories: reservations are required (and included in the ticket price) for the Eurostar, the fastest and most luxurious trains, and optional for the InterCity. You pay a supplement to use these lines, but they save time. Slower regional trains (called, strangely enough, *diretto, espresso, regionale* or *interregionale*) stop at many stations.

You should book a seat if you plan to travel by rail to towns outside Rome. Do this either at a travel agent *(agenzia di viaggio)* in the city, or in Stazione Termini, where there are plenty of easy-to-understand ticket machines. You can also book by credit card online (www.trenitalia.com) or by phone (tel: 892021, no prefix; from landline phones only; 24-hours daily, press 2 to speak to an operator). You can then pick up your tickets at machines at Termini Station or on the train (ask for the "ticketless" option when booking). Both the website and phone service offer in-depth timetable information. If you're planning a lot of rail travel, it pays to look into various rail-pass offers at home and in Italy.

Train tickets are valid for two months after the date of issue, and must be stamped on the day you travel at one of the machines at the head of each platform, otherwise you will be fined. The only exception is Eurostar tickets, which always have a booking time printed on them.

Stazione Termini is the main railway terminal, the meeting point of the two metro lines and the main stop for many city buses. There is a tourist office opposite platform 4, and a hotel reservation booth opposite platform 20, as well as lost property,

ai Treni/to Trains

Polizia/Police

ABOVE AND BELOW: Termini Station, inside and out.

luggage deposit, cafés, restaurants and fast-food joints, a bookstore, a telephone office and even an art gallery.

The official taxi rank is in front of the station. Do not be tempted by offers from unofficial cab drivers in the station interior.

By Coach

Most coaches arrive at the main terminus on Via Marsala next to Stazione Termini. If you are travelling on a COTRAL bus, the network which serves the Lazio region, you will arrive and depart from a metro stop: Lepanto, Ponte Mammolo for the north or Anagnina and EUR Fermi for the south.

By Car

European (EU) driving licences are valid in Italy. Travellers from other countries normally require an international driving licence. Carry your licence, plus the vehicle registration and insurance (Green Card) documents with you when driving. If driving your own car, you may wish to take out extra insurance to cover home recovery in case of a breakdown.

Tolls are payable on motorways, including the A1. Pay in cash or with magnetic cards, available at service stations.

Motorists arriving in Rome

from all directions will first hit the Grande Raccordo Anulare (GRA), the ring road. It is busy and can be alarming, but is usually the quickest way to reach one of the entry roads into the centre. During rush hour, however, there are frequently traffic jams.

The A1 Autostrada del Sole leads into the GRA from both north and south, as does the A24 from the east. If you arrive on the Via del Mare from the coast (Ostia), you can either switch to the GRA or continue straight on into the centre.

When leaving the GRA, follow white signs for the road you want (blue ones usually lead away from the centre). The city centre sign is a white point in a black circle on a white background.

GETTING AROUND

From the Airport

From Fiumicino, there are frequent train services to the city – every 15–30 minutes to Trastevere Station and every 30 minutes to Stazione Termini. Trains to Stazione Termini (the Leonardo Express) run from 6.37am to 11.37pm; the journey takes 35 minutes and the ticket costs €11. If you're travelling to

ACCOMMODATION

SHOPPING

ACTIVITIES

A – Z

LANGUAGE

ABOVE: one of Rome's few remaining tram lines.

one of the suburban rail stations such as Trastevere, Ostiense and Tiburtina, take one of the trains bound for Orte, which run from 6.27am to 11.27pm; tickets cost €5. It's a short taxi or bus ride to most hotels from Termini and a 15-minute tram ride or slightly longer taxi ride from Trastevere Station. At night there's a COTRAL bus that leaves from the international arrivals terminus every 75 minutes bound for the Termini and Tiburtina railway stations. In 2006, the Rome authorities capped the taxi rates; a taxi from Fiumicino to the centre should cost no more than €40. If you suspect you are being fleeced, ostentatiously make a note of the driver's licence number and report any problems to the freephone helpline, tel: 06-0606.

From Ciampino, the best way to reach the centre is to take the Terravision coach which departs from outside the arrivals building and drops you off at Via Marsala, by Stazione Termini. The journey takes 40 minutes and tickets cost €8. Book online at www.terravision.it (at least 24 hours before departure) to be sure of a seat, or buy on the coach; there is a coach for every scheduled

BUS TOURS

ATAC's double-decker open-top service (the 110 Open) leaves every 10 minutes from Termini Station and tours the city's principal monuments. The service operates daily from 8.40am to 7.40pm, and the whole journey lasts about 2 hours; it's a hop-on, hop-off ser-vice, and tickets (€13) are valid for the whole day and for as many trips as you choose to make. A special night-time ver-sion of the tour departs at 9pm in summer and 8pm in winter. Tickets can be bought at the ter-minus in Piazza dei Cinquecento (or on board if you get on at one of the other 10 stops). Archeobus is a small, eco-friendly minibus that serves the historic Appia Antica park. It departs every 40 minutes from Termini Station between 9am and 4pm. The ticket (€8) is valid all day, and the route, which lasts roughly two hours, takes in the catacombs, the Appian Way, the tomb of Cecilia Metella and the Villa dei Quintili. Freephone for both buses: 800-281281; www.trambusopen.com. A combined two-day ticket for both bus tours is also available (€20).

Ryanair and easyJet arriving or departing flight. Alternatively, taxi prices from Ciampino to the centre have been capped; a taxi into the centre should set you back no more than €30.

Schiaffini buses leave from outside the airport at 10.30am, 1pm, 3pm, 5pm, 7pm, 12.15am and 12.30am and go to Stazione Termini (ticket price €5; www.schiaffini.com).

Orientation

It sometimes seems that all Roman roads lead to Piazza Venezia. This can produce traffic chaos, but from a visitor's point of view the square is a useful orientation point at the centre of ancient, medieval and modern Rome.

To the south of Piazza Venezia, the three roads, Via dei Fori Imperiali, Via di San Gregorio and Via delle Terme thread between the greatest monuments of Ancient Rome to the Terme di Caracalla. Northwards, Via del Corso runs through the commer-cial heart of modern Rome to Piazza del Popolo. To the west, Corso Vittorio Emanuele II leads through the heart of medieval Rome and across the Tiber (Tevere) to St Peter's and the Vatican. Eastwards Via

Nazionale, Piazza della Repub-blica and Piazza dei Cinquecento lead to Stazione Termini.

An easy and pleasant way to get an overview of the city is to walk or catch a bus up the Gianicolo (Janiculum hill) behind Trastevere.

Public Transport

Public transport is quite efficient and inexpensive, but overcrowded at peak hours. Tickets are avail-

BELOW: traffic cops have their work cut out in Rome.

able from bars, tobacconists and newspaper kiosks that display the ATAC (city bus company) emblem, and from vending machines in metro stations and bus terminals. Once validated in the metro turnstile or machine at the back of the bus, single-use tickets (BIT), costing €1, are good for unlimited bus or tram rides and/or one metro ride for 75 minutes. One-day tickets (BIG), which cost €4, weekly tickets (carta settimanale), which cost €16, and monthly tickets (abbonamento mensile), which cost €30 and are only valid for the calendar month in which the ticket was bought, are also available.

Passengers caught without a ticket will be fined €51 on the spot. The amount doubles if you cannot pay immediately.

Buses and Trams

Bus and tram services run from 5.30am to midnight, with an all-night service on 22 bus lines, denoted by the letter "N" after the number. Bus and tram stops are clearly marked, and most list route numbers, the main destinations along each route and lines with night service.

Board buses at either the front or rear doors and stamp your ticket immediately. Ring the

bell to request the next stop and exit through the centre doors.

The 40 Express is the quickest way to get from the station to the city centre and then St Peter's. Along with the 64 (a slower version of the 40 Express with more stops), it is one of the city's most popular bus routes, so watch out for pickpockets.

Five electric minibuses serve the narrow streets of the Centro Storico: the most useful are the 116 which passes through or alongside Campo de' Fiori, Piazza Farnese, Piazza Navona, the Pantheon and Piazza Barberini; the 119, which serves the area

around Piazza del Popolo and Piazza di Spagna; and the 117, which goes from Piazza del Popolo to Basilica San Giovanni in Laterano.

Bus 81 runs from the Colosseum to Piazza del Risorgimento near the Vatican Museums. If you are visiting the catacombs, take bus 118 from the Piramide metro stop to the Via Appia. The No. 8 tramline links Largo Argentina in the centre to Trastevere and Monteverde in the west. From Piazza di Spagna to Stazione Termini, take metro line A. For the Colosseum, do the same and change at Termini to line B.

For information on trams,

BELOW: the new Fiat 500; an ideal city runaround.

CAR HIRE

Prices per day at all the major international firms start at approximately €60 for the smallest cars. Expect to pay a generous surcharge if you want unlimited mileage, and check exactly what is included in the insurance you are offered. All the major firms have offices at the airports and railway station, and most of them have online booking services as well as sections where you can work out how much the rental will cost. Avis, Europcar and Hertz probably provide the best cover, but Italy Rent, which also has an office at

the airport, has the lowest rates. The main rental companies are:
Avis
Tel: 06-4521 08391
www.avisautonoleggio.it
Europcar
Freephone 199-307030
www.europcar.it
Hertz
Tel: 199-112211
www.hertz.it
Maggiore
Tel: 06-488 0049
www.maggiore.it
Italy Rent
Freephone 800-930032
www.italyrent.it

Several airlines also have on online car-hire booking service, though this is usually more expensive:
easyJet
Tel: +44-11-3388 3329; lines open 365 days a year for bookings.
www.europcar4easyjet.com
Opodo (a company jointly owned by a number of European airlines)
Tel: +44-0871-277 0090
www.opodo.com
KLM Royal Dutch Airlines
Internet bookings only:
www.klm.com

ABOVE: pleasure boat on the Tiber.

buses or the metro call free-phone 800-431 784, Mon–Sat 8am–8pm, or go to www.atac.roma.it, which has a useful route planner.

COTRAL runs regional buses that connect Rome to the airports, the rest of the province and the Lazio region (www.cotralspa.it).

Metro

The metro operates from 5.30am to 11.30pm and until 12.30am on Saturday night. The city is served by two metro lines (A and B), which intersect at Stazione Termini. There are only two lines because of the problems of circumnavigating the numerous unexcavated ruins underground. A third metro line is slowly being constructed, but it is likely to be years before it is operational.

Due to much-needed renovation works, line A currently closes down at 9pm every day (and is due to do so until 2008). Two shuttle bus services – the MA1 and MA2 – replace Metro A above ground after 9pm, following roughly the same route and running roughly every 5 minutes.

Boats

The public riverboat service that operates along the Tiber makes a pleasant, tranquil change from Rome's often overcrowded buses and metros. The service makes

six stops between the Isola Tiberina (the stop is called Callata Anguillara) and the Duca d'Aosta Bridge near the Olympic Stadium.

Tickets cost €1 for a single journey of up to six stops, and can be bought on board or at any of the tourist information points *(see page 317)*. The same company organises tourist cruises of about an hour, with commentary; romantic night-time cruises with dinner; and a boat service to the site of Ostia Antica that leaves from Marconi Bridge at 9.15am Fri, Sat and Sun. It costs €13 for a return ticket, and there is a two-hour stopover. Ask at the tourist information points for more details or contact Battelli di Roma, tel: 06-9774 5498.

Taxis

Licensed taxis are white and always have a meter. If you are approached inside railway stations or at the airport by someone muttering "Taxi, taxi," always refuse as they are likely to charge you far more than the official rate.

There are ranks outside Termini Station, outside both airports, and in many parts of the Centro Storico, such as Largo di Torre Argentina and Piazza Venezia. Otherwise you can always hail a taxi on the street as long as it has a light on, indicating it is free; or call one of the following radio taxi services – tel: 06-

3570, 06-8822 or 06-4994.

Prices for licensed taxis are fixed and start with a minimum fee of €2.33. Surcharges are made for each large piece of luggage and for journeys after 10pm and on public holidays. By law every taxi should have a card (usually in the pocket of one of the front seats) listing the various rates and charges. Outside the city centre and beyond the Grande Raccordo Anulare (the ring road) the rate per kilometre also goes up.

Driving

Generally, a car is of little use within the city. Parking is hard to find, one-way systems are complex and much of the city centre is closed during business hours, and parts of it in the evening. If you need to reach a hotel in a traffic-restricted area you must make arrangements with the reception before arriving. Local drivers have a very personal set of rules and codes which allow for much flashing of lights, tooting of horns and rampant acceleration at what looks like vastly inopportune moments to anyone non-Roman. During the day most cars in the city centre obey the traffic lights. However, some of Rome's traffic lights are switched to flashing amber at night: this indicates caution, although not all drivers seem to understand this.

If you are not deterred by such problems or if you wish to make extensive trips out of town, you might want to hire your own vehicle *(see panel opposite)*. Note that all cars are required by law to keep their low-beam lights on at all times on motorways and dual carriageways.

There is a large car park under Villa Borghese (entrance at the top of Via Veneto) and one on the Gianicolo hill near the Vatican called Terminal Gianicolo (entrance from Piazza della Rovere). Several of the four- and five-star hotels in the centre have their own garage or protected parking: ask when booking. Few two- or three-star hotels are able to help with parking.

Given the lack of parking spaces, it is not surprising that a lot of cars are towed away in Rome – over 10,000 a year – so if your car is no longer where you left it, this, rather than theft, may be the reason. The Ufficio Rimozione of the traffic police (Vigili Urbani) will be able to tell you if this is the case. The fines you will have to pay to get your car back are high. Contact: Vigili Urbani, 4 Via della Consolazione; tel: 06-67691.

A lot of cars are clamped. If this happens to you, a note on the windscreen will give you the number to call.

If you think that your car has been stolen, you can report it at the nearest police station.

Breakdown Service

The Italian Automobile Association (ACI) provides an emergency breakdown service. If you need repairs, look in the Yellow Pages *(Pagine Gialle)* for the nearest mechanic *(Autofficine)*, or ask the ACI. ACI breakdown and information service, freephone: 803-116. ACI information, tel: 06-491115.

BELOW: cycling in Villa Borghese.

Bicycles and Mopeds

Romans tend to cycle, if at all, on weekends away in Tuscany with their mountain bikes. However, on car-free Sundays (which usually take place once a month) you will see them darting along the Via dei Fori Imperiali. You can hire a bicycle by the hour, the day or the week. Riding in one of the parks is a pleasant alternative to the city streets.

Sundays are a good time to cycle along the Appian Way as traffic is restricted. You can rent a bike from the visitors' centre *(see page 241)*.

Bicycle rental companies in the city include:
Bici & Baci
5 Via del Viminale
Tel: 06-482 8443 (mopeds also)
Collalti
82 Via del Pellegrino
Tel: 06-6880 1084
Touring Rome by moped or Vespa is not advisable for beginners or the nervous. You will need to show your licence when hiring a moped, and leave a deposit. Motorcycle rental companies include:
Happy Rent
3 Via Farini
Tel: 06-481 8185
Scooters for Rent

ABOVE: two wheels are better than four.

84 Via della Purificazione
Tel: 06-488 5485

On Foot

In much of the city centre the best way to get around is on foot. Most of the main sights are within easy walking distance of each other, although there are some for which you may want to use public transport.

Some parts of the centre are for pedestrians only, such as the second half of Via del Corso, roughly from the Piazza San Silvestro to Piazza del Popolo and Piazza Navona. This pedestrianised area includes the section that goes from Largo Argentina past the Pantheon to the Parliament.

Moped riders in particular, but also some car drivers, often decide that they are exempt from this rule and drive along pedestrian zones.

Cross the road with confidence, staring down nearby drivers. If you wait timidly at a pedestrian crossing for the traffic to stop, you will spend the whole day there.

Most of the centre of Rome is reasonably safe, even at night, though the areas around Stazione Termini (particularly Via Giolitti) can be deserted and, despite recent improvements, are still rather seedy and should be avoided.

TRANSPORT **ACCOMMODATION** **SHOPPING** **ACTIVITIES** **A – Z** **LANGUAGE**

A CCOMMODATION

WHERE TO STAY

Even if Milan is the fashion capital par excellence, Rome can compete in cool hotels and old-school splendour. The peeling *pensione* of old has been supplanted by a wide choice of eclectic guesthouses. Diehard design junkies will find avant-garde interiors behind conventional façades. At the grander end of the scale, gracious, timeless hotels like Hotel de Russie retain their cachet. But for those not on an imperial budget there are plenty of welcoming guesthouses and family-run hotels, while self-catering apartments and bed and breakfasts are increasingly popular options.

Choosing a Hotel

The APT office *(see Tourist Information, page 317)* publishes an annual list *(Annuario Alberghi)* showing star categories, facilities and prices of all Rome hotels. This may be obtained from the Rome APT or through the Italian national tourist offices.

Hotels are rated by stars, but these ratings correspond to facilities and services, not to the quality, which is often disappointing compared with what you would expect from similarly rated hotels in other major European cities. Since many hotels are located in renovated medieval or Renaissance *palazzi* in the centre, the rooms and bathrooms can be a bit on the small side, and noisy, too.

There has been a recent explosion of designer and luxury hotels in Rome, which offer great views, memorable food, striking decor and often a health spa; prices are high, but deals can be found on their websites.

Bed & Breakfasts

The bed & breakfast sector in Rome is flourishing. Some offer the amenities of a hotel in noble *palazzi* for more competitive prices; others are nothing more than a private room in someone's home. The APT office on Via Parigi and tourist information points have full listings of registered establishments. The Bed and Breakfast Italia agency (tel: 06-687 8618; www.bbitalia.it) has hundreds of options in Rome, which it vets and awards with a crown system. The standard rates are posted on its website.

Self-catering

It's worth considering renting a self-catering apartment, especially if you're travelling as a group or family. Among the many operators in this field are Homes in Rome (tel: 06-3975 1474; www.homesinrome. com) and Roman Homes (www.romanhomes.com).

Hotel Areas

Rome offers countless places to stay, in every imaginable category. The following list gives a selection. The area around Piazza Navona, the Pantheon and Campo de' Fiori offers the best introduction to the city, since you are right in its medieval heart and within easy reach of most main sights. However, there are relatively few hotels in the area, and these tend to be booked up early. This area is always lively, and that means it is also noisy.

The Aventine Hill is quieter, although a little further out. The Via Veneto district has a number of large hotels at the higher end of the scale. It is a convenient location, although the area is no longer the fashionable centre. Around Piazza di Spagna there is a more varied selection.

The Monteverde district on Gianicolo Hill is dotted with turn-of-the-century villas, converted into welcoming guesthouses.

TRANSPORT

Many hotels can be found around Stazione Termini. This is not the most attractive area, but it is well connected with the rest of the city by public transport. A lot of the cheaper hotels are here, but there are a few in the middle and luxury ranges. The area south of the station is rather insalubrious and best avoided.

Hotels slightly out of the centre may offer more facilities, such as swimming pools and parking, and they are quieter.

Prices & Booking

Prices are high and do not always reflect what is on offer. A two-star can be as good if not better than a three- or even four-star. Expect to pay anything between €80 and €250 for a three-star (depending on the season), and don't expect views for less then €200.

High season is pretty much year-round in Rome, so book ahead. November to March and August are quieter and prices

are lower. Bookings can be made online or by phone; sometimes a confirmation fax will be requested, as well as your credit card details. If you want to cancel, do it a few days in advance. Prices usually include breakfast, although it is rarely included in the luxury and five-star category. In bed & breakfast accommodation, guests typically pay €40–100 per night for a double room, but prices can go as low as €25 and as high as €200.

ACCOMMODATION LISTINGS

FONTANA DI TREVI, VIA VENETO & VILLA BORGHESE

Aldrovandi Palace
15 Via Ulisse Aldrovandi
Tel: 06-322 3993
[off map p335, E1]
www.aldrovandi.com
This beautiful hotel near Villa Borghese has sumptuous rooms and suites, lush gardens, a spectacular outdoor pool and a restaurant run by a Michelin-starred chef. €€€€€
Aleph
15 Via di San Basilio
Tel: 06-422901
[p336, A3]
www.boscolohotels.com
This stylish hotel has an intriguing "heaven and hell" theme, from its flame-red entranceway to its soothing "Paradise Spa". Bedrooms are inspired by 1930s design and have hi-tech touches. €€€€€
Ambasciatori Palace
62 Via Vittorio Veneto
Tel: 06-47493
[p336, A2]
www.ambasciatoripalace.com
Central and comfortable large hotel. Caters to a mainly business crowd, but the staff are friendly and efficient. €€€€€

Bernini Bristol
23 Piazza Barberini
Tel: 06-488931
[p336, A3]
www.berninibristol.com
In an imposing building overlooking Piazza Barberini, this attractive hotel has elegant rooms, a spa and a prestigious restaurant, l'Olimpo. €€€€
Daphne Inn (A&B)
20 Via degli Avignonesi
and 55 Via di San Basilio
Tel: 06-8745 0087
[p336, A3]
www.daphne-rome.com
This hotel in two locations excels in its level of service – friendly, knowledgeable staff, and laptops (one per floor) and mobile phones (one per room) are provided – an unexpected bonus in this price bracket. €€–€€€
Eden
49 Via Ludovisi
Tel: 06-478121
[p336, A2]
www.hotel-eden.it
This is a discreet, elegant and ultra-refined hotel with excellent, unsnooty service and a

prestigious roof garden restaurant. €€€€€
Fontana
96 Piazza di Trevi
Tel: 06-678 6113
[p335, E3]
www.hotelfontana-trevi.com
In a 13th-century monastery opposite the Fontana di Trevi. A tad pricey, but it has a beautiful rooftop breakfast room. €€€–€€€€
Jolly Vittorio Veneto
1 Corso Italia
Tel: 06-84951

[p336, A2]
www.jollyhotels.it
Modern, with all amenities, including conference rooms. Soundproofed. €€€€

BELOW: the Aleph.

ACCOMMODATION

SHOPPING

ACTIVITIES

A – Z

LANGUAGE

Lord Byron
5 Via Giuseppe De Notaris
Tel: 06-322 0404
[off map p335, E1]
www.lordbyronhotel.com
Built into a former
monastery, this small
hotel has the atmos-
phere of a private club,
and enjoys a serene
location away from the
city centre, in the well-
heeled Parioli district.
Sumptuous decor, and
the restaurant is fabu-
lous. €€€€–€€€€€

Parco dei Principi
5 Via G. Frescobaldi
Tel: 06-854421
[off map p335, E1]
www.parcodeiprincipi.com

Two minutes' walk from
Villa Borghese, this
hotel is not in the thick
of things, but a great
choice if you want tran-
quillity and luxury. The
excellent restaurant
overlooks the park and
the city. €€€€

Residenza A
183 Via Veneto
Tel: 06-486700
[p336, A2]
www.hotelviaveneto.com
A sleek grey colour
scheme with contem-
porary art providing the
odd splash of colour
characterises this hotel.
Rooms have a luxurious
feel, with flat-screen

computers and swanky
bathrooms. €€€–€€€€

Residenza Cellini
5 Via Modena
Tel: 06-4782 5204
[p336, B3]
www.residenzacellini.it
With rooms that are
unusually large for this
price bracket, this hotel
is deservedly popular.
All bathrooms have
jacuzzis or hydro-
massage showers. €€€

Splendide Royal
14 Via di Porta Pinciana
Tel: 06-421689
[p336, A2]
www.splendideroyal.com
Sweeping staircases,
marble floors and

dazzling chandeliers
give this hotel a gener-
ous dose of *Dolce Vita*
glamour. Ask for one of
the rooms with views
over nearby Villa Bor-
ghese. There's also a
swanky restaurant,
Mirabelle, and a lovely
rooftop terrace. €€€€€

Westin Excelsior
125 Via Vittorio Veneto
Tel: 06-47081
[p336, A2]
www.starwood.com
Part of the 1950s *Dolce
Vita* scene, the Excel-
sior, recently renovated,
offers the ultimate in
opulence and service.
€€€€€

PIAZZA DI SPAGNA AND TRIDENTE

Hotel Art
56 Via Margutta
Tel: 06-328711
[p335, E2]
www.hotelart.it
Set in a converted sem-
inary, this upmarket
hotel is a blend of old
and new. The reception
area is contained within
two futuristic pods, and
the sleek lounge area
(an exercise in style
over comfort) is laid out
in the former chapel
beneath frescoed
vaulted ceilings. €€€€€

Barocco
4 Via della Purificazione
Tel: 06-487 2001
[p336, A3]
www.hotelbarocco.com
Rooms at this charm-
ing, bijou hotel on a
side street off busy
Piazza Barberini, are
decorated with sumptu-
ous fabrics and elegant
furnishings. Try booking
one of the superior
rooms, as standard
rooms tend to be on the
small side. €€€€

Casa Howard (A&B)
18 Via Capo le Case
and 149 Via Sistina
Tel: 06-6992 4555
[p335, E3]
www.casahoward.com
Each of the 10 rooms in
this stylish hotel has a
different theme; those
in the newer Via Sistina
location all have bath-
rooms en suite and are
slightly more luxurious.
Turkish bath available
at both sites. This is
"*residenza*" accommo-
dation: there is no
reception – guests are
given a set of keys. €€€

De Russie
9 Via del Babuino
Tel: 06-328881
[p335, D2]
www.hotelderussie.it
This is Rome's original
designer hotel, housed
in a *palazzo* by Valadier.
It is chic, modern and
understated. The inter-
nal courtyard overlook-
ing a tiered garden is
magical, and the luxuri-
ous spa is one of the

best in town. Ask for a
room with a view of
Piazza del Popolo.
€€€€€

D'Inghilterra
14 Via Bocca di Leone
Tel: 06-699811
[p335, E3]
www.royaldemeure.com
Old-fashioned and trad-
itional, with unfussy
service. The rooms,
furnished with antiques,
are cosy if on the dark
side. Top-floor rooms
are brighter and have
terraces. Good position
just off the Corso.
€€€€–€€€€€

Fontanella Borghese
84 Largo Fontanella Borghese
Tel: 06-6880 9504
[p335, D3]
www.fontanellaborghese.com
This elegant hotel, once
the residence of the
noble Borghese family,
is well located for shop-
ping in the Piazza di
Spagna and Via dei
Condotti area. Rooms
have beautiful old tiles
or hardwood floors;

those overlooking the
internal courtyard are
quieter. €€€

Gregoriana
18 Via Gregoriana
Tel: 06-679 4269
[p335, E3]
www.hotelgregoriana.it
This ex-convent has a
striking Art Deco interior
with a wonderful gold-
and-black lift and
original 1930s room
numbers by the Russian
fashion designer Erté.
Near the Spanish
Steps, it has only 22
rooms. €€€

Hassler
6 Piazza Trinità dei Monti
Tel: 06-699340
[p335, E3]
www.hotelhasslerroma.it

ABOVE: the contemporary Hotel Art.

Situated above the Spanish Steps, this historic establishment is still one of Rome's most alluring luxury hotels, its olde-worlde glamour a real contrast with the sleek minimalism of some of the city's new 5-stars. The restaurant, with roof gardens and views over the city, is particularly beautiful. €€€€

Inn at the Spanish Steps
85 Via dei Condotti
Tel: 06-6992 5657
[p335, E3]
www.atspanishsteps.com
A luxury boutique hotel right in the middle of shoppers' heaven. A sister hotel, the View at the Spanish Steps, along the same road at No. 95, is similarly luxurious, though slightly more pared-down in style. €€€€

Locarno
22 Via della Penna
Tel: 06-361 0841
[p335, D2]
www.hotellocarno.com
Appealing Art Deco touches (the ornate cage lift alone is memorable), though some of the rooms have a slightly shabby feel. De luxe rooms in the new wing are lovely but cost more. Breakfast served in the garden or on the roof terrace when warm. Oodles of charm and class, and the location, two minutes from Piazza del Popolo, can't be beaten. Bicycle rental included in the price. €€€

Margutta
34 Via Laurina
Tel: 06-322 3674
[p335, E2]
On a cobbled street near Piazza del Popolo. Rooms are small but pleasant, especially the three on the top floor which have a great view and terraces. Well priced for the area. €€

Modigliani
42 Via della Purificazione
Tel: 06-4281 5226
[p335, E3]
www.hotelmodigliani.com
A lovely hotel with great views from top-floor rooms and a garden in an inner courtyard. Check the website for last-minute deals. €€€

Nazionale
131 Piazza Montecitorio
Tel: 06-695001
[p335, D3]
www.nazionaleroma.it
This hotel has an impressive roster of illustrious past guests, Simone de Beauvoir and Jean-Paul Sartre among them. These days, the hotel more often hosts politicians and city types. €€€€

Il Palazzetto
8 Vicolo del Bottino
Tel: 06-6993 4301
[p335, E2]
www.wineacademyroma.com
The chic rooms at the International Wine Academy's 19th-century Il Palazzetto have lovely views of the Spanish Steps. Breakfast is served in the luxurious Hassler, its sister hotel, and guests can use the Hassler's gym free of charge. €€€€

Hotel Panda
35 Via della Croce
Tel: 06-678 0179
[p335, E3]
www.hotelpanda.it
A rare budget option a stone's throw from the Spanish Steps, Panda's rooms, though small and pretty basic, have been attractively decorated, and some have wood-beamed ceilings. Book early. €

Portrait Suites
23 Bocca di Leone
Tel: 06-6938 0742
[p335, E3]
www.lungarnohotels.com
Opened in 2006, this boutique hotel has become a favourite with the fashion set – it's owned by the Italian couturier Ferragamo. Rooms are as stylish as you'd expect, and there's plenty of fashion memorabilia from the designer's archives. The decked terrace with underfloor heating and bar is a great place for an *aperitivo*. €€€€€

Regno
330 Via del Corso
Tel: 06-6697 6361
[p335, E4]
www.hotelregno.com
More tranquil than you might expect for its location, Hotel Regno is a reliable mid-range option right in the centre of town. The rooms are pleasant despite the slightly outdated decor. €€€€

Scalinata di Spagna
17 Piazza Trinità dei Monti
Tel: 06-679 3006
[p335, E3]
www.hotelscalinata.com
A small hotel in a beautiful town house at the top of the Spanish Steps. Breakfast on rooftop terrace in summer. Book early. €€€–€€€€

Suisse
54 Via Gregoriana
Tel: 06-678 3649
[p335, E3]
www.hotelsuisserome.com
This charming hotel near the Spanish Steps has a cosy, welcoming feel and is great value. Rooms are large, with sturdy wooden furnishings and classic decor. Breakfast is served in the rooms. €€

Valadier
15 Via della Fontanella
Tel: 06-361 1998
[p335, D2]
www.hotelvaladier.com
This family-run hotel is moments from the Spanish Steps. Rooms are grandly styled, with luxurious furnishings and marble bathrooms. €€€€

PRICE CATEGORIES

For a double room in high season:
€ = under €100
€€ = €100–180
€€€ = €180–260
€€€€ = €260–450
€€€€€ = over €450

THE VATICAN AND PRATI

Atlante Star
34 Via Vitelleschi
Tel: 06-687 3233
[p334, B3]
www.atlantehotels.com
One of the capital's bastions of luxury. The wood-panelled rooms are decorated with antiques, and the marble bathrooms all have jacuzzis. The rooftop terrace is famous for its view of St Peter's and for the haute-cuisine Les Etoiles restaurant.
€€€€

Bramante
24 Vicolo delle Palline
Tel: 06-6880 6426
[p334, B3]
www.hotelbramante.com
Rooms at this charming hotel near St Peter's are elegantly furnished and quiet, and the small terrace is a pleasant place to unwind. €€€

Cavalieri Hilton
101 Via Cadiolo
Tel: 06-35091
[off map p334, A1]
www.cavalieri-hilton.it
Luxury hotel situated on top of Monte Mario, just north of the Vatican. It is quiet and spacious, and offers amenities that more central hotels lack – tennis courts and indoor and outdoor swimming pools among them – as well as one of Rome's best restaurants (La Pergola) on the top floor, which spreads onto the terrace in summer. €€€€€

Colors
31 Via Boezio
Tel: 06-687 4030
[p334, C2]
www.colorshotel.com
Bright, clean, modern hotel on three floors,

ABOVE: Cavalieri Hilton.

with individual rooms, with or without en-suite bathroom, and dormitory accommodation. The newest rooms, on the third floor, are slightly more expensive but offer extras such as breakfast, satellite TV and air conditioning. There is a fully equipped kitchen should you want to cook, laundry facilities, a roof terrace and no curfew for dorm accommodation. The staff are very helpful. €€€€

Columbus
33 Via della Conciliazione
Tel: 06-686 5435
[p334, B3]
www.hotelcolumbus.net
On the main street leading up to St Peter's, this ex-monastery has retained some of its original features, including a large, vaulted dining room, frescoes, and a garden planted with orange trees where you can sit and dine in summer. This is a large, comfortable hotel with its own parking area. Prices go down a fair bit off season. €€€€

Dei Mellini
81 Via Muzio Clementi
Tel: 06-324771
[p335, D2]
www.hotelmellini.com
Close to the river in Prati, a short walk from Castel Sant'Angelo and St Peter's, and just across the bridge from the Via del Corso and the Tridente shopping district. Rooms are spacious and elegant if a little old-fashioned. There is a pleasant rooftop terrace. Good facilities for the disabled. €€€–€€€€

Farnese
30 Via Alessandro Farnese
Tel: 06-321 2553
[p335, C2]
www.hotelfarnese.com
This upmarket, four-star hotel occupies a grand old aristocratic residence. The attention to detail and period furnishings are what make it so special. The reception desk is a 17th-century altar from a deconsecrated church. The rooms are elegantly decorated with antiques, terracotta tiling, marble bathrooms and Murano lamps. The breakfast is excellent, and there is a pretty roof terrace. Lepanto metro station is nearby, and the hotel is within walking distance of St Peter's. €€€€

Franklin
29 Via Rodi
Tel: 06-3903 0165
[p334, A1]
www.franklinhotelrome.it
This modern hotel has airy, pleasant rooms, all with a musical theme. There are state-of-the-art CD players in all rooms, with an exten-

sive collection of music for guests to borrow in the reception area, plus bicycles for guests' use, should you want to explore the Vatican on two wheels. €€€€

Gerber
241 Via degli Scipioni
Tel: 06-322 1001
[p334, C2]
www.hotelgerber.it
Rooms suffer slightly from floral overload but are comfortable and quiet, and the hotel is close to the Vatican. There is a nice terrace too. Good value. €€

Ostello del Foro Italico
61 Viale delle Olimpiadi
Tel: 06-323 6267
[off map p334, B1]
www.ostellionline.org
Advance reservations are strongly advised, as this 334-bed hostel is the only real hostel in Rome. It's open all year round, has a midnight curfew and is located some way out of the centre (but is accessible by bus). €

Sant'Anna
133 Borgo Pio
Tel: 06-6880 1602
[p334, B3]
www.hotelsantanna.com
Housed in a 16th-century building, this hotel has comfortable rooms with a slightly old-fashioned feel. Service is attentive and friendly. €€€

PIAZZA NAVONA AND THE PANTHEON

Abruzzi
69 Piazza della Rotonda
Tel: 06-9784 1369
[p335, D4]
www.hotelabruzzi.it

Directly opposite the Pantheon, this hotel is not quiet in summer but all rooms have air conditioning and double glazing. Rooms are modest but clean, and almost all have breathtaking views of the Pantheon. There's no breakfast room, but breakfast – taken in a nearby café – is included. €€€

Due Torri
23 Vicolo del Leonetto
Tel: 06-6880 6956
[p335, D3]
www.hotelduetorriroma.com

A delightful hotel in a former cardinal's palace tucked away down a narrow cobbled street. Rooms are small and cosy; those on the top floor have terraces; quiet by Rome standards. €€€

Grand Hotel de la Minerve
69 Piazza della Minerva
Tel: 06-695201
[p335, D4]
www.grandhoteldelaminerve.com

Built within a 17th-century *palazzo* overlooking the lovely Piazza della Minerva. Vast areas of Venetian glass create spectacular public spaces. Rooms are large, and there are splendid views from the roof terrace. €€€€

Navona
8 Via dei Sediari
Tel: 06-686 4203
[p335, D4]
www.hotelnavona.com

This family-run hotel on the second floor of an attractive *palazzo* has a welcoming atmosphere. Rooms are fairly simple, but represent very good value for the area. €€

Raphael
2 Largo Febo
Tel: 06-682831
[p335, D4]
www.raphaelhotelrome.com

A distinctive ivy-covered exterior, antique furnishings, artworks and stunning views. The Richard Meier-designed "Executive" rooms on the third floor are sleek and modern, while the rest of the hotel has a classic feel. Some rooms don't quite live up to expectations, but facilities, rooftop restaurant, bar and views do. €€€€

Relais Palazzo Taverna
92 Via dei Gabrielli
Tel: 06-2039 8064
[p335, C4]
www.relaispalazzotaverna.com

Rooms at this new guesthouse near the antiques shops of Via dei Coronari have stylish, modern decor with contemporary wallpaper and white-painted beams. Excellent value for this part of town. €€€

Santa Chiara
21 Via Santa Chiara
Tel: 06-687 2979
[p335, D4]
www.albergosantachiara.com

The Santa Chiara is in a large building behind the Pantheon with three wings, 96 rooms and three rooftop suites; its rooms are more luxurious than the price would suggest. Ask for a

room with a terrace. €€€–€€€€

Sole al Pantheon
63 Piazza della Rotonda
Tel: 06-678 0441
[p335, D4]
www.hotelsolealpantheon.com

This 500-year-old hotel, a stone's throw from the Pantheon, has been renovated without spoiling the atmosphere. Front rooms have memorable views but are quite noisy. Quieter rooms overlook an internal courtyard. The decor is serene and fresh, with tiled floors, high ceilings and frescoes. €€€€–€€€€€

Teatro Pace 33
33 Via del Teatro Pace
Tel: 06-687 9075
[p335, D4]
www.hotelteatropace.com

This 17th-century building on a quiet, cobbled alley boasts a magnificent Baroque staircase (there's no lift) and high-ceilinged, wood-beamed rooms decorated in classic style. €€€

BELOW: the Raphael, with views of St Peter's from the rooftop restaurant.

PRICE CATEGORIES

For a double room in high season:
€ = under €100
€€ = €100–180
€€€ = €180–260
€€€€ = €260–450
€€€€€ = over €450

CAMPO DE' FIORI, THE GHETTO AND TRASTEVERE

Antico Borgo Trastevere
7 Vicolo del Buco
Tel: 06-588 3774
[p339, D2]
www.hotelanticoborgo.it
Though on the small side, rooms in this hotel are tastefully decorated, and have wood beams and tiled floors. Breakfast is served at nearby sister hotel the Domus Tiberina, on a piazza overlooking the river. **€€**

Arco del Lauro
27 Via dell'Arco de' Tolomei
Tel: 06-9784 0350
[p339, D2]
www.arcodellauro.it
This mini-hotel, with just four rooms, has recently opened in a quiet residential area in Trastevere. Rooms are decorated in a fresh, simple style. Breakfast is served in a nearby bar. **€€**

Barrett
47 Largo Torre Argentina
Tel: 06-686 8481
[p339, D1]
www.pensionebarrett.com
Located between Campo de' Fiori and the Pantheon, with large, comfortable rooms and big en-suite bathrooms,

this is one of the best-value hotels in Rome and has been run by the same family for 40 years. Breakfast is not included but can be arranged for an extra fee; alternatively, the area is full of cafés. No credit cards. **€€**

Campo de' Fiori
6 Piazza del Biscione
Tel: 06-6880 6865
[p339, C1]
www.hotelcampodefiori.com
A stone's throw from Campo de' Fiori, this recently renovated hotel has a beautiful terrace and intimate, individually decorated rooms with bijou en-suite bathrooms. The hotel management also rents several apartments in the area. **€€**

Della Lunetta
68 Piazza del Paradiso
Tel: 06-686 1080
[p339, C1]
www.albergodellalunetta.it
Comfortable, clean but very basic, this hotel is extremely well situated between Piazza Navona and Campo de' Fiori. Breakfast is not provided, but there are any number of cafés in the

area for your morning cappuccino. There's a pleasant, panoramic communal terrace that can be used for sunbathing and reading. **€–€€**

Pomezia
12 Via dei Chiavari
Tel: 06-686 1371
[p339, D1]
The rooms in this small hotel just off the Corso Vittorio Emanuele were renovated after the millennium, as were the reception and breakfast areas. They are basically furnished but comfortable, and all have en-suite bathrooms with power shower. There is a lift and a room equipped for people with disabilities. **€€**

Ponte Sisto
64 Via dei Pettinari
Tel: 06-686310
[p339, C1]
www.hotelpontesisto.it
Aside from its excellent, central location, this hotel is pleasant and luminous, with elegant rooms and a peaceful, palm tree-lined courtyard. **€€€€**

Residenza Arco de' Tolomei
26c Via dell'Arco de' Tolomei
Tel: 06-5832 0819
[p339, D2]
www.inrome.info
This beautifully decorated guesthouse on a quiet Trastevere street has just five rooms, three with terraces. Breakfast is a real event here, with homemade baked goods and jams served in a light-filled breakfast room. **€€€**

Residenza in Farnese
59 Via del Mascherone

Tel: 06-6889 1388
[p339, C1]
www.residenzafarneseroma.it
Rooms in this converted convent are spacious and attractive, some with original frescoes and hand-painted furniture. Ask for a room overlooking the gardens of Palazzo Spada or, on the other side, the magnificent French Embassy. **€€€€–€€€€€**

Rinascimento
122 Via del Pellegrino
Tel: 06-687 4813
[p335, C4]
www.hotelrinascimento.com
This pleasant family-run hotel has well-equipped, comfortable rooms and bathrooms, although they are a bit cramped. Ask for the room which has a stunning, direct view of the Chiesa Nuova – although it naturally gets booked early. A few of the rooms are really tiny with not a lot of light, so make sure you avoid these. **€€–€€€**

Ripa
3 Via degli Orti di Trastevere
Tel: 06-58611
[p339, C3]
www.ripahotel.com
Cutting-edge, clean and functional design characterise this hotel near the Porta Portese end of Trastevere. The Ripa is well located for Testaccio and Ostiense

BELOW: tucked away down this quaint Trastevere alley is the lovely Hotel Santa Maria.

(the city's hippest clubbing areas), the Aventine and Circus Maximus, and has all the usual extras to be found in this price range, including a fusion restaurant and its own trendy nightclub (open Saturdays only). The street it's located in is a bit of an eyesore, however. €€€€

San Francesco
7 Via Jacopa de' Settesoli
Tel: 06-5830 0051
[p339, C3]
www.hotelsanfrancesco.net
This hotel benefits from being set back a little from the bustle of central Trastevere, and its rooms are good-sized and comfortable. There's also a stunning roof terrace where breakfast is served in warm weather. €€€

Santa Maria
2 Vicolo del Piede
Tel: 06-589 4626
[p339, C2]

www.htlsantamaria.com
Behind firmly closed gates in this quiet and typical Trastevere alleyway lies a refurbished 16th-century cloister. All the rooms are large and comfortable, with terracotta tiling and a view out onto a large, sunny central courtyard planted with orange trees. €€€

Smeraldo
9 Vicolo dei Chiodaroli
Tel: 06-687 5929
[p339, D1]
www.smeraldoroma.com
A good-value hotel in a central location in a narrow street between Largo Argentina and Campo de' Fiori. Its rooms are clean and comfortable, if on the small side, and some of those on the upper floors have lovely views over the rooftops. If these are booked up you can enjoy the views from the two roof gardens. Avoid the rooms

overlooking the courtyard as they are on the gloomy side. €€–€€€

Sole
76 Via del Biscione
Tel: 06-6880 6873
[p339, C1]
www.solealbiscione.it
The main draw of this cosy hotel is its central location near Campo de' Fiori. It has quiet, if basic rooms, a pretty inner garden and a small roof terrace offering lovely views of the domed church of Sant' Andrea della Valle. It's very popular, so book well ahead. There's no breakfast service, and no credit cards are accepted. €€

Teatro di Pompeo
8 Largo del Pallaro
Tel: 06-6830 0170
[p339, D1]
www.hotelteatrodipompeo.it
Built on the site of the ancient Theatre of Pompey (the remains of which can still be seen in the breakfast room),

this is a charming, friendly hotel with comfortable, classically decorated rooms. €€€

Trastevere
24a–25 Via L Manara
Tel: 06-581 4713
[p339, C2]
www.hoteltrastevere.net
With clean, simple rooms overlooking the Piazza San Cosimato market square, this charming but down-to-earth little hotel, at the cheaper end of this price range, is a great deal for the area. €€

Villa della Fonte
Via della Fonte dell'Olio
Tel: 06-580 3797
[p339, C2]
www.villafonte.com
Five pleasant rooms make up this hotel, on a picturesque cobbled street in the heart of Trastevere. The first-floor garden terrace is a great place to soak up the sun. €€

AVENTINO AND TESTACCIO

Abitart
10–20 Via P. Matteucci
Tel: 06-454 3191
[p339, D4]
www.abitarthotel.com
A very modern hotel set in the heart of trendy Testaccio, and well positioned for the full-on nightlife that the area is famous for. The rooms are highly slick and contemporary, though some have a slightly bland, corporate feel. €€€

San Pio
19 Via di Santa Melania
Tel: 06-570057
[p339, D3]
www.aventinohotels.com

The quiet residential area of the Aventino may not be the obvious choice as a base to explore the city, but it's well connected and very peaceful – ideal for those who want a break from the noisy chaos of the city centre. This hotel consists of three separate buildings which share the same attractive gardens. It has elegant, spacious rooms with antique furnishings and generous bathrooms with jacuzzis. €€€

Sant'Anselmo
2 Piazza Sant'Anselmo

Tel: 06-570057
[p339, D3]
www.aventinohotels.com
Nestling in a peaceful garden on the leafy and exclusive Aventine Hill, this hotel has recently been lavishly redecorated. Each room has been given its own imaginative theme, and details such as four-poster beds, free-standing baths and frescoes make it a very special place to stay. The main drawback is its distance from the centre, though it's just a short walk from Testaccio and the

Piramide metro stop.
€€€–€€€€

TERMINI, MONTI AND ESQUILINO

Antica Locanda
84 Via del Boschetto
Tel: 06-484894
[p336, A4]
www.antica-locanda.com
As the name suggests (*locanda* means inn), this is a cosy, wood-panelled wine bar with rooms to rent upstairs. The elegant rooms, named after famous composers and artists, are all individually furnished. Breakfast is served in the wine bar, and guests can use the roof terrace at any time of day. €€€

The Beehive
8 Via Marghera
Tel: 06-4470 4553
[p336, C3]
www.the-beehive.com
Rooms at this appealing budget option all have shared bathroom, but are clean and stylishly decorated with some impressive designer furnishings in communal areas. There's also a small restaurant, a yoga space and a patio. €

Capo d'Africa
54 Via Capo d'Africa
Tel: 06-772801
[p340, B2]
www.hotelcapodafrica.com
This hotel's dramatic,

palm-tree-lined entrance bodes well, and its 65 rooms are comfortable and contemporary. Views are delightful, especially from the stunning rooftop breakfast room, and the Colosseum is only a five-minute walk away. €€€€

Celio
35c Via dei Santissimi Quattro
Tel: 06-7049 5333
[p340, B2]
www.hotelcelio.com
This delightful, quirkily decorated hotel close to the Colosseum has twenty rooms and a lovely rooftop terrace. Frescoes and dramatic drapes throughout make it a great place to stay. €€€€

Des Artistes
20 Via Villafranca
Tel: 06-445 4365
[p336, C3]
www.hoteldesartistes.com
Quality of accommodation tends to dip around the station, but Des Artistes is an exception: though its rooms are simple, they're comfortable and clean, and staff are friendly and helpful. The hotel also has dorm accommodation. €€

Domus Sessoriana
10 Piazza Santa Croce in Gerusalemme
Tel: 06-706151
[p341, D2]
www.domussessoriana.it
Attached to the church of Santa Croce in Gerusalemme, this hotel offers elegant, simple accommodation to a largely business clientele. There's a roof terrace with great views of San Giovanni in Laterano and beyond. €€€

Exedra
47 Piazza della Repubblica
Tel: 06-489381
[p336, B3]
www.boscolohotels.com
Among the most opulent of the city's five-star hotels, the Exedra is chic and glamorous, with luxurious, no-expense-spared rooms. There's also a rooftop bar, restaurant, pool and a swanky spa. €€€€€

Forum
25–30 Via Tor de' Conti
Tel: 06-679 2446
[p340, A1]
www.hotelforumrome.com
This luxurious, old-fashioned hotel is ideally located for the Forum, and has a wonderful view from its roof-garden restaurant. €€€–€€€€

Hotel 47
47 Via Petroselli
Tel: 06-678 7816
[p339, D2]
www.47hotel.com
Near Piazza Venezia, this new hotel is located on a street of imposing government offices. The Teatro di Marcello is at one end, and it leads out to the Temple of Vesta and the Bocca della Verità at the other. The hotel is set in an austere 1930s building which has been tastefully converted and filled with repro furniture and contemporary artworks. The views are wonderful, as is the rooftop bar-restaurant. €€€€–€€€€€

Inn at the Roman Forum
30 Via degli Ibernesi
Tel: 06-6919 0970
[p340, A1]
www.theinnattheromanforum.com
This brand-new boutique hotel offers spacious, luxurious rooms with canopied beds, a prime location and even its own ancient Roman crypt, currently being excavated. €€€€€

Lancelot
47 Via Capo d'Africa
Tel: 06-7045 0615
[p340, B2]
www.lancelothotel.com
This friendly, family-run hotel has light, airy rooms and enjoys an

BELOW: Radisson SAS es. Hotel in Termini.

enviable position, a few minutes' walk from the Colosseum. €€

Montreal
4 Via Carlo Alberto
Tel: 06-445 7797
[p336, B4]
www.hotelmontrealrome.com
The Montreal's 27 rooms are bright and spacious. This is an ever-popular mid-range option, so book ahead; check the website for off-season deals. €€

Nerva
3 Via Tor de' Conti
Tel: 06-678 1835
[p340, A1]
www.hotelnerva.com
The decor of this family-run hotel is nothing to get excited about, but it is quiet and well located on the border between the Imperial Fora and the hilly bohemian Monti district. €€€

Radisson SAS es. Hotel
171 Via Filippo Turati

Tel: 06-444841
[p336, C4]
www.rome.radissonsas.com
This cutting-edge-design hotel is seriously minimalist: rooms are pure white with the odd splash of green. A spectacular decked rooftop terrace has a restaurant and a pool (in summer). Its location – right opposite the station – is convenient but far from picturesque. €€€€

St Regis Grand
3 Via V.E. Orlando
Tel: 06-47091
[p336, B3]
www.starwood.com/stregis
Situated between the station and Via Veneto, the recently restored St Regis Grand provides a taste of 19th-century *belle époque* grandeur. If you can't afford to stay here, at least try to drop in for high tea or cocktails. €€€€€

EXCURSIONS FROM ROME

Ostia Antica
Rodrigo De Vivar
18–19 Piazza della Rocca
Tel: 06-5651939
www.rodrigodevivar.com
Near the excavations at Ostia Antica, and inside the medieval *borgo*, this upmarket country house hotel has 10 rooms and four suites, all luxuriously finished, with Persian carpets and Murano chandeliers. The hotel also organises activity days, with courses in everything from archery to restoration to painting. €€€

Tivoli
Hotel Adriano
194 Via di Villa Adriana
Tel: 0774-535028
www.hoteladriano.it
Just outside the entrance to Hadrian's Villa, this pleasant hotel offers 10 rooms, of which three are suites; most requested is Suite 14, where Marguerite Yourcenar stayed when she wrote her classic novel *Memoirs of Hadrian*. There's also a restaurant, and nearby, an array of facilities that can be used by guests of

the hotel, including a golf course, swimming pool and tennis court. €€

Hotel Sirene
4 Piazza Massimo
Tel: 0774-330605
This romantic villa hotel is set right in the centre of Tivoli, well sited for the Villa d'Este. Ask for a room with a view of the nearby Roman temples, or of Villa Gregoriana. The breakfast room here is a real selling point – it's carved out of the rock. €€

Castelli Romani
Hotel Flora
8 Viale Vittorio Veneto, Frascati
Tel: 06-941 6110
www.hotel-flora.it
The fresh, bright bedrooms and luxurious marble bathrooms at this hotel, built in the late 19th century and decorated in "Liberty" style, make it an appealing option if you're looking to stay in central Frascati. There's a pretty courtyard shaded by palm trees where you can take breakfast in warm weather. €€

Grand Hotel Villa Tuscolana
Via del Tuscolo km 1,500, Frascati
Tel: 06-942900
www.villatuscolana.it
Just east of Frascati, this beautiful hillside villa has been lavishly restored and turned into a hotel with 110 rooms. The bedrooms are spacious and elegant, and the common areas – which include a restaurant (La Rufinella) and bar – impressively grand. There's also an indoor pool. €€€

Il Cortile
9, Via Giulia, Nemi
Tel: 06-9368147
Two quaint rooms with en-suite bathroom, sharing a kitchenette in this quaint B&B. Fresh breakfast delivered to your door every morning by the friendly owner, who is a mine of information on the area.

Castelli Romani
B&B Casa di Anna
5/6 Largo della Boccetta, Cerveteri
Tel: 06-994 3837
Right in the heart of the old town, this is a sim-

ple, no-frills B&B. Bedrooms are comfortable, though, with en-suite bathrooms, and the breakfast is generous. Buses to the Necropolis are nearby. €

Residenza del Teatro
13, Piazza G. Verdi, Viterbo
Tel: 0761-345439
www.residenzadelteatro.it
This lovely, light-filled palazzetto on three floors has five spacious and elegant doubles with wood-beamed ceilings. It also boasts a great location, right in the medieval historic centre of Viterbo. €€

PRICE CATEGORIES

For a double room in high season:
€ = under €100
€€ = €100–180
€€€ = €180–260
€€€€ = €260–450
€€€€€ = over €450

TRANSPORT

ACCOMMODATION

SHOPPING

ACTIVITIES

A – Z

LANGUAGE

SHOPPING

BEST BUYS

Rome is the place for quality rather than bargains, so its best buys tend to be at the luxury end of the market, principally in the form of designer clothes and accessories, antiques and objets d'art. That said, careful shoppers may still come away with affordable buys: attractive books on art and architecture, classic leather shoes and bags, striking kitchenware, herbalists' concoctions, distinctive marbled notepaper, old prints, market bric-a-brac and a whole host of gourmet treats, all represent good value.

WHAT TO BUY

Clothing

All the major designers and national retail chains are represented in Rome, and you don't have to be super-rich to kit yourself out in style. If Via Condotti and the Bulgari brigade are not in your budget, mid-range Italian labels including Liu Jo (188 Via Cola di Rienzo/137 Via del Corso), Stefanel (219 Via di Cola Rienzo/122 Via del Corso), and Carla G (134 Via Cola di Rienzo) offer high-quality styles ranging from chic to subdued, at prices that won't make you cringe. For reliable and reasonably priced staples, head to Benetton and sister-store Siseley, Class, or Spanish imports Zara and Mango. Peruse boutique originals and home-grown start-up collections along Via Governo Vecchio and around Campo de' Fiori.

Shoes and Accessories

Before the introduction of the euro, a Fendi baguette or a pair of Prada shoes were the Italian shopping essentials. These days you're better off shopping in your home country first for designer bargains. For a great brand and price range, cruise the shops on Via Nazionale and Via Cola di Rienzo. Savvy shoe-shoppers should take advantage of the flashy, indie brands like Joseph Debauc (19 Vicolo del Cinque) and trendy, upscale shoe shop Alexandra (19 Via Paolo Emilio). For bags, Via Giubbonari (Campo de' Fiori) is lined with colourful boutiques, including Momento (Piazza Cairoli, end of the street), and Best Seller (No. 96). Aim for quality and originality in your adornments. "Made in Italy" is no longer a guarantee. In their quest to join ranks with the big guns, newer names on the Rome style scene, such as AVC and Casanita, are far more likely to sell you something that will last and impress.

ABOVE: classic Italian style in an Alessi kettle.

Leather

Italian leather is still the best in the world, and you'll find it everywhere. Big leather vendors can be found on Via del Corso, Via Nazionale, and throughout the Tridente, whereas smaller, artisan leather goods are scattered throughout the city, and require a good eye to ascertain the quality. To get you started, check out Artigiano del Cuoio (90 Via Belsiana), where your own handbag designs are ready in under a week, and Claudio Sanò (67a Largo degli Osci), whose audacious hand-stitched bags are made on site. Leather-bound notebooks and photo albums make gorgeous souvenirs. You can snatch them up at Cartoleria Pantheon and Papiro.

MONEY BACK?

As a general rule, it's next to impossible to return merchandise for a refund. While sales clerks are notoriously unrelenting, by law, unused items may be exchanged on site.

And More...

Rome is characterised by the olde-worlde values of artisan craftsmanship, artful design and good food, which define the shopping cityscape. Striking kitchenware abounds, from cute Alessi utensils and coffee service to elaborate appliances and hand-painted ceramics by Modigliani (24 Via Condotti). Stock up on top-of-the-line linens from Casa del Tessuto (64/66 Via del Statuto) and luxury bedding and window treatments from Frattelli Bassetti (73 Corso Vittorio Emanuele II).

Foodies will revel in the city's delis and speciality food shops. Castroni and Volpetti are mainstays for Italian and international delicacies, coffee and chocolate; wine and liqueurs are available at Trimani, Arcioni and many more around town.

WHERE TO BUY

Shopping Centres

Several shopping centres outside the city are good places to find last season's wares (mainly clothing) with discounts of up to 70 percent.

Castel Romano, south of EUR, has over 90 stores, including designer and mid-market brands such as Dolce & Gabbana, Versace, Calvin Klein, Diesel and Bruno Magli. **Fashion District** in Valmontone southeast of Rome (trains leave hourly from Termini) has over 200 shops selling mostly mid-market brands. For more information *see page 301*.

For a mall within city limits, check out **Galleria Alberto Sordi** on Via del Corso. The arcade has just been restored to its original grandeur after years of closure and neglect. Many new shops include Rome's first Zara, a large Feltrinelli book and music store, and a megastore called Jam, dedicated to young fashion.

Margutta Arcade (3 Via Margutta) is new and exclusive, with boutiques selling upmarket jewellery, antiques and clothing.

Department Stores

Department stores are few and far between in Rome, but there are four main chains.

COIN, 7 Piazzale Appio (San Giovanni). Dependable, with some well-made and imaginative linen and household items.

La Rinascente, Piazza Fiume and 20 Largo Chigi (level with Piazza Colonna). The most elegant of the stores, with a vast range of goods, especially fashion for women and children.

Oviesse, 62 Viale Trastevere. Basic store for household goods, clothes and cosmetics.

Upim, 172 Via del Tritone and Piazza Santa Maria Maggiore. Economical store for household goods, cosmetics and children's clothes.

MAS (Piazza Vittorio) is an emporium of cheap and often tacky essentials. You'll have to get your hands dirty, but rare gems are known to reside within.

Fashion

Cult Couture

Those into serious shopping and couture names head to the Piazza di Spagna area and explore the high-fashion temples that are Via Condotti, Via Bocca di Leone and Via Borgognona. Ateliers succeed one another in dizzying fashion and prices to match. Here's a quick reference.
Costume National, 106 Via del Babuino

Dolce & Gabbana, 51–52 Via Condotti/D&G 93 Piazza di Spagna
Fendi, 36–37a & 39–40 Via Borgognona/(women) 419 Largo Goldoni
Gianfranco Ferrè, 70 Piazza di Spagna
Gianni Versace, 26 Bocca di Leone
Giorgio Armani, 77 Via Condotti/ 140 Via del Babuino/(Armani Jeans) 137 Via Tomacelli
Gucci, 8 Via Condotti/7d Via Borgognona
Hogan, 45 Via Borgognona
Laura Biagiotti, 43 Via Borgognona
Max Mara, 28 Via Frattina
Prada, 90 Via Condotti/ 91 Via del Babuino
Roberto Cavalli, 7a Via Borgognona/Just Cavalli 82–83 Piazza di Spagna
Valentino, 13 Via Condotti/ (men) 15 Bocca di Leone

Mid-Range Clothing

Nearby **Via del Corso** is far more budget-oriented. Although crass in parts, it holds some pearls for high-street fashion fanatics, such as Diesel (No. 186), Miss Sixty (No. 510), Benetton (No. 422–23)

BELOW: Tad concept store.

SIZE CHART

Women's dresses

Italian	UK	US
38	8	6
40	10	8
42	12	10
44	14	12

Men's shirts

Italian	UK	US
36	14	14
38	15	15
41	16	16
43	17	17

Women's shoes

Italian	UK	US
37	4	6
38	5	7½
39	6	8½
40	7	9

Men's shoes

Italian	UK	US
40	6½	7½
41	7	8
42	8	8½
43	9	9½

and two Zara stores (Galleria Alberto Sordi and No. 129–35). Via del Corso ends (or begins) at Piazza del Popolo, but cross the river at Ponte Margherita to **Via Cola di Rienzo** for more wallet-friendly shops, including many sister stores. There's Benetton (No. 193–209), COIN department store (No. 173) as well as: **Blunauta**, No. 303–309. Flowing designs in silk and cashmere.

Iron G, No. 5. Get club-ready and a bit extravagant at this twenty-something magnet.

Mango, No. 198. Spain's answer to Benetton and Gap has everything basic and trendy.

Onyx, No. 225. A paradise for pre-teens and the wishfully young at heart. Warning: avoid a break-down and go up a size or two.

Diesel, No. 247–248. Best-known for jeans and ultra-urban style.

Miss Sixty, No. 235. Skinny jeans and all things long and lean, in daring colours and prints. Great accessories, too.

Chic Boutiques

For those in search of cool collections, one-of-a-kind styles and all-in-one concept stores, Rome is full of gems.

Angelo Nepi, 28 Via Dei Giubbonari, sells colourful fitted jackets, wide linen trousers and beautiful dresses and scarves.

Arsenale, 64 Via del Governo Vecchio, is the place for local designer Patrizia Pieroni's eye-catching creations.

Carla G, 121 Via del Babuino, sells garments that are classy, well cut and very sassy.

Ethic, 11 Piazza B. Cairoli (end of Via dei Giubbonari) is one of many branches of a casualwear company that mixes styles, genres and fabrics with a penchant for the ethnic or unusual. Great looking, well priced.

Kristina Ti, 40 Via Mario de' Fiori, makes sexy and feminine dresses and bikinis.

Patrizia Pepe, 1 Via Frattina, is a Florentine designer who creates modern, feminine wear at user-friendly prices.

Maga Morgana, 27 and 98 Via del Governo Vecchio, specialises in Luciana Iannace's hand-knitted garments and old-fashioned dresses.

Momento, 9 Piazza Cairoli (Via dei Giubbonari). Choose from flowing boho dresses, original designs, and enough shoes and bags to fill a million closets.

Nuyorica, 36–37 Piazza Pollarola. Something out of the U this boutique is also a shoe-lover's dream, with selections by Marni, Balenciaga, Rodolphe Menudier and Sigerson Morrison. Very hip, pretty pricey.

Bags, Shoes and Accessories

AVC, 88 Piazza di Spagna/(outlet) 1 Largo del Pallaro/141 Via Frattina. Roman designer Adriana V. Campanile is up on the trends and far lower on the prices.

Boccanera, 36 Via Luca della Robbia (Testaccio). All the big Italian (and some foreign) brands under one roof: Hogan, Tod's, Prada, Sergio Rossi and Pollini.

Borsalino, 72a Via di Campo Marzio. A time-honoured hat-maker.

Bruno Magli, 6 Via Condotti. Prestigious shoemaker for over 70 years, experiencing a major rebirth.

Calzature Fausto Santini, 165 Via Santa Maria Maggiore. His main store is on Via Frattina, but this is where you get Santini's gems from past collections at half-price.

Casanita, 8 Via del Biscione. Upstairs resembles decade-old Gap designs for teenagers, but the shoes downstairs are a well-hidden wealth of comfort, style and adorable colours.

Coccinelle, 255 Via Cola di Rienzo. Luxuriously soft leather bags and pocketbooks in the colours of the season.

Fratelli Rossetti, 59 Via Condotti. Another classic Italian footwear-maker, from Milan.

Furla, 22 Piazza di Spagna, and other branches around Rome, is Italy's mid-market answer to the bag dilemma, with a widely varied, constantly changing range of leather bags and accessories. Good quality, and pleasingly (almost) modest prices.

Geox, 3 Via Frattina. Comfortable, wearable and sexy shoes – a bit like Camper shoes.

Ibiz, 39 Via dei Chiavari. Handmade and wonderfully whimsical

SHOPPING ♦ **301**

TRANSPORT

ACCOMMODATION

SHOPPING

ACTIVITIES

A – Z

LANGUAGE

TOP: Fratelli Rossetti for men.
ABOVE AND LEFT: Prada on Via Condotti.

leather accessories of all sorts are made on site.
Mandarina Duck, 59 Via Due Macelli/272 Cola di Rienzo. Bolognese designer of pretty and functional bags and luggage.
Pollini, 22–24 Via Frattina. Classic shoes and handbags.
Sermoneta, 61 Piazza di Spagna. Gloves in a multitude of colours.
Tod's, 56a–57 Via Fontanella Borghese. Diego Della Valle's shoes and bags, sold here, have become cult items.
See also **Tad** *(page 302).*

Vintage

Via Governo Vecchio is your first destination. Check out Abiti Usati (No. 35), Omero & Cecilia (No. 110), and Vestiti Usati Cinzia (No. 45). The **Micca Market**, at the Micca Club lounge (7a Via Pietro Micca) is a veritable jumble sale starting every Sunday from 6pm on. **Pulp** (14 Via del Boschetto) is a small but treasure-packed second-hand shop in Monti. **People** (4 Piazza Teatro di Pompeo) is where the fashion-conscious head for original accessories.

Jewellery

Buccellati, 31 Via Condotti. Famous Florentine jewellers, best-known for their elaborately worked silver pieces.
Bulgari, 10 Via Condotti. The supreme jeweller to royalty and the stars.
Giokeb, 79 Via della Lungaretta. A favourite for affordable baubles, the chunky gems – especially amber – and silver settings will blow your mind and not your wallet.
Ivano Langella, 73a Via di Ponte Sisto. Not your run-of-the-mill jeweller, Langella moulds chunks of silver, gold and bronze into unusual and stunning pendants, rings and necklaces .
Massimo Maria Melis, 57 Via dell'Orso. Custom-made jewellery, inspired by Roman and Etruscan artefacts.
Tempi Moderni, 10 Via del Governo Vecchio. A funky collection of vintage treasures; get your Art Deco here.

Books

Almost Corner Bookshop, 45 Via del Moro. Australian-run, with well-chosen and reasonably priced titles.
Anglo-American Book Co, 102 Via della Vite. Novels, art books, travel tomes and a section for kids, all in English; friendly staff.
Bibli, 28 Via dei Fienaroli. Large Italian-language bookshop and café; has an internet point and does very good Sunday brunches.
The English Bookshop, 248 Via di Ripetta. A good range of travel, non-fiction and children's books, plus a café.
Feltrinelli International, 84 Via V.E. Orlando. A large selection of English-language books.
Herder, 117 Piazza di Montecitorio. A good selection of travel books and classics.
Libreria del Viaggiatore, 78 Via del Pellegrino. Travel books in Italian and English.
Lion Bookshop, 33 Via dei Greci 33. The oldest English bookshop

in Rome, with a wide assortment and a coffee shop.

Gifts

Via della Conciliazione, linking the Vatican with Castel Sant' Angelo, offers a wide range of religious artefacts including Vatican coins, statues, stamps, religious books and souvenirs. Similar objects are on sale around the Vatican itself and on Via dei Cestari, between the Pantheon and Largo Argentina.
Ai Monasteri, 72 Corso Rinascimento. In an old pharmacy; it sells teas, honeys, liqueurs, ointments and potions made by monks from all over Italy.
Al Sogno, 53 Piazza Navona. Historic toy store specialising in soft toys of all shapes and sizes.
Cartoleria Pantheon, 15 Via della Rotonda. A well-stocked card store featuring hand-bound leather notebooks.

BARGAIN PICKS

Ablue Cachemire, Via di San Francesco (Trastevere). Good-quality second-hand cashmere, silk and linen garments They are not exactly cheap, but they are good value.
Danielle and Outlet, Piazza Risorgimento. A great selection of all kinds of shoes at reasonable prices. The outlet sells overstock from Danielle at rock-bottom prices.
Habana, Via del Corso and all over town. You'll pay next to nothing for cool, cotton essentials and sundresses, and you'll get about a season or two of wear out of them.
Mas, Piazza Vittorio (Esquilino). Definitely for the determined, this cheap and often tacky department store is worth a rummage.
Tessuti Camiceria, 92 Viale Mazzini (Prati). Handmade shirts and blouses in 100 percent cotton.

ABOVE: Roman deli.

Città del Sole, 65 Via della Scrofa. A store for progressive parents and their progeny, crammed with educational toys, games and books.

Il Papiro, 5 Via del Pantheon. A stationery store featuring Florentine stationery, quill pens, and beautiful notebooks and albums.

Fabriano, 173 Via del Babuino. Quality writing paper, photo

OUTDONE YOURSELF?

Chances are your suitcase will be bursting at the seams. Luckily for you, baggage of all shapes, sizes and prices is on offer citywide. The budget luggage hub is conveniently located on **Via Nazionale**, near Termini Station.

Diomedi, 99 Piazza San Bernardo. An old-fashioned shop selling exquisite beauty cases, suitcases and brief-cases.

Segue, 160 Via Nazionale/ 94 Via dei Giubbonari. The bag mecca by Benetton. This is the place for those hard and happy-coloured cases and matching carry-alls and carry-on bags.

Tedeschi Salvatore Paolo, 160 Via Nazionale. A fine selection of small and large suitcases in all price ranges. *See also* **Mandarina Duck** *on page 301.*

albums, wallets and travel diaries, plus a section with drawing products for children.
Musicali, 473 Via del Corso, www.messaggeriemusicali.it. Huge music shop with a good video and DVD selection. Also sells concert tickets and international magazines. Open late.
Tè e Teiere, 85 Via del Pellegrino. A tea-lover's haven in a coffee-oriented city, with expert staff to boot. The teas, pots and cups range from the modern and colourful to the traditional made out of bamboo and cast iron, and come from all over the world.

Food

Castroni, 196 Via Cola di Rienzo/55 Via Ottaviano. The hands-down favourite for Italian speciality items, international treats and amazing gifts. A tin of their roasted and ground espresso will not go unappreciated.
Innocenzi, 31 Via Natale del Grande. An old-fashioned treasure trove of a deli selling rice and grain out of big canvas sacks, many organic products, and ethnic foods from all over the world, as well as regional Italian delicacies.
Panella, 4 Largo Leopardi. A bread and pastry shop straight out of one's dreams.
Volpetti, 47 Via Marmorata. Probably the best deli in Rome.

Drink

Arcioni, 11–13 Via della Giuliana. Friendly and knowledgeable staff will help you find a bottle in your price range.
Constantini, 16 Piazza Cavour. Over 2,000 Italian wines to choose from.
Enoteca al Parlamento, 1 Via dei Prefetti. Hundreds of bottles in a mind-boggling selection.
Trimani, 20 Via Goito. Good selection of wines and tempting delicacies, and one of Rome's oldest wine vendors.

Interior Design

Architettura D'Interni, 27–29 Via Bissolati. A striking store where interior design and architecture blend seamlessly.
MCM900, 10 Vicolo del Cedro (Trastevere). At the foot of the Gianicolo, this lovely shop is dedicated to 1900s period pieces. Staff are informed and friendly.
Sisters, 143 Via dei Banchi Vecchi. Three women run this eccentric and opulent space selling mirrors, lights, vases and some furniture.
Spazio Sette, 7 Via dei Barbieri. One of Rome's premier furniture and home-furnishings stores.
Tad, 155a Via del Babuino. A so-called "concept store" with all the designer lifestyle must-haves: fashion, footwear, cosmetics, magazines, furniture. There's also a florist, hairdresser and a café.
Thè Verde, 23 Via Vittoria. A lovely store selling ethnic and oriental fabrics for the home.

Kitchenware

Art'e, 3 Piazza Rondanini. A fine collection of slick, modern Italian names in kitchenware and colourful appliances.
C.U.C.I.N.A. 65 Via Mario de' Fiori. Trendy, good-quality kitchenware with an appealing mix of prices.
Gusto, 9 Piazza Augusto Imperatore. Attached to the 'Gusto mega-restaurant *(see page 134)*, this is a delightful store with the most unusual and well-made cooking utensils and gadgets, as well as a range of cookery books and magazines.
Leone Limentani, 47 Via del Portico d'Ottavia. A wide variety of discounted ceramics, crystal, china and cutlery, and Alessi products, in a dusty and rambling warehouse.
Moa, 1–3 Via Leone IV. A houseware emporium carrying exclusive lines of dishes and tableware. *See also* **Tè e Teiere** *(above).*

ACTIVITIES

THE ARTS, NIGHTLIFE, FESTIVALS, SHOPPING AND SPORTS

Romans know how to have fun – *La Dolce Vita*, the city's celebrated "good life", is still lived in the city. The best time for live music and cultural events is the summer, when classical ruins, Renaissance squares, villa gardens and parks play host to Estate Romana, an extravaganza of film, music, theatre, dance and much more. Rome's nightlife has never been as vibrant as it is today, and for sheer excitement and atmosphere you cannot beat an Italian football match at the Stadio Olimpico.

THE ARTS

Theatre

As plays are nearly always performed in Italian, an evening at the theatre is only recommended for fluent Italian-speakers. A notable exception are theatrical events related to the Roma Europa Festival *(see Festivals, page 309)* or some of the original-language performances put on at the ever-reliable **Teatro Argentina** (56 Largo Argentina, tel: 06-6840 0345, www.teatrodiroma.net). However, in some cases it is worth attending a classical drama or play in translation, if the venue itself provides the drama – particularly summer events held outdoors, whether in amphitheatres, such as the one at **Ostia Antica** (Scavi di Ostia Antica, 117 Viale dei Romagnoli, tel: 06-6840 0345), or at other classical sites *(see Summer Spectacle, below)*. Roman

theatre embraces mainstream and contemporary, but the emphasis is on the tried and trusted Italian dramatists, such as Carlo Goldoni and Luigi Pirandello, musicals, or lighter, frothier stuff, often translated. However, the university theatres and smaller venues do stage experimental or fringe productions (known as "Teatro off"). One of the most interesting of these is the recently revamped **Teatro Palladium** (8 Piazza Bartolomeo Romano, tel: 06-5706 7761, www.teatro-palladium.it) which is attached to the University Roma 3 and puts on an interesting range of readings, films, dance and theatre events. The theatre season runs from October to early June, but there are numerous summer events linked to specific Roman festivals *(see Estate Romana, page 309)*. Rome also has a last-minute theatre box office where unsold tickets can be bought on the same day for up to 50 percent off. The counter is located at 20

WHAT'S ON WHERE

For the most comprehensive listings of what's on in Rome, pick up *Roma C'è*, a weekly booklet that comes out on Wednesday and is available from news-stands. Listings are in Italian with an abbreviated section in English. The Thursday edition of the national daily *La Repubblica* carries a supplement called *TrovaRoma* that contains full listings for the upcoming week, and the fortnightly English magazine *Wanted in Rome* (available at news-stands) also has a listings section. The tourist information office and booths *(see page 317)* provide a multitude of leaflets, including the monthly guide *L'Evento* and a booklet called *Tourist's Passepartout*. Online, www.trovacinema.it lists all the films currently playing.

TRANSPORT

ACCOMMODATION

SHOPPING

ACTIVITIES

A – Z

LANGUAGE

Via Bari (Piazza Salerno, Policlinico metro stop line B); Tue–Sat 2–8pm (closed July and August).

The English Theatre of Rome (tel: 06-444 1375, www.rome theatre.com) has an interesting and varied programme of small-scale productions, with five English-language productions per season, usually put on at the intimate Teatro L'Arciliuto in the Centro Storico.

Opera and Ballet

The opera and ballet season runs from October to June at the Teatro dell'Opera, 1 Piazza Beniamino Gigli, tel: 06-4816 0255, www.operaroma.it. The ticket office is open Tue–Sat 9am–5pm, Sun 9am–1.30pm, but tickets can also be bought on its website and picked up at the opera house on the night of the performance. Ticket prices run from reasonable to exorbitant. The outdoor summer opera series (same numbers as above) has been held in a variety of venues in past years, including the Baths of Caracalla. Rome's New Opera Festival (tel: 06-561 1519, www.newoperafestivaldiroma.com) puts on classic Italian operas in the atmospheric setting of the Basilica di San Clemente near the Colosseum, most nights from

BELOW: sculpture of Constantine's hand at the Museo Capitolino.

mid-June to mid-August; ticket prices are reasonable.

The best bet for international and contemporary dance is the **Teatro Olimpico** (17 Piazza Gentile da Fabriano, tel: 06-326 5991, www.teatroolimpico.it). Ticket office is open daily 11am–7pm.

Classical Music

There is a wide range of venues for classical music. The season runs from October to June, but with special summer concerts there's something going on just about all year round.

The renowned, high-profile Accademia di Santa Cecilia (www.santacecilia.it), and its symphonic and chamber orchestras, hosts all its principal concerts from October to May at the new **Auditorium-Parco della Musica** (30 Viale Pietro de Coubertin, tel: 06-8024 1281, www.auditorium. com). Designed by Genoese architect Renzo Piano, it opened in December 2002 and features three concert halls with excellent acoustics. A 10-minute tram-ride from Piazzale Flaminio (just above Piazza del Popolo), the complex also features a large inner courtyard, which is used for outdoor concerts and events.

For more information, visit www.santacecilia.it or the Auditorium's website. There are many other venues for classical music, including churches and outdoor venues all over Rome in summer, many of them part of the Estate Romana series of events *(see Festivals, page 309)*. Some of the most atmospheric venues are the Terme di Caracalla, the Teatro di Marcello, the Fori Imperiali and the Terrazza del Pincio. Ask at a tourist information point for the monthly guide to cultural events, called *L'Evento*, or check the local press for more information on classical music events.

Museums and Galleries

The Roma Pass is an integrated ticket which costs €20, lasts three days and gives you free entrance to the first two museums and archaeological sites you visit (most major sites are included in the scheme; call 06-8205 9127 or see www.romapass.it for details); the card entitles you to reduced admission on any further sites you visit. Full access to the public transport system is also included in the price. The pass is sold at all of the sites involved, and at tourist information kiosks and Fiumicino Airport's tourist information office in Terminal C.

A €9 Museum Card, valid for three days, is available and covers all the sites of the Museo Nazionale Romano; a €20 ticket (Roma Archeologia Card), valid for seven days, covers the sites of the Museo Nazionale Romano and the Colosseum, the Palatine, the Baths of Caracalla, the Tomb of Cecilia Metella and the Villa of the Quintili. They can be bought from any participating site.

Most museums are closed on Monday, though there are some exceptions. Important art exhibitions are usually open daily.

NIGHTLIFE

Roman nightlife tends to be fun rather than frenzied. Apart from a few privileged or exclusive clubs, the nightclub scene is far less adventurous than in Berlin, London or New York. In common with other capital cities, door policy determines whether you even get to cross the threshold of a club. If your look is not right you will either not get in or not fit in. As a general rule, however, in Rome it is safer to dress up rather than down, even if it makes rejection all the more humiliating.

You may be required to obtain temporary membership (a *tessera*, or membership card, should be available at the door). Entry price may include a free drink, but drinks are normally quite expensive. Groups of young men together are usually not welcome and, in some clubs, a man may be turned away unless accompanied by a woman.

Trastevere is still a reliable destination for Romans in search of a good time. Slightly more alternative is Testaccio, which is clubland central, and a burgeoning gay, alternative and commercial scene is happening even further south in the industrial Ostiense quarter.

The historic quarters around Piazza Navona (around Via di Tor Millina), the Pantheon and Campo de' Fiori contain popular bars and clubs. The Via Veneto, scene of Fellini's *Dolce Vita*, is still home to certain elegant nightclubs and piano bars, which tend to be patronised by middle-aged, moneyed Americans.

Most nightclubs don't get going until midnight; most close Monday night, some on Sunday too. Several of the better ones are around Via di Monte Testaccio. Recently there's been an upsurge in so-called *discobar* and *ristodisco*, which as their names suggest mean bars and restaurants where there are also DJ sets and you can dance until late.

In summer, much young nightlife moves to the beach resorts south of the city. However, the glut of summer city festivals ensures that Rome remains lively. Apart from these, the best and most typical forms of Roman nightlife tend to be centred on a leisurely meal, a musical event or chatting and drinking at one of the many outdoor bars.

ABOVE: the recline-as-you-dine Supperclub in Piazza Navona.

to house with live music nights that vary from rock to Latin music.

Nightclubs

Akab
69 Via di Monte Testaccio
Tel: 06-5725 0585
www.akabcave.com
Ever-popular club with two floors and a terrace garden. The music is mainly commercial dance.

Alpheus
36 Via del Commercio
Tel: 06-574 7826
www.alpheus.it
Everything from R&B and hip hop

Anima
57 Via di Santa Maria dell'Anima (Piazza Navona)
Tel: 347-850 9256
A trendy, narrow bar and disco with mezzanine and sofas; serves cocktails to an R&B, dance and soul soundtrack.

Art Cafe
33 Viale del Galoppatoio (Villa Borghese)
Tel: 06-3600 6578
This slick, trendy club, which plays mainly commercial dance, attracts a well-heeled, party-loving crowd whose aim is to see and be seen.

Caruso
36 Via di Monte Testaccio (Testaccio)
Tel: 06-574 5019
www.carusocafedoriente.com
Latin American music is the order of the day at this cosy club, which bursts with enthusiastic salsa-dancing couples most nights. There's also a pleasant roof terrace for a breath of fresh air in the summer months.

Fake
64 Via di Monte Testaccio (Testaccio)
Tel: 06-4544 7627
www.faketheclub.com
Opened in 2005, this club has proved a success with the city's fashion crowd – thanks to its all-white, futuristic design, pop-art touches and mainly electronica music.

La Maison
4 Vicolo dei Granari (Piazza Navona)
Tel: 06-683 3312
Very hip centrally located club with a 1970s-retro feel to the decor and ambience.

La Saponeria
20 Via degli Argonauti (Ostiense)
Tel: 393-966 1321
www.lasaponeria.com
Industrial location with a retro-1970s design and music nights that range from hip hop to house.

Le Coppelle
52 Piazza delle Coppelle (Piazza Navona)
Tel: 06-683 2410
A so-called discobar with an enviably central location and a great line in cocktails. Outdoor seating on giant sofas in summer and a very cosmopolitan vibe.

Supperclub
14 Via de' Nari (Piazza Navona)
Tel: 06-6830 1011
www.supperclub.com
This futuristic restaurant with a clubby feel also hosts themed events and arty performances.

Music Venues

aBlueNote
113 Via Fabio Massimo (Prati)
Tel: 06-323 1005
This small, intimate venue hosts jazz concerts. Closed Mon.

Alexanderplatz
9 Via Ostia (Prati)
Tel: 06-3974 2171
www.alexanderplatz.it

When the big names come to town, they often come to this jazz club and restaurant, which runs the summer jazz series at the Villa Celimontana.

Beba do Samba
8 Via dei Messapi (San Lorenzo)
Tel: 339-8785 214
www.bebadosamba.it
In the student district of San Lorenzo, this is a buzzy venue with live music (generally jazz or world) most nights.

Big Mama
18 Via San Francesco a Ripa (Trastevere)
Tel: 06-581 2551
www.bigmama.it
The blues club in Rome, but also hosts jazz and rock musicians.

Brancaleone
11 Via Levanna (Nomentana)
Tel: 06-8200 4382
www.brancaleone.it
One of the liveliest of Rome's *centri sociali*, attracting high-quality DJs and live acts.

La Palma
35 Via Giuseppe Mirri (near the Tiburtina metro stop)
Tel: 06-4359 9029
www.lapalmaclub.it
Live bands playing new jazz and ethnic music and DJ sets.

Palalottomattica
Piazzale dello Sport (EUR)
Tel: 199-128 800
Refurbished architectural landmark; hosts indoor concerts.

The Place
27 Via Alberico II (Prati)
Tel: 06-6830 7137
www.theplace.it
This sophisticated club has a stage for live acts – mainly jazz bands (mostly Italian, some international).

Cinema

Virtually all films on general release are dubbed into Italian. For English-speaking cinema, try the following (films are marked VO – *versione originale*):
Alcazar, 14 Via Cardinale Merry del Val. Tel: 06-588 0099. Current film playing is shown in its original version on Monday.

ABOVE: at the Villa Borghese zoo.

Metropolitan, 7 Via del Corso. Tel: 06-320 0933. Multi-screen cinema with one screen devoted to original-version films.
Nuovo Olimpia, 16g Via in Lucina. Tel: 06-686 1068. Art-house movies occasionally shown, as well as original-language films.
Warner Village Moderno, 45–46 Piazza della Repubblica. Tel: 06-477 7911. Frequent original-version films on one screen.

CHILDREN'S ACTIVITIES

Explora-Il Museo dei Bambini, 82 Via Flaminia; Tue–Sun 9.30am–7pm; visits by prior booking only on weekends, four slots daily; entrance fee; tel: 06-361 3776, www.mdbr.it. Rome's only children's museum. With four sections dedicated to humans, the environment, communications and society, there are plenty of signs and material in English. Kids can star in their own TV show and have fun with the interactive displays. There's also a nice restaurant.

Time Elevator, 20 Via SS Apostoli; daily screenings 11am–7.30pm; entrance fee; tel: 06-9774 6243, www.time-elevator.it. Touted as a multimedia experience that illustrates the history of Rome. You sit on a moving platform, wearing headphones, for a cinematic roller-coaster ride through history with various protagonists (such as Nero and Michelangelo) playing major parts, and a narrator to help with the chronology. Quite cheesy, but a fun introduction to the Eternal City. Memorable moments include watching Rome burn.

Museo Criminologico, 29 Via del Gonfalone; Tue–Sat 9am–1pm, Tue and Thur 2.30–6.30pm; entrance fee; tel: 06-6830 0234, www.museocrimino logico.it. The Criminological Museum covers the history of the prison system in Italy, how criminal cases are solved, and how criminals were punished over the centuries, but the part (older) children will enjoy best is the section with torture instruments and paintings depicting various and gruesome forms of punishment.

Luneur, Via delle Tre Fontane EUR; open June–Sept, see website for times; tel: 06-592 5933, www.luneur.it. Rome's amusement park is not central, but worth knowing about when all else fails to amuse the little darlings. More than 70 attractions from Roller Coaster rides to Punch and Judy shows.

ANNUAL EVENTS

Many festivals are linked to the Catholic Church. The tourist office *(see page 317)* can help.

January

6 January: culmination of Christmas fair in Piazza Navona *(see December)* celebrating **Epiphany** (**Befana**), the traditional festival when good children receive presents and naughty children are given coal-shaped sweets.
17 January: **La Festa di Sant' Antonio Abate**. Blessing of animals in the church of Sant'Eusebio all'Esquilino.

February

Late February/early March:
Carnevale. Roman children put on fancy dress and take to the streets; clubs organise themed fancy-dress events.

March

9 March: **Festa di Santa Francesca Romana**. Cars and mopeds are driven to the church of Santa Francesca Romana in the Foro Romano to be blessed by the patron saint of motorists.
La Festa della Primavera. The arrival of spring is marked by the decoration of the Spanish Steps with a sea of azaleas.
Late March/early April: **Giornate FAI**. The Fondo Ambientale Italiano (Environmental Fund of Italy; www.fondoambiente.it) organises a weekend when usually closed churches, monuments and gardens can be visited.
Maratona di Roma. The marathon takes place on the third or fourth Sunday in March. www.maratonadiroma.it.
March/April: Easter week is huge, from the big Mass on Palm Sunday and the distribution of palm fronds to the mass pilgrimages for **Holy Week** (**Settimana Santa**) and concerts all over the city. The Pope also leads an outdoor **Mass at the Colosseum on Good Friday**, followed by a procession passing the Stations of the Cross. The week culminates on Easter morning with the Pope's Urbi et Orbi speech. Call the Vatican tourist office for more info *(see page 317)*.

April

21 April: **Il Natale di Roma**. Rome celebrates its legendary founding with fireworks, music and other events. Festivities are centred around the Campidoglio.
25 April: **La Festa della Liberazione**. Public holiday commemorating liberation of Italy by Allied forces at the end of World War II.
Late April or May: **Settimana della Cultura**. Cultural Week all over Italy, when entrance is free to all state-run museums and historical sites, as well as many exhibitions, see www.beniculturali.it.

May

May Day is widely celebrated in Rome – it's the one day of the year when no buses run. A huge free concert is held in front of San Giovanni in Laterano.
Sporting Events – the Italian Open Tennis Championship is usually held in the first half of May, and the International Horse Show is at the end of the month in the Villa Borghese.

June

29 June: **San Pietro e San Paolo**. The founders of the Catholic Church are honoured with a public holiday. Special Masses are held in their basilicas.
Estate Romana starts in June *(see Festivals, page 309)*.

July

Summer Opera. Opera and ballet in the open air at the Baths of Caracalla (also in August).
Festa de' Noantri. A street festival in Trastevere that runs for two weeks from mid-July.
Roma Alta Moda. A series of fashion shows featuring the new lines from the major design houses, with shows against striking historical backdrops around the city; the spring/summer previews are held over a few days in January.

August

5 August: **La Festa della Madonna della Neve**. Rose petals fall onto the congregation to commemorate the miraculous snowfall on this day in the year 352.

September

La Notte Bianca. A Saturday night mid-month when many museums, clubs, cinemas and shops stay open all night; some museums extend the event to include the night before too, when queues are more manageable.

October

Symphonic music season begins at the Auditorium, www.auditorium.com.

November

2 November: **Giornata dei Defunti**, or Day of the Dead, when the Pope celebrates Mass at the Verano cemetery.

BELOW: Rome's marathon begins and ends in Via dei Fori Imperiali.

ABOVE: Radisson SAS es. Hotel.

December

8 December: **Immacolata Concezione**. The Immaculate Conception of the Virgin is celebrated around the statue of the Madonna in Piazza di Spagna. **Christmas**. Major shopping streets are beautifuly decorated and *presepi* (Nativity scenes) set up in churches around the city. **Mercatino di Natale a Piazza Navona**. Christmas arts-and-crafts fair with stalls selling food opens the second week of December.
31 December: **San Silvestro**: fireworks and free concerts in Piazza del Popolo and other squares.

SPORT

Spectator Sports

You can find information on sporting events in two national papers devoted solely to sport: *Corriere dello Sport* and *Gazzetta dello Sport* – easy enough to understand even if you speak no Italian. Many local sporting events are also listed in Rome editions of the daily papers.

Football

Sporting life in Rome revolves around football *(calcio)*. Rome's Olympic Stadium is home to both the local clubs, SS Lazio and AS Roma, who play there from September to May. For fixtures, ticket information and official team paraphernalia, go to the Lazio Point, 34 Via Farini (near Termini) or the AS Roma Store, 360 Piazza Colonna.

Major Events

The two major sporting events that take place in Rome during the year and attract international stars and audiences are:
Concorso Ippico Internazionale (International Horse Show) at Piazza Siena in the gardens of the Villa Borghese in May (ask at a tourist information point or log on to www.piazzadisiena.com).
Also in May is the **Italian Tennis Open** (www.internazionalibnlditalia.it), held at the Foro Italico.

Participant Sports
Gyms

The sport Romans are most interested in is weight training at a local *palestra* (gym). The largest gym in the centre (which also has two Olympic indoor pools) is the **Roman Sport Center**, 33 Viale del Galoppatoio, tel: 06-320 1667 on the edge of Villa Borghese (access from the car park at the top of Via Veneto).
Farnese Fitness, 35 Vicolo delle Grotte, tel: 06-687 6931, near Campo de' Fiori, offers a decent range of classes in a 16th-century building.

Swimming

For a hot city, Rome is decidedly under-provided with swimming pools, and most that do exist are privately run. The few city council pools are booked up with slot systems that are incomprehensible and inaccessible even for many Romans. Some of the luxury hotels (especially those outside the historic centre) offer access to their pools. If you choose this option be prepared to pay for it; make an afternoon of it and enjoy a pleasant cocktail by the pool.
Cavalieri Hilton Hotel, 101 Via Cadiolo (Monte Mario), tel: 06-35091 *(see page 292)*.
Hotel Parco dei Principi, 5 Via G. Frescobaldi, tel: 06-854421. On the edge of the Villa Borghese, this pool is a tranquil oasis *(see page 290)*.
Radisson SAS es. Hotel, 171

Via Filippo Turati, tel: 06-444 841, www.eshotel.it. A truly stunning rooftop pool with a unique view of Termini's train tracks and the city below *(see page 297)*.
Piscina delle Rose, 20 Viale America, tel: 06-5926717. Take the metro to EUR Palasport. An Olympic-sized outdoor pool with rose gardens nearby. May to September only.
Other possibilities for swimming are the beaches and the lakes. The lakes are more pleasant than the beaches closest to Rome. Swimming is possible in Lago di Bracciano, the lakes of the Castelli Romani and several other smaller lakes.

Tennis

Most tennis courts belong to private clubs and are open to members and their guests only. Check with your hotel or tourist office for clubs that allow non-members to play.

How to Get Tickets

Venues have ticket offices, phone booking lines and online booking possibilities. Failing that, the best agencies for tickets are:
Hello Ticket
Tel: 06-4807 8400
Freephone: 800-907 080
www.helloticket.it (tickets can also be bought online and picked up at the venue beforehand).
Ricordi Mediastores
506 Via del Corso
Tel: 06-321 6860.
Orbis Servizi
37 Piazza Esquilino (behind Santa Maria Maggiore)
Tel: 06-474 4776.
Messaggerie Musicali
473 Via del Corso
Tel: 06-6819 2349.

FESTIVALS

Over the past few years the number of cultural events and festivals in Rome has almost tripled, and many new buildings and museums have helped this process. The two most established festivals, which nevertheless grow every year, are the Roma Europa Festival (www.romaeuropa.net or www.teatro-palladium.it) and the Estate Romana.

The **Roma Europa Festival** is a cutting-edge event which takes place every year from mid-September to at least mid-November and covers dance (usually modern), theatre, readings, cinema and music. Every year the festival has a different theme, and the performers are a highly interesting mix of well-established international performers and emerging or avant-garde troupes.

The **Estate Romana** (literally, Roman Summer) is the umbrella name for the huge programme of events sponsored by the local council from June to September which sees some of the city's most attractive parks and piazzas become venues for rock, ethnic and jazz concerts, theatre performances (in Villa Ada, Villa Celimontana, at the Fori Imperiali, Piazza del Popolo, to cite but a few), outdoor cinema (for example, in Piazza Vittorio

Emanuele II and San Lorenzo), dance lessons, and other cultural events such as readings, book fairs and gastronomic evenings. Every night various Roman piazzas and venues all over town host something to suit absolutely all tastes, and some of the locations are truly spectacular. See the local press and ask at the tourist information points for details, or log on to www.romeguide.it.

Rome's **International Photography Festival** (www.fotografiafestival.it) started in 2002 and has been such a success that it has expanded. It puts on a very wide range of photographic shows in the most diverse settings, from historic monuments to avant-garde back-street galleries. Also initiated in 2002, the **International Literature Festival** of Rome (www.festivaldelleletterature.it) hosts writers in the historic and mesmerising setting of the Basilica di Massenzio; past guests have included Günter Grass, Jonathan Coe, Alice Sebold, Paul Auster, Don Delillo, Hanif Kureishi and Salman Rushdie. Readings and debates are accompanied by live music.

SIGHTSEEING TOURS

Walking and sightseeing tours are organised by a number of travel agencies and tour guides, both licensed and unlicensed. The quality of what's on offer varies wildly. Recommended is **Enjoy Rome**, 8a Via Marghera, tel: 06-445 1843, www.enjoyrome.com, a friendly English-speaking office near the station that organises walking tours of Rome. They range from the Vatican to the Jewish Ghetto and Trastevere, and also offer a night tour of the ancient sites. Day trips to the ruins of Pompeii are organised in the summer months, and they also offer a free accommodation booking service.

Context:Rome (tel: 06-482 0911, www.contextrome.com) is a network of architects, historians and art historians who lead walking seminars for discerning travellers in order to share their love of the city, its history and culture. Taking one of these tours (which should be booked in advance) is a great way of making contact with people who really know the city inside out.

BELOW: *Les Chevaux du Vent* performing at the Roma Europa Festival.

A–Z

AN ALPHABETICAL SUMMARY OF PRACTICAL INFORMATION

A Admission Charges 310
B Budgeting for Your Trip 310
  Business Hours 311
C Climate 311
  Crime & Safety 311
  Customs 312
D Disabled Travellers 312
E Electricity 312
  Embassies/Consulates 312

  Emergencies 313
  Entry Requirements 313
G Gay & Lesbian Travellers 313
H Health & Medical Care 313
I Internet 314
L Lost Property 314
M Maps 314
  Media 314
  Money 315

P Postal Services 315
  Public Holidays 315
R Religious Services 316
S Student Travellers 316
T Telephones 316
  Toilets 317
  Tourist Information 317
U Useful Addresses 317
W Websites 317

A dmission Charges

Museum admission fees vary, but the major ones start at about €7 while the minor ones cost about €4. Most state or municipal museums offer free entrance to EU citizens under 18 or over 65. The entrance ticket to the Palatine can be used to visit the Colosseum. Entrance to the Roman Forum, the Pantheon and all basilicas and churches is free, as are the Vatican Museums on the last Sunday of the month (expect long queues).

B udgeting for Your Trip

Prices have rocketed in Rome in recent years, with many blaming the euro and lack of government control when it was introduced.

Things have calmed down a bit, and some prices have normalised, but hotels and restaurants were two of the worst-hit sectors, and in some cases prices have doubled. Expect to pay at least €150 a night for a double room if you want to stay in the city centre somewhere decent. For a more elegant hotel the prices are well over €200 a night. The cost of eating out varies hugely; a three-course evening meal with wine costs about €40 a head, on average, at a decent restaurant in the Centro Storico, but it's also possible to pay as little as €15 if you're happy to settle for a no-frills meal (pizza being an ever-popular budget option). You will also pay a bit less at lunchtime, or if you find a neighbourhood trattoria in the

suburbs or something off the beaten track, and more if you are in blatant tourist territory or in a modern minimalist restaurant with a "creative" menu.

One thing that remains very cheap is public transport. A single tickets costs €1 and can be used for 75 minutes, and a number of passes are available. There are one-day, three-day and seven-day passes, called *Biglietto Integrato Giornaliero*, *Biglietto Turistico Integrato* and *Carta Integrata Settimanale*, which are good for unlimited metro, bus and local train or regional bus travel. They need to be validated only on first use. Month-long passes, *Abbonamento Mensile*, are also available. COTRAL, the regional bus company, offers a regional day-pass *(BIRG)*, which

TRANSPORT

ACCOMMODATION

SHOPPING

ACTIVITIES

A – Z

LANGUAGE

CLIMATE CHART

- ☐ Maximum temperature
- ■ Minimum temperature
- — Rainfall

covers your round trip and in-city travel. Taxis are also cheaper than in most other capital cities, with a trip from the station to the centre (Piazza Navona) costing about €12–15 depending on the traffic; fares go up at night.

Business Hours

Business hours vary greatly, but in general shops open Mon–Sat 9am–1pm and 3.30–7.30pm. Many close on Monday morning. Recently, in the touristy areas, many shops have started opening on Sunday and through lunch. Hairdressers and barbers are open all day but closed on Monday. In general the small food shops are open 8am–1.30pm and 5.30–8pm, and closed Saturday afternoon in summer and Thursday afternoon the rest of the year. Many shops and restaurants close for two weeks in August.

Churches generally open 7am–7pm with a three-hour lunch break; the four main basilicas open 7am–7pm with no lunchtime closure.

Banks open Mon–Fri 8.30am–1.30pm and 2.45–4pm; a few in the city centre also open Saturday morning. Most currency exchange bureaux open until 7.30pm Mon–Sat, and in very touristy areas even later.

State and city museums are closed on Monday, but there are a few exceptions: the Colosseum, the Roman Forum and the Imperial Fora, the Vatican Museums and the Galleria Doria Pamphilj are all open on Monday.

C limate

Despite some very unusual weather in the past few years (snow and hail in July, heatwaves in May), Rome can still be said to have a classic Mediterranean climate: mild-ish winters and very hot, long summers. July and August are the hottest and most humid months, when it is advisable to stay indoors or in the shade in the middle of the day.

When to Visit

April, May, September and October are the best months to visit as the weather is usually sunny and warm but devoid of that heavy, airless quality. In August many Romans go on holiday (especially around the Feast of the Assumption on 15 August), but for the past few years the city council has put on an incredible range of world-class outdoor concerts and other cultural events from June to September, and the city is less deserted than it used to be.

What to Wear

Light summer clothes are suitable from spring to autumn. The Roman heat is sometimes alleviated by a light breeze which can produce cool evenings even in summer, so a cardigan or jacket is useful. Wear a hat if you are sensitive to heat. Sunglasses are essential.

In summer, the likelihood of rain is slight: sometimes there is no rainfall in Rome for more than

NO   YES

three months. If it does rain, it will probably be a downpour in a thunderstorm. There is little point in preparing for this: just run for cover. At other times of the year, some form of waterproofing is worth considering, but not worth a lot of weight in your luggage. The most likely times for rain are autumn and spring.

In winter, warmer clothes are needed, including a heavy overcoat, as it can be very cold. Indoors, you may find the heating levels are below your expectations. In response to the climate, Roman building design has always concentrated on keeping heat out, rather than creating cosy interiors.

If visiting churches, and particularly St Peter's, remember that bare arms or shorts (on men or women) and short skirts are not acceptable, and you will be refused admittance. If wearing a short-sleeved or sleeveless garment, carry a light shirt/blouse or scarf with you.

Romans, like most Italians, consider clothes important. Most will dress smartly for an evening out, a restaurant meal or a visit to the theatre. Rome is accustomed to casually dressed tourists, but you may wish to follow local habits.

Dress codes for discos and bars vary enormously and change with the seasons and fashions. In general, however, dress is still likely to be slightly more formal than would be expected in much of Northern Europe or the US.

Crime and Safety

The main problem tourists experience in Rome is petty crime: pickpocketing and bag-snatching, together with theft from parked cars. Reduce the possibility of theft by taking elementary precautions. Leave money and valuables, including airline tickets, in the hotel safe. Carry your camera out of sight and always be discreet with your money or wallet.

If you are carrying a handbag, keep it on the side away from the road, and when sitting in a café, place it firmly on your lap; one Roman speciality is the motorbike snatch. Backpacks, while convenient, make easy targets: take them off or sling them under your arm in crowds. Always keep a separate record of credit card and cheque numbers just in case. A photocopy of your passport is also a useful precaution.

On the streets and especially near the main tourist attractions, keep an eye on beggars, particularly the small children who crowd around you with boxes in their hands. Take extra care on crowded buses and the metro and on bus routes frequented by tourists, such as the No. 40 Express and the No. 64.

Put a car with a foreign number plate in a garage overnight. Take your radio out, even if your insurance company will replace it, because fixing a broken windscreen means wasted time and trouble. Don't leave any items visible in the car.

If you are unlucky enough to have something stolen, report the theft *(furto)* to the police as soon as possible: you will need the police report for any insurance claim and to replace stolen documents. For information on the nearest police station call the central station, the Questura Centrale, 15 Via San Vitale, tel: 06-46861. Report the loss of travellers' cheques or credit cards to your credit card company, and of passports to your consulate or embassy.

Customs

Visitors from EU countries are not obliged to declare goods imported into or exported from Italy if they are for personal use, up to the following limits: 800 cigarettes, 200 cigars or 1 kg of tobacco; 10 litres of spirits (over 22 percent alcohol) or 20 litres of fortified wine (under 22 percent alcohol).

For US citizens, the duty-free allowance is 200 cigarettes, 50 cigars; 1 litre of spirits or 2 litres

of wine; one 50 g bottle of perfume and duty-free gifts to the value of US\$175.

D isabled Travellers

Rome is a difficult city for people with disabilities. Most churches, museums and archaeological sites have steps; streets and pavements are often uneven or cobbled, and pavements in the medieval centre are frequently too narrow for a wheelchair or have cars parked on the access ramps. However, things are improving, and the following attractions have installed ramps and lifts: the Vatican Museums, Galleria Doria Pamphilj, Castel Sant'Angelo, Palazzo Venezia, St Peter's, Galleria Borghese, Galleria Nazionale d'Arte Moderna and the Bioparco-Zoo. Ask at the tourist information points for other sites with facilities for people with disabilities.

Some trains have access for the disabled, but check with the railway before travelling; train timetables have a wheelchair symbol next to accessible trains. Seats at the front of city buses are reserved for the disabled, and many have designated wheelchair areas in the centre. The newest trams and buses all have large central doors and access ramps. On the metro, most of the central stations on line A are inaccessible, but all stations on line B have lifts, disabled toilets and designated parking spaces, except for Circo Massimo, Colosseo and Cavour. The metro website (www.metro roma.it) has information on wheelchair-accessible stations.

If travelling by car, there are free parking spaces for drivers

DISABILITY SERVICE

To find out more about a special transport service for people with disabilities, which is free if you carry proof of your disability, tel: 06-46954001, www.trambus.com/trasportodisabili.htm.

with disabilities displaying an official placard.

Restaurants are usually helpful, but call in advance to ask about access. A number of hotels claim to offer access to travellers with disabilities, but check with the individual hotel – be as precise as possible about your needs and ask detailed questions.

For more information, contact Roma Per Tutti (tel: 06-5717 7094, www.romapertutti.it), an English-speaking general information line.

E lectricity

Standard is 220 volts AC, 50 cycles. Sockets have either two or three round pins. For UK visitors, adaptors can be bought before you leave home, or at airports and main railway stations. Travellers from the US will need a transformer.

Embassies & Consulates

Consulates generally have answering machines on which you can leave a message in the event of a query or problem. If your passport is lost or stolen you will need to obtain a police report and have proof of your identity and suitable photos in order to get a new one.

Australia
5 Via Antonio Bosio
Tel: 06-852 721
www.italy.embassy.gov.au
Britain
80a Via XX Settembre
Tel: 06-4220 0001
www.britain.it
Canada
30 Via Zara
Tel: 06-854441
www.canada.it
Ireland
3 Piazza Campitelli
Tel: 06-697 9121
www.ambasciata-irlanda.it
New Zealand
28 Via Zara
Tel: 06-441 7171
www.nzembassy.com

TRANSPORT

ACCOMMODATION

SHOPPING

ACTIVITIES

A – Z

LANGUAGE

EMERGENCY NUMBERS	
Police	113
Carabinieri	112
Fire	115
Ambulance	118

South Africa
14 Via Tanaro
Tel: 06-852541
www.sudafrica.it
United States of America
119a Via Veneto
Tel: 06-46741
www.usembassy.it
(Consulate: 121 Via Veneto,
tel: 06-46741)

Entry Requirements
Visas and Passports
EU passport-holders do not require a visa; a valid passport or ID card is sufficient. Visitors from the US, Canada, Australia or New Zealand do not require visas for stays of up to three months; non-EU citizens need a full passport.

Nationals of most other countries do need a visa. This must be obtained in advance from the Italian Consulate. For addresses of embassies and consulates in Rome, *see above*.

G ay & Lesbian Travellers
Rome has an active and vibrant gay community. For information on cultural events and news, contact:
Circolo di Cultura Mario Mieli, Via Efeso 2a, tel: 06-541 3985, www.mariomieli.org.
Arci-Lesbica Roma, 15 Via Stefanini, tel: 06-4180211, www.arcilesbica.it, is a group that runs a helpline and organises social get-togethers for lesbians.
Babele, 116 Via dei Banchi Vecchi, tel: 06-6876628, is a gay bookshop and a good source of information (closed Sunday and Monday morning).
Alibi, 40–44 Via di Monte Testaccio, tel: 06-5743448, is a predominantly gay disco. Closed Mon–Wed.

Coming Out, 8 Via San Giovanni in Laterano (near the Colosseum), tel: 06-700 9871, is a mainstay of the Roman gay scene – it is often as crowded on the pavement outside as inside.
Hangar, 69a Via in Selci (near Via Cavour), tel: 06-488 1397, is a well-established gay club. Closed Tuesday.
Luna e L'altra, 1a Via San Francesco di Sales (in Trastevere), tel: 06-6840 1727, is a women-only evening restaurant in the recently renovated Casa Internazionale delle Donne (International House of Women; www.casainternazionaledelledonne.org). Closed Sunday.

H ealth & Medical Care
EU residents are entitled to the same medical treatment as an Italian citizen. Visitors will need to complete an EHIC form (see www.ehic.org.uk for information) before they go. This covers medical treatment and medicines, although it is still necessary to pay prescription charges and a percentage of the costs for medicines. Note that the EHIC does not give any cover for trip cancellations, nor does it provide repatriation in case of illness. For this, you will need to take out private insurance. US citizens are advised to take out private health insurance. Canadian citizens are also covered by a reciprocal arrangement between the Italian and Canadian governments.

If you are covered by a reciprocal scheme and need to visit a doctor while in Italy, take the EHIC form (if an EU resident) or proof of citizenship and residence (eg passport) to the local health office (Unità Sanitaria Locale), which will direct you to a doctor covered by the state system and supply the necessary paperwork. Not all doctors work in the state scheme, and those who do are often busy, so be prepared to wait. A consultation with a private doctor may be quicker (and certainly requires less preparatory paperwork) but costs more, so private insurance is a good idea.

If you need emergency treatment, call 118 or tel: 06-5510 (Red Cross) for an ambulance or to get information on the nearest hospital with an emergency department *(pronto soccorso)*. The most central is **Ospedale Fatebenefratelli**, Isola Tiberina, tel: 06-68371. If your child is sick go to the **Ospedale Pediatrico Bambino Gesù**, 4 Piazza Sant'Onofrio, tel: 06-68591, on the Gianicolo hill.

Medical Services
The **International Medical Center** (tel: 06-488 2371) is a private referral service with English-speaking doctors who are on call for house visits 24 hours a day. The **Rome American Hospital** (69 Via Emilio Longoni, tel: 06-22551), 30–40 minutes out of the town centre by taxi, has English-speaking doctors and

dentists. The **George Eastman Hospital** (287 Viale Regina Elena, tel: 06-844831) is Rome's only 24-hour dental hospital.

Chemists

Chemists *(farmacia)* can easily be identified by a green cross. Opening hours are usually Mon–Sat 8.30am–1pm and 4–8pm. A rotating system ensures there is always a chemist within walking distance which is open at night; a list outside every chemist indicates which it will be. Purchases at night carry a surcharge.

Some chemists are also open 24 hours a day. A couple of the most central are **Farmacia della Stazione**, 51 Piazza dei Cinquecento (corner of Via Cavour), tel: 06-488 0019, and **Farmacia Piram Omeopatia**, 228 Via Nazionale, tel: 06-488 0754.

Internet

Many of the city's green spaces are now wireless hotspots; you can surf the internet free in Villas Borghese, Pamphili, Ada and Torlonia (see www.romawireless.com for further information). There is no shortage of internet cafés in Rome:
Easy Everything
2 Via Barberini
Tel: 06-4290 3388
www.easyeverything.com
Open daily 8am–2am. More than 250 computers on three floors; offers some of the cheapest

rates in town (especially at night). Has a café selling light snacks and hot and cold beverages.
The Netgate
25 Piazza Firenze
Tel: 06-689 3445
Open Mon–Sat 7am– 9pm. Trained staff and 37 hi-tech computers. Also has a café.

Lost Property

For property lost on trains anywhere in Rome ask at the Termini Station's left-luggage office *(see below)*. For property lost on public transport (except trains) contact the ATAC bus and tram network lost property office; at the time of writing, the office is in the process of moving to new premises, but can be reached on 06-581 6040 (Mon, Wed, Fri 8.30am–1pm, Tue 3–5pm, Thur 8.30am–5pm).

Left Luggage

The left-luggage office in Termini Station is below ground level (level –1) at the side of platform 24 (daily 6am–midnight). Fiumicino Airport has 24-hour left-luggage facilities in the international terminals.

Maps

Free city maps are available from the main tourist information offices dotted around town *(see page 317)*. Free and comprehensive bus maps of the city centre are available from **ATAC** at 59 Via

Volturno (Mon–Fri 9am–1pm, Tue and Thur also 2.30–5pm). Detailed transport maps of the city and outskirts called Roma Metro-Bus can be bought at any newsstand.

Most news-stands sell city maps, as do museum shops. At the latter ask for the Mondadori maps, available in various languages and very durable.

Media
Newspapers and Magazines

Most important European dailies are available on the day of publication from street kiosks, as is the *International Herald Tribune*.

The main Rome-based Italian newspapers are *La Repubblica* and *Il Messaggero*. Other Italian newspapers such as *Il Corriere della Sera* publish Rome editions with local news and entertainment listings. *La Stampa* offers serious economics coverage.

The best way to find out about what's on in Rome is *Roma C'è*, a comprehensive weekly guide to everything in the city, from museums to art exhibitions, shopping, eating, films, etc. It comes out on Wednesday and can be bought from any newsstand throughout the week. Listings are in Italian, but there is an abbreviated section in English.

Wanted in Rome, a fortnightly magazine in English, is another good source of information. The website (www.wantedinrome.com) is updated regularly.

Porta Portese (www.porta portese.com) comes out on Tuesday and Friday, with thousands of classified ads, including a large accommodation section.

The American Magazine (www.theamericanmag.com) is a monthly magazine on Italian cultural life, available from news-stands in the centre.

Television

Italy has six major networks (three owned by state broadcaster RAI and three by the

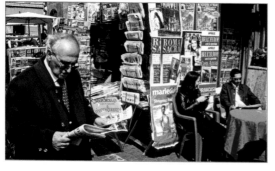

Media Set group owned by the Berlusconi family) and another two that are increasingly popular, MTV Italia and La7. MTV is the Italian version of the ever-popular US music channel, and La7 offers a worthy alternative to the other six channels, which are all connected in some way to former premier Silvio Berlusconi.

Most hotels also offer guests CNN, BBC World, and some French or German channels.

Radio

The three state-owned channels, RAI 1 (89.7 Mhz FM), RAI 2 (91.7 Mhz FM) and RAI 3 (93.7 Mhz FM), offer popular music, classical music, chat shows and news (RAI 3 is the most serious); see www.rai.it for a list of programmes.

The most popular music channels are Radio Capital (95.8 Mhz FM, www.capital.it) and Radio Deejay (101 Mhz FM, www.deejay.it).

Vatican Radio One-O-Five Live (105 Mhz FM, www.vaticanradio.org) offers news, commentary and spiritual programmes in English.

Money

The unit of currency in Italy is the euro (€), which is divided into 100 cents. There are €5, 10, 20, 50, 100, 200 and 500 notes, coins worth €1 and €2, and 1, 2, 5, 10, 20 and 50-cent coins.

Changing Money

You need your passport or identification card when changing money, which can be a slow operation. Not all banks will provide cash against a credit card, and some may refuse to cash

Lost Credit Cards

American Express
Freephone: 800-914912
Diner's Club
Freephone: 800-864064
MasterCard
Freephone: 800-870866
Visa
Freephone: 800-819014

travellers' cheques in certain currencies. On the whole, the larger banks (those with a national or international network) will be the best for tourist transactions.

Travellers' cheques are the safest way to carry money, but not the most economical, since banks charge a commission for cashing them, and shops and restaurants give unfavourable exchange rates if they accept them at all.

Credit Cards

Major credit cards are accepted by most hotels, shops and restaurants in Rome but are less easy to use in the countryside. Very few petrol stations accept credit cards or travellers' cheques.

Automated cash dispensers (ATMs), called Bancomat, can be found throughout central Rome, and are linked with several international banking systems, including Cirrus. The transaction fee will depend on your home bank, but rates are generally the best. The daily withdrawal limit is €250.

Tipping

Service is not included in a restaurant bill unless noted on the menu. It is customary to leave a modest amount as a tip, but nothing like the 10–15 per cent common in other countries. Romans usually leave between €1–5, depending on how satisfied they were with the service; tourists are expected to be slightly more generous.

By law, the old cover charge, called pane e coperto (bread and table linen), has been abolished, but still appears on many menus. Keep an eye out: in many cases it has turned into a charge for bread, which you may refuse if you wish.

When you take a taxi, just round the fare up to the nearest euro.

P ostal Services

Post offices are generally open Mon–Fri 8.30am–1pm; central post offices are generally open in the afternoon too (see below).

Public Holidays

Banks and most shops are closed on the following holidays, and banks may close early on the preceding day.
New Year's Day (Capodanno): 1 January
Epiphany (Befana): 6 January
Pasqua (Pasqua): variable, March–April
Easter Monday (Pasquetta): variable, March–April
Liberation Day (Anniversario della Liberazione): 25 April
May Day (Festa del Lavoro): 1 May
Patron Saints of Rome (San Pietro e San Paolo): 29 June
August Holiday (Ferragosto): 15 August
All Saints' Day (Ognissanti): 1 November
Immaculate Conception (Immacolata Concezione): 8 December
Christmas Day (Natale): 25 December
Boxing Day (Santo Stefano): 26 December

Stamps (francobolli) for postcards and standard-weight letters to most destinations can be bought at many tobacconists (tabacchi) and bars that sell tobacco products. Often you can buy stamps when you buy your postcards. You will only need a post office for more complicated transactions, such as sending a parcel, express letter or fax, or collecting Posta Restante.

Italian postboxes are red or yellow, but several blue boxes specifically for foreign letters have been set up in the centre. Postboxes have two slots, per la città (for Rome) and tutte le altre destinazioni (everywhere else). The Italian postal system has improved considerably in recent years and now runs a pretty efficient priority post service (ask for posta prioritaria when buying your stamps). If posting valuables or important documents, send them registered

A – Z ◆ 315

TRANSPORT

ACCOMMODATION

SHOPPING

ACTIVITIES

A – Z

LANGUAGE

(raccommandata). If sending an urgent parcel ask for *posta celere,* a courier-style service that is slightly slower than the private companies but far cheaper.

The Vatican runs its own postal service. When visiting St Peter's, buy Vatican-issued stamps for your postcards and post them immediately: they are only valid in the Vatican City's blue postboxes.

The main post office is in Piazza San Silvestro, just off Via del Corso (Mon–Sat 8am–7pm). The post office at Stazione Termini is also open Mon–Sat 8am–7pm. For more information visit www.poste.it or tel: 803 160, Mon–Sat 8am–8pm. There are many other post offices: ask at your hotel or in a local bar for the nearest – *Dov'è l'ufficio postale più vicino?*

R eligious Services

Anglican
All Saints' Anglican Church
153b Via del Babuino
Tel: 06-3600 1881
Sunday Eucharist: 8.30 and 10.30am

Catholic
Santa Susanna (American)
15 Via XX Settembre
Tel: 06-4201 4554
Sunday Masses: 9am and 10.30am (also 6pm Saturday).
San Silvestro (British)
1 Piazza S. Silvestro
Tel: 06-679 7775
Sunday Masses: 10am, 5.30pm.
St Patrick's (Irish)
60 Via Boncompagni
Tel: 06-420 3121
Sunday Mass: 10am

Episcopal
St Paul's within the Walls
58 Via Napoli
Tel: 06-488 3339
www.stpaulsrome.it
Sunday services: 8.30am and 10.30am

Islamic
Moschea di Roma
(Centro Islamico)
Viale della Moschea (Parioli)
Tel: 06-808 2167

Jewish
Tempio Maggiore
(Comunità Ebraica)
Lungotevere Cenci
Tel: 06-684 0061

Presbyterian
St Andrew's Church of Scotland

7 Via XX Settembre
Tel: 06-482 7627
Sunday service: 11am

S tudent Travellers

The Centro Turistico Studentesco (CTS) is a chain of travel agents designed to meet the needs of young and student travellers. The main branch is at 16 Via Genova, tel: 06-462 0431, but its website (www.cts.it) lists the others. It can provide you with student discount cards, hostel membership and bookings, cheap flights and language courses.

T elephones

Several companies provide public payphones, but the most ubiquitous phones are the silver ones run by Telecom, which accept phonecards *(scheda telefonica)* only. You can buy them in various denominations from *tabacchi* and from many newsstands. Some payphones accept credit cards, and many bars have coin-operated payphones. Additionally, there are a number of far cheaper

AN AUDIENCE WITH THE POPE

For many, the highlight of a visit to Rome is attending Mass in St Peter's or even a Wednesday morning audience with the Pope. Mass is celebrated daily in St Peter's in several different languages. Confessions are heard in English and many other languages in all four main Roman basilicas: St Peter's, San Giovanni in Laterano, San Paolo fuori le Mura and Santa Maria Maggiore.

To attend an audience with the Pope, you need to write in advance to the Prefettura della Casa Pontificia, 00120 Città del Vaticano, tel: 06-6988 3273 (open Mon–Sat 9am–1.30pm), or fax them on 06-6988 5863. Specify the date you would like to attend and give a local phone

number and address (your hotel) where tickets can be delivered. Alternatively, go to the *prefettura* offices in St Peter's Square (same hours as above) and get the tickets in person.

The general audiences are held either in St Peter's Square or in the Audience Room or, during the summer, at Castel Gandolfo, the Pope's summer residence in the Castelli Romani. There is no charge for attending an audience.

If you are in Rome for Christmas or Easter and want to attend Midnight Mass or Holy Week celebrations, ask the tourist information service for times and other information, as you may need tickets for some events.

TRANSPORT

international phonecards available from many news-stands, and there are call centres where you can make your call and pay later, particularly in the area around Stazione Termini. Currently the best for the UK and US are Europa and Eurocity.

Landlines in Rome have an 06 area code which you must use whether calling from within Rome, from outside Rome or from abroad. Numbers in Rome have four to eight digits. Toll-free numbers start with 800.

Mobile phone numbers begin with 3, for example 338, 340, 333, 348, and cost a lot more. If you bring your mobile phone with you, remember that if you are calling a local number you will need to dial the international access code as well as the country code before putting in the area code and subscriber number.

For a number outside Italy, first dial 00 (the international access code), then the country code, the area code (omitting the initial 0, if applicable) and then the subscriber number.

For international directory enquiries, 892 412; for operator-assisted national and international calls, 170.

Time Zone

Italy follows Central European Time (GMT+1). From the last Sunday in March to the last Sunday in September, clocks are advanced one hour (GMT+2). The following times apply in summer, when it is noon in Rome:

New York	6am
London	11am
Johannesburg	noon
Paris	noon
San Francisco	3am
Sydney	8pm

Toilets

Bars are obliged by law to let you use their toilets. This doesn't mean that they will do so with good grace; if you don't consume something at the bar first they may throw you a look. However, if you ask politely you should not have any problems. In many cases bar toilets are locked and you will need to ask for the key *(chiave)* at the till; once inside you may find out that there is no soap or toilet paper. In the past few years public and modern toilets have been opened near most of the major sights and monuments, for which you have to pay a small fee.

Tourist Information

The main Rome Tourist Office (**APT**) is at 5 Via Parigi, tel: 06-4889 9200, but it's open to the public only, Mon and Thur 9.30am–1pm, 2.30–4.30pm. The APT also runs an English-speaking tourist information call centre which you can call daily 9am–7.30pm, tel: 06-8205 9127. The Hotel Reservation Service, in Stazione Termini opposite platform 24 (daily 7am–10pm), tel: 06-699 1000, www.hotelreservation.it, makes commission-free reservations.

PIT (*punto informativo turistico* or tourist information points) are open daily from 9.30am–7.30pm:
Piazza Pia (Castel Sant'Angelo)
Piazza del Tempio della Pace (Via dei Fori Imperiali)
Piazza delle Cinque Lune (Piazza Navona)
Via Nazionale (Palazzo delle Esposizioni)
Piazza Sonnino (Trastevere)
Piazza San Giovanni in Laterano
Via dell'Olmata (Santa Maria Maggiore)
Via Marco Minghetti (Fontana di Trevi)

There is also an information point in Stazione Termini, in front of platform 4, which is open daily 8am–9pm.

The Vatican tourist office (Ufficio Pellegrini e Turisti) is in Braccio Carlo Magno, Piazza San Pietro (to the left of the basilica), tel: 06-6988 1662 (Mon–Sat 8.30am–6.30pm).

U seful Addresses

Italian Tourist Offices Abroad
Canada: 175 Bloor Street E, Suite 907, Toronto M4W3R8, tel: 416-925 4882.
Irish Republic: 47 Merrion Square, Dublin 2, tel: 01-766397.
UK: 1 Princes Street, London W1B 8AY, tel: 020-7408 1254.
US: 630 5th Avenue, Suite 1565, New York, NY 10111, tel: 212-245 4822/5618.

Travel Agents in Rome
American Express, 38 Piazza di Spagna, tel: 06-67641.
CIT Italia, 65 Piazza della Repubblica, tel: 06-482 5219.

Airline Contacts
Air France, 40 Via Sardegna, tel: 06-487 911.
Alitalia, 11 Via Bissolati, tel: 06-2222.
British Airways, Fiumicino Airport, tel: 06-6501 1575; call centre, tel: 199-712 266 (no office in the city).
Air Canada, Fiumicino Airport, tel: 06-6501 1462.
Delta Airlines, 40 Via Sardegna, freephone: 800-477 999.

W ebsites

www.romaturismo.com (official Rome tourism site)
www.comune.roma.it (Rome city council)
www.vatican.va (Vatican)
www.trenitalia.com (train information)
www.adr.it (airport information)
www.atac.roma.it (public transport)
www.trovacinema.it (cinema programmes for all Italy)
www.2night.it (regularly updated, hip nightlife and entertainment guide)
www.pierreci.it (art and culture)

ACCOMMODATION

SHOPPING

ACTIVITIES

A – Z

LANGUAGE

L ANGUAGE

UNDERSTANDING THE ITALIANS

Basic Rules

Here are a few basic rules of grammar and pronunciation: *c* before *e* or *i* is pronounced "ch" as in *ciao*. *Ch* before *i* or *e* is pronounced as "k", eg *la chiesa*. Likewise, *sci* or *sce* are pronounced as in "sheep" or "shed" respectively. *Gn* in Italian is rather like the sound in "onion", while *gl* is softened to resemble the sound in "bullion".

Nouns are either masculine (*il*, plural *i*) or feminine (*la*, plural *le*). Plurals of nouns are most often formed by changing an o to an i and an a to an e, e.g. *il panino*, *i panini*; *la chiesa*, *le chiese*.

Words are stressed on the penultimate syllable unless an accent indicates otherwise.

Italian has formal and informal words for "You". In the singular, *Tu* is informal while *Lei* is more polite. It is best to use the formal form unless invited to do otherwise.

Basic Phrases

Yes *Si*
No *No*
Thank you *Grazie*
Many thanks *Mille grazie/ tante grazie/molte grazie*
You're welcome *Prego*
All right/That's fine *Va bene*
Please *Per favore/per cortesia*

Excuse me (to get attention) *Scusi* (singular), *Scusate* (plural); **(to attract attention from a waiter)** *Senta!* **(in a crowd)** *Permesso;* **(sorry)** *Mi scusi*
Can I help you? (formal) *Posso aiutarla?*
Can you help me? (informal) *Può aiutarmi, per cortesia?*
Could you help me? (formal) *Potrebbe aiutarmi?*
Certainly *Ma, certo*
I need... *Ho bisogno di...*
I'm lost *Mi sono perso/a*
I'm sorry *Mi dispiace*
I don't know *Non lo so*
I don't understand *Non capisco*
Do you speak English/French? *Parla inglese/francese?*
Could you speak more slowly? *Può parlare più lentamente, per favore?*
Could you repeat that please? *Può ripetere, per piacere?*
here/there *qui/là*
yesterday/today/tomorrow *ieri/oggi/domani*
now/early/late *adesso/ presto/tardi*
What? *Quale/Come...?*
When/Why/Where? *Quando/ Perché/Dove?*
Where is the lavatory? *Dov'è il bagno?*

Greetings

Hello (good day) *Buon giorno*
Goodbye *Arrivederci*

Good afternoon/evening *Buona sera*
Goodnight *Buona notte*
Hello/Hi/Goodbye (familiar) *Ciao*
Mr/Mrs/Miss S*ignor/Signora/ Signorina*
Pleased to meet you (formal) *Piacere di conoscerla*
I am English/American/ Irish/Scottish/Canadian/ Australian *Sono inglese/ americano(a)/ irlandese/ scozzese/canadese/ australiano(a)*
I'm here on holiday *Sono qui in vacanze*
Is it your first trip to Rome? *É il suo primo viaggio a Roma?*
Do you like it here? (formal) *Si trova bene qui?*
How are you (formal/informal)? *Come sta (come stai)?*
Fine, thanks *Bene, grazie*
See you later *A più tardi*
See you soon *A presto*
Take care (formal/informal) *Stia bene/Sta bene*
Do you like Italy/Florence/ Rome/Venice? *Le piace Italia/Firenze/Roma/Venezia?*
I like it a lot *Mi piace moltissimo*

Telephone Calls

I'd like to make a reverse-charge (collect) call *Vorrei fare una telefonata a carico del destinatario*

the area code *il prefisso telefonico*
May I use your telephone? *Posso usare il telefono?*
Hello (on the telephone) *Pronto*
My name's *Mi chiamo/Sono*
Could I speak to...? *Posso parlare con...?*
Sorry, he/she isn't in *Mi dispiace, è fuori*
Can he call you back? *Può richiamarLa?*
I'll try later *Riproverò piu tardi*
Can I leave a message? *Posso lasciare un messagio?*
Please tell him I called *Gli dica, per favore, che ho telefonato*
Hold on *Un attimo, per favore*
a local call *una telefonata urbana*
Can you speak up please? *Può parlare più forte, per favore?*

In the Hotel

Do you have any vacant rooms? *Avete delle camere libere?*
I have a reservation *Ho fatto una prenotazione*
I'd like... *Vorrei...*
a single/double room *una camera singola/doppia*
a room with twin beds *una camera a due letti*
a room with a bath/shower *una camera con bagno/doccia*
for one night *per una notte*
for two nights *per due notti*
How much is it? *Quanto costa?*
On the first floor *Al primo piano*
Is breakfast included? *E compresa la prima colazione?*
Is everything included? *E tutto compreso?*
half/full board *mezza pensione/pensione completa*
It's expensive *E caro*
Do you have a room with a balcony/view of the sea? *C'è una camera con balcone/con vista del mare?*
a room overlooking the park/the street/the back *una camera con vista sul parco/che da sulla strada/sul retro*
Is it a quiet room? *E una stanza tranquilla?*

The room is too hot/cold/noisy/small *La camera è troppo calda/fredda/rumorosa/piccola*
We have one with a double bed *Ne abbiamo una doppia/matrimoniale*
Could you show me another room please? *Potrebbe mostrarmi un altra camera, per favore?*
Can I see the room? *Posso vedere la camera?*
What time does the hotel close? *A che ora chiude l'albergo?*
I'll take it *La prendo*
big/small *grande/piccola*
What time is breakfast? *A che ora è la prima colazione?*
Please give me a call at... *Mi può chiamare alle...*
Come in! *Avanti!*
Can I have the bill, please? *Posso avere il conto, per favore?*
Can you call me a taxi, please? *Può chiamarmi un taxi, per favore?*
dining room *la sala da pranzo*
key *la chiave*
lift *l'ascensore*
towel *un asciugamano*
toilet paper *la carta igienica*

At a Bar

I'd like... *Vorrei...*
coffee:
(small, strong and black) *un caffè espresso*; **(with hot, frothy milk)** *un cappuccino*; **(weak, served in tall glass)** *un caffè lungo*; **(with alcohol, probably brandy)** *un caffè corretto*
tea *un tè*
lemon tea *un tè al limone*
herbal tea *una tisana*
hot chocolate *una cioccolata calda*
(bottled) orange/lemon juice *un succo d'arancia/di limone*
orange squash *aranciata*
freshly squeezed orange/lemon juice *una spremuta di arancia/di limone*
mineral water (fizzy/still) *acqua minerale gassata/naturale*
with/without ice *con/senza ghiaccio*
red/white wine *vino rosso/bianco*
(draught) beer *una birra (alla spina)*

a bitter (Vermouth, etc) *un amaro*
milk *latte*
(half) a litre *un (mezzo) litro*
bottle *una bottiglia*
ice cream *un gelato*
cone *un cono*
pastry/brioche *una pasta*
sandwich *un tramezzino*
roll *un panino*
Anything else? *Desidera qualcos'altro?*
Cheers *Salute*

In a Restaurant

I'd like to book a table *Vorrei prenotare una tavola*
I have a reservation *Ho fatto una prenotazione*
lunch/supper *pranzo/cena*
we do not want a full meal *Non desideriamo un pasto completo*
Could we have another table? *Potremmo spostarci?*
I'm a vegetarian *Sono vegetariano/a*
Is there a vegetarian dish? *C'è un piatto vegetariano?*
May we have the menu? *Ci dia la carta?*
wine list *la lista dei vini*
What would you recommend? *Che cosa ci consiglia?*
What would you like as a main course/dessert? *Che cosa prende di secondo/di dolce?*
What would you like to drink? *Che cosa desidera da bere?*
a carafe of red/white wine *una caraffa di vino rosso/bianco*
fixed-price menu *il menù a prezzo fisso*
dish of the day *il piatto del giorno*
home-made *fatto in casa*
VAT (sales tax) *IVA*
cover charge *il coperto/pane e coperto*
that's enough/no more/thanks *basta così*
the bill, please *il conto per favore*
Is service included? *Il servizio è incluso?*
Where is the lavatory? *Dov'è il bagno?*
Keep the change *Va bene così*
I've enjoyed the meal *Mi è piaciuto molto*

Menu Decoder

Antipasti – Starters

antipasto misto **mixed hors d'oeuvres: cold cuts, cheeses, roast vegetables (ask for details)**
buffet freddo **cold buffet**
caponata **aubergine, olives, tomatoes**
insalata caprese **tomato and mozzarella salad**
insalata di mare **seafood salad**
insalata mista/verde **mixed/ green salad**
melanzane alla parmigiana **fried or baked aubergine with parmesan and tomato**
mortadella/salame **similar to salami**
pancetta **bacon**
proscuitto **ham**
peperonata **grilled peppers drenched in olive oil**

Primi – First Courses

gli asparagi **asparagus (in season)**
brodetto **fish soup**
brodo **broth**
crespolini **savoury pancakes**
gnocchi **potato and dough dumplings**
la minestra **soup**
il minestrone **thick vegetable soup**
pasta e fagioli **pasta and bean soup**
il prosciutto (cotto/crudo) **(cooked/cured) ham**
i supplì **rice croquettes**
i tartufi **truffles (fresh in season, otherwise bottled or vacuum-packed)**
la zuppa **soup**

Secondi – Main Courses

La Carne **Meat**
allo spiedo **on the spit**
arrosto **roast meat**
ai ferri **grilled without oil**
al forno **baked**
al girarrosto **spit-roasted**
alla griglia **grilled**
involtini **skewered veal, ham, etc**
stagionato **hung, well aged**
ben cotto **well done (steak)**

media cottura **medium**
al sangue **rare**
l'agnello **lamb**
la bresaola **dried salted beef**
la bistecca **steak**
il capriolo/cervo **venison**
il carpaccio **wafer-thin beef**
il cinghiale **wild boar**
il controfiletto **sirloin steak**
le cotolette **cutlets**
il fagiano **pheasant**
il fegato **liver**
il filetto **fillet**
la lepre **hare**
il maiale **pork**
il manzo **beef**
l'ossobuco **shin of veal**
il pollo **chicken**
le polpette **meatballs**
il polpettone **meat loaf**
la porchetta **roast suckling pig**
la salsiccia **sausage**
il saltimbocca (alla Romana) **veal escalopes with ham**
le scaloppine **escalopes**
lo stufato **braised, stewed**
il sugo **sauce**
la trippa **tripe**
il vitello **veal**

Frutti di Mare **Seafood**
affumicato **smoked**
alle brace **charcoal-grilled**
al ferro **grilled without oil**
fritto **fried**
alla griglia **grilled**
ripieno **stuffed**
al vapore **steamed**
acciughe **anchovies**
l'anguilla **eel**
l'aragosta **lobster**
il baccalà **dried salted cod**
i bianchetti **whitebait**
il branzino **sea bass**
i calamaretti **baby squid**
i calamari **squid**
la carpa **carp**
le cozze **mussels**
i crostacei **shellfish**
il fritto misto **mixed fried fish**
i gamberetti **shrimps**
i gamberi **prawns**
il granchio **crab**
il merluzzo **cod**
le ostriche **oysters**
il pesce **fish**
il pescespada **swordfish**
il polipo **octopus**

il risotto di mare **seafood risotto**
le sarde **sardines**
le seppie **cuttlefish**
la sogliola **sole**
surgelati **frozen**
il tonno **tuna**
la triglia **red mullet**
la trota **trout**
le vongole **clams**

I Legumi/La Verdura – Vegetables

a scelta **of your choice**
gli asparagi **asparagus**
la bietola **(similar to spinach)**
i carciofini **artichoke hearts**
il carciofo **artichoke**
le carote **carrots**
il cavolo **cabbage**
la cicoria **chicory**
la cipolla **onion**
i contorni **side dishes**
i fagioli **beans**
i fagiolini **French beans**
fave **broad beans**
il finocchio **fennel**
i funghi **mushrooms**
l'indivia **endive/chicory**
l'insalata mista **mixed salad**
l'insalata verde **green salad**
la melanzana **aubergine/ eggplant**
le patate **potatoes**
le patatine fritte **chips/fries**
i peperoni **peppers**
i piselli **peas**
i pomodori **tomatoes**
le primizie **spring vegetables**
il radicchio **red, bitter lettuce**
i ravanelli **radishes**
ripieno **stuffed**
rughetta **rocket**
spinaci **spinach**
la verdura **green vegetables**
la zucca **pumpkin/squash**
zucchini **courgettes**

La Frutta – Fruit

le albicocche **apricots**
le arance **oranges**
le banane **bananas**
le ciliege **cherries**
il cocomero **watermelon**
i fichi **figs**
le fragole **strawberries**
frutti di bosco **fruits of the forest**
i lamponi **raspberries**
la mela **apple**
la pera **pear**

la pesca **peach**
le uve **grapes**

I Dolci – Desserts

al carrello **desserts from the trolley**
la cassata **Sicilian ice cream with candied peel**
il dolce **dessert/sweet**
le fritelle **fritters**
un gelato (di lampone/limone) **(raspberry/lemon) ice cream**
una granita **water ice**
una macedonia di frutta **fruit salad**
un semifreddo **semi-frozen dessert (many types)**
il tartufo (nero) **(chocolate) ice-cream dessert**
il tiramisù **cold, creamy rum and coffee dessert**
la torta **cake/tart**
zabaglione **sweet dessert made with eggs and Marsala**
zuccotto **ice-cream liqueur**
la zuppa inglese **trifle**

Basic Foods

aceto **vinegar**
aglio **garlic**
burro **butter**
formaggio **cheese**
frittata **omelette**
grissini **bread sticks**
marmellata **jam**
olio **oil**
pane **bread**
pane integrale **wholemeal bread**
parmigiano **parmesan cheese**
pepe **pepper**
riso **rice**
sale **salt**
senape **mustard**
uova **eggs**
zucchero **sugar**

Sightseeing

abbazia (badia) **abbey**
basilica **church**
biblioteca **library**
castello **castle**
centro storico **old town/ historic centre**
chiesa **church**
duomo/cattedrale **cathedral**
fiume **river**
giardino **garden**
lago **lake**

mercato **market**
monastero **monastery**
monumenti **monuments**
museo **museum**
parco **park**
pinacoteca **art gallery**
ponte **bridge**
ruderi **ruins**
scavi **excavations/ archaeological site**
spiaggia **beach**
torre **tower**
ufficio turistico **tourist office**
il custode **custodian**
il sacristano **sacristan**
Aperto/a **Open**
Chiuso/a **Closed**
Chiuso per la festa/per ferie/per restauro **Closed for the festival/ holidays/restoration**

At the Shops

What time do you open/close? *A che ora apre/chiude?*
Pull/Push (sign on doors) *Tirare/Spingere*
Entrance/Exit *Entrata/Uscita*
Can I help you? (formal) *Posso aiutarla?*
What would you like? *Che cosa desidera?*
I'm just looking *Sto soltanto guardando*
How much is this? *Quanto viene?*
Do you take credit cards? *Accettate le carte di credito?*
I'd like... *Vorrei...*
This one/that one *questo/quello*
Have you got...? *Avete...?*
We haven't got (any) *Non (ne) abbiamo*
Can I try it on? *Posso provare?*
the size (for clothes) *la taglia*
What size do you take? *Qual'è la sua taglia?*
the size (for shoes) *il numero*
Is there/do you have...? *C'è (un/una)...?*
Yes, of course *Si, certo*
No, we haven't (there isn't) *No, non c'è*
That's too expensive *È troppo caro*
Please write it down for me *Me lo scriva, per favore*
cheap *economico/a buon prezzo*

Do you have anything cheaper? *Ha niente che costa di meno?*
It's too small/big *È troppo piccolo/grande*
brown/blue/black *marrone/ blu/nero*
green/red/white/yellow *verde/rosso/bianco/giallo*
pink/grey/gold/silver *rosa/ grigio/oro/argento*
No thank you, I don't like it *Grazie, ma non è di mio gusto*
I'll take it/I'll leave it *Lo prendo/lo lascio*
This is faulty. May I have a replacement/refund? *C'è un difetto. Me lo potrebbe cambiare/rimborsare?*
Anything else? *Altro?*
The cash desk is over there *Si accomodi alla cassa*
Give me some of those *Mi dia alcuni di quelli lì*
(half) a kilo *un (mezzo) kilo*
100 grams *un etto*
200 grams *due etti*
more/less *più/meno*
with/without *con/senza*
a little *un pochino*

Types of Shops

antique dealer *l'antiquario*
bakery/cake shop *la panetteria/ pasticceria*
bank *la banca*
bookshop *la libreria*
boutique/clothes shop *il negozio di moda*
butcher *la macelleria*
chemist *la farmacia*
delicatessen *la salumeria*
dry cleaner *la tintoria*
fishmonger *la pescheria*
florist *il fioraio*
food shop *l'alimentari*
greengrocer *l'ortolano/ il fruttivendolo*
grocer *l'alimentari*
hairdresser *il parucchiere*
ice-cream parlour *la gelateria*
jeweller *il gioiellere*
leather shop *la pelletteria*
market *il mercato*
news-stand *l'edicola*
post office *l'ufficio postale*
shoe shop *il negozio di scarpe*
stationer *la cartoleria*
tobacconist *il tabaccaio*
travel agency *l'agenzia di viaggi*

Travelling

aeroplane *l'aereo*
airport *l'aeroporto*
arrivals/departures *arrivi/partenze*
boarding card *un biglietto di bordo*
boat *la barca*
bus *l'autobus/il pullman*
bus station *l'autostazione*
coach *il pullman*
couchette *la cucetta*
connection *la coincidenza*
ferry *il traghetto*
ferry terminal *la stazione marittima*
first/second class *la prima/seconda classe*
flight *il volo*
left-luggage office *il deposito bagagli*
platform *il binario*
port *il porto*
porter *il facchino*
railway station *ferrovia (la stazione ferroviaria)*
return ticket *un biglietto andata e ritorno*
single ticket *un biglietto solo andata*
sleeping car *la carrozza letti/il vagone letto*
smokers/non-smokers *fumatori/non-fumatori*
station *la stazione*
stop *la fermata*
ticket office *la biglietteria*
train *il treno*
WC *il gabinetto*

At the Station

(trains, buses and ferries)
Can you help me please? *Mi può aiutare, per favore?*
Where can I buy tickets? *Dove posso fare i biglietti?*
at the ticket office/at the counter *alla biglietteria/allo sportello*
What time does the train leave/arrive? *A che ora parte/arriva il treno?*
Can I book a seat? *Posso prenotare un posto?*
Are there any seats available? *Ci sono ancora posti liberi?*
Is this seat free/taken? *È libero/occupato questo posto?*

I'm afraid this is my seat *È il mio posto, mi dispiace*
You'll have to pay a supplement *Deve pagare un supplemento*
Do I have to change? *Devo cambiare?*
Where does it stop? *Dove si ferma?*
You need to change in Rome *Bisogna cambiare a Roma*
Which platform does the train leave from? *Da quale binario parte il treno?*
The train leaves from platform one *Il treno parte dal binario uno*
When is the next train/bus/ferry for Naples? *Quando parte il prossimo treno/pullman/traghetto per Napoli?*
How long does the crossing take? *Quanto dura la traversata?*
What time does the bus leave for Siena? *Quando parte l'autobus per Siena?*
How long will it take to get there? *Quanto tempo ci vuole per arrivare?*
Next stop, please *La prossima fermata per favore*
Is this the right stop? *È la fermata giusta?*
The train is late *Il treno è in ritardo*
Can you tell me where to get off? *Mi può dire dove devo scendere?*

Directions

right/left *a destra/a sinistra*
first left/second right *la prima a sinistra/la seconda a destra*
Turn to the right/left *Gira a destra/sinistra*
Go straight on *Va sempre diritto*
Go straight on until the traffic lights *Va sempre diritto fino al semaforo*
Is it far away/nearby? *È lontano/vicino?*
It's 5 minutes' walk *Cinque minuti a piedi*
It's 10 minutes by car *Dieci minuti con la macchina*
opposite/next to *di fronte/accanto a*
up/down *su/giù*
traffic lights *il semaforo*
junction *l'incrocio, il bivio*

building *il palazzo* (could be a palace or a block of flats)
Where is...? *Dov'è...?*
Where are...? *Dove sono...?*
Where is the nearest bank/petrol station/bus stop/hotel/garage? *Dov'è la banca/il benzinaio/la fermata di autobus/l'albergo/l'officina più vicino?*
How do I get there? *Come si può andare?* (or: *Come faccio per arrivare a...?*)
How long does it take to get to...? *Quanto tempo ci vuole per andare a...?*
Can you show me where I am on the map? *Può indicarmi sulla cartina dove mi trovo*
You're on the wrong road *Lei è sulla strada sbagliata*

Health

Is there a chemist nearby? *C'è una farmacia qui vicino?*
Which chemist is open at night? *Quale farmacia fa il turno di notte?*
I feel ill *Sto male/Mi sento male*
Where does it hurt? *Dove Le fa male?*
It hurts here *Ho dolore qui*
I suffer from... *Soffro di...*
I have a headache *Ho mal di testa*
I have a sore throat *Ho mal di gola*
I have a stomach ache *Ho mal di pancia*
Have you got something for air sickness? *Ha/Avete qualcosa contro il mal d'aria?*
Have you got something for sea sickness? *Ha/Avete qualcosa contro il mal di mare?*
It's nothing serious *Non è niente di male*
Do I need a prescription? *Ci vuole la ricetta?*
antiseptic cream *la crema anti-settica*
insect repellent *l'insettifugo*
sticking plaster *il cerotto*
sunburn *scottato dal sole*
sunscreen *la crema antisolare*
tissues *i fazzoletti di carta*
toothpaste *il dentifricio*
upset-stomach pills *le pillole anti-coliche*

FURTHER READING

History and Society

The Early History of Rome, by Livy (Penguin Classics).
Daily Life in Ancient Rome, by Jérôme Carcopino (Penguin History, Yale US).
The Roman Emperors, by Michael Grant (Weidenfeld and Nicolson).
The Caesars, by Allan Massie (Secker & Warburg).
The Decline and Fall of the Roman Empire, by Edward Gibbon (Dent and Penguin).
A History of Rome, by Michael Grant (Faber & Faber).
Rome: Biography of a City, by Christopher Hibbert (Penguin).
The Italians, by Luigi Barzini (Penguin).
La Bella Figura: A Field Guide to the Italian Mind, by Beppe Severgnini (Broadway Books).
The Dark Heart of Italy, by Tobias Jones (Faber & Faber).
Rubicon: the Triumph and Tragedy of the Roman Republic, by Tom Holland (Abacus and Anchor).

Art and Literature

The Aeneid, by Virgil (Penguin).
Meditations, by Marcus Aurelius (Penguin).
Lives of the Artists, by Giorgio Vasari (Penguin).
The Life of Benvenuto Cellini, by Benvenuto Cellini (Macmillan).
Rome, by Emile Zola (Paris and New York).
Michelangelo and the Pope's Ceiling, by Ross King (Pimlico).
Portrait of a Lady, by Henry James (various).
The Woman of Rome and *Roman Tales*, by Alberto Moravia (Oxford University Press).
A Violent Life, by Pier Paolo Pasolini (Carcanet).

Fellini on Fellini, by Federico Fellini (New York).
I Claudius, Claudius the God by Rupert Graves (Penguin)

Food and Wine

The Encyclopedia of Italian Wines, by Oz Clarke and Maureen Ashley (Prentice Hall and IBD).
Italian Food, by Elizabeth David (Penguin Cookery Library).
The Essentials of Classic Italian Cooking, by Marcella Hazan (Macmillan).

FEEDBACK

We do our best to ensure the information in our books is as accurate and up-to-date as possible. The books are updated on a regular basis, using local contacts, who add, amend and correct as required. However, some mistakes and omissions are inevitable and we are ultimately reliant on our readers to put us in the picture. We would welcome your feedback on any details related to your experiences using the book "on the road". The more details you can give us (particularly with regard to addresses, e-mails and telephone numbers), the better. We will acknowledge all contributions, and we'll offer an Insight Guide to the best letters received.

Please write to us at:
Insight Guides
PO Box 7910
London SE1 1WE
United Kingdom
Or: insight@apaguide.co.uk

Famous Travellers

Pictures from Italy, by Charles Dickens (Penguin Classics).
Italian Journey, by Johann Wolfgang von Goethe, translated by W.H. Auden & Elizabeth Mayer (Pantheon Books and Penguin).
Italian Hours, by Henry James (Penguin Classics).
The Fountains of Rome and *A Traveller in Rome*, by Henry V. Morton (Methuen).
Byron in Italy, by Peter Quenell (Viking Press, New York).
The Grand Tour, by Christopher Hibbert (G.P. Putnam, New York).

Other Insight Guides

Insight Guide: Italy covers the whole country, with features on food and drink, culture and the arts. Other titles cover Northern Italy, Southern Italy, Venice, the Italian Lakes, Florence, Tuscany, Sicily and Sardinia.
Insight Pocket Guides, including a pull-out map, feature tailor-made itineraries and are ideal for short breaks. Guides in the Italian series include: Venice, Rome, Milan, Florence, the Italian Lakes, Sicily, Sardinia, Umbria and Tuscany.
Insight Compact Guides are inexpensive, mini-encyclopaedias with a star-rated system of all the sites worth seeing. Titles include Florence, Milan, Rome, Tuscany, Venice, the Italian Riviera and the Italian Lakes.
Insight Fleximaps combine clear, detailed cartography with essential travel information. The laminated finish makes the maps durable and weatherproof. Italian maps include *Florence*, *Milan*, *Rome*, *Tuscany*, *Umbria* and *Venice*.

ART & PHOTO CREDITS

c.20thC.Fox/Everett/Rex Features 45L
4Corners Images 9TR & BL, 16/17, 76/77, 83/1, 264, 269B
akg-images 29L, 33BR, 34B, 36TL, 43T
Alamy 12B, 78/79, 80, 130BR, 180B, 187BR, 217B, 223B, 265, 270B, 280
Alessi 298
The Art Archive 27, 30TC & TR, 31CL, 32L, 37TL, 40CR & BL, 49B, 122T, 204B, 239
Gaetano Barone 35TR, 41C
The Bridgeman Art Library 10CR, 28T, 29R, 30B, 32R, 33TR, 34T, 35TL, TC & CL, 36TR, 37TR, 40TL, 41TR & BL, 42C & BR, 102B, 105BR, 109TL, 112B, 113C, 121T, 126B, 139CL, 140T, 141TC, 142 (all), 156B, 158TR, 160T, 161C, 163B, 186T, 192B
Casa Howard 13TL & TR
Cavalieri Hilton 145, 292
Cephas 13C
Corbis 8CL, 10CL, 14/15, 23, 24B, 25TL, 26, 31TR, 38 (all), 39 (all), 40C, 42TL & BL, 43CL & BR, 45R, 46, 49T, 50/51T, 52TL & B, 68, 82/1, 109TR, 116, 122B, 130CL, 163TR, 179TL, 187BL, 193CR, 195B, 196T, 224BL, 226TR, 254T, 274T, 276T, 277T & BR, 309
Jerry Dennis/APA 66CL
Giovanna Dunmall 235BR
Mary Evans Picture Library 28B, 31TL, 33TL, 104C, 106TR
Getty Images 119B
Patrizia Giancotti 268TR, 270TL, 274B, 277BL
Frances Gransden/APA 8CL, 9CL, 53CL, 82/3, 82/5, 89T, 106TL, 173T, 177T, 241TR, 256
Albano Guatti 273
John Heseltine 50CR, 51TR, 184, 251, 254B
Jim Holmes 53TR
Hotel Aleph 289
Italian Cultural Institute 111C
Britta Jaschinski/APA 1, 3, 6T, 8B, 9C & BR, 11 (all), 18, 19, 20 (all), 21 (all), 22 (all), 24TL & TR, 25TR, 37B, 41TL, 47, 48B, 51B, 53TL, 56, 57, 59R, 62, 63, 64 (all), 65 (all), 66T & B, 67 (all), 69, 70CR & B, 71R, 81, 82/2, 82/3, 83/5, 86, 87, 88TR & B, 89B, 90 (all), 91, 97, 98T & B, 99B, 100, 101L, 102T & C, 103B, 104B, 106B, 107 (all), 108C, 110T, 111T, 112TI & TR, 113T & B, 117,

118L, 120T, 121C & B, 123 (all), 125, 126C, 127B, 128T & B, 129T, 130T, 131 (all), 132T, 133 (all), 135, 136, 137, 138TR, 139BL, 140B, 141TR, 143 (all), 144, 150, 153 (all), 154T & BR, 155CL & B, 156C, 157T, 158TL & B, 159CL & BR, 160T & B, 162C, 164 (all), 165 (all), 167, 169, 170 (all), 171 (all), 172BR, 176T, 178 (all), 179TR, 181, 183 (all), 185, 186B, 187T, 188 (all), 189 (all), 191TL & TR, 192C, 193TL, 197 (all), 201, 202CL, 203 (all), 204T, 206CL, 207T, 208, 210, 211, 212R, 213 (all), 214 (all), 215CL, 217TL, 218, 219, 220, 221, 222L, 223CL, 224T & BR, 225 (all), 226TL & B, 228, 229, 231 (all), 232 (all), 233B, 236, 246/247, 250, 252 (all), 253 (all), 255 (all), 257, 258 (all), 259 (all), 260 (all), 261 (all), 266 (all), 267 (all), 268TL & B, 270TR, 271 (all), 272, 275 (all), 276B, 278 (all), 279, 282 (all), 283, 284 (all), 285, 286, 287, 288, 291, 296, 300, 303, 304, 305, 306, 308, 311, 313, 317
The Kobal Collection 44T
Marka/Kay Reese & Associates 43C, 128C
Mockford & Bonetti/APA 8T, 9TL, 10B, 12T, 48TL & TR, 50TL, 58L, 83/2, 96, 99T, 101R, 105T, 108/109, 124, 127T, 141B, 154BL, 155T, 157B, 159BL, 163TC, 168, 172BL, 173B, 174 (all), 175 (all), 177L, 179B, 191B, 193B, 196B, 202T, 205CL & CR, 206BL & BR, 207B, 212L, 216 (all), 217TR, 222R, 233T & C, 234 (all)
Cathy Muscat 119T, 120B, 160B, 172TL & CL, 182, 194B, 195T, 227, 307
Peter Namuth 36B
Gerd Pfeifer 269T
Pierluigi/Rex Features 44B
Andrea Pistolesi 105BL, 126T
Raphaël Hotel 293
Mark Read/APA 7T
Alessandra Santarelli/APA 9CR, 12CL, 58R, 59L, 70TL & TR, 71L, 83/3, 83/4, 111B, 132B, 151, 162B, 173C, 176B, 194C, 200, 215B, 235T & CL, 238, 240, 241TL & B, 242 (all), 243 (all), 299, 301 (all), 302, 314
Superstock 7B, 30TL, 205B
Bill Wassman/APA 88TL, 98CR, 103T, 118R, 129B, 138TL, 139BR, 177R, 180CL, 316

ROME STREET ATLAS

The key map shows the area of Rome covered by the atlas
section. An index of street names and places of interest
shown on the maps can be found on the following pages. For
each entry there is a page number and grid reference.

Map Legend

▭▭▭	Autostrada with Junction
▭ ▭ ▭	Autostrada (under construction)
▭▭▭	Dual Carriageway
▭▭▭	Main Road
▭▭▭	Secondary Road
▭▭▭	Minor Road
──	Track
── ▪▪	International Boundary
── ──	Province/State Boundary
▪── ▪▪	National Park/Reserve
── ──	Ferry Route

⊖	Border Crossing
✈ ✈	Airport
✝ ✝	Church (ruins)
✝	Monastery
⛫ ⛫	Castle (ruins)
∴	Archaeological Site
∩	Cave
★	Place of Interest
⌂	Mansion/Stately Home
☀	Viewpoint
⚑	Beach

▭▭▭	Autostrada
▭▭▭	Dual Carriageway
▭▭▭	} Main Roads
▭▭▭	} Minor Roads
──	Footpath
▭▭▭	Railway
▭	Pedestrian Area
▭	Important Building
▭	Park

Ⓜ	Metro
🚌	Bus Station
❶	Tourist Information
✉	Post Office
✝	Cathedral/Church
☾	Mosque
✡	Synagogue
👤	Statue/Monument
▯	Tower
⚡	Lighthouse

A   B

Monte
di Gallo

Stazione
S. Pietro

Via delle Fornaci

Chiesa dell'
Annunziata

Faro

Carcere di Regina Coeli

L.go
L. Perosi

S. Ma
Monse

Via S. Silverio
P.za
F. Borgoncini

Maria
Addolorata

Via d. Orti d'Albert

Ponte
G. Mazzini

Lgt.
dei

Lgt. della Tevere

S. E
Pa
Falc

Villa
Lovatti

Vic. di S. Francesco di Sales.

Via della
Penitenza

VILLA Villa
Farnesina

Collegio
Pontificio Pio

Via dei Riari

Palazzo
Corsini

FARNESINA

Farne

Torre
dell Drago

VILLA

P.le Anita
Garibaldi

Villa
Lante

ORTO
BOTANICO

S.
S. Giova
d. Malv

ABAMELEK

P.le
Giuseppe
Garibaldi

CORSINI

S. Mar
d. Scal

P.za d
S. Egid

M. Gianicolo

Via Garibaldi

Collegio
S. Pietro

VILLA
AURELIA

Vicolo del
Cedro

Museo
di Roma in
Trastevere

Via Aurelia Antica

VILLA
Villa
Medici

Porta
S. Pancrazio
(Museo Garibaldino)

Fontana d.
Acqua Paola

S. Pietro
in Montorio

P.za S. Pietro
in Montorio

Via
di F

Palazzo
Congre

Casino

Ambasciata
d. Belgio

Via Aurelia

Il Vascello

MEDICI

S. Pancrazio

P.le
Aurelio

Via A. Masina

Via

Mauseleo
Ossario
Gianicolense

Bramante's
Tempietto

Via

P.za
S. Cosi

Accademia
d'America

I QUATTRO

Via
G. Bruzzesi

Via
de L. Mercantini

Via Trenta Aprile

Via Nicola Fabrizi

Viale

VENTI

L.go
Cocchi

TRASTEVERE

Minis
d. Pub
Istruz

P.za
S. Pancrazio

Via A. Algardi

Via Carini

F. Bonnet

Via P. Roselli

Via Wurts Calandrelli

VILLA

Glori

Basilio Bricci

Via E.
Guastalla

Via G.
Livraghi

Via Giacinto

Viale Wenn

Viale A. Kirscher

Via L. Cairoli

VILLA
DORIA

Via Vitellia

Via F. Bolognesi

Via F. Pamphili

Via O. Regnoli

Via Gianicolensi

SCIARRA

Via Aurelio

Satti

PAMPHILI

P.za
Ottavilla

Via B. Vici

Via F. S.

Via G. Rossetti

Via di Mura Gianicolensi

Villa
Sciarra

Via Cesmo
De Torres

Via di Monreale

Via

P.za
Rosolino
Pilo

Via G. Bassini

Viale Aurelio Saffi

Via U. Bassi

P.za
Anzani

Via dei
Pamphili

Via Innocenzo X

L.go
Vitetti

Via Giovagnoli

Via M.

Cavallotti

Quadrio

F. Torre

Via Aurelio Saffi

Via Dandolo

Via P. Sterbini

P.za
Ippolito
Nievo

Clivo di Porta
S. Pancrazio

P.za
Fonteiana

S. Maria
Regina Pacis

Via A. Coluutti

Poerio

Via Francesco

Via G. Carini

Via F. Daniele

Via G. B.

Via F. Benaglia

L.go
G. Toja

Via Pig. Foà

Via Pietro Paolucci

Via di Donna Olimpia

Via V. Brunetti

Via di Orti
di Galba

Via Sesto
Celere

S. Maria
d. Prov.

Via S. Sebastiano

Via
Giulio

Via Barrili

Via Nicolini

Via F. D. Guerrazzi

Via Francesco

Via Alessandro

Via di Trastevere

Via di Trastevere

L.go
Parboni

Via I. Nievo

L.go
Ripari

Via N. Hellig

P.za A.
Ugone

Via Federico Ozanam

Via Fonteiana

P.za A.
Donna Olimpia

Via Decilio
Quinto

Via Giovanni
Battista Falda

Via R. Paolucci

Via Calandi

Via di Donna Olimpia

Via G. Jemiscalchi

Via degli
Orti
di Galba

P.le
Quattro
Venti

Via Anton

L.go
A. Orlandi

Via C. Pisacane

Via F. Rosazza

Via C. Pascarella

Via Rolli

Via Ettore

Via Nicol
Bettoni

Per.
Per
Testi

MONTEVERDE

F. Cornaro

Viale di Quattro

NUOVA

N. S. de
la Salette

Missione
di Salette

Via G.
Guinzelli

L.go
Giuseppe
Leti

Via G. Bartoli

Via Revere

Via A. Traversari

Via G. Ponziano

Via V. Bonghi

Via C. Porta

Via Portuense

A   B

D

E

Pal. della
ancelleria
P.za S. Andrea
della Valle
Museo
Barracco
P.za
Vidoni
Palazzo
Altieri
Plebiscito
Palazzo
Vidoni
Museo
Barracco
S. Andrea
della Valle
V. Emanuele II V.d.
S. Marco
P.za
Venezia
Prefettura
L.go
Magnana-
poli
Villa
Aldobrandini

Col. Traiana
Foro di
Traiano
SS. Domenici
e Sisto

Teatro di
Pompeo
Area Sacra
dell'Argentina
Chiesa
del Gesù
Palazzo
Venezia
Monumento a
Vittorio Emanuele II
(Vittoriano)
Fori
Imperiali

S. Carlo
ai Catinari
Palazzo
Mattei
Via delle Botteghe Oscure
S. Maria
in Aracoeli
Foro
di Augusto

Palazzo d.
Monte di Pietà
Palazzo
Mattei
Crypta Balbi -
Museo Naz.
Romano
Palazzo
Nuovo
SS. Luca
e Martina

Palazzo
Spada
Palazzo
Cenci
Musei
Capitolini
Palazzo
Senatorio
Arco di
Settimio
Severo
Basilica
Aemilia

Ministero di
Grazia e Giustizia
Pal. dei
Conservatori
Basilica
Giulia
Basilica di
Massenzio

Ospedale
Fatebenefratelli
M. Capitolino
Foro Romano
Tempio di
Venere e
Roma

Isola Tiberina
S. Nicola
in Carcere
P.za
Consolazione
S. Teodoro
Arco di Tito

della
G. G. Belli
S. Bartolomeo
all'Isola
Ponte
Rotto
Uffici di
Comune
S. Giorgio
in Velabro
ORTI
FARNESIANI
Arco di
Costantino

S. Maria
in Trast.
Ponte Palatino
Tempio di
Fortuna Virile
Arco di Giano
M. Palatino

S. Crisogono
Tempio
di Vesta
S. Anastasia
Domus
Flavia
Casa
di Livia

Monopoli
S.
Cecilia
Uffici
Comunali
Domus d.
Augustana
Stadio di
Domiziano
Antiquarium

di Stato
S. Maria
in Cosmedin
Terme
Severare

Palazzo
d'Esami
S. Vincenzo
de Paoli
Circo
S. Gregorio
Magno

S. Francesco
a Ripa
Monumento
a. G. Mazzini
Circo Massimo
Torre
d. Molette
Largo di
Caduti di Magno
Nassiriya

P.ta Portese
Porta Portese
PARCO
SAVELLO
Ugo La Malta
CIRCO
MASSIMO
Obelisco
di Axum

S. Sabina
S. Alessio
Pietro
d'Illiria
S. Prisca
Aventino
F.A.O.

Ponte
Sublicio
P.za
dell'Emporio
S. Maria d.
Priorato di Malta
Tempio Diana
S. Saba
PARCO
DI PORTA
CAPENA

Tevere
M. Aventino
S.
Anselmo
P.za
Albania
S. Balbina

Testaccio
S. Maria
Liberatrice
Mercato
PARCO DELLA
RESISTENZA
DELL 8 SETT.
S. Saba

MARCO al
Mattatoio
L.go
Manlio
Gelsomini
P.za Porta
S. Paolo

MONTE
TESTACCIO
CIM
ACATTOLICO
Museo di
Via Ostiense
Piramide di
Caio Cestio
P.ta
S. Paolo
Ostiense

332

0 100 200 300 400 500 m

0 100 200 300 400 500 yds

TUSCOLANO

Key
- Hotel
- Restaurant

Museo Canonica
VILLA
PARCO D. DAINI
Galleria Borghese
P.za di Siena
P.le del Museo Borghese
P.le del Cav. Marini
BORGHESE
Tempio d. Diana

VILLA GEORGIO
Mausoleo d. Lucillo Petro
Villa Albani
VILLA ALBANI
SALARIO
Museo d'Arte Contemporanea di Roma (MACRO)
Corpus Domini

Casina d. Rose
Jolly Vittorio Veneto
Casa del Cinema
GALOPPATOIO
P.le Brasile
Chiesa Luterana
Teatro delle Arti
S. Teresa d' Italia
Campania
P.ta Salaria
SS. Redent.
Ministero d. Lavori Pubblici
Ministero d. Trasporti

P.ta Pinciana
Papà Baccus
Residenza A
Girarrosto Fiorentino
Doney
S. Camillo
VILLA BONAPARTE
Porta Pia
P.ta Pia
P.za della Croce Rossa

Westin Excelsior
Splendide Royal
Eden
La Terrazza dell'Eden
Ambasciatori Palace
Pal. Margherita (American Embassy)
Istituto Naz. Assicurazioni
Ministero Lavoro
Cantina Cantarini
Ambasciata Gran Bretagna

S. Isidoro
S. Maria della Concezione
Aleph
Medigliani
Daphne
Casa Howard
Convento d. Cappuccini
Suisse
Barocco
Bernini Bristol
Gall. Naz. d' Arte Antica
Palazzo Barberini
Daphne
S. Susanna
Pza di S. Bernardo
Ministero Agricoltura e Foreste
S. Maria d. Vittoria
St Regis Grand
S. Maria d. Angeli
Chiostro d. Certosa
Museo Nazionale Romano (Palazzo Massimo)
Africa
Des Artistes
The Beehive
S. Cuore

Al Presidente
GIARDINO DEL QUIRINALE
Palazzo del Quirinale
M. Quirinale
Palazzo d. Drago
S. Carlo alle Quattro Fontane
S. Andrea
Ministero d. Difesa
Dagnino
Residenza Cellini
P.za della Repubblica
Exedra
Teatro dell'Opera
Terme di Diocleziano-Museo Nazionale Romano
L. Einaudi
P.za dei Cinquecento
Palazzo Massimo - Museo Nazionale Romano
Stazione Roma Termini

Palazzo delle Esposizioni
S. Vitale
Palazzo d. Consulta
Palazzo Pallavicini Rospigliosi
Ministero degli Interni
S. Prudenzia
Cavour

Scuderie del Quirinale
Palazzo Koch
S. Silvestro
L.go Magnana-poli
Villa Aldobrandini
Il Guru
Antica Locanda
Hasekura
F.I.S.H.
SS. Domenicani e Sisto
Foro di Traiano
P.za dell' Esquilino
S. Maria Maggiore
Radisson SAS es.
Radisson SAS es. Hotel
Montreal
Agatà e Romeo
S. Prassede
Hang Zhou
Vineria Monti DOL
Accademia Alfonsiana
Trattoria Monti
S. Eusebio

A   B

335

337

D **E**

0 100 200 300 400 500 m
0 100 200 300 400 500 yds

■ *Hotel*
■ Restaurant

Arancia Blu
Formula Uno
SS. Immacolata
P.le Tiburtino
P.za di P.ta S. Lorenzo
Da Franco ar Vicoletto
S. Bibiana
Scalo Merci S. Lorenzo
Il Palazzo del Freddo di Giovanni Fassi
Via di Porta Maggiore
Giolitti
Via Prenestina
P.za Prenestina
P.za di Porta Maggiore
P.ta Maggiore
Hostaria degli Artisti
Villa Altieri
Via S. Quintino
Acquedotto Neroniano
VILLA WOLKONSKI
Domus Sessoriana
S. Croce in Gerusalemme
Casilina
P.za del Pigneto
Anfiteatro Castrense
Viale
P.za Lodi
Scala Santa
P.za Porta S. Giovanni
Spezia
P.za Camerino
Algiero
P.za Castroreale
L.go Brindisi
P.le Appio
P.ta Asinaria
S. Giovanni
SS. Immacolata
SS. Fabiano
P.za di Villa Fiorelli
Appia
Taranto
P.za Lugo
S. Maria d. Orto
L.go Magna Grecia
P.za dei Re di Roma
L.go Vercelli
Via Vercelli
L.go Frassinetti
P.za Asti
P.za Ragusa
RE DI ROMA
Nuova
Via Etruria
Ognissanti
Staz. Roma-Tuscolana F.S.
P.za Tuscolo
PONTE LUNGO
Via Etruria
Via Albenga
P.za di Ponte Lungo
P.za Zama
Istituto Antoniano di Roma
Circonvallazione
P.za Fibocchiaro Aprile
Appia Nuova
TUSCOLANO

D **E**

STREET INDEX

A

Abruzzi, Via 328 A2
Accademia d. Romania 327 D1
Accademia d'America 330 B2
Accademia della Scienze 326 A3
Accademia di Belle Arti 327 D2
Acireale, Via 333 D2
Acquedotto Neroniano 333 C2
Acqui, Via 333 D4
Adalberto, Via 329 E2
Adda, Via 328 B1
Adelaide, Via M. 327 D2
Adria, Via 333 E4
Adriana, P.za Augusto 327 C3
Adriana, Piazza 326 C3
Africa, Via Capo d' 332 B2
Agrigento, Via 329 D2
Alba, Via 333 D4–E4
Albani, Via di Villa 328 B1
Albania, P.za 331 E3
Albenga, Via 333 D4
Albenzio, Via Fra' 326 A2
Alberici, Via di Villa 326 A4
Alberico II, Via 326 B3
Albert, Via d. Orti d' 326 C4
Alberto, Via C. 328 B4
Alcamo, Via 333 E2
Alesia, Via 332 B3–C4
Alessandria, P.za 328 B2
Alessandria, Via 329 C1
Alessandrina, Via 331 E1
Alfieri, Via 332 C1
Algardi, Via A. 330 A3
Alghero, Via 333 E2
Allegri, Via G. 328 B1
Alpi, Via della 329 C1
Amato, Via 326 A1
Amedeo, Ponte Pr. 326 C4
Amedeo, Via Principe 328 B4–C4
Amelia, Via 333 E4
Amendola, Via G. 328 B3
Amiterno, Via 333 C3
Amore, Via D. 327 D3
Anamari, Via degli 333 D1
Ancona, Via 328 B2
Andreoli, Via 326 B1
Anfiteatro Castrense 333 D2
Angelica, Via di P.ta 326 B3
Angelico, Borgo 326 B3
Angelico, Viale 326 B1
Anglona, Via 332 B3
Anguillara, Lgt. S. 331 C2–D2
Anicia, Via 331 D2
Aniene, Via 328 B1
Annia, Via 332 B2
Annibaldi, Via d. 332 A1
Antica, Via Aurelia 330 A2
Antiquarium 331 E2
Antonina, Via 332 A3
Antoniniana, Via 332 A4–B4
Anzani, L.go 330 C4
Aosta, Via 333 D3
Appia Nuova, Via 333 D3–E4
Appio, P.le 333 C2

Aprile, P.za Finocchiaro 333 E4
Aprile, Viale Trenta 330 B2
Aprile, Vialle XXI 329 E1
Apuania, Via 329 E1
Apuli, Via d. 329 D4
Apulia, Via 332 C3
Aquila, Via L' 333 E2
Aquitania, Via 332 C4
Ara Pacis 327 D3
Aracoeli, P.za d' 331 D1
Aradam, Via Amba 332 B3
Aranciera, Viale della 327 E1
Arancio, Via dell' 327 D3
Arborea, Via E. d' 329 E2
Archetto, Via dell' 327 E4
Archivio di Stato 327 D4
Arco di Giano 331 E2
Arco di Costantino 331 E2
Arco di Settimio Severo 331 E1
Arco di Tito 331 E2
Ardea, Via 333 C3
Ardeatina, Viale di Porta 331 E4
Arduino, Via 329 E2
Area Sacra dell'Argentina 327 D4
Arenula, Via 331 D1
Arezzo, Via 329 D2
Argentina, Via di T. 327 D4
Ariosto, Via L. 332 C2
Armenia, P.za 333 C4
Armi, Lgt. d. 327 C1
Arno, Via 328 C1
Arrigo VII, L.go 331 D3
Asciaghibi, L.go 331 C3
Asinaria, P.za 333 C3
Assisi, Via 333 E4
Astalli, Via 327 E4
Asti, P.za 333 E3
Astura, Via 333 C4
Atrio d. Vestali 331 E1
Auditorio di Mecenate 332 B1
Augusta, Lgt. in 327 D2
Aula delle Udienze Pontificie 326 B3
Aurea, Viale d. Domus 332 B2
Aurelia, Via della Cava 330 A1–A2
Aurelia, Via 326 A4
Aureliana, Via 328 B2
Aurélie, Viale delle Mura 330 B1
Aurelio, P.le 330 B2
Aurelio, Via M. 332 B2
Aurora, Via 328 A2
Aurunci, V. degli 333 D1
Ausoni, Via d. 329 D4
Aventina, Via 331 E3
Aventino, Lgt. 331 D3–D2
Aventino, Viale 331 E3
Avezzana, Via Giuseppe 327 C1
Azeglio, Via M. D' 328 B4
Azuni, Via D. A. 327 D1

B

Babuino, Via del 327 E2
Baccelli, Viale Guido 331 E3
Baccina, Via 331 E1

Bafile, Via A. 326 B1
Baglivi, Via G. 329 D2
Baiamonti, Via 326 B1
Balbo, Via C. 328 B4
Baldinotti, V. G. 331 E4
Balilla, Via 333 C1
Bandiera, Via F. 330 B4–B3
Barberini, Via 328 A3
Barberini, P.za 328 A3
Bargoni, Via 330 C4
Bari, Via 329 D2
Barletta, Via 326 B2
Barrili, Via Anton Giulio 330 B4
Bartoli, Via 330 B4
Barzellotti, Via G. 326 A2
Basento, Via 328 B1
Basilica Aemilia 331 E1
Basilica di Massenzio 331 E1
Basilica di San Pietro 326 A3
Basilica Giulia 331 E1
Basilica S. Giovanni in Laterano 332 C3
Bassi, Via U. 330 C3
Battista, Via Giovanni 329 D1
Beccaria, Via C. 327 D1
Belisario, Via 328 B2
Bella, Via G. della 329 E2
Belli, P.za G. G. 331 C2
Belli, Via G. G. 327 D2
Belluno, Via 329 D1
Belsiana, Via 327 E2
Beltrami, Via C. 331 E4
Belvedere, Via d. 326 B3
Benaglia, Via F. 330 C4
Berengario, Via 329 C2
Bergamo, Via 328 B2
Bernadotte, Viale F. 327 E1
Berniero, Via G. 331 D3
Bernini, P.za G. L. 331 E4
Bertinoro, Via C. di 329 E2
Bettolo, Via G. 326 B2
Bettoni, Via Nicolò 330 C4
Biancamano, Via Umberto 333 C2
Bianchi, Via G. 331 C3
Biblioteca Nazionale Centrale 329 C2
Biella, Via 333 E3
Bissolati, Via L. 328 B3
Bixio, Via Nino 333 C1
Boario, Viale Campo 331 C4
Bobbio, Via 333 D3
Bocca d. Verità, P.za 331 D2
Bodoni, Via Giovan Battista 331 C4
Boezio, Via 326 C2
Boiardo, Via M. 332 C2
Bologna, P.za 329 E1
Bolognesi, Via F. 330 A3
Boncompagni, Via 328 A2
Bonghi, Via R. 332 B2
Boni, Via G. 329 E1
Bonnet, Via F. 330 B3
Borelli, Via A. 329 D2
Borghese, L.go F. 327 D3
Borghese, P.le del Museo 328 A1
Borghese, P.za Paolina 327 E1
Borghese, Via F. 330 A3
Borghese, Viale del Museo 328 A1
Borghetto, Vic. del 327 D2
Borgognona, Via 327 E3
Borsieri, Via P. 326 B1

Boschetto, Via del 328 A4
Bosio, Via Antonio 329 D1
Botta, Via C. 332 B1
Bottazzi, Via F. 330 A4
Bovio, Via G. 326 A1
Bramante's Tempietto 330 C2
Branca, Via Giovanni 331 C4
Brasile, P.le 328 A2
Brescia, Lgt. A. da 327 D1
Brescia, Via 328 B1
Brianzo, Via M. 327 D3
Bricci, Via Basilio 330 B3
Brindisi, Via A. 327 D2
Brofferio, Via A. 326 C1
Brunetti, Via A. 327 D2
Bruno, Via Emilio Faà di 326 B1
Bruno, Via G. 326 A1
Bruzi, Via dei 333 D1
Bruzzesi, Via G. 330 B2
Buccari, Via 326 A1
Buonarroti, Via 332 B1

C

Caballini, P.za 333 E2
Caccini, Via 328 B1
Caduti, P.za Parco 329 D4
Caetani, Via 331 D1
Cagliari, Via 328 C1
Cairoli, P.za 331 D1
Cairoli, Via 333 C1
Calabria, Via R. 329 D1
Calandrelli, Via 330 B3
Calboli, Via P. de 326 B1
Caltanissetta, Via 333 E2
Camene, Via Valle delle 332 A3
Cameria, Via 332 C4
Camerino, P.za 333 D2
Camillo Re, P.za 333 D4
Camillo, Via F. 333 E4
Camozzi, Via 326 B1
Campanella, Via T. 326 A2
Campani, Via d. 333 D1
Campania, Via 328 B2
Campidano, P.za dei 329 E1
Campidoglio, P.za del 331 D1
Campitelli, P.za di 331 D1
Campo de' Fiori 331 C1
Cancelleri, La B. 326 B3
Candia, Via 326 A2
Canestre, P.za 327 E1
Canneti, Via del 329 E2
Canonica, Viale Pietro 327 E1
Canossa, Via M. di 329 E2
Cantoni, Via di Q. 328 B4
Capizucchi, P.za 331 D1
Cappadocia, Via 333 D4
Cappella Sistina 326 B3
Cappellari, Via d. 331 C1
Cappellini, Via 328 C4
Capponi, P.za Americo 326 B3
Capranica, P.za 327 D4
Caprara, Via 333 E1
Caracalla, Via delle Terme di 332 A3–B4
Caracciolo, Via F. 326 A2
Carcani, Via M. 331 C3
Carcere Regina Coeli 326 C4
Carducci, Via G. 328 A3
Carini, Via Giacinto 330 B3
Carnia, Via 329 E2
Caro, Via L. 327 C2
Carrara, Via F. 327 D1
Carrozze, Via d. 327 E3

Casa del Cinema 328 A1
Casa di Goethe 327 D2
Casa di Keats-Shelley 327 E3
Casa di Livia 331 E2
Casa Madre d. Mutilati 327 C3
Casa Ordine Frati Minori 326 A4
Case, Via C. le 327 E3
Casentino, Via 329 E1
Caserta, Via 329 D2
Casilina, Via 333 D2
Casina Bessarione 332 B4
Casina dell'Orologio 328 A1
Casina Valadier 327 E2
Casini, Via F. 330 C3
Casino 330 A2
Casino dell'Aurora 328 A2
Casoria, Via 333 D3
Cassiodoro, Via 327 C2
Castel Sant'Angelo 326 C3
Castelfidardo, Via 328 B2
Castello, L.go di Porta 326 C3
Castello, Lgt. 327 C3–D3
Castrense, Viale 333 D2
Castroreale, P.za 333 E3
Catalana, Via 331 D1
Catania, Via 329 D2
Catanzaro, Via 329 D2
Catone, Via 326 B2
Cattaneo, Via C. 328 B4
Caudini, Via 329 C4
Cava, Via della 326 A4
Cavalleggeri, Via d. P.ta 326 A4
Cavalleggeri, P.ta 326 B3
Cavallo, P.za Ferro di 327 D2
Cavallotti, Via Felice 330 B4
Cavour, P.za 327 C3
Cavour, Ponte 327 D3
Cavour, Via 328 B4
Cedro, Vicolo del 330 C2
Cefalo, Vicolo 326 C4
Celani, Via 330 A4
Celere, Via Sesto 330 A4
Celimontana, P.za 332 B3
Celimontana, Via 332 B2
Celso, Via C. 329 D2
Cenci, Lgt. dei 331 D1–D2
Cenci, P.za dei 331 D1
Ceneda, Via 333 C3
Cerchi, Via dei 331 E2
Ceriani, Via A. 330 A1
Cernaia, Via 328 B3
Cernuschi, Via E. 330 A4
Cervantes, P.za 327 E1
Cerveteri, Via 333 C3
Cesalpino, Via 329 C2
Cesare, Viale Giulio 326 B2
Cesena, Via 333 D3
Cesi, Via F. 327 C2
Cestari, Via d. 327 D4
Cestia, Via P. 331 D4
Cestio, Ponte 331 D2
Cestio, Via C. 331 D4
Chiarini, L.go Giovanni 332 A4
Chiesa del Gesù 327 E4
Chiesa dell' Annunziata 330 B1
Chiesa Luterana 328 A2
Chiesa Nuova 327 C3
Chiesa Valdese 327 C3
Chiesa, Via C. A. Dalla 326 B1
Chieti, Via 329 D2

Chioggia, Via 333 E3
Chiostro d. Certosa 328 B3
Cicerone, Via 327 C2
Cilone, Fabio L. 331 E4
Cimarra, Via 328 A4
Cinquecento, P.za del 328 B3
Cipro, Via 326 A2
Circo Massimo 331 E2
Circonvallazione 333 D4
Città Universitaria 329 D3
Cittaduc, Via 333 E3
Claterna, Via 333 C3
Claudia, Via 332 B2
Clementi, Via M. 327 D3
Clodio, P.za le 326 B1
Clotilde, Via Pr. 327 D2
Cocchi, L.go 330 B2
Colautti, Via A. 330 B3
Collazia, Via 333 C4
Collegio Pontificio Pio
 330 B1
Collina, Via 328 B2
Colonna, P.za 327 E3
Colonna, Via M. 327 C2
Colonna, Via V. 327 D3
Colosseo 331 E1
Colosseo, P.za del 332 A2
Colosseo, Via del 332 A1
Como, Via 329 D2
Conciliazione, Via d. 326 B3
Concordia, Via 333 C4
Condotti, Via dei 327 E3
Confalonieri, Via 326 C1
Confienza, P.za 329 C3
Consolazione, P.za 331 D2
Consolazione, Via d. 331 E1
Consulta, Via della 328 A4
Conti, Corte d. 326 B1
Conti, Via T. de 331 E1
Convento d. Cappuccini
 328 A3
Coppelle, Via della 327 D3
Cornaro, Via F. 330 A4–B4
Coronari, P.za 327 C3
Coronari, Via dei 327 C4
Corpus Domini 328 C2
Corridori, Via 326 B3
Corsi, Via dei 329 D4
Corso Trieste 329 C1
Corso, Via del 327
 D2–D3–E3
Cosenza, Via 329 D2
Cossa, Via P. 327 D2
Cottolengo, Via del 326 A4
Crema, Via 333 E3
Cremera, Via 328 B1
Cremona, Via 329 E1
Crescenzio, Via 326 B2
Crispi, Via F. 327 E3
Cristina, Via M. 327 D2
Croce, Via d. 327 E3
Crociate, P.ze della 329 E2
Crocifisso, Via d. 326 A4
Crypta Balbi-Museo Naz.
 Romano 331 D1
Cucchi, P.za 330 B3
Cuma, Via 333 C3
Cunfida, Via 326 A1
Cupa, Via 329 E2
Cutilia, Via 333 C4

D

Dacia, Via 333 C4
Daini, P.le dei 328 A1
Dalmati, Via d. 329 D4
Dalmazia, P.za 328 C1
Dalmazia, Via 329 C1
Damiata, Via 326 C1

Dandolo, Via 330 C3
Dante, P.za 332 C1
Dataria, Via della 327 E4
Dauni, Via 329 D4
Deciane, Via Terme 331 E3
Decii, Via d. 331 D3
Depretis, Via A. 328 B4
Diana, P.za Tempio 331 D3
Dionigi, Via M. 327 D3
Domodossola, Via 333 D4
Domus Aurea 332 B1
Domus d. Augustana 331 E2
Domus Flavia 331 E2
Donati, Via P. 329 E1
Doria, Via A. 326 A2
Drago, P.za del 331 D2
Druso, Via 332 B3
Duilio, Via 326 C2

E

Einaudi, Via L. 328 B3
Elea, Via 333 C3
Elena, Vialle Regina 329 D2
Eleniana, Via 333 D2
Emanuele I, Via Carlo 333
 C2
Emanuele II, Corso V. 327
 C4–D4
Emanuele II, Ponte Vitt.
 326 C3
Emanuele II, P.za Vittorio
 332 C1
Emanuele II, V. 331 D1
Emilia, Via 328 A2
Emilia, Via Reggio 328 C1
Emilio, Via P. 326 C2
Emo, Via Angelo 326
 A3–A2
Emporio, P.za dell' 331 D3
Enna, Via 333 E3
Enotri, Via d. 329 D4
Epiro, P.za 332 C4
Equi, Via d. 329 D4
Equi, Viad. 333 D1
Eremita, Via P. l' 329 E2
Eroi, P.za le degli 326 A2
Esculapio, Viale 327 E1
Esquilino, P.za dell' 328 B4
Etruria, Via 333 C4–D4
Etruschi, Via d. 329 D4
Eugenio, Via Pr. 333 C1
Eustacchio, Via B. 329 C2
Ex Palazzo di Giustizia
 327 C3
Ezio, Via 326 C2

F

Fabbri, Via E. 326 C1
Fabbrica, Via di Porta
 326 A4
Fabretti, Via A. 329 D1
Fabricio, Ponte 331 D2
Fabrizi, Viale Nicola 330 B3
Fabrizio, P.za Girolamo
 329 C2
Falco, Via del 326 B3
Faleria, Via 333 C3
Famagosta, Via 326 B2
Farini, C., Via 328 B4
Farinone, Via 326 B3
Farnese, P.za 331 C1
Farnese, Via A. 327 C2
Farnese, Via 331 C1
Farnesina, Lgt. della 330 C1
Faro 330 B1
Farsalo, Via 332 C3
Faustina, Via Annia 331 E4
Felice, Viale Carlo 333 C2

Ferento, Via 333 D4
Fermo, Via 333 E3
Ferrari, Via G. 326 C1
Ferruccio, Via 332 B1
Fidene, Via 333 C3
Fienili, Via D. 331 E2
Filangieri, Via G. 327 D1
Filiberto, Via Emanuele
 333 C2
Filippi, Via d. 327 C4
Filippo Turati, Via 328 C4
Fiocco, P.za del 327 E1
Fiore, Via R. 326 A3
Fiorelli, P.za di Villa
 333 E3
Fiori, Campo de' 327 D4
Fiori, Via de 327 E3
Fiorini, Via F. 330 A4
Firduisi, P.za le 327 E1
Firenze, Via 328 B3
Fiume, P.za 328 B2
Fivizzano, Via 333 E2
Flaminia, Via 327 D1
Flaminio, P.za le 327 D1
Flavia, Via 328 B3
Florio, Via 331 C4
Foà, Via Pio 330 A4
Foligno, Via 333 D3
Fonseca, Via di V. 332 B3
Fontana di Trevi 327 E3
Fontana, Via della 329 C1
Fontane, Via d. Quattro
 328 A3
Fonteiana, P.za 330 A3
Fonteiana, Via 330 A4–A3
Foraggi, Via d. 331 E2
Fori Imperiali 331 E1
Forli, Via 329 D2
Fornaci, Via della 326 B4
Fornaci, Via Nuova d. 330
 B1–B2
Fornovo, Via 327 C1
Foro di Augusto 331 E1
Foro di Traiano 327 E3
Foro Romano 331 E2
Fortuny, Via M. 327 D1
Foscolo, Via U. 332 C1
Frangipane, Via 331 E1
Franklin, Via B. 331 C4
Frassinetti, L.go 333 D3
Frattina, Via 327 E3
Fregene, Via 333 C3
Frentani, Via dei 329 C3
Frez, Via d. 327 D2
Friuli, Via Cividale del
 333 D4
Friuti, Via 328 A2
Funari, Via dei 331 D1

G

Gabi, Via 333 C3
Gaeta, Via 328 C2–B3
Galazia, Via 333 C4
Galba, Via Orti di 330 A4
Galilei, Via 332 C2
Galleria Alberto Sordi
 327 E3
Galleria Borghese 328 A1
Galleria Doria Pamphilj
 327 E4
Galleria Naz. d'Arte Antica
 328 A3
Galleria Nazionale d'Arte
 Moderna 327 E1
Gallia, Via 332 B3–C3
Gallipoli, Via 333 E4
Gallo, Clivo di del 330 A1

Gallo, Clivo di Monte del
 326 A4
Gallo, Via di Monte del
 326 A4
Gallonio, Via A. 329 D1
Galluppi, Via 326 A1
Galvani, Via 331 D4
Gambero, Via 327 E3
Garibaldi, P.le Anita 330 B1
Garibaldi, P.le Giuseppe
 330 B1
Garibaldi, Ponte 331 C2
Garibaldi, Via 330 B2–C2
Gela, Via 333 E4
Gelosmini, Viale M. 331 D4
Gelsomini, L.go Manlio
 331 D4
Gelsomino, Via del 326 A4
Genova, Via 328 A4
Genovesi, Via dei 331 D2
Gerace, Via 333 D3
Germanico, Via 327 C1
Gesmundo, Via G. 326 B1
Gessi, Via R. 331 D3
Gesù, P.za 327 D4
Gesù, Via del 327 D4
Ghiberti, Via L. 331 C4
Gianicolense, Lgt. 326 C4
Gianicolensi, Via delle Mura
 330 B2–B3
Gianicolensi, Via di Mura
 330 B3–C3
Gianicolensi, Via Orti
 330 A4
Gianicolo, Passeggiata del
 326 B4
Gianicolo, Via d. 326 B4
Giannone, Via P. 326 A2
Gianturco, Via 327 D1
Giardini, Via dei 328 A3
Ginori, Via 331 D4
Gioberti, Via 328 B4
Giordano, Via M. 327 C4
Giorgio, Via M. 331 D3
Giornate, P.za Cinque
 327 C1
Giotto, Viale 331 E4
Giovagnoli, Via 330 B3
Giovanelli, Via R. 328 B1
Giovanni Giolitti, Via
 328 C4
Giovanni XXIII, P.za 326 C3
Giovanni, Via Tata 331 E4
Giubbonari, Via dei
 331 C1–D1
Giulia, Via 326 C4
Giuliana, Via della 326 B1
Giusti, Via 332 C1
Giustiniani, P.za O. 331 C4
Giustiniani, Via degli Orti
 327 D1
Giustiniani, Via 327 D4
Glorioso, Viale 330 B2
Gobetti, Viale P. 329 C3
Goethe, Viale W. 327 E1
Goito, Via 328 B3
Governatorato 326 A3
Grabau, Via C. 326 B1
Gracchi, Via dei 326 C2
Grande, Via N. D. 331 C2
Grasperi, Via A. De 326 B4
Grazioli, P.za 327 E4
Greci, Via dei 327 E3
Grecia, L.go Magna 333 C3
Grecia, Via Magna 333 C3
Gregoriana, Via 327 E3
Gregorio VII, P.za le 326 A4
Gregorio VII, Via 326 A4

Grosseto, Via 333 E2
Grotta di Lourdes 326 A3
Guardia, Viale Fiorello La
 327 E1
Guattani, Via G. A. 329 D1
Gubbio, Via 333 E4
Guerrazzi, Via Fr. D.
 330 B4
Guerrieri, Via 331 E4
Guicciardini, Via 332 B2
Guinizelli, Via G. 330 B4
Gulli, Via T. 326 B1

H–K

Helbig, Via N. 330 A4
Hugo, P.za Victor 327 E1
Iberia, Via 332 C4
Icilio, Via 331 D3
Illiria, P.za Pietro d' 331 D3
Illiria, Via V. 332 C3
Imera, Via 333 C4
Imola, P.za 333 E2
Imperatore, P.za 327 D3
Imperia, Via 329 D2
Imperiali, Via dei Fori
 331 E1
Indipenden, P.za 328 B3
Induno, Via G. 331 C3
Innocenzo III, Via 326 A4
Innocenzo X, Via 330 A3
Ippocrate, Viale 329 D2
Ipponio, P.le 332 C3
Ipponio, Viale 332 B3
Irpini, Via d. 329 D3
Isonzo, Via 328 B1
Italia, Corso d' 328 B2
Italia, P.za Giovine 326 B1
Ivrea, Via 333 D4–E4
Klitsche, Viale A. 330 B3

L

Labicana, Via di Porta
 333 D1
Labicana, Via 332 B2
Labicano, P.le 333 D2
Labriola, Via A. 326 A2
Lancisi, Via A. M. 329 C2
Lando, Via Michele d.
 329 E1
Lante, Via R. Grazioli
 326 B1
Lanusei, Via 333 E2
Lanza, Via G. 332 B1
Lateriano, Via d. F. in
 332 B3–C3
Latina, P.ta 332 C4
Latina, S. Giovanni a P.ta
 332 B4
Latina, Via di Porta 332 B4
Latina, Via 332 C4
Latine, Via d. Mura 332 C4
Latini, Via 329 D4
Laurenziano, Via d. Castro
 329 D3
Lauria, Via R. di 326 A2
Lavatore, Via d. 327 E3
Lavernale, Via di Porta 331
 D3
Lavinio, Via 333 D3
Lazio, Via 328 A2
Lecce, P.za 329 D1
Leone IV, Via 326 B2
Leone, Via Bocca di 327 E3
Leonina, P.za Città 326 B3
Leonina, Via 332 A4
Leopardi, L.go Giacomo
 332 B1
Lepanto, Via 326 C1

Leti, L.go Giuseppi 330 B4
Letizia, Viale Madama
327 E1
Libertà, P.za della 327 C2
Liburni, Via d. 329 D3
Liceo 331 E1
Licia, Via 332 C3
Licinia, Via 331 E3
Ligorio, Via P. 331 E4
Liguria, Via 328 A3
Littore, Via T. 330 A4
Livenza, Via 328 B1
Livorno, Via 329 E1
Locri, Via 333 C3
Lodi, P.za 333 E2
Lollis, Via C. de 329 D4
Lombarda, Via Lega 329 E2
Lombardi, L.go dei 327 D3
Lombardia, Via 328 A2
Lotario, P.za 329 E1
Lubin, Via 327 D1
Lucani, Via de 333 D1
Lucania, Via 328 B2
Lucca, Via 329 D2
Lucchesi, Via 327 E4
Luce, Via della 331 D2
Luceri, Via dei 329 D4
Lucullo, Via 328 A2
Ludovico II, Via 329 E2
Ludovisi, Via 328 A2
Ludus Magnus 332 B2
Lugo, P.za 333 E3
Lune, P.za Cinque 327 D3
Lungara, Via della 326 C4
Lungaretta, Via della 331 D2
Lungo, P.za di Ponte 333 E4
Lupa, Via d. 327 D3
Lusitania, Via 332 C4
Luzzatti, L. 333 D2

M

Macchiavelli, Via 332 C1
Macelli, Via Due 327 E3
Macerata, Via 333 E2
MACRO al Mattatoio 331 C4
Maderno, Via B. 331 E4
Magenta, Via 328 C3
Maggio, Via XXIV 327 E4
Maggiore, P.ta 333 D2
Maggiore, P.za di Porta
333 D1
Maggiore, Via di Porta 333
D1
Magnanapoli, L.go 327 E4
Magnifico, Via Lorenzo 329
E1
Magno, P.ta 331 E3
Magno, Via Pompeo 327 C2
Magnolie, Viale della 327 E2
Malfa, P.le Ugo La 331 E3
Malta, P.za Cavalieri di 331
D3
Mameli, Via G. 330 C2
Mamiani, Via 328 C4
Manara, Via L. 331 C2
Manin, Via 328 B4
Mantellate, Via d. 326 C4
Mantova, Via 328 B1
Manuzio, Via Aldo 331 C4
Manzoni, Viale 333 C1
Maratta, Via 331 E4
Marcella, Via 331 D3
Marcello, Via del Teatro di
331 D2–D1
Marche, Via 328 A2
Marghera, Via 328 C3
Margherita, P.za Regina
328 C1

Margherita, Ponte 327 D2
Margherita, Viale Regina
328 B1
Margutta, Via 327 D2
Maria, Via Gesù e 327 D2
Marina, P.za della 327 D1
Marini, P.le dei Cav. 328 A1
Marini, Viale dei Cavalli
328 A1
Mario, Via C. 326 B2
Marmorata, Via 331 D3
Marrucini, Via d. 329 D4
Marsala, Via 329 C4
Marsi, Via di 329 D4
Marsica Via della 329 E1
Marsigli, Via 333 E1
Martini, L.go Monte 328 B3
Marzio, Lgt. 327 D3
Marzio, P.za in Campo
327 D3
Marzio, Via d. C. 327 D3
Mascherino, Via 326 B3
Masina, Via A. 330 B2
Massime, L.go di Villa
329 D1
Massimo, P.za Valerio
329 E3
Massimo, Via del Circo
331 E2
Mastai, P.za 331 C2
Matera, Via 333 D3–E3
Maticotti, Ponte G. 327 C1
Mattei, P.za 331 D1
Mattonato, Via dei 330 C2
Mauritania, Via 332 C4
Mausoleo di Lucillo Petro
328 B1
Mausoleo di Adriano 326 C3
Mausoleo Ossario
Gianicolense 330 B2
Mazzarino, Via 328 A4
Mazzini, P.za G. 326 C1
Mazzini, Ponte G. 331 C1
Mazzini, Viale Giuseppe
326 B1
Mecenate, Via 332 B1
Medici, Via G. 330 B2
Melfi, Via 333 E1
Mellini, Lgt. 327 D2
Meloria, Via 326 A2
Menotti, Via C. 327 C1
Mentana, Via 328 C2
Mercanti, P.za 331 D2
Mercantini, Via L. 330 B2
Mercede, Via d. 327 E3
Merulana, Via 332 C2
Mesia, Via G. 332 C4
Messina, Via 328 C2
Metaponto, Via 332 C1
Metronia, Via 332 B3
Metronia, P.za Via P.ta 332 B3
Metronio, P.le 332 B3
Metronio, Viale 332 B4
Miani, Via G. 331 E4
Michelangelo, Lgt. 327 C1
Michelangelo, Viale B. di
326 B2
Mignanelli, P.za 327 E3
Milano, Via 328 A4
Milazzo, Via 328 C3
Milizie, Viale della 326
B2–C1
Mille, Via d. 328 C3
Minerva, P.za 327 D4
Mingazzini, Via G. 329 D2
Mirabello, Via C. 326 B1
Mirandola, Via 333 E3
Missori, Via G. 330 B1

Mocenigo, Via 326 A2
Modena, Via 328 A3
Modica, Via 333 E4
Mompiani, Via G. 326 B1
Mondovi, Via 333 D4
Monferrato, Via C. 333 D4
Monopoli di Stato 331 D2
Monreale, Via L. di 330
A4–A3
Monserrato, Via di 327 C4
Montebello, Via 328 B3
Montecitorio, P.za di 327 D3
Montepulciano, Via 333 E3
Monterone, Via 327 D4
Monti, P.za Trinità dei
327 E3
Monti, Via Madonna d.
331 E1
Monti, Viale Trinita dei
327 E2
Monumento a Vittorio
Emanuele II (Vittoriano)
331 E1
Monumento a. G. Mazzini
331 E3
Monza, Via 333 D3
Monzambano, Via 329 C3
Mordini, Via A. 326 C1
Morgagni, Via G. B. 329 C2
Morin, Via C. 326 B1
Moro, P.le Aldo 329 D3
Moro, Via d. 331 C2
Moroni, Via G. 329 E1
Morosini, Via E. 331 C2
Mura, Viale della 326 B4
Muratori, Via L. 332 B2
Muratte, Via d. 327 E4
Murri, Via A. 329 D2
Musa, Via A. 329 C2
Musei Capitolini 331 D1
Musei Vaticani 326 B3
Museo Barracco 327 D4
Museo Canonica 327 E1
Museo Carlo Bilotti 327 E1
Museo d'Arte Contemporanea
di Roma (MACRO) 328 B1
Museo di Roma in
Trastevere 330 C2
Museo di Via Ostiense
331 D4
Museo Napoleonico 327 D3
Museo Naz. d'Arte Orientale
332 B1
Museo Naz. d. Paste
Alimentari 327 E3
Museo Nazionale Romano
(Palazzo Massimo) 328 B3
Musolino, Via B. 330 C3

N

Napoleone I, P.za le 327 D2
Napoleone III, Via 328 B4
Napoli, Via 328 A3
Nassiriya, Largo di Caduti
di 332 A3
Navi, Lgt. d. 327 D1
Navicella, Via d. 332 B3
Navona, P.za 327 D4
Nazareno, Via 327 E3
Nazionale, Via 328 A4
Nenni, Ponte P. 327 C1
Niccolini, Via G. B. 330 B3
Nicolo V, Via 326 B4
Nicosia, P.za 327 D3
Nicotera, Via G. 327 C1
Nievo, P.za Ippolito 330 C3
Nievo, Via I. 330 C4
Niso, Via 333 E4

Nizza, Via 328 B1–C1
Nola, Via 333 D2
Nomentana, Via 328 C2
Nona, Lgt. Tor di 327 C3
Norico, Via 332 B3
Novara, Via 329 C1
Novembre, Via IV 327 E4
Nuoro, Via 333 E2
Nuova, Via Appia 333 C3
Nuovi, Via d. Banchi 327 C4

O

Obelisco di Axum 331 E3
Obelisco, Viale dell' 327 D2
Oca, Via dell' 327 D2
Ognissanti 333 D4
Olbia, Via 332 C3
Olimpia, P.za Donna 330 A4
Olimpia, Via di Donna 330
A4
Olmata, Via d. 328 B4
Ombrellari, Via 326 B3
Ongaro, Via Francesco dall'
330 B4–C3
Oppio, Via del M. 332 A1
Oppio, Viale del Monte
332 B1
Orazio, Via 327 C2
Orfeo, Via 326 B3
Oristano, Via 333 E2
Orlando, Via V. E. 328 B3
Oro, Viale delle Medaglie d'
326 A2
Orsini, Via Virg. 327 C2
Orso, Via dell' 327 D3
Orto, Via Madonna dell'
331 D2
Orvieto, Via 333 D3
Osci, L.go degli 329 D4
Oscure, Via delle Botteghe
331 D1
Ostiense, P.za 331 E4
Ostilia, Via 332 B2
Otranto, Via 326 B2
Ottavia, Via del Portico d'
331 D1
Ottaviano, Via 326 B2
Ottavilla, P.za 330 A3
Ovidio, Via 326 C2
Ozanam, Via Federico
330 A4
Ozieri, Via 333 E2

P

Pace, Via d. 327 D4
Pace, Via d. T. 327 D4
Padova, Via 329 D2
Paisiello, V. G. 328 B1
Palatino, Ponte 331 D2
Palazzo Altemps 327 D3
Palazzo Altieri 327 D4
Palazzo Barberini 328 A3
Palazzo Bernini 327 E3
Palazzo Bonaparte 327 E4
Palazzo Borghese 327 D3
Palazzo Braschi 327 D4
Palazzo Cenci 331 D1
Palazzo Chigi 327 E3
Palazzo Colonna 327 E4
Palazzo Corsini 330 C1
Palazzo d. Congregaz. 328 A4
Palazzo d. Consulta 328 A4
Palazzo d. Drago 328 A3
Palazzo d. Esami 331 C3
Palazzo d. Monte di Pietà
331 C1
Palazzo dei Conservatori
331 D1

Palazzo del Gov. Vecchio
327 C4
Palazzo del Quirinale
327 E4
Palazzo del Sant'Uffizio
326 B3
Palazzo della Borsa 327 E4
Palazzo della Cancelleria
327 D4
Palazzo delle Esposizioni
328 A4
Palazzo Falconieri 330 C1
Palazzo Farnese 331 C1
Palazzo Fiano 327 D3
Palazzo Giraud 326 B3
Palazzo Koch 328 A4
Palazzo Lateranense 332 C2
Palazzo Madama (Senato)
327 D4
Palazzo Margherita
(American Embassy)
328 A2
Palazzo Massimo 327 D4
Palazzo Massimo-Museo
Nazionale Romano 328 B3
Palazzo Mattei 331 D1
Palazzo Montecitorio 327 D3
Palazzo Odescalchi 327 E4
Palazzo Pallavicini
Rospigliosi 328 A4
Palazzo Pamphilj 327 D4
Palazzo Poli 327 E3
Palazzo Ruspoli 327 D3
Palazzo Sacchetti 326 C4
Palazzo Senatorio 331 E1
Palazzo Spada 331 C1
Palazzo Spagna 327 E3
Palazzo Taverna 327 C4
Palazzo Venezia 327 E4
Palazzo Vidoni 327 D4
Palermo, Via 328 A4
Palestrina, Via P. da 327 D2
Palestro, Via 328 B2–C3
Palladio, Via A. 332 C4
Palline, Via 326 B3
Pamphili, Via dei 330 A3
Pamphili, Viale di Villa
330 A3–A4
Pandosia, Via 332 C4
Panetteria, Via d. 327 E3
Panico, Via 327 C3–C4
Panisperna, Via 328 A4
Pannonia, L.go 332 B4
Pannonia, Via 332 B3
Pantheon 327 D4
Pantheon, Via del 327
D3–D4
Paola, Via 326 C3
Paolina, Via 328 B4
Paolo II, Via 326 A4
Paolucci, Via R. 330 A4
Paradiso, P.za del 331 C1
Parboni, Via 330 C4
Parigi, Via 328 B3
Parione, Via d. 327 D4
Parlamento, P.za 327 D3
Parma, Via 328 A4
Paruta, Via P. 333 D4
Pascarella, Via C. 330 C4
Pasquino P.za d. 327 D4
Passaglia, Via G. 326 A2
Passamonti, L.go 329 D4
Pastini, Via dei 327 D4
Pastrengo, Via 328 B3
Patrizi, Via di Villa 329 C2
Pavia, Via 329 D2
Pelasgi, Via 329 D4
Peligni, Via 329 D4

Pellegrino, Via dell 326 B3, 327 C4
Pellicia, Via 331 C2
Penitenza, Via della 330 B1
Penitenzieri, Via dei 326 B3
Penna, Via della 327 D2
Pepoli, Via di Villa 331 E4
Peretti, L.go di Villa 328 B3
Peri, Via J. 328 B1
Perosi, L.go L. 327 C4
Perugia, Via 333 E2
Peruzzi, Via B. 331 E4
Pesaro, Via 333 E2
Pescara, Via 333 E3
Petrarca, Via 332 C1
Pettinari, Via 331 C1
Pfeiffer, Via 326 B3
Pia, P.le Porta 328 B2
Pia, P.ta 328 B2
Piacenza, Via 328 A4
Piasani, Via V. 326 A2
Piatti, Via G. B. 333 D2
Piave, Via 328 B2
Piazza, Via C. B. 329 D1
Piccolomini, Via Ottavio 333 E1
Piceni, Via dei 329 D4
Piceno, Via A. 333 E2
Piemonte, Via 328 A2
Pierleoni, Lgt. D. 331 D2
Pietra, P.za di 327 D4
Pigneto, P.za del 333 E2
Pigneto, Via del 333 E2
Pigorini, Via L. 329 E1
Pilo, P.za Rosolino 330 B3
Pilotta, P.za 327 E4
Pinciana, Via 328 A2
Pinciana, Via 328 A1
Pinciana, Via Porta 327 E2
Pinerolo, Via 333 D3
Pio, Borgo 326 B3
Piramide di Caio Cestio 331 D4
Pisa, Via 329 E1
Pisacane, Via C. 330 B4
Pisanelli, Via G. 327 D1
Piscinula, P.za in 331 D2
Pistoia, Via 333 E3
Platone, Viale 326 A1
Plauto, Via 326 B3
Plebiscito, V. d. 327 E4
Plinio, Via 326 C2
Po, Via 328 B1
Poerio, Via Alessandro 330 B4
Polesine, Via 329 D2
Poli, Via 327 E3
Poliziano, Via A. 332 B2
Pollione, Via A. 331 D4
Polverone, Vicolo d. 331 C1
Poma, C. 326 B1
Pomezia, Via 333 E4
Pompe, Via 333 C4
Pompilio, P.le Numa 332 B4
Pomponazzi, Via P. 326 A2
Pontelli, Via B. 331 E4
Pontif. Ateneo Lateranense 332 C3
Ponziani, P.za dei 331 D2
Ponziano, Via 330 B4
Popolo, P.le del 327 D1
Popolo, P.za del 327 D2
Populonia, Via 332 C4
Pordenone, Via 333 D3
Porta S. Pancrazio (Museo Garibaldino) 330 B2
Porta, Via C. 330 C4
Portese, P.ta 331 C3

Portese, P.za Porta 331 C3
Porto di Ripa Grande 331 D3–D2
Porto, Via del 331 D2
Portoferraio, Via 333 D3
Portogruaro, Via 333 E3
Portuense, Lgt. 330 C4, 331 C3
Portuense, Via 330 C4, 331 C3
Portuensi, V. le d. M. 331 C3
Prati, Lgt. 327 D3
Prefetti, Via dei 327 D3
Premuda, Via 326 A1
Prenestina 333 E1
Prenestina, P.za 333 D1
Prenestina, Via 333 D1
Pretoriano, Viale 329 C4
Pretorio, Via Castro 328 C3
Pretorio, Viale C. 328 C2
Prisco, Via Tarq. 333 E4
Procida, Via G. da 329 E2–E1
Progresso, Via d. 331 D1
Propaganda Fide 327 E3
Properzio, Via 326 B3
Provincie, P.le delle 329 E2
Provincie, Viale delle 329 E2
Publicii, Clivo de 331 D2–E3
Puccini, Via 328 A1
Puglie, Via 328 B2
Pulci, Via Luigi 329 E1
Purificazione, Via 328 A3

Q
Quadrio, Via M. 330 B3
Quercia, P.za d. 331 C1
Quinto, P.za Cecilio 330 A4
Quirinale, P.za del 327 E4
Quirinale, Via del 328 A4
Quiriti, P.za dei 326 C2

R
R. Melis, Via P. 333 E2
Racchia, Via 326 B1
Radio Vaticana 326 A3
Ragusa, P.za 333 E3
Raimondi, Via P. 328 A1
Ramni, Via dei 329 C4
Ranocchia, Via della 329 E4
Rasella, Via 328 A3
Rattazzi, Via 328 B4
Ravenna, L.go 329 D1
Ravenna, Via 329 D1
Recina, Via 333 C4
Redi, Via F. 329 C1
Regnoli, Via O. 330 B3
Regolo, Via A. 326 C2
Remo, Via S. 333 E3
Remuria, P.za 331 E4
Renella, Via 331 C2
Repubblica, P.za della 328 B3
Reti, Via dei 329 D4
Revere, Via 330 B4
Riari, Via dei 330 B3
Riboty, Via A. 326 B1
Ricasoli, Via B. 328 C4
Ricci, L.go Corrado 331 E1
Ricciotti, Via N. 326 C1
Ricotti, Via di Villa 329 D1
Rienzo, P.za Cola di 327 C2
Rienzo, Via Cola di 326 B2
Rieti, Via 328 B1
Rimini, Via 333 D3
Rinascimento, Corso del 327 D4

Ripa, Lgt. 331 D2
Ripa, Via A. 328 B2
Ripari, Via P. 330 C4
Ripetta, P.za Porta 327 D3
Ripetta, Via di 327 D2–D3
Risorgimento, P.za del 326 B2
Rodi, Via 326 A1
Rogazionisti, Via d. 333 E3
Rolli, Via Ettore 330 C4
Roma, P.za dei Re di 333 D3
Romagna, Via 328 B2
Romagnosi, Via G. 327 D1
Romano, P.za Collegio 327 E4
Rosa, Via E. 331 E4
Rosazza, Via F. 330 C4
Rose, Casina d. 328 A2
Roselli, Via P. 330 B3
Rossa, P.za della Croce 328 C2
Roselli, Via Fra. 326 B1
Rossetti, Via G. 330 B3
Rossetti, Via R. 326 A1
Rossi, Via di Villa Massimo de 329 D1
Rosso, Via C. 328 C2
Rotonda, P.za d. 327 D4
Rotonda, Via d. 327 D4
Rotto, Ponte 331 D2
Rovere, P.za D. 326 B4
Roverella, Via B. 330 A1
Rovigo, Via 329 D2
Rubattino, Via 331 D2
Ruffin, Via J. 326 C1
Rutario, Clivo 330 A3–A4
Rutoli, Via dei 329 D4

S
S. A. dei Goti, V. di 332 A1
S. A. Magno, Via 331 D3
S. Agnese in Agone 327 D4
S. Agostino 327 D3
S. Alessio 331 D3
S. Alessio, Via 331 D3
S. Anastasia 331 E2
S. Andréa d. Fratte 327 E3
S. Andréa d. Valle 327 D4
S. Andréa della Valle, P.za 327 D4
S. Andréa 328 A3
S. Angelo, Ponte 327 C3
S. Anselmo 331 D3
S. Anselmo, P.za 331 D3
S. Anselmo, Via 331 D3
S. Antonio d. Portoghesi 327 D3
S. Antonio de Padova 332 C2
S. Balbina 331 E3
S. Bartolomeo all'Isola 331 D2
S. Basilio, Via d. 328 A3
S. Bernardo, P.za di 328 A3
S. Bibiana 329 C4
S. Calepodio, Via 330 A3–B4
S. Calisto 331 C2
S. Calisto, P.za 331 C2
S. Camillo 328 A2
S. Carlo ai Catinari 331 D1
S. Carlo al Corso 327 D3
S. Carlo alle Quattro Fontane 328 A3
S. Castulo, Via 333 E2
S. Cecilia 327 D2
S. Cecilia, Via 331 D2
S. Cesareo 332 B4
S. Claudio 327 E3
S. Clemente 332 B2

S. Clemente, P.za 332 B2
S. Cosimato, P.za 330 C2
S. Cosimato, Via di 331 C2
S. Crisogono 331 C2
S. Croce in Gerusalemme 333 D2
S. Croce in Gerusalemme, P.za di 333 D2
S. Croce in Gerusalemme, Via di 333 C1
S. Cuore 328 C3
S. d'Alando, Via 329 E1
S. de Saint Bon, Via 326 B1
S. di Lauro, P.za 327 C3
S. Domenico, Via 331 D3
S. Egidio, P.za di 330 C2
S. Eligio 327 C3
S. Erasmo, Via di. 332 B3
S. Eusebio 328 C4
S. Eustachio 327 D4
S. Eustachio, P.za 327 D4
S. F. di Sales, Via di 330 B1
S. Francesca Romana 331 E1
S. Francesco a Ripa 331 C3
S. Francesco a Ripa, Via di 331 C2
S. Francesco d'Assisi, P.za 331 C3
S. Francesco di Sales, Vic. di 330 B1
S. Giacomo 327 D2
S. Giacomo, Via 327 D2
S. Gioacchino 326 C2
S. Giorgio in Velabro 331 E2
S. Giosafat, Via 331 D3–E3
S. Giovanni d. Fiorentini 326 C4
S. Giovanni d. Malva, P.za 330 C1
S. Giovanni in Laterano, P.za 332 C2
S. Giovanni in Laterano, Via di 332 B2
S. Giovanni, P.ta 333 C3
S. Giovanni, P.za Porta 333 C2
S. Giuseppe 326 A1, 329 C1
S. Grandis, Via 333 D2
S. Gregorio Magno 331 E2
S. Gregorio VII 326 A4
S. Gregorio, Via di 331 E2
S. Ignazio 327 E4
S. Ippolito 329 C2
S. Ippolito, Via d. 329 E2
S. Isodoro 327 E3
S. Ivo 327 D4
S. Lorenzo in Lucina 327 D3
S. Lorenzo 329 D4
S. Lorenzo, P.te 329 D3
S. Lorenzo, P.za di P.ta 329 C4
S. Lorenzo, Via d. Scalo 333 D1
S. Lorenzo, Via di Porta di 329 C4
S. Lucio, Via 330 A2
S. Luigi d. Francesi 327 D4
S. M. ai Monti, Via 328 B4
S. M. in Cappella, Via 331 D2
S. M. Liberatrice, P.za 331 D4
S. M. Maggiore, Via di 328 B4
S. Macuto 327 E4
S. Mancini, Via P. 327 D1
S. Marcellino 332 C2

S. Marcello 327 E4
S. Marco 327 E4
S. Maria alle Fornaci 326 B4
S. Maria alle Fornaci, P.za di 326 B4
S. Maria Ausiliatrice 329 D4
S. Maria d. Angeli 328 B3
S. Maria d. Anima 327 D4
S. Maria d. Grazie 326 A2
S. Maria d. Grazie, P.za di 326 A2
S. Maria d. Monserrato 327 C4
S. Maria d. Orto 333 E3
S. Maria d. Pace 327 D4
S. Maria d. Popolo 327 D2
S. Maria d. Priorato di Malta 331 D3
S. Maria d. Prov. 330 A4
S. Maria d. Scala 330 C2
S. Maria d. Vittoria 328 B3
S. Maria dei Mirac. 327 D2
S. Maria del Carmine 326 C3
S. Maria della Concezione 328 A3
S. Maria in Aracoeli 331 E1
S. Maria in Cosmedin 331 D2
S. Maria in Domnica 332 B3
S. Maria in Montesanto 327 D2
S. Maria in Traspontina 326 C3
S. Maria in Trast., P.za 331 C2
S. Maria in Trastevere 331 C2
S. Maria in Via 327 E3
S. Maria Liberatrice 331 D4
S. Maria Maggiore 328 B4
S. Maria Maggiore, P.za 328 B4
S. Maria Mediatrice 326 A3
S. Maria Mediatrice, Via di 326 A4
S. Maria Regina Pacis 330 B3
S. Maria s. Minerva 327 D4
S. Martin, P.za le Jose di 327 E1
S. Martino ai Monti 332 B1
S. Martino d. B., Via 328 C3
S. Massimo, Via 328 B2
S. Melania, Via di 331 D3
S. Michele 326 B3
S. Michele, Via di 331 D3
S. N. da Tolentino, Via 328 A3
S. Nerco e Achilleo 332 B3
S. Nicola in Carcere 331 D1
S. Onofrio 326 B4
S. Onofrio, Sal. di 326 B4
S. Onofrio, Vic. di 326 B4
S. Orsola 329 E1
S. Orsola, Via 329 E1
S. P. della Croce, Via 332 A2
S. Pancrazio 330 B2
S. Pancrazio, P.ta di 330 B2
S. Pancrazio, Via di P.ta 330 B2
S. Paolo a. Reg., Via di 331 C1
S. Paolo de Brasile, Viale 327 E2
S. Paolo, P.ta 331 D4

S. Paolo, P.za Porta 331 D4
S. Pellico, Via 326 B1
S. Pietro in Montorio 330 B2
S. Pietro in Montorio, P.za 330 C2
S. Pietro in Vincoli, P.za 332 A1
S. Pietro, Via Stazione di 326 B4
S. Porcari, Via 326 B3
S. Prassede 328 B4
S. Prisca 331 E3
S. Prisca, P.za 331 E3
S. Prisca, Via di 331 E3
S. Prudenzia 328 B4
S. Quintino, Via 333 C2
S. Rocco 327 D3
S. Saba 331 E4
S. Saba, Via di 331 E3
S. Sabina 331 D3
S. Sabina, Via di 331 D3
S. Salvatore 327 C3
S. Sebastiano, Via di Porta 332 B4
S. Silverio, Via 330 A1
S. Silvestro 327 E3, E4
S. Silvestro V, P.za 327 E3
S. Simeone 327 D3
S. Sisto Vecchio 332 B3
S. Sonnino, P.za 331 C2
S. Spirito in Sassia 326 B3
S. Spirito, Borgo 326 B3
S. Spirito, P.ta 326 B4
S. Sprovieri, Via F. 330 B3
S. Stefano Rotondo 332 B3
S. Stefano Rotondo, Via di 332 B2
S. Susanna 328 A3
S. Susanna, L.go di 328 A3
S. Teodoro 331 E2
S. Teodoro, Via 331 E2
S. Teresa 328 B2
S. Teresa, Via d. 328 B2
S. Tommaso d'Aquino, Via 326 A2
S. Vecchia, Via d. 331 E1
S. Veniero, Via 326 A2
S. Vincenzo d. Paoli 327 C2
S. Vincenzo Pallotti, P.za 331 C1
S. Vitale 328 A4
S. Vito, Via 328 B4
S. Vittore, Via 330 A4
Sabelli, Via dei 329 D4
Sabotino, Via 326 B1
Sacchi, Via G. 330 C2
Saffi, Viale Aurelio 330 B3–C3
Salandra, Via A. 328 B2
Salaria, P.ta 328 B2
Salaria, Via 328 B1
Salentini, Via d. 329 D4
Salento, Via 329 E1
Salerno, P.za 329 D2
Saliceto, Via G. 329 C2
Sallustiana, Via 328 B2
Sallustio, P.za 328 B2
Salumi, Via dei 331 D2
Saluzzo, Via 333 D4
Salvi, Via N. 332 A1–B1
San Lorenzo fuori le Mura 329 E3
San Pietro in Vincoli 332 A1
San Pietro, P.za 326 B3
Sanatoria il Tivoli 326 A2
Sangallo, Lgt. 326 C4
Sannio, Via 333 C3

Sanniti, P.za dei 329 D4
Santamaura, Via 326 A2
Sant'Angelo, Borgo 326 B3–C3
Santo Eugenio, Via di 327 D1
Santo, Via Monte 326 B1
Sanzio, Lgt. del R. 331 C2
Sardegna, Via 328 A2
Sardi, Via dei 329 D4
Sassari, P.za 329 D2
Sassia, Lgt. in 326 C3
Saturnia, Via 332 C4
Sauro, Via N. 326 A1
Savello, P.za Monte 331 D2
Savoia, Via di Ludovico 333 C2
Savoia, Via F. di 327 D2
Savoia, Via L. di 327 D2
Savoia, Via 328 B1–C1
Savona, Via 333 E3
Savonarola, Gir. 326 A2
Scala, Via d. 330 C1
Scarpa, Via A. 329 D2
Scauro, Clivo di 332 A2
Schiavoni, L.go 327 D3
Scialoia, Via d. 327 D1
Scienze, Viale d. 329 D3
Scipioni, Via degli 326 B2
Scrofa, Via della 327 D3
Scuderie del Quirinale 327 E4
Sebastiano, Via E. 330 A4
Sebeto, Via 328 B1
Segneri, Via P. 330 B4
Selci, Via in 332 B1
Sella, Via O. 328 B2
Seminario 327 D4–E4
Sepolcro d. Scipioni 332 B4
Sermide, Via 333 D3
Serpenti, Via dei 328 A4
Serra, Via L. 331 C3
Servili, P.za 331 D4
Sesia, Via 328 B1
Sessoriana, Via 333 D2
Settembre, Via XX 328 B2
Settembrini, Via L. 327 C1
Severano, Via G. 329 D1
Sforzesca, Via d. 329 C3
Sibari, Via 332 C3
Sicilia, P.za Ruggero di 329 E1
Sicilia, Via 328 A2–B2
Siciliani, P.za Vespri 329 E1
Siculi, P.za 329 D4
Siena, P.za di 327 E1
Silla, Via 326 B2
Silveri, Via D. 326 B4
Simeto, Via 328 B1
Sinuessa, Via 333 C4
Siracusa, Via 329 D2
Siria, Via 333 D4
Sistina, Via 327 E3
Sisto V, P.le 329 C4
Sisto, Ponte 331 C1
Sivori, Via F. 326 A3
Soana, Via 333 D4
Socrate, P.za le 326 A1
Solunto, Via 333 D4
Sommeiller, Via G. 333 D2
Sondrio, Via 333 E2
Sopraelevata 333 D1–E1
Sora, Via 327 C4
Spagna, P.za di 327 E2
Spallanzani, Via Lazzaro 329 C1
Speri, Via T. 326 C1
Spezia, Via La 333 D2

Spoleto, Via 333 E3
Sportivi 326 A4
Squarcialupo, Via Fr. 329 E1
SS. Apostoli 327 E4
SS. Apostoli, P.za dei 327 E4
SS. Domenicani e Sisto 328 A4
SS. F. e Venanzio, Via 333 E3
SS. Fabiano 333 E3
SS. Giovanni e Paolo 332 A2
SS. Immacolata 333 D1, D3
SS. Luca e Martina 331 E1
SS. Quattro Coronati 332 B2
SS. Quattro 332 B2
SS. Redent. 328 B2
SS. Rosario 326 B2
SS. Trinità dei Monti 327 E2
Stamira, Via 329 E1
Statilia, Via 333 C2
Statuto, Via 332 B1
Stazione Flaminio 327 D1
Stazione Laziali 329 C4
Stazione Roma–Termini 328 B3
Stazione Roma-Tuscolana F.S. 333 E4
Stazione S. Pietro 326 B4
Stazione Vaticana 326 A3
Sterbini, Via P. 330 B3
Storza, Via 328 B4
Strozzi, P.za Prati degli 326 B1
Sublicio, Ponte 331 D3
Sudario, Via del 327 D4
Suessola, Via 333 D4
Sulmona, P.za 333 D3
Susa, Via 333 D4

T

Tacito, Via 327 C2
Talamo, L.go E. 333 D1
Talentino, V. lo 328 A3
Taranto, Via 333 D3
Tarquinia, P.za 333 C3
Tasso, Via Torquato 332 C1
Taurini, Via di 329 D4
Tazzoli, Via E. 326 C1
Teatro Adriano 327 C2
Teatro Argentina 327 D4
Teatro delle Arti 328 A2
Teatro dell'Opera 328 B3
Teatro di Marcello 331 D1
Teatro di Pompeo 327 D4
Teatro Valle 327 D4
Tebaldi, Lgt. dei 330 C1
Telesio, Via B. 326 A2
Tempio d. Diana 327 E1
Tempio d. Esculapio 327 E1
Tempio di Fortuna Virile 331 D2
Tempio di Venere e Roma 331 E1
Tempio di Vesta 331 D2
Teramo, Via 333 E2
Terme di Caracalla 332 A4
Terme di Diocleziano, Via d. 328 B3
Terme di Diocleziano-Museo Nazionale Romano 328 B3
Terme di Traiano 332 B1
Terme Severare 331 E2
Terni, Via 333 D3
Testaccio, Lgt. 331 C4
Testaccio, P.le Ponte 330 C4
Testaccio, P.za 331 D4
Testaccio, Ponte 331 C4

Testaccio, Via Monte 331 D4
Tevere, Via 328 B1
Tibullo, Via 326 B3
Tiburtina, Via 329 E3–E2
Tiburtino, Viale di Porta 329 C4
Tiburtino, P.le 329 D4
Tirso, Via 328 B1
Tito, Via delle T. di 332 A1
Tizi, Via d. 329 D4
Toja, L.go A. 330 C4
Tola, Via P. 333 D4
Tolemaide, Via 326 B2
Tomacelli, Via 327 D3
Tomassetti, Via 329 D1
Torino, Via 328 B4
Torlonia, Via Alessandro 329 D1
Torre d. Molette 331 E3
Torre dell Drago 330 A1
Torre, Via d. F. 330 B3
Torricelli, Via 331 C4
Torto, Viale del Muro 327 E2
Tortona, Via 333 D4
Toscana, Via 328 A2
Tracia 332 B3
Traforo, V. del 327 E3
Traiana, Col. 331 E1
Traiano, Via T. di 332 B1
Trapani, Via 329 D2
Trastevere, Via d. O. di 331 C3
Trastevere, Viale di 330 C4, 331 C2
Traversari, Via A. 330 B4
Trento, P.za 328 C1
Treviso, Via 329 D2
Triboniano, Via 327 C3
Tribunali, P.za 327 C3
Trilussa, P.za 331 C1
Trionfale, L.go 326 B2
Trionfale, Via 326 A1
Tritone, Via del 327 E3
Tunisi, Via 326 A2
Turati, Via Filippo 329 C4
Turchi, Via L. 330 C4
Tuscolana, Via della Staz. 333 E3
Tuscolana, Via 333 E4
Tuscolo, P.za 333 C3

U

Uccelliera, Viale dell' 328 A1
Udine, Via 333 D2
Ugone, Via A. 330 A4
Ulpiano, Via 327 D3
Umberto, P.za 327 D3
Umberto, Ponte 327 D3
Umberto, Via P. 333 C1
Umilta, Via dell' 327 E4
Unità, Piazza dell' 326 B2
Universita, Viale dell' 329 D3
Urbana, Via 328 B4
Urbaniana, Pont. Univ 326 B4
Urbino, Via 333 D3
Urbisaglia, Via 332 C4

V

Valadier, Via 327 C2
Valenziani, Via A. 328 B2
Vallati, Lgt. dei 331 C1
Vantaggio, Via del 327 D2
Vanvitelli, Via 331 C2
Varese, Via 328 C3
Varisco, Via Bern. 326 A1

Vascello, Via del 330 B3
Vaticano, Viale 326 A3–A2
Vecchi, Via Banchi 327 C4
Vecchio, Via d. Governo 327 C4–D4
Veio, Via 333 C3
Veneto, Via Vitt. 328 A2
Venezia, P.za 327 E4
Venti, P.le Quattro 330 B4
Venti, Viale de Quattro 330 B4–B3
Venticinque, Via G. 326 C2
Verano, P.le del 329 D3
Verano, Viadel 329 E4
Verbania, Via 333 E4
Vercelli, L.go 333 D3
Vercelli, Via 333 D3
Verde, Via Conte 332 C1
Vergini, Via della 327 E4
Verona, Via 329 D2
Versilia, Via 328 A3
Vesalio, Via A. 329 C2
Vescia, Via 333 C4
Vespasiana, Via 326 B2
Vespucci, Via A. 331 C4
Vetulonia, Via 332 C4
Vibenna, Via C. 332 A2
Vicariato di Roma 330 C2
Vicario, Via d. U. d. 327 D3
Vicario, Vicolo del 330 A1
Vicenza, Via 328 C3
Vico, Via B. 330 A3
Vigliena, Via 327 C1
Vigoni, Via 331 E4
Villa Aldobrandini 328 A4
Villa Altieri 332 C1
Villa Farnesina 330 C1
Villa Lante 330 B3
Villa Lovatti 330 A1
Villa Medici 327 E2
Villa Ruffo 327 D1
Villa Sciarra 330 B3
Villari, Via 332 B2
Villini, Via dei 329 C2
Viminale, P.za del 328 B4
Viminale, Via del 328 B4
Vincenzo de Paoli 331 D2
Virgilio, Via 326 C2
Visconti, Via Ennio O. 327 C2
Vite, Via della 327 E3
Vitelleschi, Via G. 326 B3
Vitellia, Via 330 A3
Vitetti, L.go 330 A3
Vittoria, Via 327 D2
Vittorio, Borgo 326 B3
Voghera, Via 333 D2
Volsci, Via dei 329 D4
Volta, Via A. 331 D4
Volterra, Via 333 E3
Volturno, Via 328 B3
Vulci, Via 332 C4

W–Z

Washington, Viale 327 D1
Wern, Viale 330 B3
Wurts, P.le 330 B3
Zabaglia, Via Nicola 331 D4
Zama, P.za 333 C4
Zanardelli, Via 327 D3
Zingari, P.za 328 A4
Zingari, Via degli 328 A4
Zoccolette, Via d. 331 C1
Zoologico, P.le del Giardino 328 A1
Zoologico, Viale del Giardino 327 E1

GENERAL INDEX

A page reference in **bold**
indicates the main entry
in the book.

A

Abbazia di San Nilo
(Grottaferrata) 267–8
Abbazia delle Tre
Fontane 216
Accademia Britannica
191
Accademia di San Luca
118
accommodation 13,
288–97
admission charges 310
Adrian VI 160
Agro Romano 59
air travel 282
Alban Hills 265, 268
Albano Laziale 269
Aldobrandini family 266
Alexander VI 33, 146–7,
171
Alexander VII 127, 137,
140
Anfiteatro Castrense 234
Anguillara 278
Anzio 254
aperitivi 64
Apolodorus of Damascus
49
Appian Way see Via
Appia Antica
Ara Pacis 23, 60, **133**
Archaeological Area of
Veio 274
Archeobus 241
Arco di Constantino 50,
112
Arco di Dolabella 226
Arco di Settimio Severo
103
Arco di Tito 108
Area Sacra 172, **173**
Arricia 269
art and architecture 25,
47–61
ancient 48–50
baroque 35, **52–5**
fascist 37, **58**, 196, **216**

modern 60–1
Renaissance 33, 34,
50–2
art galleries see museums
and galleries
arts, performing 23–4,
303–6
Auditorio di Mecenate
232
Auditorium-Parco della
Musica 24, 60, 61,
196, **304**
Augustus 23, 28, **30**, 48,
99, 110, 125, 133,
157, 175, 180, 251
Aula Ottagona 233
Aventino 211–14

B

Badoglio, Marshal 38
baldacchino (San Pietro)
139, 140, 154, 160
ballet 304
barbarians 32
Barberini family 51, 122,
140, 142, 160, 275
Basilica Aemilia 102
Basilica Cristiana (Ostia)
253
Basilica di Massenzio e
Constantino 107
Basilica di San Pietro 10,
24, 51, 54, **138–41**
Basilica Giulia 105
Baths see Terme
Battistero Lateranense
222
beaches 11, **254**
bed & breakfast 288
Belli, G.G. 204
Benedict XVI 24, 39
Berlunconi, Silvio **39**, 45
Bernini, Gianlorenzo 53,
54–5, 120, 121, 126,
130, 155, 230, 234,
269
Blessed Ludovica
Albertoni 204
Ecstasy of St Teresa 10,
122, 187
Fontana dei Quattro
Fiumi 9, **159**
Ponte Sant'Angelo 143,
165

Vatican 11, 137, 139,
140, 154, 160
Biagiotti, Laura 73, **132**
bicycle hire 241, **287**
Bilotti, Carlo 23, 188–9
boat trips 178, 286
Bocca della Verità 180
Borghese family 36, 51,
188, 193, 198–9
Borghetto Flaminio 25,
75
Borgia, Cesare 33
Borgo 144
Borgo Santo Spirito 144
Borromini 53, 54, **55**,
120, 121, 176, 178,
179, 222
Bramante, Donato 102,
126, 138, 170
Tempietto 51, **206**, 207
breakdown services 287
Bruno, Giordano 170,
171
buses 20, 70, 241, **285**
tours 284
Byron, Lord 94, 114,
130, 131, 214

C

Caesar, Julius 29–30, 48,
98–9, 103, 106, 162,
169, 172
Caffè Capitolino 10
Caligula 30, 270
Campo de' Fiori 9, 72,
74–5, **170–1**
Campus Martius 48,
151, 169
Canopus (Villa Adriana)
261
Capanna di Romolo 109
Capitoline Hill 87–95
Capitolium Curia (Ostia)
253
Capocotta 254
Capucci, Roberto 132
Capuchin friars 186, 187
car hire 285
Caracalla 103
Caravaggio 10, **52**, 93,
126, 157–8
Carcere Mamertino 90
Carcere Regina Coeli
204

Carceri Nuove 178
Casa del Cinema 189
Casa di Livia **109**, 233
Casa di Diana (Ostia)
253–5
Casa di Goethe 128
Casa di Lorenzo Manilo
175
Casale Rotondo 243
Casina delle Civette 195
Casina Valadier 189
Casino dell'Aurora 187
Casino Borghese 193,
199
Castel Gandolfo 269
Castel Sant'Angelo 10,
11, **143**
Castelli Romani 265–71
Castello di Giulio II 255
Castello Orsini 277, 278
Castello di Vignanello
263
catacombe 12, **241–2**,
244–5
di Domitilla **242**, 245
di Priscilla **193**, 245
di San Callisto **241**,
244, 245
di San Pancazio 207
di San Sebastiano **242**,
245
Santa Maria delle
Concezione 186, **187**
Sant'Agnese fuori le
Mura **195**, 245
Catedrale di San Lorenzo
(Viterbo) 279
cats 12, **172**
Cattedra di San Pietro
140
Celio Hill 225–6
Cenci, Beatrice 175–6
Centro Storico 151–83
Cerveteri 11, 276–7
Charlemagne 32
Charles V 34, 89, 157
chemists 314
Chigi, Agostino 34, 126,
205–6
children 11, **306**
Christianity 31–2
churches
Basilica di San Pietro
10, 24, 51, 54,
138–41

Basilica di Santa Maria ad Martyres 9, **154**
Catedrale di San Lorenzo (Viterbo) 279
Chiesa di Dio Padre Misericordioso 60, **235**
Chiesa Nuova 53, **164**
Chigi Chapel 126
Domine Quo Vadis 241
Gesù 53, **173**
Jubilee Church 60, **235**
Madonna del Rosario (Marino) 269
Oratorio dei Filippini 164
San Bartolomeo 179
San Carlino 121
San Carlo alle Quattro Fontane 55, **120–1**
San Clemente 224–5
San Crisogono 204
San Filippo 178
San Francesco a Ripa 204
San Giovanni dei Fiorentini 121, **178–9**
San Giovanni in Laterano 24, 52, 102, **221–3**
San Gregorio Magno 227
San Lorenzo in Damaso 170
San Lorenzo fuori le Mura 235
San Lorenzo in Lucina 128
San Luigi dei Francesi 10, 157–8
San Marcello al Corso 129
San Marco 91
San Martino ai Monti 232
San Pancrazio 207
San Paolo fuori le Mura 218
San Pietro in Montorio 207
San Pietro in Vincoli 10, **231**
San Saba 213
San Tommaso in Formis 226
San Vitale 122
Santa Bibiana 234
Santa Cecilia in Trastevere 204–5
Santa Costanzia 195
Santa Croce in Gerusalemme 52, **234**

Santa Francesca Romana 108
Santa Maria degli Angeli 232
Santa Maria dell'Anima 161
Santa Maria Antiqua 106
Santa Maria in Aracoeli 88–9
Santa Maria della Cima (Genzano) 270
Santa Maria della Concezione **185–6**, 187
Santa Maria in Cosmedin 180
Santa Maria in Domnica 226
Santa Maria di Grottaferrata 268
Santa Maria Maggiore 52, **230**
Santa Maria dell' Orazione e Morte 178
Santa Maria della Pace 52, **161**
Santa Maria del Popolo 10, 52, **125–6**
Santa Maria sopra Minerva 54, 55, **155**
Santa Maria in Trastevere 10, **202–3**
Santa Maria della Verità (Viterbo) 279
Santa Maria in Via Lata 128–9
Santa Maria della Vittoria 10, 55, 122, **187**
Santa Prassede 10, 230
Santa Prisca 213
Santa Pudenziana 231
Santa Sabina 211–12
Sant'Agnese in Agone 55, **159**
Sant'Agnese fuori le Mura 195
Sant'Alessio 212
Sant'Andrea al Quirinale 54, 120
Sant'Andrea della Valle 172
Sant'Angelo in Pescheria 175
Sant'Eligio degli Orefici 178
Santi Cosma e Damiano 107

Santi Giovanni e Paolo 103, **226–7**
Santi Nereo e Achilleo 52
Santi Quattro Coronati 223–4
Sant'Ignazio 53, **155**
Sant'Ivo 162
Santo Spirito in Sassia 144
Santo Stefano Rotondo 52, 225–6
Sistine Chapel 8, 34, 141, **142**, **148–9**
Tempietto 51, **206**, 207
Trinità dei Monti 57, **129**
Cinecittà 44–5
cinema 24, 25, 38, **44–5**, **306**
Circo di Massenzio 242
Circo Massimo 110–11, 125
Città del Gusto 60
Città Universitaria 58, **235**
classical music 24, 304
Claudius 251
Clement VII 34, 51, 155, 157
climate 311
Cloaca Maxima 100, **102**
Colonna Decennalia 105
Colonna family 123, 275
Colonna di Foca 104
Colonna di Marco Aurelio 128
Colonna Traiana 100
Colosseum 8, 49, **111–12**, **114–15**
Constantine the Great 31, 112, 139, 142, 196, 221, 224, 251
Colossus of Constantine 92–3, 107
Constantius II 158
Corso Italia (Viterbo) 279
Corso Vittorio Emanuele II 59, 165, **169**, 172
Counter-Reformation 34–5, 52–3
credit cards 315
crime 311–12
Crypta Balbi 25, 161, **173**
Curia 102
Curia Pompeia 172
customs regulations 312
cycling 241, 287

D

de Sica, Vittorio 38, 44
Decumanus Maximus (Ostia) 253
Diocletian 31, 105
disabled travellers 312
Dome, Pantheon 154
Dome, San Pietro 140–1
Domine Quo Vadis 241
Domitian 49, 104, 109, 114, 158, 159
Domus Augustana 110
Domus Aurea 30, 49, **112–13**
Domus Flavia 109–10
Domus, Roman 103
dress code 311
driving 286–7

E

electricity 312
embassies & consulates 312–13
emergency numbers 313
English ghetto 130–1
ES Hotel 61
Esquilino 229, **232–7**
d'Este, Cardinal Ippolito 257–8
Etruscans 11, 27, 28, 192
Cities for the Dead 277
Etruscan towns 273–9
EUR 11, 20, 58, 60, **216**
European Union 38
events *see* festivals and events
Excelsior hotel 187

F

Farnese family 51, 109, 172, 173, 177
fascism 37–8, 58, 175, 216
fashion 69–71, 73, 131, **132**, **299–301**
Fellini, Federico 20, 25, 38, 44, 45, 122, 185
Fendi 12, 73, **132**
festivals and events 306–8
Christmas 159, 308
Cinema Festival 24
Easter week 12, **24**, **307**
Estate Romana 12, 13, 25, 303, 307, **309**

Frascati 266
Infiorata (Genzano) 270
International Literature Festival 309
International Photography Festival 12, **309**
Il Natale di Roma 12, 27, 307
Notte Bianche 22, 307
RomaEuropa 12, 218, **309**
Settimana della Cultura 13, 307
strawberry festival (Nemi) 270
Fontana 132
Fontana, Domenico 221, 222
food and drink 13, 37, **63–7**
menu decoder 320–1
football 308
Fori Imperiali 97, **98–100**
Foro di Augusto 99
Foro di Cesare 97, **98–9**
Foro Italico 58, **196**
Foro (Ostia Antica) 253
Foro Romano 8, **48**, **100–8**
Foro di Traiano 49, **99**
Fosse Ardeatine 241
fountains
dell'Acqua Paola 207
delle Api 122
of Fauns 191
Mascherone 177
del Moro 55, **159**
del Nettuno 159
dei Quattro Fiumi 9, **159**
delle Tartarughe 174
di Trevi 9, 11, 57, **117**
del Tritone 122, 185
Villa d'Este (Tivoli) 257–9
Frascati 57, **265–7**
Fregene 11, **254**
Fuksas, Massimiliano 60

G

Galopatoio 189
Garbatella 59, 217–18
Garibaldi, Giuseppe 36, 37, 207
gay & lesbian travellers 313
Genzano 270
Ghetto 169, **174–5**
Gianicolo 10, **206–7**

giardino see **parks and gardens**
Gibbon, Edward 36
Gibson, Mel 45
gladiators 111–12, 114–15
Globe Theatre Roma 25
Goethe 36, 47, 94, 127, **128**, 214
Grand Tour 36, **130**
Great Schism 33
Gregory the Great 32
Gregory VII 33
Grottaferrata 267–8
gyms 308

H

Hadid, Zaha 23, 60, 61, 196
Hadrian 21, 31, 143, 154, 165, 260–1
Hawthorne, Nathaniel 94, 117
health 313–14
Henry IV 33
history 27–43
Holy Roman Empire 32–4
hotels 13, **288–97**
House of the Vestal Virgins 106

I

ice cream 12, **66**
Imperial Fora see **Fori Imperiali**
Innocent X 159
internet access 314
Isola Tiberina 179

J

Jesuits 35, 53, 173
Jewish Ghetto see **Ghetto**
John Paul II 21, 38, 39, 175
Julius II 34, 51, 138, 142, 148, 177, 231, 255
Justinian 32

K

Keats, John 36, 125, 214
Keats-Shelley House 130–1
Knights of Malta 212–13
Koolhaas, Rem 60, 217

L

Lacus Juturnae 105
Lago di Albano 269
Lago di Bracciano 263, **278**
Lago di Nemi 270
language 318–22
Lapis Niger 102–3
Largo di Torre Argentina 172–3
Laterano 221–5
law, Roman 28
Lazio
beaches 11, **254**
Etruscan Towns 273–9
parks and gardens 262–3
Leo I 32
Leo III 32
Leo IV 142, 144
Leo X 35, 51, 155, 157
Lido di Ostia 254
Livy 27–8, 30, 92
Loggia della Benedizione (Castel Gandolfo) 269
lost property 314
Ludovisi, Cardinal 161
Ludus Magnus 111–12
Luneur 11, **216**
Lungotevere 59

M

Machiavelli 33
Maderno, Carlo 121, 139, 172, 178, 179, 187, 205, 266, 269
magazines 314
Magnani, Anna 44
Manilo, Lorenzo 175
maps 314
Marcus Aurelius 21, 31, 89, 92, 95, 128
Marinetti, Filippo 37
Marino 269
Marius 29, 274
markets **74–5**, 144, 205, 217
Mattatoio 215, 217
Mattiolo, Gai 132
Mausoleo di Augusto 133
Mausoleo di Romolo 242
Maxentius 47, 105, 107, 112, 196, 242
Mazzini, Giuseppe 36
Mazzoni, Angiolo 58, 233
medical services 313–14

Medici family 51, 138, 142, 155, 157, 191
Meier, Richard 60, 133, 235
menu decoder 320–1
Mercati Generali 217
Mercati di Traiano 99–100
Metro 286
Michelangelo 51, 95, 155, 177
Basilica di San Pietro 138–9
Campidoglio 89
Moses 10, 231
Pietà 10, **139**
Sistine Chapel 8, 34, 142, **148–9**
Miliarum Aureum 103
Mithras 224, 225
money 315
money-saving tips 13
Monte Cavo 268–9
Monte Testaccio 215
Monteverde Vecchio 207
Monti 229–31
mopeds 287
Moravia, Alberto 21, 47
Moretti, Nanni 45
Mosque 194
museums and galleries **304**
Ara Pacis Museum 23, 60, **133**
Carlo Bilotti Museum 23, **188–9**
Casa di Goethe 128
Centrale Montemartini 61, **217**
Children's Museum 11
Criminology Museum 178
Crypta Balbi Museum 173
Etruscan Museum (Vatican) **146**, 279
Galleria dell'Accademia di San Luca 118
Galleria Borghese 55, **192–3**, **198–9**
Galleria Doria Pamphilj 129, **156**
Galleria Nazionale d'Arte Antica 23, **121–2**, **206**
Galleria Nazionale d'Arte Moderna 191
Galleria Spada 176
Keats-Shelley House 130–1

MACRO 24, 61, **194**, **217**
MACRO al Mattatoio 217
MAXXI 23, 60, 61, **196**
Musei Capitolini 8, **89**, **92–5**
Museo dell'Alto Medioevo 216
Museo d'Arte Contemporanea di Roma 24, 61, **194**, **217**
Museo Barracco 23, **171–2**
Museo Civico (Viterbo) 279
Museo della Civiltà Romana 216
Museo Etrusco di Villa Giulia **192**
Museo Henrik Christian Andersen 191
Museo delle Mura 239, **240–1**
Museo Napoleonico 165
Museo delle Navi Romane (Nemi) 270
Museo Nazionale Archeologica di Palestrina 275–6
Museo Nazionale d'Arte Orientale 231–2
Museo Nazionale delle Arti del XXI Secolo 23, 60, 61, **196**
Museo Nazionale delle Arti Tradizioni Popolari 216
Museo Nazionale Cerite (Cerveteri) 277
Museo Nazionale delle Paste Alimentari 67, **118–19**
Museo Nazionale Preistorico-Etnografico Luigi-Pigorini 216
Museo Nazionale Romano 161, 173, 232, 233
Museo Nazionale degli Strumenti Musicali 234
Museo Nazionale Tarquinense (Tarquinia) 278
Museo Palatino 110
Museo di Palazzo Venezia 91
Museo Pio-Clementino (Vatican) 146, 147

Museo del Risorgimento 91
Museo di Roma 163
Museo di Roma in Trastevere 203
Museo Storico Nazionale dell'Arte 144
Museum of Jewish Culture 175
Ostia Antica 255
Palazzo Colonna 122, **123**
Scuderie del Quirinale 119–20
Tusculano Museum (Frascati) 267
Vatican Museums 8, **141–2**, **146–9**
music 24, **304**, **305–6**
Mussolini, Benito 37–8, 44, **58**, 91, 97, 137, 144, 162, 195, 196, 207, 216

N

Napoleon 35–6, 165, 191, 198
Napoleon III 36
Necropoli della Banditaccia 276–7
Necropoli dei Monterozzi (Tarquinia) 277–8
Nemi 270
Neri, St Filippo 53, 164
Nero 24, 31, 97, 108, 126, 226
Golden House **30**, 49, **112–13**
Nettuno 254
newspapers 314
Nicholas V 51
nightlife 22–3, **304–6**
Ninfa 11, **263**, 270

O

obelisks 52, 128
elephant 150, 154, 155
Palazzo di Montecitorio 157
Piazza Navonna 159
Piazza del Popolo 125
Piazza di San Giovanni 223
Piazza San Pietro 137
Santa Maria Maggiore 121

opening hours 311
museums and galleries 304
shops 70
opera 304
Oppio 231–2
Ospedale Santo Spirito 144
Ostia 255
Ostia Antica 11, 251–5
Ostiense 217
Ozpetek, Ferzan 45

P

palaces see **palazzi**
Palatine Hill 48, **108–10**
palazzi
Altemps 161–2
Banco di Santo Spirito 165
Barberini 52, 53, 54, **121–2**
Borsa 157
Braschi 163
Cancelleria 169–70
Cenci 175–6
Chigi 127
Chigi (Arriccia) 269
Civiltà del Lavoro 58, **216**
Colonna 122, **123**
Colonna-Barberini (Palestrina) 275
Conservatori 89, 90, **92–3**
Consulta 120
Corsini 206
Doria Pamphilj 52, 53, **159–61**
Esposizioni 122
Falconieri 178
Farnese 172, 176, **177**
Giustizia 144
Governo Vecchio 165
Koch 122
Lateranense 221, 223
Madama 157
Margherita 187
Massimo alle Colonne 163–4
Massimo alle Terme 161, **233**
Mattei 174
Monte di Pietà 176
Montecitorio 53, 57, 127, **156–7**
Nuovo 94–5

Papale (Castel Gandolfo) 269
Papale (Viterbo) 278–9
Pupazzi 169
Quirinale 61, **119**
Sapienza 162
Senatorio 89
Spada 176
Venezia 91
Palestrina 274–6
Pamphilj family 51, 129, 159
Pantheon 9, 21, 25, 151, **154**, 160
papacy 32–6, 53, 160, 221, 269
Palazzo Lateranense 221, 223
Palazzo Papale (Castel Gandolfo) 269
Palazzo Papale (Viterbo) 278–9
papal audiences 139, 316
papal insignia 142
Vatican City 137–49
parks and gardens
Castello di Vignanello 263
Giardini della Landriana 262
Giardino del Lago 191
Giardino Zoologico 192
Horti Sallustiani 186–7
Lazio **262–3**
Luneur 11, **216**
Oasi di Ninfa 11, **263**, 270
Oasi di Porto 263
Orte Farnesiani 108
Orto Botanico 206
Parco del Celio 225
Parco Savello 211
Parco degli Scipioni 239
Parco di Veio 274
Parco di Villa Gregoriana (Tivoli) 259
Pincio Gardens 10, **189–91**
San Liberato 263
Vatican Gardens 140, 141
Villa Borghese Gardens 9, 11, 25, **188**
Villa d'Este (Tivoli) 11, **257–9**, 263
Villa Pamphili Park 207
Villa Sciarra 207

Pasolini, Pier Paolo 44
passetto 143
passports 313
Paul II 91, 127
Paul III 34, 51, 89, 139
Paul IV 174
Paul, St 216, 218
Pecile (Villa Adriana) 260-1
Peter, St 241
phrase book 318-22
Piacentini, Marcello 58, 216
Piano, Renzo 60, 61, 196
Piazza Augusto Imperatore 75
Piazza Barberini 53, **122**, 185
Piazza Bartolomeo Romana 218
Piazza della Bocca della Verità 180
Piazza del Campidoglio 11, 51, 87, **89**, 95
Piazza di Campo Marzio 151
Piazza dei Cavalieri di Malta 212-13
Piazza Cavour 144
Piazza della Chiesa Nuova 164
Piazza Colonna 127-8
Piazza di Siena 191
Piazza Farnese 11, **177**
Piazza Fiume 72
Piazza della Fontanella Borghese 153
Piazza G.G. Belli 204
Piazza Mattei 11, 173-4
Piazza Matteotti (Marino) 269
Piazza del Mercato (Frascati) 266
Piazza Mincio 194
Piazza Navona 9, 11, 53, 54-5, 72, **158-9**
Piazza dell'Olmo (Frascati) 266
Piazza di Pasquino 160, **163**
Piazza di Pietra 153
Piazza del Plebiscito (Viterbo) 279
Piazza del Popolo 52, 72, **125**
Piazza del Quirinale 119-20
Piazza Regina Margherita (Palestrina) 276

Piazza della Rotonda 153
Piazza San Cosimato 75, 203
Piazza di San Giovanni 221
Piazza San Pietro 11, 24, 54, **137**
Piazza San Pietro (Frascati) 266
Piazza Santa Maria in Trastevere 11, **202**
Piazza Sidney Sonnino 204
Piazza di Spagna 11, 57, **129-30**
Piazza Testaccio 214
Piazza Venezia 10, **90**, 126, 127
Piazza Vittorio Emanuele II 59, 73, 229, **234**
Piazzale delle Corporazioni (Ostia) 253
Piazzale Garibaldi 206-7
Pincio Gardens 10, **189-91**
Piramide di Caio Cestio 214
Pius IX 36
Pius XI 38, 137
pizza **13**, 66
Pomarancio, Niccolò 52
Pompey 29, 30, 49, 172
Pomponio Hylas 239
Ponte Cestio 179
Ponte Fabricio 179
Ponte Milvio **195**, 196
Ponte Palatino 179
Ponte Rotto 179
Ponte Sant'Angelo 53, 54, **143**, **165**
Ponte Sisto 51
Ponte Vittorio Emanuele 169
Pontin archipelago 253
Ponza 253
Porta Flaminia 126
Porta Maggiore 234
Porta Pia 122
Porta Pinciana 188, 189
Porta Portese 73, 74, 75, **204**, **205**
Porta San Paolo 214
Porta San Sebastiano 239, 240
Porta Settimiana 205
Portico d'Ottavia 174, **175**

postal services 315-16
Praeneste *see* Palestrina
Prati 144
Priorato di Malta 213
Prodi, Romano 39
Protestant Cemetery 214
public holidays 315
public transport 20, 70, 241, **284-5**
puppet theatre 11, **206**

Q

Quartiere Coppedè 59, **194**
Quirinal Hill 119-22

R

radio 315
rail travel 282-3
Raphael 10, 51, 126, 154, 161, 178, 206
Raphael Rooms (Vatican) 141, **142**, 146
Rebecchini, Salvatore 38
Regia 106
religion 21
religious services 316
Republic, Roman **29**, 48
restaurants 63-6
see also end of each chapter
Risorgimento **36**, 91, 207
road travel 283
Rocca di Papa 268
Rocca Priora 268
Roma Pass 304
Roman Empire
architecture 48-50
history 30-2
Romans
ancient 27-32
modern **19-25**, 201
Romulus and Remus **27-8**, 89, 92, 102-3, 109, 242
Rossellini, Roberto 38, 44
Rostra 103
Rutelli, Francesco 59

S

Sabaudia 254
safety 311-12
Salvi, Nicola 57, 117

San Lorenzo 235
San Pellegrino quarter (Viterbo) 279
La Sapienza 162
Scala Santa 223
Schola di Traianum (Ostia) 253
Scipio family 239
Scorsese, Martin 45
Scuderie Aldobrandini (Frascati) 267
Scuderie del Quirinale 119-20
Sepolcro degli Scipioni 239
Septimius Severus 103, 205
Servian Walls 233
Shelley, Percy Bysshe 130-1, 214
shopping 12, 24-5, **69-75**, 131, **298-302**
sightseeing tours 309
Sistine Chapel 8, 34, 141, **142**, **148-9**
Sixtus IV 51, 92, 148
Sixtus V 52, 137, 221
Sordi, Alberto 45, 201
Spanish Steps 9, 57, **129-30**
Sperlonga 254
sport 308
Stadio dei Marmi 196
Stadio Olimpico 25, **196**
Stazione Termini 21, 57, 58, 61, 232, **233-4**
student travellers 316
Sulla 29, 274
swimming 216, **308**
Swiss Guards 137, 138, 269
Synagogue 175

T

Tabularium 10, **89**, 93, 94, 99
talking statues 91, 128-9, **160**, 163, 203
Tarquinia 277-8
Tarquinius Superbus 29, 274
taxis 286
Teatro Argentina **172**, 303
Teatro di Marcello 48, **180**
Teatro Marittimo (Villa Adriana) 261

Teatro (Ostia Antica) **253**, 303
Teatro Palladium 218, 303
Teatro di Pompeo 172
telephone services 316–17
television 314–15
Tempietto 51, **206**, 207
temples
di Antonino e Faustina 107
di Castore e Polluce 105
di Cesare
della Concordia 104
Hercules 180
di Minerva Medica 234
di Minerva (Veio) 274
Mithras **225**, 245
Portunus 180
di Romolo 107
Sanctuary of Fortuna Primigenia (Palestrina) 274–5
di Saturno 104
di Venere e Roma 108
di Vespasiano 104
di Vesta 106
di Vesta (Tivoli) 259
tennis 308
Terme di Caracalla 25, **227**
Terme di Diocleziano 161, **232–3**
Terme di Nettuno (Ostia) 253
Terme Severiane 110
Terme (Villa Adriana) 261
Testaccio 21, 24, 61, **214–15**
theatre 303
Tiber, River 59, 151, 195, 215, 251, 286
boat trips 178, 286
Tiber Island 179
Tiberius 30, 104
tickets 308
Tiepolo, Paolo 35
time zone 317

tipping 315
Titus 49, 104, 108, 111, 114, 174, 186
Tivoli 11, **257–61**
toilets 317
Tomb of Cecilia Metella 243
tombs, Etruscan 276–8
Tor Tre Teste 235
Torre delle Milizie 50
tourist information 317
tours 11, 20, **284**, **309**
Trajan 31, 49, 99–100, 251
trams 285
transport 19, 20, 70, 241, **282–7**
Trastevere 9, 20, 73, 179, **201–6**
Trent, Council of 34, 52
Trevi Fountain 9, 11, 57, **117**
Tridente 125–35
Trilussa 203
Tusculum 267

U

Umberto I 199
Umbilicus Urbis 103
Urban VIII 140, 154, 160, 204, 269

V

Valentino 12, 73, **132**
Vatican City 53, **137–49**, 221
Vatican Museums 8, **141–2**, **146–9**
Veio 274
Veltroni, Walter 39, 59
Vespasian 49, 104, **105**, 111, 114, 186
Vestal Virgins 106
Via Andrea Doria 75, 144
Via Appia Antica 59, **239–45**
Via del Babuino 51, 72, 125, 131

Via dei Banchi Vecchi 169
Via Bocca di Leone 131
Via della Caffarella 241
Via dei Cappellari 171
Via Cavour 57, 229
Via dei Cestari 153
Via Cola di Rienzo 72
Via della Conciliazione 58, 144
Via dei Condotti 24, 72, **131**, 132
Via dei Coronari 153, 164, **165**
Via del Corso 24, 72, 125, **126–9**
Via Flaminia 195
Via dei Fori Imperiali 58, 97–8
Via Frattina 131
Via Galvani 214–15
Via Garibaldi 205, 206, **207**
Via Giulia 52, **177**
Via della Lungara 205
Via Maddalena 153
Via Margutta 131
Via di Monte Testaccio 215
Via Nazionale 59, 73, 229
Via dell'Orso 153, **165**
Via Ostiense 217, 251
Via del Pantheon 153
Via dei Pastini 153
Via del Pellegrino 169
Via della Pilotta 123
Via del Quirinale 120
Via Regina Margherita (Frascati) 266
Via di Ripetta 51, 125, **133**
Via Sacra **101–2**, 108
Via Salaria 72, 193
Via Sannio 75
Via Sistina 52
Via Trionfale 144
Via Vittorio Veneto 122, **185–7**

Viale di Trastevere 204
Victor Emmanuel II **36**, 90, 91, 174, 193
Victor Emmanuel III 37
Villa Ada 193, 194
Villa Adriana (Tivoli) 11, 94, 95, **260–1**
Villa Aldobrandini 122
Villa Aldobrandini (Frascati) 266–7
Villa Borghese 9, 11, 25, 53, **188–93**, **199**
Villa Celimontana 225
Villa Colonna 123
Villa d'Este (Tivoli) 11, **257–9**, 263
Villa Doria Pamphilj 53
Villa Farnesina 51, 126, 196, **205–6**
Villa Giulia **192**, 279
Villa Gregoriana (Tivoli) 259
Villa di Massenzio 242
Villa Medici 191
Villa dei Quintili 243
Villa Sciarra 207
Villa Torlonia 194–5
Villa Torlonia (Frascati) 266
Villagio Globale 215
Virgil 27, 30
visas 313
Viterbo 278–9
Il Vittoriano 90–1

W

websites 317
wine **65–6**
Frascati **266**, 267
Marino 269
women, Roman 28
World War I 37
World War II 38, 175, 241, 265

Z

Zoo 192

Vatican (Vaticano)

Via Frà' Albenzio
S. Maria d. Grazie
P.za di S. Maria delle Grazie
Via Sebastiano Veniero
Viale Vaticano
Viale B. di
Via Vespasiano
V. Ottaviano
Via Marcantonio Bragadin
Via F. Sivori
Via Melona
Erno
V. Pisani
Ingresso
Sport
Salita del Giardini
Piazza del Risorgimento
Via D. Millerin
Via
Via
Angelo
Viale delle
Musei Vaticani (Vatican Museums)
Michelangelo
Officine
Osservatore Romano
Via di Porta Angelica
Via
S. Maria Mediatrice
Viale Vaticano
Viale delle Zitella
Pinacoteca
Stradone dei Giardini
Musei Vaticani (Vatican Museums)
Via della Posta
Via della Tipografia
Sant' Anna
Bo
Civico d. Mura Vaticane
Serre
GIARDINO QUADRATO
Museo Storico (sotterraneo)
Viale Centrale del Bosco
Ufficio Centrale delle Poste
Tipografia Papale
Bo
GIARDINI VATICANI
Madonna della Guardia
Fontana dell' Aquilone
Accademia della Scienze
Via del Belvedere
Caserma degli Svizzeri
Viale Benedetto
Viale del Giardino Quadrato
Fontana del Sacramento
Loggia di
P.za S. Leon
Madonna d. Guardia
Radio Vaticano (Direzione)
Monumento a San Pietro
Stanze di Raffaello
Cortile di San Damaso
L.go S. Martino
Viale dell' Osservatorio
P.za del Forno
Cappella Sistina (Sistine Chapel)
Raffaello
L.go Colona
Piazzale Grotta di Lourdes
Collegio Etiopico
S. Marta
Via del Governatorato
Via del Fondamenta
Basilica di San Pietro
Portone di Bronzo Scala Regis
P.za
Viale Vaticano
Via d. Olivi
Grotta di Lourdes
Mura di Leone IV
Radio Vaticano
Via del Seminario Etiopico
Ple Governatorato
S. Stefano
San Pietro
L.go Ali
Eliporto
Governatorato
P. d. Protomartiri Romani
Ingresso
L.go
Via Maccarani
Scuola d'Arte Mosaica
Palazzo di Giustizia
L.go S. Stefano
Sagrestia
Camposanto Teutonico
i
Viale Vaticano
L.go Giov. XXII
Pio XII
L.go Capanna Cinese
Stazione Vaticana
Museo d'Arte Storico (tesoreria)
P.za S. Marta
Ufficio Scavi Nekropole
S. Maria della Pietà
L.go Paolo VI
Via d. S. Uff
Via Aurelia
Via Nicolò V
Via d. Staz. Vaticana
Palazzo dell' Arciprete
Palazzo Santa Marta
Aula delle Udienze Pontificale
Palazzo del Sant' Uffizio
P.za del S. Uffizio
Pe
P.ta Cavalleggeri

0 ——— 250 m
0 ——— 250 yds

N

Forum (Foro Romano)

Foro di Cesare (Caesar's Forum)
V. della Curia
Curia (Senate House)
Argilentum
Basilica Aemilia
Entrance
SS. Luca e Martina
Arco di Settimio Severo (Arch of Septimius Severus)
Tempio di Antonino e Faustina (Temple of Antoninus & Faustina)
Tempio della Concordia (Temple of Concord)
Lapis Niger (Black Stone)
Via Sacra
Palazzo Senatori
Umbilicus Urbis
Colonna di Diocleziano
Rostra (Speaker's Platform)
Colonna Decennalia
Colonna di Foca (Column of Phocas)
Tempio di Cesare (Temple of Caesar)
Via d. Foro Romano
Curtain Lake
Tempio di Vespasiano (Temple of Vespasian)
Miliarum Aureum (Golden Milestone)
Regia
Tempio di Saturno (Temple of Saturn)
Portico degli Dei Consenti (Portico of the Dii Consentes)
Arco di Augusto (Arch of Augustus)
Tempio di Vesta (Temple of Vesta)
Atrio d.
(House of the
MONTE CAPITOLINO
Basilica Giulia (Basilica Julia)
Tempio dei Castore e Polluce (Temple of Castor & Pollux)
Lacus Juturnae (Fountain of Juturna)
Via
Santa Maria Antiqua